Sweet Freedom's Plains

Race and Culture in the American West
Quintard Taylor, Series Editor

Sweet Freedom's Plains

African Americans on the Overland Trails, 1841–1869

SHIRLEY ANN WILSON MOORE

UNIVERSITY OF OKLAHOMA PRESS : NORMAN

Library of Congress Cataloging-in-PublicationData

Names: Moore, Shirley Ann Wilson, 1947– author.
Title: Sweet freedom's plains : African Americans on the Overland Trails, 1841–1869 / Shirley Ann Wilson Moore.
Other titles: African Americans on the Overland Trails, 1841–1869
Description: Norman, OK : University of Oklahoma Press, [2016] | Series: Race and culture in the American West ; volume 12 | Includes bibliographical references and index.
Identifiers: LCCN 2016007764 | ISBN 978-0-8061-5562-3 (hardcover) ISBN 978-0-8061-9011-2 (paper) Subjects: LCSH: African Americans—West(U.S.)—History—19th century.| Frontier and pioneer life—West (U.S.) | Overland Trails—Description and trvel. | Overland journeys to the Pacific—History—19th century. | AfricanAmericans—West (U.S.)—Biography. | West (U.S.)—Race relations.
Classification: LCC E185.925 .M66 2016 | DDC 305.896/073078—dc23
LC record available at https://lccn.loc.gov/2016007764

Sweet Freedom's Plains: African Americans on the Overland Trails, 1841–1869 is Volume 12 in the Race and Culture in the American West series.

Source of book epigraph (page vii): William Wells Brown, "The Flying Slave," in *The Anti-Slavery Harp: A Collection of Songs for Anti-Slavery Meetings Compiled by William W. Brown, A Fugitive Slave* (Boston: Bela Marsh, No. 25 Cornhill, 1848), 47. Digital reprint, http://www.fullbooks.com/The-Anti-Slavery-Harp.html(accessedSeptember 29,2010).

The paper in this book meets the guidelines for permanence and durability of the Committee on Production Guidelines for Book Longevity of the Council on Library Resources, Inc. ∞

Copyright © 2016 by Shirley Ann Wilson Moore. Published by the University of Oklahoma Press, Norman, Publishing Division of the University. Paperback published 2022. Manufactured in the U.S.A.

All rights reserved. No part of this publication may be reproduced, stored in a retrieval system, or transmitted, in any form or by any means, electronic, mechanical, photocopying, recording, or otherwise—except as permitted under Section 107 or 108 of the United States Copyright Act—without the prior written permission of the University of Oklahoma Press. To request permission to reproduce selections from this book, write to Permissions, University of Oklahoma Press, 2800 Venture Drive, Norman, OK 73069, or email rights.oupress@ou.edu.

For my husband, Joe Louis Moore

The Flying Slave

The night is dark, and keen the air,
And the Slave is flying to be free;
His parting word is one short prayer;
O God, but give me Liberty!
Farewell—farewell!
Behind I leave the whips and chains,
Before me spreads sweet Freedom's plains

    William Wells Brown, *The Anti-Slavery Harp*, 1848

Contents

List of Illustrations		xi
Acknowledgments		xiii
Introduction		3
1	The Early Black Presence in the West	18
2	On the Eve of Overland Migration: Antebellum Slavery and Freedom	32
3	The Jumping-Off Places	54
4	The Providential Corridor	75
5	Community and Work on the Trails	109
6	Life, Death, and Acts of Kindness	130
7	Sweet Freedom's Plains	157
8	Place of Promise	193
Epilogue		229
Notes		233
Bibliography		313
Index		357

Illustrations

Figures

James P. Beckwourth	96
Emily Fisher and her gravesite marker	96
Hiram Young wagon replica	97
Alvin Aaron Coffey, ca. 1887	97
Mahala Tindall Coffey	98
Coffey descendants	98
Peter and Nancy Gooch	99
Monroe family in front of the Monroe house	99
Howard Estes	100
Hannah Estes and children	100
Sylvia Stark	101
Charles and Nancy Alexander	101
Charles and Nancy Alexander's descendants	102
Bridget "Biddy" Mason	102
Lewis Southworth and his violin	103
Lewis Southworth at his fireplace	103
Clara Brown	104
Barney Ford	104
Sugg family pictures	105
Sugg family house	105
Ben Palmer	106
Richard McDonald	107
Mary Harris McDonald	107
The McDonalds' tin box	108
Keepsakes from the McDonalds' tin box	108

Map

Overland Trails	6–7

Acknowledgments

I AM INDEBTED TO A HOST of scholars, archivists, librarians, curators, public historians, preservationists, and private individuals who unstintingly shared their time, knowledge, and resources with me. Their expertise and insight on the subjects of the overland trails, western history, and the African American experience have enriched this book.

Many thanks to Lee Kreutzer, Frank Norris, Guy Washington, Aidan Smith, and Aaron Mahr of the National Park Service, who contributed their vast hands-on knowledge of the overland trails and provided me with a wealth of trails resources when I began this project as a report for the National Park Service. I am also grateful for the assistance of Jeremy McReynolds, Michael Okey, Barry Smith, and Holly Thane at Marshall Gold Discovery State Historic Park, Coloma, California, for giving me access to the Gooch-Monroe family photographs and for their support of the Hiram Young overland wagon project that grew out of this work. I offer my sincerest thanks to Will Bagley, Salt Lake City, Utah; Travis Boley and Cathy Conway, Oregon-California Trails Association, Independence, Missouri; Richard Boyden, National Archives, San Bruno, California; Clarence Caesar, California State Parks historian (retired); Ronald G. Coleman, University of Utah, Salt Lake City; Joellen ElBashir, Moorland-Spingarn Research Center, Howard University, Washington, D.C.; Marcia Eymann, Sacramento (California) History Museum; Mary Gallagher, Benton County Historical Society and Museum, Philomath, Oregon; Mark L. Gardner, University of New Mexico, Albuquerque; Peter Hanff, Bancroft Library, Berkeley, California; Richard Jenkins, Moorland-Spingarn Research Center, Howard University, Washington, D.C.; Patricia Johnson, Center for Sacramento History; William Loren Katz, New York City; Gary Kurutz, California State Library, Sacramento; John Mark Lambertson, National Frontier Trails Museum, Independence, Missouri (retired); Michael N. Landon, Salt Lake City, Utah; Rick Moss, African American

Museum and Library, Oakland, California; Anna Nelson, Blair-Caldwell, African American Research Library, Denver, Colorado; Kenneth N. Owens, California State University, Sacramento (emeritus); Rachel Phillips, Gallatin Historical Society and Pioneer Museum, Bozeman, Montana; Kimberly Roberts and Jessica Maddox, Special Collections, University of Nevada, Reno; Michael J. Schmandt, California State University, Sacramento; and Jack Smith, California State University, Sacramento. My thanks as well to the staffs at the El Dorado County Historical Museum, Placerville, California; the Kansas State Historical Society, Topeka; the Leavenworth County Historical Society, Leavenworth, Kansas; the Los Angeles (California) Public Library; and the Salt Spring Island Archives, British Columbia.

I greatly appreciate the invaluable contributions of William and Annette Curtis, Independence, Missouri; Denise I. Griggs, Sacramento, California; Sharon McGriff Payne, Vallejo, California; Sylvia Alden Roberts, Sonora, California; Rush Speddin, Salt Lake City, Utah; and Gail Schontzler, *Bozeman Daily Chronicle,* Bozeman, Montana. Special thanks to Joanna Nute, Bozeman, Montana, for sharing the McDonald family photographs from her personal collection, and to Lindell Price, Cameron Park, California, for transcription services, clerical help, and unflagging good cheer. I wholeheartedly thank Quintard Taylor, Kathleen A. Kelly, Steven Baker, and Bethany R. Mowry of the University of Oklahoma Press, and freelance copy editor Ursula Smith, for their professionalism, guidance, and patience.

I am especially indebted to the descendants of the African American overlanders who graciously opened their homes to me and shared priceless resources and insights regarding their pioneer ancestors. Many thanks to Jeannette Molson, Davis, California; Charles and Gay Alexander and family, San Jose, California; Constance Moore Richardson, Los Angeles, California; Celeste Rountree and family, Vallejo, California; James Williams and family, Vallejo, California; and Michelle Thompson and family, Walnut Creek, California.

I offer my sincerest thanks to Andrew and Sonya St. Mary, Rocklin, California; Rick B. and Lana K. Wilson Combs, Sacramento, California; Helene Burgess and Cy Epstein, Richmond, California; and

Lynn Cooper, Berkeley, California, who were an enthusiastic and affirming audience for readings of portions of this manuscript and who offered me solace during very difficult times.

Finally, my most profound gratitude is reserved for my husband, Joe Louis Moore, whose unfaltering love and strength sustained me.

Sweet Freedom's Plains

Introduction

THE WESTWARD MIGRATIONS THAT CARRIED NEARLY 500,000 emigrants over the Oregon, California, and Mormon Trails from 1841 to 1869 (the year the transcontinental railroad was completed) constituted, in the words of historian Merrill J. Mattes, "one of the largest peacetime mass migrations in human history."[1]

Despite the passage of time, the story of western migration continues to influence popular imagination and our national culture. In the public's perception, western emigration is replete with tales of rugged individualism, perseverance, ingenuity, heroism, and their opposites. The popular understanding of the movement evokes iconic, albeit mistaken, images of straining teams of oxen and mules yoked to creaking wagons driven by hardy pioneers of European stock who steadfastly piloted their "prairie schooners" through relentless plains, searing deserts, and heart-stopping mountain passes.[2] However, the traditional narrative of western expansion, no matter how compelling, falls short of the real story of overland migration and the diversity and conflict that characterized the undertaking. African American men, women, and children were western pioneers too. Enslaved and free, they also joined the human tide that flowed out onto the trails to begin the long journey across the continent. Nevertheless, the journals, diaries, and letters of white emigrants, with few exceptions, typically show indifference to the black emigrants who traveled overland just as white emigrants did, sharing the same hazards and dangers that constituted daily life on the trails.

These African Americans, like their white counterparts, crossed plains, deserts, and mountains for myriad personal, economic, social, and political reasons. Both whites and blacks shared aspirations driven by the lure of free land, new business opportunities, and personal autonomy; but African American emigrants were not merely "black white [men]," as some American Indians saw them and some white Americans expected them to be.³ African American emigrants also trekked westward for reasons rooted in their unique circumstances as black people in the nineteenth-century United States, a nation that had relegated them to a subordinate status that affected every aspect of their lives. Slaves usually had no choice and no voice in the decision to go west. Each unwilling step down the trail separated them from their families and loved ones. An enslaved overlander's only solace was the thought that he or she might somehow gain freedom at the end of the trail—his or her own freedom or eventually freedom for kin left behind, or both. That cherished hope, so different from the hopes of white emigrants, sustained enslaved overland pioneers as they trudged westward. Free black emigrants set out on the overland journey largely to escape social injustice and economic repression, believing that the "wild" West, especially tumultuous gold rush California, was a place where industriousness and ingenuity might trump lines of race, caste, and class.

Whether they came across the trails under the dominion of westbound white slave owners or as free people, African Americans undertook the trip with an abiding conviction that they were more than disposable chattels or anonymous laborers. For them, the journey held out the possibility that in the West they could establish themselves as human beings worthy of freedom, dignity, and respect.

Sweet Freedom's Plains: African Americans on the Overland Trails, 1841–1869 centers on African Americans in the great overland migrations, placing black men and women firmly within the story of western expansion and settlement. It offers a model for African American migrational history that links nineteenth-century black overland emigrants to the migrations of African-descended people who, some two centuries earlier, had moved northward from the empires of New Spain and Mexico into what would become the American Southwest. This book grounds the African American overlander experience in what historian Anne F. Hyde has called the "human complexity" of the western frontier, which in the eighteenth and nineteenth centuries was, in the words of historian Albert L. Hurtado, a "cosmopolitan place—a meeting ground for people of disparate cultures and conflicting motives."⁴

On the trek west, African Americans entered a diverse arena where Native, Hispanic, Afro-Latino, and European populations had been a continuous presence for centuries. African American emigrants now became players in a heterogeneous milieu where racial and cultural comingling and constantly shifting power dynamics had eroded the rigid categories of race and color that held sway in the eastern and southern United States. Like everything else on the overland trails, the racial binary of black and white that proscribed the lives of African Americans in the nineteenth century was tested and eventually transformed, but not without a fight that assumed many forms and spanned generations. Black overlanders' expectations of the West—expectations for positive change—were the driving engine of that fight on and off the trails.

Sweet Freedom's Plains attempts to move beyond the paradigm of African Americans *in* the West—ground that has been covered admirably and amply by other historians to whom I am deeply indebted.[5] Rather, this work focuses on the goals and objectives that motivated innumerable African American slaves and free people to trek the Mormon, California, and Oregon Trails (and lesser-known routes); arrive in the Rocky Mountain region, the Pacific Coast, the Great Basin; and enter the Oregon Country, Utah Territory, New Mexico Territory, Colorado Territory, Arizona Territory, Idaho Territory, and other western territories (and the states that later were carved from them) to become permanent settlers or sojourners.[6] Moreover, this study addresses how, why, and whether the factors that pushed and pulled them across the plains, deserts, and mountains differed from those that drove white overlanders.

Three interrelated themes form the core of this book, and all point to the need for a reconceptualization of the emigration narrative. The first theme involves the experiences and skills of African Americans in the jumping-off places and along the trails. The second explores black perceptions of the journey, and the last theme addresses African Americans' expectations of the West and their new communities. All themes deal to some degree with the question of numbers—that is, how many black people actually journeyed overland? Unfortunately, the answer to this question probably never will be known, for a variety of reasons.

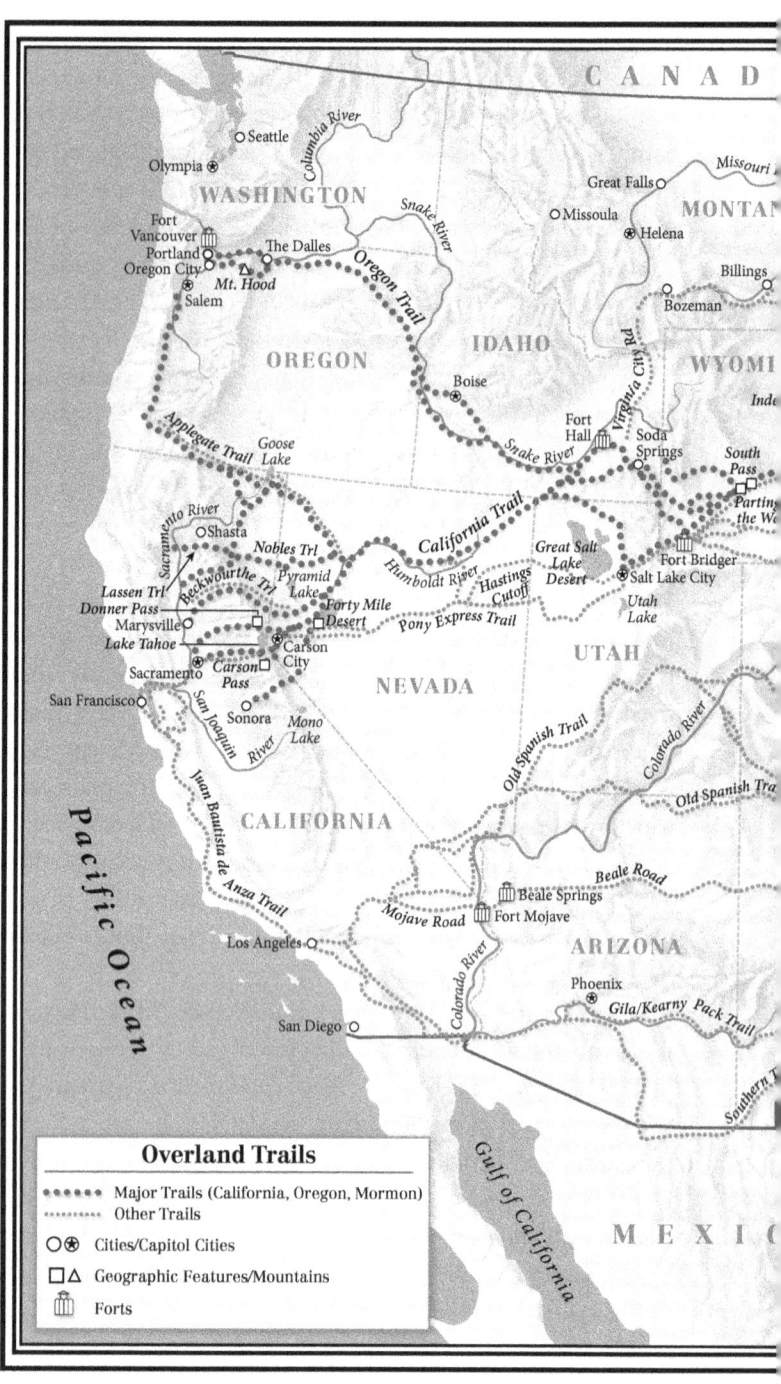

Base map courtesy of the Oregon-California Trails Association. Cartography by Gerry Krieg. Copyright © 2016 University of Oklahoma Press. All rights reserved.

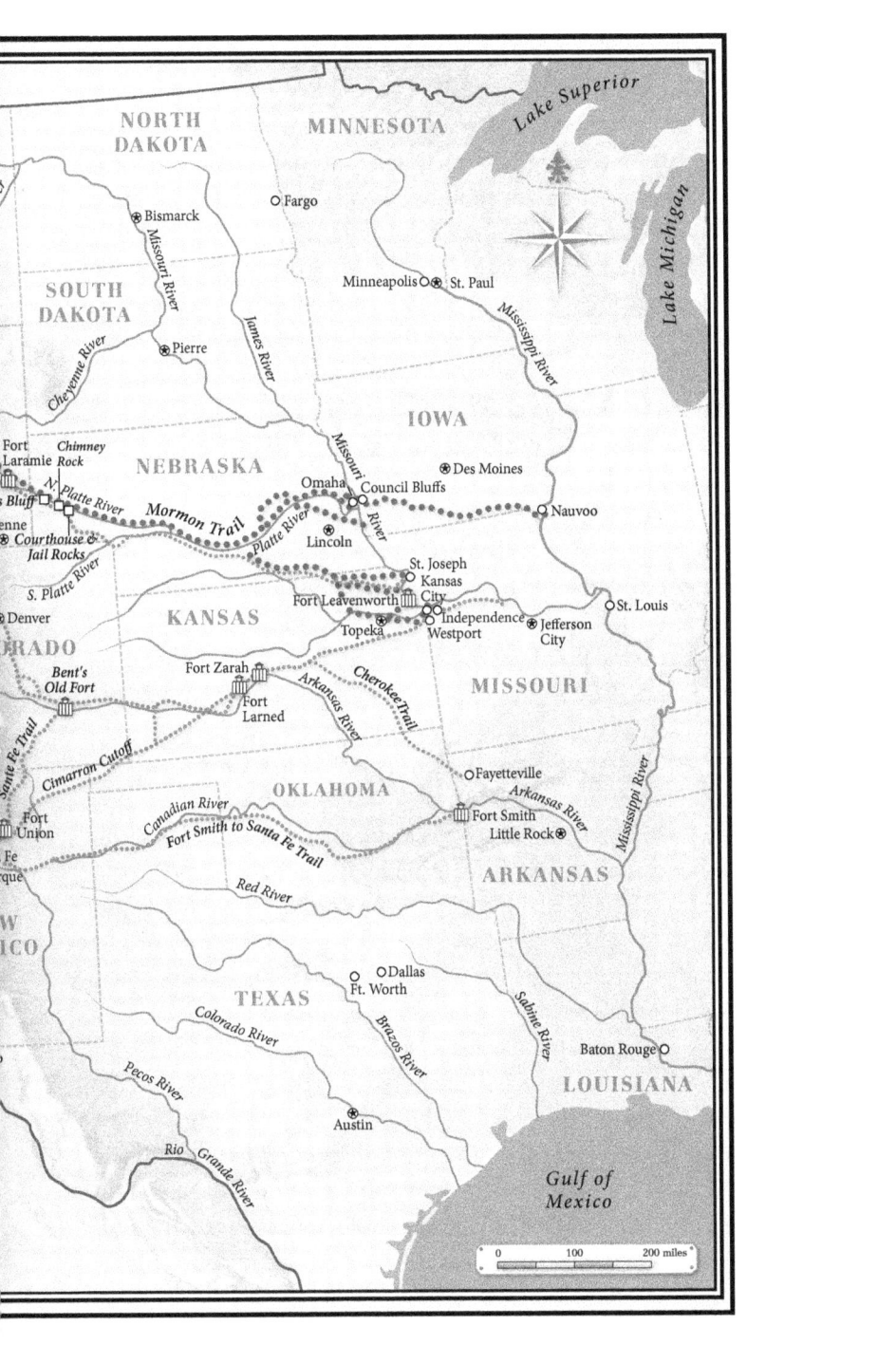

Estimates of the number of overland emigrants in general vary, and the task of calculating the actual number of black emigrants is made even more problematic by the indifference of official record keepers and toll takers whose reckonings routinely ignored and discounted their presence. The research presented in this book, however, suggests that every African American overlander identified by name in the trails narratives and other literature is representative of scores, if not hundreds, of other, anonymous black travelers. This challenges the popular assumption that the African American presence in overland emigration was negligible.[7]

Related to the question of quantity is the problem of identity. Just who were these black travelers? Although slaves made up a portion of African American overlanders, an unknown number of free black people also took to the trails. Some of their names and experiences have found their way into the general narrative, but undoubtedly many more free black men and women who remain anonymous undertook the journey as well.

In addition to the problems of numbers and identity, another concern of this book is the question of how African American travelers determined the end of their journey—the reasons they decided to stop where they did. In contrast to whites, it appears that the journey for most African Americans became an open-ended proposition, consisting in many cases of a series of sojourns along, and detours from, the trails. Their decision to permanently settle somewhere depended on the prevailing racial climate of the region they entered. While black and white emigrants often shared similar expectations for advancement and prosperity and perceived the long trek as a means to those ends, African Americans tended to define those things in terms unique to their circumstances as enslaved and racially persecuted people. For them, the trip marked the beginning of liberation and transformation. This was true for slaves and free people alike and was particularly relevant to black women, who struggled under the dual burden of racial and gender prejudice. Thus, freedom, safety, and opportunity became the overriding factors marking the end of the trail for black people—some of whom were willing to push beyond the borders of the United States in pursuit of these goals. Unquestionably, pragmatism motivated most black overlanders, but it appears that, in addition, less tangible, nonquantifiable aspirations (expressed in the writing and art of a few African American overlanders) set some on the trails.

No matter what expectations African Americans held, however, they often came into sharp conflict with real-world conditions on the trails and in their new homes. This book examines the often painful clash between African Americans' hopes and western realities by looking at the experiences of some African Americans (prominent and lesser known) whose stories are representative of the challenges most faced and sometimes surmounted. I use the term "representative" with caution, however, well aware that the accounts presented in this book demonstrate that the black men and women who trekked overland did so under unique and varied circumstances, and their experiences on and off the trails underscore their individuality. To impose the burden of representativeness on them risks obscuring this crucial point and diminishes the centrality of African Americans in the narrative of overland emigration. With this caveat at the forefront, it is possible, however, to view the men and women discussed in this book as "representative" in the sense that they, like all black overlanders regardless of status or the circumstances that placed them on the trails, shared common experiences in their struggles for freedom, equality, and opportunity—both en route and long after the journey ended.

Chapter 1, "The Early Black Presence in the West," discusses the presence of people of African ancestry in the West before the first Africans arrived in Jamestown, Virginia, in 1619. This chapter links the nineteenth-century black overlander experience to the earlier migrations of African-descended people who settled in the present-day southwestern United States and argues that the migrations of earlier African-descended people are fundamental to an understanding of nineteenth-century black overland emigration and the issue of race. This chapter examines the experiences of some early black explorers and settlers of New Spain whose mixed racial heritage of European, American Indian, and African characterized Spanish settlement in the West and contributed to the emergence of a sociopolitical system that allowed African-descended people more social and economic mobility than did the settlements established by the English or Dutch. This chapter also assesses the gender implications of early western settlement and looks at the contributions of African-descended women who were part of the expeditions that trekked to New Spain's northernmost outposts. It concludes with a discussion of the role played by black mountain men—many of whom were of mixed ancestry and whose lives epitomized the racial fluidity of the early frontier period—whose trailblazing efforts helped pave the way for overland emigration and settlement.

Chapter 2, "On the Eve of Overland Migration: Antebellum Slavery and Freedom," examines the issue of race and the impact of the "one-drop rule" on African Americans. It offers a brief overview of slavery and freedom at the dawn of the great overland migrations and discusses the conditions under which enslaved and free black people lived, focusing on the slave codes and black laws that existed in the Deep South, border states, Texas, Indian Territory, the North, and the Far West. The chapter also examines the unique situation of African Americans in Mormon Utah and argues that regardless of location or religious persuasion, black men and women, slaves or not, lived under constant threat of slavery, were isolated by racial prejudice, and faced white hostility that frequently erupted into violence against them. It concludes with a discussion of the tensions produced by the spread of slavery, the proliferation of black laws that culminated in the infamous *Dred Scott* decision, and white fear of workplace competition—tensions that worked as push-pull factors setting many free blacks on the trails west and making enslaved black overlanders, who were subject to their owners' will, reluctant but hopeful travelers.

Chapter 3, "The Jumping-Off Places," examines the bustling river towns where blacks and whites outfitted themselves for the trail. This chapter contends that these towns were cosmopolitan, commercial venues where a few entrepreneurial black people facilitated western migration, established themselves financially, engaged in community building, and served as models for freedom's possibilities for African American overlanders. The chapter also argues that black sojourners in the jumping-off places, unlike their white counterparts, encountered complications that impeded their progress even before setting foot on the trail. It explores African Americans' vulnerability in these towns to slave hunters, foul play, and racially prejudiced wagon-train companies. Applying the concept of what historian Douglas Daniels has called "travelcraft," this chapter also discusses some of the strategies blacks employed to help them negotiate the often perilous racial terrain of the jumping-off towns.[8]

Chapter 4, "The Providential Corridor," reviews the complex of overland trails, including the main Oregon, California, and Mormon Trails and the less traveled routes, focusing on the experiences of African Americans on these roads. It also looks at the trailblazing efforts of African American explorer Jacob Dodson in establishing the routes that opened the West to emigration and settlement, and examines the impact of the extraordinary Oregon-California Trails map produced by African American cartographer T. H. Jefferson.

Chapter 5, "Community and Work on the Trails," looks at the mutually beneficial trail society that eventually emerged from the disparate individuals who began the overland trek. Focusing on the work and responsibilities that African Americans took on in westbound wagon train and pack companies, this chapter argues that black overlanders, though confined to roles of servants, laborers, and slaves, nevertheless performed a variety of duties and held positions of authority and trustworthiness that went far beyond those categories. Whether free or enslaved, black emigrants, in the course of performing the work of the trails, sometimes were specifically targeted for racial violence or found themselves caught in the middle of conflicts that erupted among their white trailmates. African American women, who worked their way west regardless of status, were also vulnerable to sexual predation.

Chapter 6, "Life, Death, and Acts of Kindness," looks at black emigrants' interactions—positive and otherwise—with the Native peoples they encountered. It argues that though African Americans, because of their skin color, occasionally received deferential treatment from them, American Indians often regarded African Americans (and the whites with whom they traveled) as intruders to be repelled by force, irrespective of skin color. Reinforcing this perception was the fact that African Americans and whites frequently shared the same prejudices against Native people, and blacks sometimes joined whites in committing reprehensible acts against them. This chapter also examines the need for security on the trails and the roles played by African Americans, including the Buffalo Soldiers, in safeguarding the trails and the westbound wagon trains and pack companies that clattered across them. It discusses the life-and-death situations in which black overlanders, voluntarily or otherwise, battled Native peoples and others to protect themselves, their wagon-train communities, and trailmates on the road and after the journey had come to an end.

The chapter discusses the accidents, illnesses, and other trail hazards that endangered overlanders' lives and accounted for thousands of fatalities. It contends that black emigrants, because of their subordinate status, often were more vulnerable to those calamities and likely succumbed to them at rates equal to or greater than those of their white counterparts. Chapter 6 concludes with a discussion of the reciprocal acts of kindness and selflessness that occasionally occurred among blacks, whites, and Native peoples, on and off the trails. These benevolent exchanges were precipitated most often by dire necessity, sometimes by friendship, and occasionally by simple human compassion that transcended, however briefly, prejudice and suspicion.

Chapter 7, "Sweet Freedom's Plains," discusses the "invisibility" of African Americans in the western emigration narrative and the difficulty of determining their numbers despite their obvious presence. Using the stories of famous, little-known, and anonymous black overlanders, slaves and free people, this chapter examines the reasons they trekked to the West and assesses their expectations. It argues that although racist attitudes and practices attempted to cloak them in invisibility, African Americans headed west as self-aware human beings, harboring hope that the journey would open up new options. The western trek represented a fresh start for most people regardless of race, but for black men and women, it held out the possibility of deliverance from bondage, an end to racial persecution, and the opportunity to improve their economic situation.

This chapter looks at the degree to which African American emigrants' expectations of the West were fulfilled, and using an extraordinary set of letters from Rachel Brown, an African American woman (who never traveled the trails) to her husband, David Brown, in gold rush California, examines the impact of emigration on the loved ones who remained behind. The names and deeds of the African Americans highlighted in this chapter have been preserved and are a matter of record. They, like countless unrecorded and unacknowledged black emigrants, were pushed and pulled across "sweet freedom's plains" by the common goals of liberty, security, and advancement.

Chapter 8, "Place of Promise," contends that the driving force in black western emigration, for slaves and free people alike, was the opportunity to live and work in communities free of the racial prohibitions that had plagued them in their former homes. Their experiences demonstrate that community building was foundational to the promise of the West. Topping the list of community-building efforts was the task of establishing themselves as free people and carving out places in the emerging economies of the region. This chapter argues that black westerners, linking economic progress to civil rights, created institutions that challenged the racial status quo and became the staging ground for their concerted attacks on the laws and practices that denied them legal equality and prevented them from pursuing their vision of the good life in the West.

The epilogue assesses the significance of black overland emigration and revisits the notion of travelcraft as it is reflected in the experiences of African American emigrants in the jumping-off places, on the trails, and in their new western communities. Whether enslaved or free, black overlanders—pragmatic, adaptable, and optimistic about the long-term—drew on an array of skills and strategies that helped them negotiate the complex of overland trails to the West and confront the legal, economic, and social barriers that attempted to limit them once they arrived at their destinations. The experiences and perspectives of African American overlanders are essential to a fuller and more accurate understanding of western expansion, one of the most iconic and transformative events in the nation's history. To that end, I have made every effort to hear the voices of African American emigrants and to let them speak for themselves. This has been both a rewarding and frustrating task, primarily for reasons having to do with the availability of sources. Because of the paucity of firsthand accounts written by African American overlanders, most of the descriptions of black people on the trails, by necessity, have come from contemporary white diarists and commentators, the most prolific chroniclers of the overland emigrations. Although most of these sources tend to be racially condescending, dismissive, and not necessarily representative of the reality of African Americans' contributions to the process of overland emigration, they are nonetheless tremendously useful in gleaning information about the black men and women who trekked over the trails. No matter how indifferent or disdainful, white diarists and journalists frequently revealed the important roles blacks played in the wagon-train and pack companies that crossed the continent. What emerges from the brief references to African Americans in white-penned diaries, journals, and reports is a picture of black agency, capability, and purpose that most white contemporaries could not or would not acknowledge but that are central themes in this work.

This book draws deeply from earlier scholarship on African Americans in the West. Delilah Beasley's pioneering *Negro Trail Blazers of California* has been the source of a wealth of detail about black western settlers. Beasley, a self-taught researcher and historian, produced one of the earliest and best works (though not without its methodological problems) to take a professional approach to the subject of African Americans in the West. The personal stories, manumission papers, and other primary sources included in her book are priceless. Other early scholarship of the black western experience has been of great help in the preparation of this book. Such works include Kenneth Wiggins Porter's edited volume, *The Negro on the American Frontier*; the works of W. Sherman Savage published in the *Journal of Negro History;* and the work of Sue Bailey Thurman.[9]

Since the 1970s, a renewed interest in the West and in African American western history has produced an abundance of outstanding scholarship. The works of Jack Forbes, William Loren Katz, Rudolph Lapp, James Fisher, John W. Ravage, and Lawrence B. de Graaf represent some of the most meticulous research and writing on western African Americans. Their works have lifted the veil of "invisibility" that had surrounded the black western experience and have pointed the way to rich new areas for future study. I am indebted to all of them. Of course, Quintard Taylor's groundbreaking 1998 book, *In Search of the*

Racial Frontier: African Americans in the American West, 1528–1990, set a new standard for all scholars working in the field of African American western history. Anne F. Hyde's *Empires, Nations, and Families: A New History of the North American West, 1800–1860,* a compelling and accessible work of scholarship, emphasizes the diversity and interrelatedness of the peoples and regions of the West and is a model of history as story. Other touchstones in western and overland trails scholarship are the works of John D. Unruh Jr., Merrill J. Mattes, Dale L. Morgan, William H. Leckie, and Will Bagley. Richard V. Francaviglia's remarkable book, *Mapping and Imagination in the Great Basin: A Cartographic History,* has added tremendously to my understanding of the landscape and geography of the American West.[10]

Sweet Freedom's Plains also incorporates census records, maps, government documents, and other primary and secondary sources to get at the stories of African American emigrants that are embedded in the general narrative of overland migration. In addition, oral history plays an important role in this work. Because many (if not most) black overlanders could not read or write, their experiences have been preserved in the oral tradition passed down through generations of family members. The descendants of African American overland emigrants, though removed in time from the actual events, are the living archives of that history.

I have conducted interviews with the descendants of several black overlanders and have used oral histories, interviews, and reminiscences already recorded with other black emigrants and their descendants. Oral history can pose certain problems for historical accuracy (for instance, memory dims with the passage of time, secondhand accounts can be unreliable, or the interviewee can have a selective memory), but it is a valuable tool for illuminating the personal, gaining alternate perspectives, and allowing the marginalized to enter the mainstream. I have included them, fully aware of these inherent shortcomings, yet convinced of their usefulness in gaining insight into what black emigrants believed about themselves, unfiltered through the biases of whites. My objective here, as nearly as possible, is to let African American voices be heard, to let them tell us what they valued and what they experienced.

The primary focus of *Sweet Freedom's Plains* is African American overlanders' goals and their campaigns for freedom, opportunity, and dignity on and off the trails, but this is no triumphalist version of black western emigration and settlement. While trails narratives abound with tales of corrupt, treacherous, and violent whites who exploited both emigrants and Native peoples (for example, the accounts of so-called white Indians—white men who disguised themselves as American Indians, preyed on emigrant parties, then blended back in with the white population), information regarding disreputable black behavior, like everything else involving the African American overland experience, is scarce. Clearly there were no "black Indians," but occasionally the journal and diary entries of white overlanders reveal that African Americans engaged in villainous acts as well.

The accounts in this book of George Berryman, the desperate slave of an unscrupulous black owner, and the story of an anonymous "runaway slave" who was likely working in cahoots with a dubious white "sheriff" to extort money from a party of white Texas emigrants attest to this fact. Some African Americans, like whites, transported racist attitudes toward Native peoples and engaged in violence against them as they moved west. This work discusses the black man known as "negro Andy," who traveled with J. Goldsborough Bruff's gold-mining expedition and joined his white companions in the rape of an Indian woman. Andy also earned a reputation as a fierce Indian fighter who rode with a posse that hunted and killed Native people. The famed African American military units known as the Buffalo Soldiers, which served on the western frontier, left a paradoxical and tragic legacy. These soldiers, many of whom were former slaves, proudly and, for the most part, unquestioningly carried out duties that included escorting wagon trains, protecting settlements, and participating in military campaigns that dispossessed and annihilated Native people. Neither African American emigrants nor their descendants would have been likely to write about or publically disclose this less than admirable behavior—an aspect of the African American overlander experience that perhaps lies deeply buried in the family lore of generations of black pioneer families.

Mindful of all these challenges, I have attempted to retrieve the stories and deeds, laudable or otherwise, of the African American men and women who traveled the overland trails, voluntarily and as slaves, and to reclaim their presence as full participants in one of the most momentous and contested events in our history.

Chapter 1
The Early Black Presence in the West

When Esteban got away from [Marcos de Niza] . . . he craved to gain honor and fame in everything and to be credited with the boldness and daring of discovering, all by himself, those terraced pueblos, so famed throughout the land.

Pedro de Castañeda, 1640

The forts that now afford protection to the traveler were built by ourselves at the constant peril of our lives, amid Indian tribes nearly double their present numbers. Without wives and children to comfort us on our lonely way; without well-furnished wagons to resort to when hungry; no roads before us but trails temporarily made.

James P. Beckwourth, 1856

AFRICAN AMERICANS WHO SET OUT on the overland trails in the mid-nineteenth century were not the first African-descended people to journey across the continent in search of freedom, riches, land, and adventure. People of African ancestry had been a presence on the American continent since the early days of Spanish and other European exploration; their presence in what is now known as the American West predates the arrival of Africans in Jamestown, Virginia, in 1619.[1] The nineteenth-century overland migrations that brought countless African American emigrants westward mark a critical point in the migrational arc of African-descended people into the western region—an arc that would continue well into the twentieth century. The roots of the movement are found in the sixteenth century, as explorers and settlers of African ancestry pushed northward into "the West" to establish new outposts for the empire of New Spain, a realm that included today's southeastern United States, stretching from west of the Mississippi River to what is now Mexico and Central America.

Explorers and Settlers

New Spain's African-descended pioneers, enslaved and free, often intermarried with the European and indigenous peoples with whom they traveled or encountered on their trek north and upon arriving at their destinations. Such interracial, cross-cultural alliances served the political and economic interests of the expanding empire, giving it a veneer of legitimacy in the region and bringing stability, however tenuous, to the all-important business of trade. Thus, most transactions—economic, political, or social—took place via intricate and interdependent networks that grew from generations of intermarriage and kinship ties and operated within a racially and culturally accommodating context.

Historian Anne F. Hyde, writing about the diversity of the western frontier before the dawn of the great overland migrations, noted that accommodation among the peoples of the area "shaped the communities they built . . . and revealed a set of deeply gendered and always contested definitions of who mattered."[2] This heterogeneous and fluid setting presented opportunities and posed problems for nineteenth-century black overland emigrants, just as it had for the African-descended pioneers who first entered the region. Both groups, though separated by time, geography, and background, fought for self-determination and justice—for inclusion among the ranks of those who "mattered"—as they blazed uncharted paths, trod the trails, and settled in what now composes the present-day American West.

Esteban and Others

Historian Quintard Taylor has written that "African American life in the West began with nature's violence" when Esteban (also known as Estevanico), the Moroccan slave of Spanish explorer Andrés Dorantes de Carranza, accompanied his owner on Pánfilo de Narváez's 1527–28 treasure-hunting expedition in the Gulf of Mexico.[3] Narváez's fleet was destroyed by a hurricane, and Esteban, cast ashore with fifteen other men, became the first African to set foot in what later became Texas and the western United States. He and his party endured many hardships, including a starvation winter on a sandbar near present-day Galveston. They were captured by coastal Native people and spent five years enslaved by them. By September 1534, Esteban was one of only four survivors of the original party. He and this small group, led by Álvar Nuñez Cabeza de Vaca, escaped their captors and fled into the interior, where they encountered friendly indigenous people. Esteban's skill and fluency in sign language thrust him into the important roles of interpreter, ambassador, and negotiator with the Native populations of the region. His efforts helped the depleted band of conquistadors survive an eight-year, 15,000-mile march across the Southwest. With the help of the Shuman Apaches, whose guidance Esteban helped secure, the group crossed the Rio Grande and trudged through Chihuahua and Sonora, finally arriving in Mexico City in July 1536.[4]

Just three years later, in March 1539, under orders from the viceroy of New Spain, Don Antonio de Mendoza, Esteban, the Franciscan friars Marcos de Niza and Onorato (whose illness prevented him from completing the journey), and a sizable retinue of Native allies set out from Culiacán (the northernmost Spanish outpost) on another expedition that sought the fabled cities of Cíbola. Esteban likely had been purchased by Friar Marcos de Niza, and was to serve as the party's guide and interpreter. Shortly before reaching their destination, Esteban sent messengers ahead to the pueblo to announce their arrival. Zuni leaders warned him not to enter the town, but Esteban pushed on to the first pueblo, where he was captured and subsequently killed.

The facts of Esteban's death are unclear, but his influence on the indigenous populations he encountered in his travels is undeniable. Believing him to be a powerful healer, they were impressed by the black man who wore "bells and feathers on his ankles and arms and carried plates of various colors." Historian Ramón A. Gutiérrez has written that the Zunis regarded him as a "black Katsina," or ancestor spirit and healer. Equally notable is Esteban's importance to early western settlement. His explorations not only reinforced the Spanish presence on the continent but helped pave the way for the founding of important towns in the West and Southwest, precipitating interaction among the various Native, Spanish, and Anglo cultures in this hotly contested area—an interaction that would have profound implications for the region's history.[5]

Over the next century, people of African ancestry served as explorers, scouts, and settlers on the frontlines of New Spain. In 1540–42, Francisco Vásquez de Coronado's expedition retraced Esteban's path to the northern frontier. Coronado's company included an entourage of more than 1,000 people, including Africans and American Indians. An unnamed free black man served as interpreter for Juan de Padilla, the friar for the Coronado expedition. When Padilla remained behind to minister to the Kansa Indians in 1541, the black interpreter stayed with him.[6]

Women of African Descent

Not all early African-descended explorers and settlers of the West were men. Women of African ancestry composed a significant portion of western settlers in the seventeenth and eighteenth centuries and were, in the words of historian Dedra S. McDonald, "more than fixtures on the high desert landscape." They participated in all aspects of settlement and community building. African-descended women joined contingents of Spanish settlers who pushed northward from Mexico to start colonies in New Mexico and Alta California (the northwestern province of New Spain), helping to establish schools, churches, and towns in those areas.[7]

The 1781 expedition recruited in Mexico by Captain Fernando X. Rivera to found a pueblo somewhere between the San Gabriel mission and the Santa Barbara presidio in Alta California included a number of women of African ancestry, their spouses, and children. Most of these recruits came from the Mexican state of Sinaloa, where nearly one-third of the inhabitants claimed African heritage. A significant number had resided in the village of Rosario where two-thirds of the residents were listed in the census as mulattoes. Persuaded by offers of "cash, supplies, tools, animals, clothing, a limited period of no taxation, and access to land," they left Alamos, Sonora, Mexico, under military escort in February 1781. After a grueling journey of several months, this band of "Indians, mulattos, and Spaniards" arrived at Mission San Gabriel where they spent a month in quarantine as a precaution against smallpox. In September 1781, the group of forty-six *pobladores* (settlers) pushed on to establish the *Pueblo de Nuestra Señora la Reina de Los Angeles de Porciuncula,* which is known today as Los Angeles.[8]

Historian Albert S. Broussard has written that women of African or partial African descent who participated in the settlement of New Spain, whether free or enslaved, tended to "live less violent lives" than their male counterparts, yet they faced other threats to their security.[9] In 1600, Isabel de Olvera, the daughter of a black father and a Native mother who resided in Querétaro, New Spain (present-day Mexico), joined the Juan Guerra de Resa expedition to the colony of Santa Fe (present-day New Mexico) as the servant of one of the Spanish women in the group. Before departing, de Olvera sought official protection of her rights as a free, single, black woman. Presenting a deposition to the *alcalde* (mayor), she declared:

> As I am going on the expedition to New Mexico and have reason to fear that I may be annoyed by some individual since I am a mulatta, and as it is proper to respect my rights in such an eventuality by affidavit showing that I am a free wom[an], unmarried, and the legitimate daughter of Hernando, a negro [sic], and an Indian named Magdalena, I therefore request your grace to accept this affidavit, which shows that I am free and not bound by marriage or slavery. I request that a properly certified and signed copy be given to me in order to protect my rights, and that it carry full legal authority. I demand justice.[10]

Isabel de Olvera's story suggests that women of African heritage in New Spain's empire remained vulnerable to racial and gender exploitation as they engaged in the work of settlement and community building. However, they could and did claim control over their lives, taking legal action to defend themselves against maltreatment.[11]

De Olvera's successful petition for safe passage to New Mexico stands in stark contrast to the situation of countless nineteenth-century African American women, enslaved and free, who traveled westward on the overland trails without protection or legal recourse against the predations of slave masters, slave hunters, unscrupulous employers, and others.

York

Some two hundred years after Isabel de Olvera submitted her legal petition before departing for Santa Fe, and more than three centuries after Esteban's harrowing march across the Southwest, a black man named York would also traverse the West. Much about him remains a mystery, but he has been described as "large, dark, agile and strong."[12] He made his journey, not as a free man intending to settle, but as the slave of Capt. William Clark, who, with Meriwether Lewis, led the exploratory Corps of Discovery expedition from St. Louis to the Pacific between 1804 and 1806. York became the first documented American slave to cross the continent, though, unlike de Olvera, he had no legal rights.

Just as Esteban had done for his party centuries earlier, York contributed crucial interpreting, trading, and scouting skills to the team. His negotiating prowess and the rapport he established with the Native peoples they encountered were vital to the expedition's success. He was recognized and treated as a full member of the Corps and engaged in all decision making, voting, and hunting activities with the group. When the journey ended, York expected to be freed and reunited with his wife in Kentucky as a reward for his considerable service. But Clark held onto him for another decade. Confronted with York's dismay and anger, Clark unsuccessfully tried to break his slave's defiance with beatings, imprisonment, and threats of sale. Finally, in 1816, York was freed but the fate of this black explorer is unclear. William Clark contended that York hated being a free man and died while attempting to return to his former master. Mountain man Zenas Leonard provides another account, one that has York living among the Crows in the 1830s as a respected member of the tribe. Still another version of the story contends that York remarried and spent a comfortable life as the owner of a drayage service operating between his home in Louisville, Kentucky, and Nashville, Tennessee.[13] Whatever path York's life may have taken after gaining freedom, his experiences in the Corps of Discovery place him among the earliest African-descended explorers and travelers to enter the West.

Mountain Men

Unlike York and Esteban, who explored the West as sojourners, or Isabel de Olvera and other settlers of New Spain's empire who traveled under government edict, a small group of African-descended men spent most of their lives in the West, far from governmental regulation and the rigid racial proscriptions that invariably accompanied settlement. These men, whose lineage often reflected the racial and ethnic diversity of the area, belonged to an exclusive fraternity of explorers, trappers, traders, interpreters, and scouts who crisscrossed the mountains, deserts, and valleys of the West. Some mountain men were employed by the large trading companies that had sprung up to supply the demand for beaver pelts; others worked independently as "free trappers," not bound to any company. All had come to the mountains to make a living in an occupation that promised, according to historian Robert M. Utley, "adventure, excitement, personal freedom, and the nearly total absence of authoritarian restraint." Not quite the unsociable, wandering loners often depicted in popular views, they nonetheless cultivated reputations as fiercely independent individuals of enormous endurance and courage.[14]

Whatever their background and motivation, mountain men of African descent were in the forefront of western exploration prior to the advent of the overland migrations. And when the fur trade began to decline, some managed to reinvent themselves, hiring out their impressive array of resources and skills to the wagon caravans that had begun to roll out over the unfamiliar and daunting complex of western trails.

Edward Rose

Edward Rose, the son of a white trader and a black-Cherokee woman, was one of the most competent and daring of the mountain men.[15] He was, in the words of Robert M. Utley, a "big, powerful man of volatile temper yet undoubted ability."[16] As a young man, Rose worked as a deckhand on a keelboat that took him from Kentucky, where he was raised, down to New Orleans. In 1805, he headed north to St. Louis where, in 1807, he joined Manuel Lisa's fur-trading expedition bound for the Bighorn River in modern-day Wyoming. Serving periodically as a guide, hunter, and trapper for a number of fur-trading companies, his knowledge of Native languages and cultures made him invaluable to the trappers who called upon him to negotiate with the indigenous peoples of the region. Charles Keemle, one of the leaders of an early 1820s trapping expedition that included Rose recalled that "he alone understood their language, and, of course, could tell them any and everything he pleased. . . . His word was law and he well knew how to give it an elevated tone."[17]

At least two Native American groups, the Absarokas (Crows) and the Arikaras, held him in great esteem. His willingness to fight alongside the Absarokas as they waged war against their enemies only solidified his standing with them, and in 1807, they adopted him into the tribe. In 1820, the Arikaras (in what is now South Dakota) bestowed the same honor on him. White trapper Zenas Leonard encountered Rose (whom he mistakenly thought was York of the Lewis and Clark expedition) in the winter of 1832–33, living in a Crow village near the mouth of the Stinking River (now called the Shoshone River in present-day Wyoming). Rose was apparently enjoying "all the dignities of a chief," surrounded by several wives.[18] Many of his white contemporaries, however, held a less favorable opinion of the black mountain man whom they regarded, despite his skills and accomplishments, as self-serving, dishonest, and untrustworthy.[19] Sometime in 1833, as Rose and two companions made their way across the frozen Yellowstone River on an ill-fated trip from Fort Cass to Fort Union, a band of Arikara warriors attacked the group, killing all three men.[20]

Peter Ranne and Polette Labross

Peter Ranne, another black mountain man, explored the Southwest and the Great Salt Lake region as a member of Jedediah Smith's trailblazing Southwest Expedition of 1826–27. Ranne, who was free-born, is credited with being the first man of African ancestry to enter the boundaries of present-day Nevada. Described in company records as a "man of color," Ranne joined Smith's trapping expedition to hunt beaver in the Cache Valley of northern Utah and southeast Idaho. He and his fellow trappers endured a grueling trip across the Mojave Desert, crossed the Colorado River, and eventually straggled into California to the villages of the Mojaves, where they recuperated for two weeks before continuing their journey northward into the San Joaquin Valley. Smith returned to Salt Lake, leaving Ranne and most of the party in California for several weeks. When he rejoined the group, the trappers began working their way up the Oregon coast in search of beaver. In Oregon, they set up camp just north of the Umpqua River, where, in July 1827, a band of Kelawatsets attacked and killed most of the company, including Ranne. Smith, who was away from camp scouting out a new river crossing with two other trappers and a Native guide, narrowly escaped the same fate.[21]

Undeterred, Jedediah Smith made another trip to the West in 1828. This time, his nineteen-man company included Polette Labross, a mulatto. Just as before, the group spent time in the villages of the Mojave, but now the Native Americans were not as welcoming as they had been a year earlier. They attacked the trappers as they crossed the Colorado River, killing nine men, including Polette Labross.[22]

James Pierson Beckwourth

Peter Ranne and Polette Labross enjoyed reputations as tough, resourceful men in the wilderness; however, mountain man Jim Beckwourth's fame was unsurpassed and had been established long before the first emigrant wagons lumbered over the plains. Born in 1797 or 1798 in Frederick County, Virginia, Beckwourth was the son of a slave woman known only as "Miss Kill" and her white owner, Jennings Beckwith.[23]

Beckwourth's western journey began in 1810, when he moved with his father to the recently acquired lands of the Louisiana Territory. There, they settled near St. Charles, Missouri. At the age of fourteen, Beckwourth was apprenticed by his father to the St. Louis blacksmiths George Casner and John L. Sutton.[24] After spending five years there, young Beckwourth ran away. Now on his own, he first hired himself out as a hunter and then went to work as a lead miner. In the fall of 1824, he signed on as a "wrangler and body servant" with William Ashley's fur-trapping expedition to the Rocky Mountains. The company set out from St. Louis that September, and within a year, Beckwourth was making his living as a trapper for Ashley.[25]

For at least two decades Beckwourth traveled western mountains and plains, working as an independent trader, an employee of Bent, St. Vrain's Company at Bent's Old Fort, and as a trapper and guide for the American Fur Company.[26] He was equally at home among many American Indian nations, including the Blackfeet and the Crows. In 1834, the Crow Nation conferred upon him the title "Chief of All Chiefs." While living with the Absarokas in Montana, he married two Indian women; then, in 1840, he married Louisa Sandoval in Santa Fe and, in 1860, he wed Elizabeth Lettbetter, an African American woman, in Denver.[27]

Most of his contemporaries regarded Beckwourth's abilities, if not his character, highly, but they branded him a "gaudy liar."[28] His exploits, greatly exaggerated in his autobiography, attest to an eventful life: He traveled with the Thomas Smith expedition along the Old Spanish Trail from Utah to southern California; operated Louis Vasquez's trading post at Fort Vasquez, Colorado; and fought with the rebel forces in the Battle of Cahuenga Pass in 1845 in a failed attempt to wrest independence for California from Mexico. In 1847, Beckwourth moved to New Mexico but was lured back to California in 1849 by the gold rush. Once there, he pursued a number of enterprises, including mining and shopkeeping but failed to strike it rich in any of them.[29]

As the fur trade began to wane and overland wagon trains started to fill the trails, Beckwourth, because of his familiarity with the western terrain and its Native populations, became a much sought-after wagon-train guide. He also became an outspoken promoter of western settlement, especially after his discovery in 1850 of a quicker, lower route through the Sierra Nevada. Now known as Beckwourth Pass, it would become the portal of a new emigrant route.[30] In late July or early August 1851, the first wagon train rolled through Beckwourth Pass, headed by the legendary black mountain man, now turned full-time wagon-train guide. Future poet laureate of California, Ina Coolbrith, a young girl in the train whom Beckwourth swept into his saddle in front of him as he led the procession, described him as "one of the most beautiful creatures that ever lived. He was rather dark and wore his hair in two long braids, twisted with colored cord that gave him a picturesque appearance."[31]

Despite its auspicious beginnings and heavy promotion, the Beckwourth Trail never became a major route for western emigrants. Beckwourth had overestimated the number of emigrants who actually would use it as an entry into California. By 1852, he had reinvented himself once again, this time as a hotelkeeper and trading-post operator. He told writer Thomas Bonner that his War Horse Ranch (located in present-day Sierra Valley, Plumas County) was the "emigrant's landing-place" and proclaimed that his place was the first one an emigrant "arrives at in the golden state, and is the only house between this point and Salt Lake." Describing the toll that the overland journey exacted from the weary emigrants who trailed into his establishment, he recalled: "Their wagon appears like a relic of the Revolution after doing hard service for the commissariat. . . . The old folks are peevish and quarrelsome, the young men are so headstrong, and the small children so full of wants, and precisely at a time when every thing has given out, and they have nothing to satisfy them with."[32]

By all accounts, Beckwourth was a generous host who took pride in the fact that, even though "numbers have put up at my ranch without a morsel of food, and without a dollar in the world to procure any," they "never were refused what they asked for at my house; and during the short space I have spent in the Valley, I have furnished provisions and other necessaries . . . to a very serious amount."[33] White overlander Henry Taylor testified to his hospitality, recalling that when his wagon company reached the ranch nearly starved in 1852, the black man greeted them warmly and informed them, "Boys, I have nothing to eat, but drink all you want, only leave me enough for tomorrow, for the train will be here then, and I will have plenty." Their host then suggested, "You're welcome to go down to the corral and kill a beef." Taylor reported, however, "we were all too tired for anything of that kind."[34]

By 1859, James Beckwourth had moved on to Colorado, pursuing the gold rush there. He started several businesses in Denver, even serving as an agent for the federal government in its negotiations with Native tribes during the Civil War. He continued to travel back and forth across the trails, until 1866, when he took a job as a scout and interpreter for the military expedition of Col. Henry Carrington, whose company set out from Fort Laramie on a mission to establish forts along the Bozeman Trail. Beckwourth died at Fort C. F. Smith in present-day Montana, at the age of sixty-seven or sixty-eight and was reported to have been buried on Crow land.[35]

Moses "Black" Harris

Moses "Black" Harris, a contemporary of Beckwourth's, also won fame as a mountain man, but virtually everything about his life is an enigma. He was born around 1800 probably in Union City, South Carolina, or somewhere in Kentucky. His parentage and his status as slave or free man is equally vague.[36] Indeed, controversy surrounds his racial background as well. Some of his contemporaries, including Beckwourth, referred to him as a white man. Another, W. H. Gray, described him as a man "of medium height, black hair, black whiskers, dark brown eyes and of very dark complexion."[37] Western artist Alfred Jacob Miller depicted Harris as the quintessential mountain man, dressed in skins and furs and having a "wiry frame, made up of bone and muscle with a face composed of tan leather and whipcord finished up with a peculiar blue black tint, as if gun powder had been burnt into his face."[38] White mountain man James Clyman's wry epitaph for his comrade seems to hint at African ancestry, alluding to the possibility that Harris's lifelong wanderlust in the West might have sprung from a desire "for the freedom of Equal rights."[39]

Fluent in several Native American languages, a consummate explorer, hunter, and guide, Harris started out as a trapper in 1822; in 1824, he joined Ashley's expedition to the Rocky Mountains.[40] Like Beckwourth, Harris turned to guiding wagon trains when the fur-trading business began to dwindle. His first interaction with westbound emigrants was as a trader transporting supplies to the annual fur traders' rendezvous in Wyoming. Then, in 1836, he led the Whitman-Spalding missionary party as far west as the Green River. By 1840, guiding wagon trains had become his full-time occupation. Harris, too, became an ardent proponent of western expansion and American settlement, even volunteering to lead a "filibustering expedition" to the internationally disputed Oregon Country.[41]

In 1844, Harris led the Gilliam-Simmons-Bush-Ford wagon company, which consisted of seven hundred wagons, one of the largest emigrant wagon trains to enter Oregon. The group contained at least eight African Americans, including free-born George W. Bush (who served as a scout for the party), his white wife, and five sons. Robin, Polly, and Mary Jane Holmes, the slaves of Nathaniel Ford, were the other known black overlanders in the company.[42] Harris guided them all into the Willamette Valley in October 1844 and remained in The Dalles, Oregon, until the spring of 1845. While preparing for another trip east that spring, he received an urgent request from Stephen Meeks, the guide of the hapless "Lost Meeks" party, who pleaded for the mountain man's help in saving his group, which had lost its way after trying a new cutoff and becoming stranded in the high desert of eastern Oregon. After gathering supplies from American Indians, Harris and others rode to the rescue, guiding the desperate emigrants safely to The Dalles on the Columbia River. In December of 1846, he once again mounted another rescue of starving emigrants coming into Oregon across the Applegate Trail.[43]

Harris left the Willamette in the spring of 1847, headed for St. Joseph, Missouri, where he advertised his services as a guide in the *St. Joseph Gazette,* then set out for Fort Laramie. When he returned to Missouri on April 18, 1849, he was on his way to St. Joseph, where he had contracted to serve as "pilot" for the fledgling Pioneer Lines, a private commercial wagon-train venture that pledged to transport overland passengers to California in the astonishing time of fifty-five to sixty days, for a flat fee of two hundred dollars.[44] While stopping over in Independence, Harris was stricken with cholera and died. In a letter to the editor of the *Independence Daily Union,* dated May 14, 1849, Pacific Line passenger Bernard Reid, using the pseudonym "Gerald," acknowledged his passing, writing that three men in Reid's Independence hotel had died in a twenty-four-hour period, the first being "Black Harris, chosen to lead us across the Rocky Mountains." Reid reported that as the mountain man lay dying, he spoke of a wife and two children living in an Indian village "in the mountain fastnesses." This is the only evidence that Moses "Black" Harris may have had a family.[45]

The explorers, settlers, and mountain men like Esteban, Isabel de Olvera, York, Edward Rose, Peter Ranne, James Beckwourth, Moses

"Black" Harris, and nameless others attest to a centuries-old presence of African-descended people in the present-day American West. Long before the great overland migrations, men and women of African ancestry, out of necessity, preference, or an affinity that sprang from diverse kinship ties, had been living and working within the "ethnic fluidity of the culture that evolved in the region."[46] The racially and culturally accommodating systems that had emerged in the preoverland migrations West gave African-descended people a remarkable degree of mobility in comparison with the settled areas of the East and South.[47]

The lives and exploits of these early westerners of African ancestry suggest that ability and fortitude could prevail over racial pedigree. African-descended women shouldered pioneering duties with their male counterparts in expeditions that would take them to the farthest outposts of settlement, blazing trails, enduring hardships, and building communities. Neither their gender nor their racial lineage disqualified them from taking part in that work or barred them from demanding and receiving legal rights. However, a different experience awaited the African American emigrants, free and enslaved, who followed the original group of African-descended pioneers. Much would change on the western frontier as national expansion brought with it the unyielding racial laws, customs, and tensions that dominated the United States during the mid-nineteenth century.

Chapter 2
On the Eve of Overland Migration
Antebellum Slavery and Freedom

Those coloured persons who are legally free, must necessarily hold their freedom by a very precarious tenure, particularly where every person tinged with an African die [sic], is presumed to be a slave, unless proven to be free.
African Observer, Philadelphia, 1827

I thought upon coming to a free State like Ohio, that I would find every door thrown open to receive me, but from the treatment I received by the people generally, I found it little better than in Virginia. . . . I found every door closed against the colored man in a free State, excepting the jails and penitentiaries, the doors of which were thrown wide open to receive him.
John Malvin, Ohio, 1827

My grandmother was her master's daughter; and my mother was her master's daughter; and I was my master's son; so you see I han't got but one-eighth of the blood. Now admitting it's right to make a slave of a full black nigger, I want to ask gentlemen acquainted with business, whether because I owe a shilling, I ought to be made to pay a dollar?
Lewis Garrard Clarke, fugitive slave, 1842

AT LEAST A CENTURY BEFORE black men and women took to the overland trails, a rigid line of racial demarcation between "white" and "other" had begun to emerge.[1] White Americans, driven by economic, social, and cultural factors, set about establishing a society in which race would be a major factor in determining who would be incorporated and who would be excluded.[2] For African Americans, race became a sign of their inferiority and servility that increasingly targeted them for enslavement. Slavery became the primary indicator of race, and "color" became "the sign of slavery."[3]

The Question of Race: The One-Drop Rule

If, at times, color made some African Americans indistinguishable from the whites who enslaved them, authorities invoked an arbitrary, scientifically unsupportable theory known as the "one-drop rule" to resolve the question. The one-drop rule was a system of racial classification that relied on an "imagined quantum of blood" and certain physical characteristics (skin, hair, nose, teeth, fingernails, and even feet) to establish racial identity. According to the one-drop rule, as little as one-fourth, one-eighth, one-sixteenth, one-thirty-second, or *one drop* of "black blood" qualified an individual as "Negro."[4] Unlike the Spanish *Sistema de Castas* (System of Castes) that delineated a hierarchy of racial classes—which included the African-descended explorers and pioneers in New Spain's empire—the one-drop rule disallowed intermediate racial categories. It held that a person with any degree of "African blood" was indeed black and presumed to *be* a slave or *suitable for* enslavement, irrespective of skin color or degree of "whiteness."[5]

Lewis Garrard Clarke, a Kentucky slave who escaped bondage and became popular on the abolitionist speaker's circuit, commented on the arbitrary and punitive nature of the one-drop rule. In a speech recounting his experiences as a slave who, like his mother and grandmother, was the child of his master, Clarke asserted: "I han't got but one-eighth of the blood. Now admitting it's right to make a slave of a full black nigger, I want to ask gentlemen acquainted with business, whether because I owe a shilling, I ought to be made to pay a dollar?"[6] The one-drop rule took precedence over parentage and birthplace, governed economic and social mobility, and served as a marker of moral character as well.[7] At the time of the great overland migrations, it had become the standard for establishing racial identity in the United States, and race provided the strongest justification for the systematic enslavement and exploitation of African Americans, whether they resided in the South, the border states, the North, or the West.

Antebellum Slavery and Freedom

In the antebellum period, African Americans lived in a nation that denied them legal rights and offered them few protections because of their race. This bleak environment pushed countless black men and women, enslaved and free, onto the overland trails to the West, seeking relief from the pervasive slave laws and black codes that controlled every aspect of their lives.

African Americans in the South

In the South, where the vast majority of African Americans resided, chattel slavery had become a deeply entrenched institution. Four million enslaved black Southerners toiled under a system that held them in lifetime, hereditary bondage. Some worked on large plantations as field hands and domestic laborers, others on smaller agricultural units, and some labored in a variety of urban factories and industries.[8] While each Southern state had its own set of slave codes, all slave codes followed a common pattern: Most prohibited slave gatherings (including religious services) without white supervision, forbade teaching slaves to read and write, and prohibited them from bearing firearms, legally marrying, or traveling without the written permission of their owners or overseers. As the pace of overland migration increased and growing numbers of slaveholders headed west, most enslaved black Southerners who set out on the trails did so as reluctant travelers, forced to do their masters' bidding and often leaving loved ones behind.

By contrast, free African Americans in the South (who composed a fraction of the region's total black population) eagerly began the trek west in pursuit of real freedom because, although they did not have masters, they were far from free. Black laws dictated that free black Southerners be prepared at all times to prove their freedom. Failure to do so could result in enslavement, as could failure to pay debts, court fines, or taxes. In addition, Southern laws prohibited free blacks from voting, holding office, or testifying in court against a white person. Georgia laws even barred them from owning property.[9]

African Americans in the Border States

Conditions for enslaved and free African Americans in the border states were much the same as in the lower South, except that large plantations were rarer in the border states, and most slaves worked on smaller units in closer proximity to their owners. However, neither plantation size nor proximity to owners altered the reality that here, as in all slaveholding regions, slaves did not have control over their own lives.

Missouri, a western border state deeply steeped in the mores, culture, and laws of the Old South, entered the Union as a slave state under the terms of the Missouri Compromise. Slaves there were owned by masters who kept only one or two slaves or a single family to work as general field hands, farmhands, and domestic servants. As in the other slaveholding regions, slavery became the mainstay of Missouri's economy.[10] Missouri's constitution recognized the institution of slavery but did not specify who could be enslaved. Yet it did, as historian Harrison Anthony Trexler has written, "fix the status of those to be considered colored," and thus effectively consigned African Americans to permanent chattel slavery. Drawing on the one-drop rule, Missouri lawmakers defined as black anyone having one-fourth or more "negro blood" and determined that such people would be governed by the same codes that regulated slaves, "negroes and mulattos."[11]

Ironically, Missouri's slave codes (which free blacks were also obliged to obey) held that slaves were simultaneously property and persons with some legal protections. As property, they could be sold in satisfaction of debt, given as gifts, and bequeathed in wills. They were required to obtain permission (written and verbal) before leaving their master's property, and their movements were strictly regulated. Gatherings larger than five people were forbidden unless overseen by whites, and runaways, including those just "lying out" (temporarily escaping to nearby woods or swamps), were jailed and "dealt with according to law." No "slave or mulatto whatsoever" was permitted to "carry any gun, powder, shot, club, or other weapons whatsoever"; and slaves engaging in "riots, routs, unlawful assemblies, and seditious speeches" would be "punished with stripes." Whites controlled all commercial transactions between slaves and free people, black or white, yet even when such transactions fulfilled every legal requirement, the deal still could be rescinded by the courts.[12]

As "persons," slaves in Missouri were guaranteed some legal protections, including protection from cruel treatment, a jury trial if charged with a felony, and the right to testify in court in "pleas of the state against negroes or mulattoes, bond or free," and in civil cases "where negroes and mulattoes shall be parties."[13] However, their most important protection was the ability to sue for freedom. Missouri law provided that any "person held in slavery" could "petition the circuit court, or judge thereof . . . to sue, as a poor person, in order to establish his right to freedom." The individual filing a "freedom suit" was required to "state in his petition the ground on which his claim to freedom is founded."[14] Most often, slaves who had resided in a free territory challenged their condition, citing the doctrine of "once free, always free" (the judicial practice that held that residence on free soil conferred freedom); others claimed that they had been granted freedom in their master's will or by purchase; and some sued on the basis of the freeborn status of their mother, arguing that the child's legal status followed that of the mother.[15]

By the 1840s, Missouri courts increasingly adjudicated unlawful enslavement claims on racial criteria. In two separate and parallel suits filed by siblings Charlotte and Pierre (who were of African American and American Indian lineage), the Missouri supreme court declared in Pierre's case that "the system [of slavery] being recognized in fact, it devolved upon the plaintiff, he being a negro, to show the law forbidding it." During the course of Charlotte's suit, the court proclaimed that the "existence of slavery in fact was presumptive evidence of its legality." In the final hearing of her case in 1857, the court held that slavery had long existed in Missouri and several other states "without any act of legislation introducing it and none was necessary" since "it was not dependent on any positive law for its recognition."[16]

In the border state of Kentucky, there was no doubt about the status of slaves or slavery. In 1849, Kentucky lawmakers approved an amendment to the state constitution establishing an "iron-bound guarantee of the preservation of slavery in the state." The 248,809 black slaves who lived there in 1850 could not sue for unlawful enslavement, nor did Kentucky laws recognize their personhood. Kentucky slave codes barred slaves from owning personal property (including his or her clothing, furnishings, and work tools), buying and selling without written permission, and entering into contracts. They were legally prohibited from testifying in court, except when making their own confessions, testifying in their own defense, or testifying in cases involving other blacks, "mulattoes, or Indians." If found guilty of giving false testimony, blacks, unlike whites, could be punished with "thirty-nine lashes."[17]

Restrictive laws also governed Kentucky's small free black population (11,000 in 1860). Kentucky black codes banned the entry of free blacks from other areas and prohibited the return of African Americans who had left the state. They required free blacks to carry "free papers," for which they were required to pay an annual registration fee. As in other slaveholding states, free black Kentuckians were denied the franchise, had no legal redress, and were subject to arrest for crimes ranging from keeping a disorderly house to owning more than one firearm. Kentucky law made it a crime for African Americans to defend themselves against white assaults regardless of the circumstances. If unable to pay the fines levied against them for these offenses, free African Americans risked being sold into slavery.[18]

The work conditions for black Kentuckians, enslaved and free, were similar to those in other border states. The absence of large plantations meant that most slaves lived and worked on smaller units, performing an array of duties and cultivating crops that included wheat and corn. However, the rise of "king cotton" stimulated Kentucky's production of hemp, used by planters and processors across the South as bale rope and bagging for cotton. Hemp production quickly eclipsed other crops, becoming the most valuable commodity grown in the state's Blue Grass region.[19]

As important as agriculture was to the economy, not all enslaved Kentuckians were agricultural workers. Many labored in mining and iron industries, worked in bridge and road construction, and served as teamsters and wagoneers. Enslaved black artisans applied their skills in the blacksmithing, shoemaking, carpentry, and weaving trades. By the 1830s, however, soaring cotton prices, the clamor of planters in the lower South for more slave labor, and declining economic conditions swept enslaved and free blacks in Kentucky and other border states into the flourishing interstate slave trade, which dragged them away to be auctioned off in slave markets across the Deep South. Between 1830 and 1860, in Kentucky alone, slaveholders sold more than 80,000 slaves farther South, reaping handsome profits in the process. This involuntary migration ripped apart black families and tore men, women, and children from the only homes most had ever known.[20]

In Virginia, where the majority of the nation's African American population lived, the situation was much the same. Economic depression, indebtedness, and exhausted farm soil forced planters to scale back operations. Taking advantage of the skyrocketing demand for slave labor, cash-strapped Virginia slave owners, like many others in the upper South, sold their "surplus" slaves farther South to markets in New Orleans, Mobile, and beyond, breaking up thousands of families and causing increasing numbers of desperate slaves to run away to escape this calamity.[21]

Virginia's agricultural and manufacturing sectors rebounded in the 1840s and 1850s, with slave labor firmly in place. Enslaved Virginians— the majority of whom lived east of the Blue Ridge in the southern Piedmont region in numbers rivaling the vast plantations of the Deep South—engaged in a variety of tasks. Some worked as field hands cultivating the wheat, corn, grain, and tobacco that composed the core of Virginia's agricultural wealth. A sizable number labored in the state's burgeoning iron, coal, salt, and railroad industries, and a smaller number of skilled black artisans worked as blacksmiths, carpenters, and cobblers. Virginia slaves (and slaves elsewhere in the Chesapeake) were allowed to "hire out" to earn money for themselves, after contracting to pay their masters a portion of their wages.[22] Hiring out allowed them to live on their own, taking responsibility for their food, clothing, and sometimes lodging. A hiring-out arrangement gave slaves a measure of independence and lessened their masters' control, but in Virginia, as elsewhere, slave codes and black laws left no doubt that whites had complete authority over African American lives.[23]

Virginia took the first step in legally regulating its slaves in 1636, adopting a measure that prohibited slaves from bearing arms. By the antebellum period, the state had put in place a battery of laws governing black Virginians—slaves and free people. Slaves could not purchase or consume alcohol, assemble unless under white supervision, travel without a written pass, or conduct religious services without a white minister (or a black one approved and supervised by a white man) being present. Following the slave revolts that terrified white Virginians in 1800 and 1831, the state further tightened its laws, banning African American ministers from preaching in the state altogether and criminalizing slave literacy. Free blacks were forbidden to obtain an education in Virginia, and those who left to be educated elsewhere were barred from returning. Emancipated slaves were not allowed to remain in the state longer than one year at the risk of re-enslavement. Special criminal courts were set up for slaves charged with crimes. There, they faced juries not of their peers but of slaveholders who owned at least three hundred dollars worth of slave property. In addition, Virginia legislators enacted laws creating and funding the slave patrols and militia that were charged with enforcing these laws.[24]

African Americans in Texas and Indian Territory

Texas, a region with both southern and southwestern roots, was, for a brief time, a haven for fugitive slaves and free blacks who fled there, encouraged by Mexico's abolition of slavery after winning independence from Spain in 1821. Despite the fact that Mexico had abolished the institution of slavery, Mexican authorities made no attempt to eliminate it in the country's northern provinces. Therefore, in the early 1820s, white Southerners moving west to join Stephen Austin's American colony in Mexican *Tejas*, carried slavery along with them. By 1825, there were 443 black bondsmen in *Tejas,* and, as Quintard Taylor has noted, by 1835, "fully 10 percent of English-speaking Texans were slaves."[25]

The Texas revolution against Mexico flared that year, largely over slavery issues, and the resulting Republic of Texas legalized the institution. In 1836, approximately 5,000 enslaved black people lived in Texas; four years later, the slave population there had soared to 11,323.[26] The republic's new constitution mandated that free blacks already living in Texas petition Congress for permission to stay, but later the Texas legislature reversed its position and allowed blacks to remain without citizenship rights. Black Texans—anyone of at least one-eighth African blood—could not vote, own property, or testify against whites in a court of law.[27] In 1845, Texas joined the Union as a slave state, and in 1860, on the eve of the Civil War, the slave population stood at 182,921, some 30 percent of the state's total residents.[28]

The expansion of African American slavery into what would become present-day Oklahoma began in the 1830s as a direct result of the federal government's forced relocation of Indian tribes from their homes in the South to "Indian Territory," which would become the "second-largest slaveholding region in the West."[29] By 1860, more than 7,000 slaves (about 14 percent of the total population) lived in Indian Territory, taken there by the Cherokee, Chickasaw, Seminole, Choctaw, and Creek (Muskogee) people who had adopted some distinctive Southern social and economic practices, including plantation agriculture and black slavery. The Cherokee alone transported several hundred black slaves to Indian Territory in 1838; of those, 175 died on the infamous Trail of Tears. So deep were the Five Tribes' Southern roots that in 1861, the Cherokee Nation issued a decree in support of the South in the "War of Northern Aggression" [the Civil War] and mustered troops to fight for the Confederacy.[30]

African Americans in the North

North of the Mason-Dixon Line, African Americans endured discrimination, prejudice, and violence with few rights or protections. White Northerners, who steadfastly opposed slavery and its spread, nevertheless passed laws designed to discourage free African Americans from settling in their communities. Massachusetts led the way on this in 1788, when it barred blacks from living there longer than two months under penalty of imprisonment, whipping, and hard labor. In addition, the fight over black male enfranchisement became a flashpoint for African American Northerners. Their efforts to gain the franchise met with mixed results.

In 1807, New Jersey law prevented black men from voting; by 1844, the state constitution specifically limited the franchise to white men. In 1818, Connecticut adopted a measure granting suffrage to black men who had voted prior to that date. In 1821, New York placed property qualifications on black male voters, requiring them to own property worth at least two hundred fifty dollars and to pay taxes; white men had only to pay taxes or serve in the state militia to meet state voting requirements. In 1845, Pennsylvania's new state constitution universally enfranchised white men but disfranchised African American men who previously had been permitted to vote in some counties of the state, subject to property qualifications. On the eve of the Civil War, African Americans in Massachusetts, like their counterparts residing in other Northern states, had won the right to vote, use public transportation, hold public office, testify in court, serve on juries, and intermarry with whites. However, black Northerners remained excluded from most public venues, were discriminated against in the workplace, and were confined to segregated neighborhoods and schools.[31]

Conditions for African Americans in the states of the Old Northwest (Ohio, Indiana, Illinois, Iowa, and Wisconsin) were even more dismal. In 1803, Indiana banned African Americans from testifying in court, voting, and serving in the militia. In addition, the legislature levied a three dollar tax on all black men residing in the state. Similarly, Ohio required African Americans to post a five hundred dollar bond upon entering the state, and in 1839, Ohio lawmakers approved a measure that forbade African Americans from petitioning for any reason whatsoever. Even Wisconsin, with the smallest black population in the Old Northwest, established an antiblack suffrage law.[32]

When the wagons began rolling westward in the antebellum period, some 200,000 African Americans lived in a state of "unfreedom" in the North. Thanks to a welter of laws that denied most of them basic legal rights and protections and precluded them from redressing their grievances, black Northerners were reduced to living as squatters in states where many of them had been born and had resided for generations.[33]

African Americans in the West

Historian William Loren Katz has observed that black laws established in the East "moved westward with the pioneer's wagons," spreading first to the western territories carved from the Old Northwest.[34] In the territories of Montana, New Mexico, Arizona, and Nevada, where African Americans made up just a small percentage of the total population, exclusionary laws and policies plagued them as well. In Montana, suffrage became the most pressing concern for blacks when the territory was created in 1864. The organic act that authorized the territory's creation restricted suffrage to white males. After intense debate, most of which centered on Wisconsin senator James R. Doolittle's contention that no blacks resided in Montana, the Senate and House of Representatives reached a compromise that removed the whites-only voting provision and broadened the franchise to male citizens of the United States. This move excluded African American men who, being barred from citizenship, could not vote in Montana or anywhere else in the country. Not until the passage of the Territorial Suffrage Act in 1867 and the ratification of the Fourteenth and Fifteenth Amendments in 1868 and 1870, respectively, did African Americans receive citizenship and black men obtain the right to vote in territorial and federal elections.[35]

In New Mexico Territory, where Native American indentured servitude and slavery and Mexican peonage constituted the major sources of coerced labor, the Compromise of 1850 played an important role in determining slave codes and black laws. A key part of the compromise provided that slavery in New Mexico (and in Utah Territory) be determined by popular sovereignty. Despite the relative absence of African Americans in New Mexico Territory (black slaves never exceeded a dozen or so in number), New Mexico legislators quickly began to pass black laws.[36] In a move to prevent an influx of fugitive and freed Texas slaves, New Mexico officials in 1856 placed a limit on the number of free blacks allowed to enter. In 1859, the territory instituted its first slave code, which restricted slave travel, barred all blacks from giving testimony in court, and forbade slaveholders from arming their slaves except in defense against Indian raids.[37]

The southern portion of New Mexico Territory, generally referred to as Arizona, was a hotbed of Southern sentiment even before the Civil War. Eventually, it enacted similar antiblack codes. In 1860, the inhabitants there took matters into their own hands and renamed the area the Territory of Arizona, making the town of Mesilla (the main route between Texas and California) the territorial capital. Pro-Confederate residents of the Territory of Arizona (both Americans and Mexicans) voted to secede from the Union in 1861, proclaiming the region to be the Confederate Territory of Arizona. In 1862, after Union forces defeated the Confederates in the crucial battle of Glorieta Pass, the federal government regained control of the area. That same year, Congress banned slavery in all U.S. territories and, in 1863, recognized Arizona (now located west of the 109th meridian) as an official territory of the United States. However, African Americans in the newly created Arizona Territory continued to suffer under legal prohibitions that denied them voting and other civil rights.[38]

Similar conditions beset the tiny African American community in the portion of Utah Territory that later became Nevada. The federal census enumerated only forty-four blacks living in the region in 1860, most clustered around the Virginia City and Gold Hill areas in the western part of the territory. They composed only 0.6 percent of the total population.[39] Yet, from the outset, Nevada was, as historian Elmer R. Rusco has written, "racist during the territorial and early statehood period." Despite substantial antislavery and pro-Union sentiment in the territory, Nevada lawmakers made it their top priority to "legislate for white men."[40] In 1861, they adopted a measure banning slavery, but subsequently passed laws that granted the franchise to white men only and prohibited nonwhites from holding office, serving on juries, testifying against whites in court, and joining the militia. No provisions were made for the public education of nonwhite children, and intermarriage between whites and nonwhites (including blacks, mulattoes, Indians, and Chinese) was criminalized. When Nevada entered the Union in 1864, officials drafted a constitution that continued earlier racial policies, but in 1865, they modified the testimony law to permit African Americans to testify in court under limited conditions. In the matter of public education, the new constitution specifically excluded African American children from attending public schools unless separate, segregated public schools had been established for them.[41]

The situation was just as bleak in the territories of the Far West. In 1844, Peter H. Burnett, a newly elected member of the Oregon provisional government, introduced a bill that banned slavery from Oregon Territory but levied severe penalties on black people attempting to enter. In June of the same year, that governing body also approved a bill known as the Oregon Black Exclusion Law—commonly called the Lash Law. This measure ordered all black people over the age of eighteen out of Oregon within two years (if male), three years (if female), or be subjected to twenty to thirty-nine lashes from a whip. This punishment would be repeated every six months "until he or she shall quit the territory." The law was amended six months later. Now, instead of whipping, African Americans who remained in Oregon beyond the specified time would be turned over to work for a white "employer" for a brief period, after which the "employer" was required to remove the black person from the territory or be fined $1,000. Oregon legislators repealed this law in 1845 before it could take effect.[42]

When Oregon became an official possession of the United States in 1846, and organized its territorial legislature three years later, in September 1849, legislators adopted a measure requiring all black and mulatto newcomers to leave the territory within forty days but exempted those already there. This decree remained in force until being replaced by the Oregon constitution of 1859, which banned black immigration into the state and prohibited African Americans from voting. In addition, Oregon's Homestead Act, in place since 1850, excluded African Americans from claiming and settling on the land that the government offered free of charge to white settlers.[43]

California entered the Union as a free state in 1850 by way of the Compromise of 1850, which outlawed slavery in the Golden State. Nevertheless, the free state of California had, by far, the largest number of "bond servants" west of Texas.[44] In 1852, some three hundred black slaves, illegally held by white owners, labored in California's goldfields, and an undetermined number worked as domestic servants. As in other western states, California lawmakers quickly established an array of laws that severely restricted African Americans' ability to earn a living and protect themselves—leaving them vulnerable to exploitation of all sorts. Denied citizenship, they could not legally settle on public land, vote, hold public office, serve on juries, attend public schools, or use public transportation. In 1852, the state passed a bill that prohibited African Americans from testifying in court against whites.[45]

That same year, California adopted its own fugitive slave law, mirroring the federal Fugitive Slave Act of 1850.[46] California's Fugitive

Slave Act denied the freedom claims of slaves who were brought into the state by gold-seeking southern whites, required that captured black fugitives be returned to their owners, and imposed a five hundred dollar fine and prison sentence on any white person who helped a former slave escape arrest. The law, in effect for one year, was extended in 1853 and again in 1854.[47] California's Fugitive Slave Act would have significant consequences for innumerable enslaved black overlanders who accompanied their owners to California expecting manumission in exchange for their labor.

Utah: Slaves and Saints

In Utah, the confluence of religion, race, slavery, and politics enmeshed African Americans in a system unlike any other in the antebellum West. The African Americans who arrived in the Salt Lake valley in 1847 as part of the Mormon western exodus were among the first blacks to enter the region. They came as slaves and free people, Mormons and non-Mormons, and their numbers increased with the arrival of each new Mormon contingent.[48] Although many of the black newcomers had adopted the Mormon faith, conversion did not grant them equality of status or legal standing. Utah became the only western territory where black slavery and slave sales were safeguarded by territorial statute and, as in New Mexico Territory, popular sovereignty dictated the context for slavery in Utah.[49] The contradictory and changing Mormon position on blacks and slavery resulted in African Americans in Utah Territory, enslaved and free, converts or not, being subordinated to whites, much like other African Americans in the West and across the nation. Mormon doctrine, which condemned all forms of human bondage and led some Mormon leaders to oppose slavery forcefully, underwent a transformation with regard to race and slavery during this time.[50]

Mormon Church founder Joseph Smith, in his 1844 presidential campaign bid, denounced the peculiar institution and called for the "break down [of] slavery" and the destruction of the "shackles from the poor black man." He stopped short of calling for African American equality, proposing instead that all slaves be emancipated and relocated to Texas (which was then part of Mexico) or to Canada.[51] After the expulsion of the Latter-day Saints from Missouri and their relocation to

Nauvoo, Illinois, Mormon opposition to slavery reached its peak. But as early as the 1830s, when anti-Mormonism had become widespread and more violent, church leaders, hoping (in part) to avert the wrath of militant antiabolitionists, began to temper their antislavery stance.[52] In 1835, church leadership approved a resolution that acknowledged their responsibility to "preach the gospel to the nations of the earth," but insisted that Mormons "do not believe it right to interfere with bond servants, neither preach the gospel to nor baptize them, contrary to the will and wish of their masters," nor did the church intend to "meddle with or influence" slaves to be "dissatisfied with their situations in this life," at the risk of "jeopardizing the lives of men."[53]

Brigham Young, who was ordained church president three years after Joseph Smith's murder, took an even stronger position in support of black enslavement, finding justification for it in church doctrine.[54] Speaking before a joint session of the legislative assembly in 1852, Young declared that the church believed that blacks were descended from "Ham and Canaan," in league with Cain and the devil, and were condemned by their lineage to be the "servant of servants." African Americans therefore would "inevitably carry the curse which was placed upon them until the same authority, which placed it there, shall see proper to have it removed."[55]

Young, who claimed to own no slaves, welcomed slaveholding Mormons into the newly established Utah Territory in 1852. Leaving no doubt about his stance on African Americans, he declared in a speech to territorial lawmakers, "I am a firm believer in slavery." Asserting that "the Negro in the Southern States are [sic] much better treated than the laboring classes of England," he declared that if "a master has a Negro, and uses him well, he is much better off than if he was free."[56] In a move designed to appease wealthy and politically connected Utah slave owners, court slaveholding Southern Mormons, and limit the importation of slaves into Utah, while currying favor with proslavery representatives in Congress, at Brigham Young's urging, the territorial legislature passed "An Act in Relation to Service," which legally recognized slavery in the Great Basin.[57]

The act elaborated Mormon views of slavery, portraying African American bondage as indentured servitude rather than chattel slavery, and cast slaveholding Mormons in the role of benevolent masters who were admonished to use their black servants with "all the heart and feelings, as they would use their own children."[58] The law also laid out Utah's slave codes, which, unlike Southern black codes, placed greater emphasis on the behavior of slave owners than on slave behavior. Utah laws prevented owners from selling their slaves out of the territory without the slaves' consent, forbade slaveholders from engaging in sexual relations "with any of the African race" under penalty of fines ranging from $500 to $5,000, and required masters to provide slaves with sufficient food, shelter, clothing, and recreational opportunities. The law also called for owners to provide schooling for slaves between the ages of "six and twenty years" for "not less than eighteen months" and required Utah slaveholders to prove that their human property had come into the territory "of their own free will and choice."[59]

Despite its benevolent veneer, the act represented the culmination of racial antipathies that had begun to emerge at least a decade before the Mormon pilgrimage to the Great Salt Lake basin. These trends intensified in the wake of Joseph Smith's murder and were codified into law within the first five years of Mormon settlement in the region.[60] By early 1852, African Americans in Utah, enslaved and free, were banned by the territorial legislature (and by municipal officials in later Great Basin settlements) from voting, holding public office, and serving in the territorial militia. These prohibitions were written into the constitution of the proposed Mormon state of Deseret, beginning in 1856 and again in 1860 and 1862.[61] Although many Latter-day Saints (including Vermont-born Brigham Young) had come to Utah from regions that were strongholds of abolitionism, the Mormon position about the place of African Americans in their unique society ultimately reflected the racial attitudes and practices embraced by the rest of white America.

Tensions over Race and Slavery

Regardless of region, African Americans were dominated by laws that enslaved, excluded, penalized, and terrorized them. Added to this was the violence that roiled through antebellum cities—violence that marked the killing and injuring of black men, women, and children and reinforced the precarious context in which all African Americans lived.

In the South, white fears of slave uprisings, "amalgamation," and economic competition subjected African Americans to punishments that included imprisonment, physical abuse, and outright murder.[62] North of the Mason-Dixon Line, whites adamantly opposed slavery and its expansion, but most were hostile to blacks settling in their cities. This hostility routinely spilled over into mob violence that targeted African Americans. Such behavior grew out of fear that a flood of cheap black labor would undercut white men's wages; later, out of many poor whites' perception that they were being drafted to fight on behalf of slaves in the Civil War; and in no small part out of white society's deep-rooted racial prejudices.

In Cincinnati, Ohio, white hostility simmered for years before finally exploding into an orgy of violence that devastated the African American community there. In 1827, Cincinnati officials, in a campaign to curb the growth of the city's African American population (2,258, or 9.4 percent of the city's total population of 24,148), began harshly enforcing state black laws. In addition, city fathers attempted to eliminate black competition in the job market by imposing fines on African Americans that barred them from skilled trades. These measures left black Cincinnatians with few economic prospects and no confidence that the situation would improve. John Malvin, a free-born black Virginian who fled the South, commented on the dismal state of affairs that greeted him upon his arrival in Cincinnati in 1827: "I thought upon coming to a free State like Ohio, that I would find every door thrown open to receive me, but . . . I found every door closed against the colored man in a free State, excepting the jails and penitentiaries."[63]

This discouraging situation prompted black Cincinnatians to organize an emigration society with the intention of relocating elsewhere; Canada seemed like a promising place.[64] In June 1829, the society elected Thomas Crissup and Israel Lewis to travel to Upper Canada and purchase land for an all-black settlement there. After meeting with and receiving encouragement from Lt. Gov. John Colbourne of Upper Canada, Crissup and Lewis bought 4,000 acres of land (at $1.50 an acre) in Biddulph Township, along the Au Sable River, less than twenty miles from Lake Huron and the Thames River and eight miles from Lake

Erie, in Ontario. They named the settlement Wilberforce, after the British antislavery champion William Wilberforce, and organized it as an independent, rural agricultural community for black farmers and cattle ranchers.[65]

In August 1829, before the black exodus got underway, white Cincinnatians embarked on a week-long rampage in which rock-throwing armed mobs destroyed black homes, buildings, and businesses. This outburst added extra urgency to African Americans' emigration plans.[66] An estimated 1,100 to 1,500 black people fled Cincinnati because of the riot; they included families who were unprepared for long-distance travel. They sought refuge in nearby cities, only to return to Cincinnati after things had calmed down.[67]

Others, however, were ready and willing to travel much farther. Some 460 to 2,000 black Cincinnatians, under the leadership of James C. Brown, a former Kentucky slave who had purchased his freedom, set out for Canada. Mobilizing all their resources for the 377-mile journey, the group traveled on foot and in wagons, rolling through Ohio, across Lake Erie from Sandusky, and on to the Wilberforce settlement in Canada. Once they arrived, however, most of the emigrants did not settle in Wilberforce, choosing instead to live in established Canadian cities, where work was more plentiful. In 1835, Cincinnati was rocked by another riot that targeted abolitionists, their newspaper presses, and African American neighborhoods and businesses. Antiblack violence exploded again in the city in 1836, 1839, and 1841.[68]

One year after the 1829 Cincinnati riot, whites in Portsmouth, Ohio, forced 80 of the town's 200 black residents to flee. In 1846, in Carthagena, Mercer County, Ohio (near Columbus), white mobs drove away 383 newly arrived African Americans who had been the slaves of Sen. John Randolph of Roanoke, Virginia. Randolph's will had manumitted them upon his death and stipulated that the freed people be relocated to a free state on land to be purchased with funds from his estate. Randolph's executor paid $38,000 for 3,200 acres of land in Mercer County to settle the former slaves, but a confrontation with hostile whites forced them to abandon their plans and seek shelter with sympathetic whites, or move on.[69]

Antiblack riots swept other Northern cities as well. African Americans in Philadelphia were the victims of recurring eruptions of violence in 1820, 1829, 1834, 1835, 1838, 1842, and 1849.[70] Riotous white mobs besieged African Americans in Pittsburg, Providence, Boston, Detroit, Utica, and Buffalo, killing and maiming scores and destroying black-owned property. However, the New York City draft riot of 1863 earned the dubious distinction of being the grimmest of all race upheavals in antebellum United States. Hundreds of angry whites, including many Irish immigrants who feared black workplace competition and resented that black men were exempted from the draft, tore through the city, hanging African Americans from lamp poles, murdering others in their homes, and burning down an orphanage for African American children. The raging horde killed upwards of one hundred black people in the four-day rampage.[71] In 1830, African Americans throughout the North, shocked and outraged by the Cincinnati riot and the upsurge of antiblack violence in the country, came together to found the American Society of Free Persons of Color. The society held its first convention in Philadelphia, where the group demanded an end to the violence and the immediate abolition of slavery, and advocated black emigration to Canada. This organization was the beginning of the free black convention movement—a movement that extended the fight for civil rights and equality westward with the African Americans who made their way over the trails.[72]

While hostility and violence continued to plague black people, tensions over the issue of slavery reached a boiling point in 1854, when the Kansas-Nebraska Act repealed the Missouri Compromise, established Kansas Territory, and permitted residents to determine by popular vote whether the territory would enter the Union as a free or slave state. Within days of the act's passage, hundreds of Missouri "emigrants" surged into Kansas to claim land and help carry the vote for slavery; nonresident abolitionists likewise flooded in to ensure that Kansas would be a free-soil state. "Bleeding Kansas"—where only 2 slaves and 625 "free colored people" had resided in 1860—became a violent flashpoint of the North-South conflict over the western expansion of slavery. Raiders of both pro- and anti-slavery persuasions crossed the Missouri-Kansas border to punish the opposition.[73]

These were the conditions that led many African Americans to seek refuge where they could—in other cities, in Canada, and on the overland trails bound for the West.

No Rights to Be Respected

The landmark *Dred Scott* decision of 1857 left no doubt about the status of African Americans in the nation wherever they resided, free or enslaved. The ruling not only denied black people basic human rights but also increased their vulnerability to kidnappers, slave hunters, and all categories of exploitation.[74]

In the 1830s, Dred Scott, a Virginia-born slave living in Missouri, accompanied his owner, John Emerson, an army doctor, to the free state of Illinois and the free territory of Wisconsin. Sometime in 1836 or 1837, while on "free soil," Scott married Harriet Robinson, a teenaged slave owned by Maj. Lawrence Taliaferro, the Indian agent for Wisconsin Territory. In October 1837, the army once again transferred Emerson from Fort Snelling (in present-day Hennepin County, Minnesota) to St. Louis, Missouri, leaving Dred and Harriet in Wisconsin to be hired out. Emerson was subsequently posted to Louisiana, where he married Eliza Irene Sanford in February 1838. The newlyweds demanded that Dred and Harriet join them in Louisiana, and the black couple voluntarily traveled back to the slave state. In September 1838, the Emersons and the Scotts stopped in St. Louis, later moving on to Fort Snelling. In May 1840, Emerson was transferred to Florida, leaving his wife and slaves in St. Louis with his father-in-law, Alexander Sanford, who hired out Dred and Harriet. In 1842, Emerson returned to St. Louis and moved to Davenport, Iowa, with his wife, but left his slaves in Missouri.[75]

Three years after Emerson's death in 1843, Dred and Harriet Scott filed separate lawsuits in the Missouri courts, demanding freedom and arguing that their stay on free soil had conferred freedom on them forever. Under the long-standing Missouri legal precedence of "once free, always free" used in adjudicating other freedom suits, what should have been a strong case for Scott turned out otherwise.[76] Dred Scott lost his first suit, won his second, lost again on appeal in the Missouri supreme court, and lost again in the U.S. circuit court. In the final appeal, *Dred*

Scott v. Sanford, the U.S. Supreme Court, with chief justice Roger B. Taney of Maryland writing for the predominantly Southern majority, ruled that African Americans "had no rights which the white man was bound to respect; and that the negro might justly and lawfully be reduced to slavery for . . . [the white man's] benefit." Moreover, the court held that Scott's sojourn on free soil did not negate the fact that he, like all slaves, was chattel property, and Congress had no authority to pass legislation (including the Missouri Compromise or the Kansas-Nebraska Act) that prevented slave owners from taking their human property into any territory whatsoever.[77]

Eventually, the Scotts' new owner, Dr. Calvin Chaffee, a Massachusetts abolitionist and member of Congress who had married John Emerson's widow, freed Dred and Harriet. The couple moved to St. Louis, where Harriet worked as a laundress and Dred was employed as a porter at the Barnum Hotel. In 1858, less than sixteen months after gaining his freedom, Dred Scott died of tuberculosis. Harriet passed away in the St. Louis home of her daughter and son-in-law in 1876.[78]

The *Dred Scott* ruling became the most important legal decision on the issues of slavery, freedom, and race in antebellum America. It legally stripped African Americans of their personhood and further entrenched the institution of slavery in the nation's economic, political, and social life, outraging abolitionists and heartening proslavery forces.[79] Before *Dred Scott* condemned African American slaves to lifetime bondage, free blacks, living in slavery's looming shadow, had only a tenuous grasp on their freedom. The *African Observer,* a Philadelphia-based abolitionist journal, noted in 1827 that "those colored persons who are legally free, must necessarily hold their freedom by a very precarious tenure, particularly, where every person tinged with an African die, is presumed to be a slave, unless proved to be free."[80] The Supreme Court ruling in 1857 only worsened their condition. It increased the risk of enslavement for all African Americans, whether they remained at home or traveled the overland routes leading west.

In the South, North, East, and West, African Americans existed on the economic and social margins of antebellum society. The scientifically untenable but legally and socially accepted "one-drop rule" provided justification for their condition. If enslaved, African American men, women, and children served as the permanent, hereditary property of their owners, without rights or legal recourse. If free, every aspect of their lives was governed by black codes that denied them suffrage and barred them access to courts, public schools, and other economic and social accommodations.

In the cities located above the Mason-Dixon Line, waves of violent eruptions that killed and displaced thousands of African Americans confirmed that most white Northerners were no more willing to accept them as equals than were whites in the slaveholding South. In the states and territories of the West, where slavery had been outlawed, white legislators nonetheless scrambled to create laws restricting the African Americans who resided there and preventing others from entering. African Americans in Mormon Utah were no more shielded from racist laws and policies than blacks in other regions. Utah's slave codes and black laws, though overlaid with religious dogma, consigned black people to enduring bondage and subservience.

Finally, the *Dred Scott* ruling represented the culmination of racial laws and attitudes that had existed for more than two centuries. It inflicted a devastating blow to African Americans' aspirations for freedom and rendered black people legally and socially inconsequential. This decision imperiled black lives by legitimizing the work of the ubiquitous slave hunters who scoured the country for runaway slaves and other vulnerable black people.

African Americans who headed west on the overland trails, free or enslaved, did so for similar reasons. Slaves, forced to follow and serve their westbound owners, often departed with mixed feelings as they reluctantly left their families behind. Free blacks voluntarily trekked west, refusing to languish in their old homes without real freedom or opportunity. All made their way with caution, acutely aware of the conditions surrounding them yet with an abiding conviction that their lives would be changed for the better once they stepped out on the trail.

Chapter 3
The Jumping-Off Places

Here might be seen the African slave with his shining black face, driving his six horse team of blood-red bays . . . some [wagons] driven by Spaniards, some by Americans resembling Indians, some by negroes, and others by persons of all possible crosses between these various races.
J. Quinn Thornton, Independence, Missouri, 1848

[A] gentleman of color from Wisconsin came here [Kanesville, Iowa] last night to join two teams which he had fitted out, well— he found his teams and was very summarily dismissed by his hired white men, one of whom drew a pistol and ordered him to vamose [sic] . . . taking advantage of the night[,] the gentlemen . . . were "bound for California at the nigger's expense."
Edward H. N. Patterson, Kanesville, Iowa, 1850

BY THE EARLY 1840S, THE MISSOURI River marked the boundary between the settled United States and the western frontier. In the era of overland migration, thousands of hopeful travelers, black and white, poured into the towns and outposts along the Missouri River, prepared to "jump off" onto the trails. From these river towns, travelers crossed the Missouri River and began their long overland trek. Historian Merrill J. Mattes has defined the jumping-off places as the "Missouri River border towns" that served as trailheads for the "feeder lines" converging onto the Great Platte River Road. They were the spots where people outfitted for the overland trip before "jumping off" into the lawless (at least initially) "Indian Territory" west of the Missouri River.[1] Some emigrants traveled directly overland from their old homes in the East, the Upper Midwest, and the South to reach the jumping-off towns, while many others boarded riverboats or traveled overland to St. Louis, at the confluence of the Mississippi and Missouri

Rivers. From St. Louis, travelers continued by steamer up the Missouri to Independence, Westport (Kansas City, Missouri), and points north, where their real adventure would begin.[2]

Getting to the Jumping-Off Places

For many travelers, the journey overland began long before arriving at the jumping-off places or setting foot on the Oregon, California, or Mormon Trails. It was grueling for everyone, but slaves who traveled with their owners experienced problems that frequently put them at greater risk than the whites with whom they trekked. In the winter of 1847, a group of enslaved African Americans began making their way west as part of the Mormon exodus. The men—Oscar Crosby, thirty-two, Hark Lay, twenty-two, Henry Brown, age unknown, and an unnamed black man owned by Mississippi Mormon John H. Bankhead—were part of an advance team for a brigade of Mormons known as the "Mississippi Saints" who were leaving the South for what later would become Utah.[3] The advance team departed Mississippi on January 10, 1847, in an initial party of two wagons that included the "four colored servants," David Powell (brother of Mormon pioneer John Powell), Daniel M. Thomas and family (who brought their two slaves, Phileman and Tennessee), and Charles Crimson. John Brown, a white Mormon convert, had been directed by Brigham Young to shepherd the group to Winter Quarters, Nebraska, where they would rendezvous with other Latter-day Saints awaiting departure to the West.[4]

The thousand-mile journey to the Mormon trailhead in Nebraska took them across Mississippi and through Tennessee, Kentucky, and Missouri. The trip exacted a heavy toll on the travelers, who were plagued by severe storms, freezing temperatures, and exhaustion. John Brown wrote in his journal, "As we traveled northward the weather became extremely cold. At St. Louis, where we were joined by Joseph Stratton and his family, we purchased more teams and wagons. A few days later Bryant Nowlin and Matthew Ivory overtook us, and we now had six wagons. But the mud was so heavy that we had to lay over several days." Brown added that the temperature turned bitterly cold, "giving us the severest kind of weather, which was extremely hard on the Negroes." He declared that "this journey from Mississippi was the hardest and severest trip I had ever undertaken," but he noted that "the negroes suffered most."[5]

Brown's journal does not indicate why the African Americans in the company were hit hardest by the brutal conditions. Certainly, everyone, regardless of race, engaged in difficult work as they made their way, and everyone was exposed to the harsh weather. However, the fact of enslavement likely exacerbated the situation for the African Americans in the party. Slaves, whether they labored on Southern plantations or in wagon trains, typically were forced to perform the most strenuous and hazardous work. In wagon companies, nearly everyone, regardless of race, walked the distance. But unlike white travelers, slaves rarely were permitted to ride; nor were their owners obliged to carry additional supplies while trudging endless miles on foot.[6] Slaves routinely cleared trails, rescued animals from icy rivers, rounded up stray livestock, and pulled stranded wagons, animals, and people from the muddy quagmires that often made roads miserable. Whites engaged in these tasks too, but slaves were on call twenty-four hours a day, compelled to do their masters' bidding under all conditions, without protest and often without sufficient food, water, clothing, shelter, or rest. There is nothing to suggest that the experiences of the "four colored servants" in the Mormon party were any different.[6]

These realities perhaps explain why two of the six slaves who embarked on the mid-winter trip from Mississippi to Nebraska succumbed to lobar pneumonia, an illness known in the antebellum period as "winter fever." Slaves were particularly susceptible to influenza and other respiratory ailments; and pneumonia was, in the words of historian Eugene Genovese, "a steady slave killer" throughout the South after 1845. By 1850, Southern "planters more or less assumed that their slaves would be troubled regularly by pneumonia and related diseases."[7] The Medical Society of the State of North Carolina conceded in 1852 that the winter and spring months were the worst time for slaves who were "much exposed to the inclemencies of the weather."[8] John Brown recorded in his journal that his slave Henry Brown "took cold and finally the winter fever set in which caused his death on the road." John Brown buried Henry Brown in Andrew County "at the lower end of the round Prairie, eight miles north of Savannah, Missouri." By the time the party reached Council Bluffs, the unnamed black man owned by John H. Bankhead also had died of winter fever. Brown does not mention the location of this slave's burial place.[9]

First Impressions

Emigrants who made it to the jumping-off towns received their first eye-opening lessons about getting set for life on the trails. Their stopover in the river towns of Independence, Westport, St. Joseph, and Kanesville (Council Bluffs) left most—black and white—both fascinated and appalled. The teeming crowds, sky-high prices, relentless cacophony, and raucous environment that greeted them were overwhelming.[10] Western adventurer and future historian Francis Parkman wrote in 1846 that in Independence, a "multitude of shops had sprung up to furnish emigrants and Santa Fe traders with necessaries for the journey." The town pulsated with the "incessant hammering and banging from a dozen blacksmiths' sheds, where the heavy wagons were being repaired, and the horses and oxen shod;" and the "streets were thronged with men, horses and mules."[11]

Similarly, a new arrival to St. Joseph observed that the town contained "some two thousand five hundred inhabitants and at present is a very busy place on account of the California emigrations which seems to center here. . . . [The] place contains four good sized Hotels, about twenty stores and the residue is made up of groceries, bakeries, & C."[12] Business owners in Independence boasted that their town offered "Provisions and Implements of every kind suited to the wants of emigrants," including "several large Wagon and Carriage Manufactories, in which are between 40 and 50 forges. These have on hand a large number of Baggage and Spring Wagons and Carriages, made expressly for emigrants, which may be bought at from $80 to $100 . . . [and] three large Saddlery establishments, which have on hand large and superior stocks of Saddles, Harness, &c., suitable for the Plains; one very extensive Hat manufactory; 2 gunsmith and two tinshops."[13]

Clearly, the jumping-off towns depended on the overlanders for economic survival, and they competed fiercely with each other to attract the business of westbound travelers.[14] The emigrants who streamed into the towns unwittingly provided economic opportunity for less reputable entrepreneurs as well. Newcomers were targeted by sharp-eyed merchants, robbers, gamblers, and other desperadoes who swarmed the outfitting towns, preying upon the "greenhorns," who often arrived with their life savings in tow. While outfitting themselves, overlanders often fell victim to scams, holdups, assaults, and even murder. Francis Parkman wrote that, even in relatively small Westport, "whiskey, by the way, circulates more freely . . . than is altogether safe in a place where every man carries a loaded pistol in his pocket."[15] Overland diarist Lucius Fairchild decried the presence in St. Joseph of "thieves enough to steal a man blind." Former slaves Richard and Mary McDonald, who jumped off in St. Joseph, heading for Montana in 1864, took precautions to safeguard their money and keepsakes in a small tin box that they buried every night along the trail from St. Joseph to Bozeman.[16]

In April 1850, an unnamed black overlander was victimized by criminals as he waited to jump off with a California-bound company in Kanesville, Iowa (near Council Bluffs). The African American man, identified only as being from Wisconsin, suffered a severe setback to his plans when the two white men he had hired to work for him on the trip stole his teams and outfitting gear. Edward H. N. Patterson, of Oquawka, Illinois, who witnessed the incident as he prepared to leave Kanesville with his own wagon company, noted in his journal that a "gentleman of color from Wisconsin came here [to Kanesville] last night to join two teams which he had fitted out, well—he found his teams and was very summarily dismissed by his hired white men, one of whom drew a pistol and ordered him to vamose [sic]." The black man left but he "set about devising some plan by which to recover his teams." Patterson also reported that "in the meantime, taking advantage of the night[,] the gentlemen who were 'bound for California at the nigger's expense' eloped, and are now in Nebraska, where I wish them no harm—but hope the Indians may strip them; their rascality deserves no better fate."[17] There is no indication that the man recovered his property or was able to continue his journey.

Cosmopolitan Crossroads

When westbound emigrants pulled into the jumping-off places, they entered a historically diverse setting. The outfitting boomtowns along the river that now catered to their travel needs had, in the words of Anne F. Hyde, "layered themselves on top of old communities." Towns like Independence, Westport, and St. Joseph were "long-lasting examples of the powerfully syncretic world of people of mixed race and practices that the fur trade had created."[18] They continued to be magnets that attracted an international assortment of hunters, trappers, roustabouts, missionaries, laundresses, cooks, traders, tourists, and adventurers of all racial and cultural backgrounds. Over time, this "heterogeneous mix" produced a distinct society of many languages, cultures, and ethnicities who engaged in international trade.[19]

Manuel Alvarez, a native of Spain and a trader on the Santa Fe Trail, viewed Missouri as "a mere way station" on a much larger international commercial trail. He sold cargoes of "textiles, sewing utensils, lace, buttons, combs, shovels, knives, and belts," purchased from firms based in London and New York, and transported them to New Mexico in wagons starting out from Independence, Westport, and St. Louis. Manuel X. Harmony, another Spaniard and partner in the New York City shipping and commission firm of P. Harmony Nephews and Company, moved English goods to Independence and freighted them to New Mexico via the Santa Fe Trail. Doña Gertrudis *"La Tules"* Barceló, the shrewd New Mexico businesswoman, famed monte dealer, and gambling impresario, invested $10,000 in the Santa Fe trade in the boom year of 1843. Charles Ilfeld, a German Jewish immigrant in New Mexico, was one of several prominent Jewish mercantilists engaged in Santa Fe Trail trade. Wyandotte Chief William Walker (elected provisional governor of Nebraska Territory, 1853) also leased a warehouse in Independence to facilitate his tribe's business ventures as Santa Fe Trail traders.[20]

White overlander J. Quinn Thornton described the multicultural makeup of Independence in 1848, where "might be seen the African slave with his shining black face, driving his six horse team of blood-red bays," and other conveyances "driven by Spaniards, some by Americans resembling Indians, some by negroes, and others by persons of all possible crosses between these various races."[21] Former Tennessee slave and wealthy St. Louis entrepreneur, James Thomas, recalled that, even in relatively tiny Westport, "there were many nationalities represented."[22] This jumble of cultures made the jumping-off towns cosmopolitan crossroads where buyers and sellers, blacks and whites, native-born and foreign-born, businesspeople and laborers, American Indians and Mexicans, men and women, residents and transients all interacted on a basis of economic self-interest, if not harmony and trust.[23]

Doing Well and Doing Good

A few African American entrepreneurs prospered from the booming economies of the region. Even though Missouri was a slave state, its relatively small free black population (3,572 in 1860) established enduring communities and institutions within slavery's shadow. On the eve of the Civil War, almost one half of Missouri's free black population lived in St. Louis, gateway to the jumping-off towns. African Americans there reportedly controlled property worth several millions of dollars. At least two black cattle dealers owned businesses whose combined worth was nearly $360,000, and transplanted Tennessean and former slave James Thomas owned real estate and other interests amounting to several thousand dollars.[24]

John Berry Meachum, a Virginia-born slave and talented carpenter, cabinetmaker, cooper, ordained minister, and one of the most prosperous and best-known figures in St. Louis, became a leader in the African American community and in the fight for abolition. After purchasing freedom for himself and his family, Meachum opened a successful cooperage business that became, as historian Lorenzo Green has written, "a training ground for freedom." Between 1826 and 1836, he bought nearly twenty slaves, put them to work in his factory, where they learned the trade and eventually bought their own freedom with their earnings. In 1827, Meachum and other community members formed the First African Baptist Church of St. Louis after splitting from the religious fellowship that had been organized by two white Baptist missionaries in 1817. The First African Baptist Church became the first black Protestant congregation in the city and the first one west of the Mississippi River. Meachum and his wife Mary, put the church and their home at the service of the Underground Railroad, conducting slaves across the Mississippi River to the free soil of Illinois.[25]

As an outspoken advocate of black education, Meachum foreshadowed Booker T. Washington's position on vocational education, encouraging black Missourians to become literate and pursue training in "manual labor schools." In 1847, the Missouri legislature outlawed all African American education, so Meachum instituted black educational programs in the guise of Sunday school classes. By 1860, all five African American churches in St. Louis had established covert educational operations that became known as "Candle Tallow Schools." Students, free or enslaved, were charged a monthly tuition of one dollar, but none were turned away for lack of funds. When lawmakers discovered these clandestine schools and shut them down, Meachum, undeterred, built a steamboat, outfitted it as a schoolhouse, and anchored it in the middle of the Mississippi River. His "floating freedom school" fell under federal jurisdiction and thus circumvented Missouri laws banning black education. Meachum continued his work in the abolitionist cause until he died at the pulpit in the First African Baptist Church on February 19, 1854.[26]

African Americans in the jumping-off towns along the Missouri River, though fewer in number than in St. Louis and less wealthy, also built viable communities. In 1850, African Americans in Westport (Kansas City) settled on land owned by Henry Clay Pate, publisher of Missouri's *Border Star* newspaper and founded a thriving black enclave known as Steptoe. In 1868, Steptoe residents opened Penn School, the first school west of the Mississippi constructed for the sole purpose of educating black children. A decade later, they built Saint Luke African Methodist Episcopal (AME) Church, and in 1883 Steptoe residents established St. James Baptist Church. By the 1920s, Steptoe was home to African American maids, cooks, railroad porters, and professionals, who lived in a "collection of neat clapboard houses." By the early twentieth century, this African American community, with its roots in the antebellum era of overland migration, had become "the best colored neighborhood in the city."[27]

Independence, Missouri, was the major jumping-off point for emigrants in the early years of western migration. However, by the 1850s, it had been eclipsed by towns like St. Joseph, Westport, and Kanesville

(Council Bluffs).[28] During Independence's heyday as a jumping-off point, some African American residents, benefiting financially from the overland traffic, were able to establish themselves and their communities, engaging in everything from constructing roads to supplying provisions and accommodations to the newcomers who flooded in.[29] Emily Fisher and Hiram Young, the most prominent African Americans in Independence at the time, helped found enduring black institutions and furthered the causes of abolition and equality while carving out comfortable livelihoods from the lucrative emigrant market. These African American entrepreneurs did not travel the overland trails themselves, yet played a pivotal but largely unexamined role in aiding western emigration and African American freedom. Their experiences raise the likelihood that other equally essential but anonymous black men and women engaged in similar work during the era of overland migration.

Emily Fisher, born a slave in Kentucky around 1808, settled in Independence in 1836 when her white master and father, Adam Fisher, purchased a farm on Jones Road, just east of Independence, in Jackson County. Emily married an enslaved man named Rowan, also owned by Adam Fisher, and the couple had two sons, Rowan Jr. and Shelby, and a daughter they named Sarah. When Emily was in her early forties, Adam Fisher manumitted her, and she began managing the hotel her father had purchased in Independence. When Adam Fisher died in 1860, Emily became the sole owner and proprietor of the hotel (located on the northeast corner of Main and Maple Streets), thus becoming Jackson County's first African American businesswoman.[30] Her culinary, housekeeping, and business skills made her establishment a success. The hotel, which "catered to Santa Fe–Oregon Trail travelers," gained a reputation for outstanding service, clean linens, and comfortable accommodations. Author Tricia Martineau Wagner has written that Fisher ran the hotel "as she saw fit," opening her establishment to blacks and whites, an unusual situation in the jumping-off towns, where hotels and restaurants vied with each other for white emigrants' business but typically refused service to African Americans. Black travelers, who generally were left on their own to secure lodging when stopping over to outfit or waiting to contract with westbound wagon trains, found a safe haven in Fisher's hotel.[31]

Emily Fisher's invention of a secret "healing salve," the recipe for which came to her "one night while [she] was sleeping," further contributed to her reputation and wealth; she did a booming business selling it to overland travelers. Economic prosperity gave Fisher the means to contribute to her community in other ways as well. She purchased and donated the first load of bricks for the construction of the Second Baptist Church, the first African American church in Independence and the oldest African American church building in the Kansas City area. Unlike Fisher's hotel, the church is still standing. Emily Fisher died in 1887 and was buried in Independence's Woodlawn Cemetery.[32]

Hiram Young, another African American entrepreneur in the Independence area, was not an overland traveler, but as historian W. Sherman Savage has noted, he "not only aided the western movement but prospered by it."[33] Young, a former slave described by one of his contemporaries as a "tall, dark skin colored man," was born in Tennessee circa 1812. He was taken to Green County, Missouri, by his owner George Young, where he purchased his freedom in 1847. Hiram Young may have bought his wife Matilda's freedom first so that their children, taking the status of their mother, would be recognized as free-born, and so that she, as a free woman, could better assist him in his business dealings.[34] Between 1847 and 1850, Hiram and Matilda Young lived in the Missouri town of Liberty (approximately twenty miles east of the Kansas border), which quickly became known as the "outfitting center of Independence."[35]

In 1850, Hiram, Matilda, and their infant daughter, Amanda, moved to Independence, where Hiram worked as a carpenter. Young, who could not read or write, relied on white businessman William McCoy (who served as Independence's first mayor) to act as his business agent. By 1851, Young had opened a modest establishment in Independence on North Liberty Street to begin the "manufactory of yokes and wagons—principally freight wagons for hauling govt. freight across the plains" and supplying drayage wagons and ox yokes for the Santa Fe Trail trade. His business grew along with the westbound overland emigrant traffic that had begun to stream out over the plains. Young's company enjoyed a virtual monopoly on ox-yoke manufacturing, turning out approximately 50,000 yokes and 800 to 900 wagons a year.[36]

Soliciting the emigrant trade that made up an increasing portion of his business, Young advertised in local newspapers that his company could outfit travelers with wagons, ox yokes, and other provisions "at the shortest notice." The wagons he produced were equipped to haul 6,000 pounds; they were pulled by six teams of oxen, and stamped on each wagon were the initials of the purchaser and a logo emblazoned with the words, "Hiram Young and Company." These wagons became enormously popular with overlanders, who commonly referred to them as "Hiram Young" wagons.[37] James Thomas, a contemporary of Young's and a businessman himself, recalled that "Wagons of his [Young's] make could be seen on the plains from Kansas City to San Francisco." Many emigrants, black and white, who outfitted in the jumping-off towns began their journey to the West in wagons built by Hiram Young and pulled by ox teams wearing yokes made in his shop.[38]

In addition to the wagon manufacturing business, which the 1860 census listed as the largest industry in Independence, Hiram Young operated a cluster of enterprises that supplied thousands of emigrants with the essentials for overland travel. His thriving foundry and blacksmith shop in Independence housed seven forges and employed twenty men. Six miles east of Independence, in the Little Blue Valley, Young's 480-acre farm employed nearly sixty workers and produced livestock, corn, and wheat for emigrants preparing to set out. The census of 1860 ranked Hiram Young as one of the wealthiest men in Jackson County, with real estate valued at $36,000 and personal property at $20,000. He simply described himself as a "colored man of means."[39]

Hiram Young's business empire provided him with a solid economic foundation, facilitated western emigration, and helped sustain the African American community. His considerable resources provided a pathway to freedom for hundreds of slaves who toiled on plantations in and around Independence. Contracting with slave speculators and local planters like Jabez Smith, the largest slaveholder in Jackson County, to supply workers for his shops, Young, undoubtedly influenced by his years in bondage, treated them as paid apprentices rather than chattel property and paid all workers, regardless of race, equal wages.[40] Hiram Young scholar, William Curtis, explained that the slaves received the "going wage of five dollars a day" and rigorous training "so that each one of them would be able to be totally independent when they were free."[41] Young gave them the opportunity to purchase their own liberty and perhaps become overlanders themselves, setting out for the West in wagons they had built and outfitted with money they had earned while working in his shop.

Although Hiram Young's business empire operated within the constraints of slavery, it challenged the foundation upon which slavery rested. This fact angered many "rank and file" whites who resented Young for his freedom and prosperity, and for encouraging enslaved African Americans to follow in his footsteps. Young's friend James Thomas recalled that "many would have liked to have a finger in his [Young's] business but all such he kept off from."[42]

Hiram Young further challenged the racial status quo by opening his "well furnished home" to any employee who needed a place to live, regardless of race. Daniel Flanagan, one of many Irish immigrants who found work in Young's shops, was the recipient of his employer's hospitality as a newcomer to Independence. Flanagan, an apprentice wagon maker who had learned the craft in New York, arrived in Independence seeking a job and eventually went to work in Young's wagon shop and became a boarder in the Young household. Flanagan's granddaughter, Josephine Flanagan Randall, recalled in an interview that her grandfather "was especially grateful because Hiram Young . . . brought a white Irishman . . . into his home to be his student." She added that Young "made [my] grandfather a prosperous merchant."[43]

Hiram Young's businesses were devastated by the Civil War, and he and his family became short-distance travelers when they fled Independence for the safety of Fort Leavenworth, Kansas, to wait out the war. In 1868, the Youngs returned to Independence "to find that much of [Hiram's] old business was destroyed and the Santa Fe Trail commerce gone." He subsequently opened a moderately successful planing mill and resumed his community involvement. A strong supporter of education, Young helped establish Independence's first and only school for African American children in the late 1860s. In 1874, he led a fund-raising campaign for the construction of the Douglass School (which was later renamed in his honor). He spent the last years of his life embroiled in lengthy, unfruitful litigation with the federal government, suing for damages done to his property by Union troops during the Civil War. He died without a will in 1882, his estate mired in debt. He, like Emily Fisher, was buried in Woodlawn Cemetery.[44]

The experiences of Hiram Young and Emily Fisher highlight the importance of African Americans who never set foot on the trails, yet facilitated the great overland migrations. These black entrepreneurs achieved economic success and helped sustain their communities by catering to the emigrants who flooded into the jumping-off towns, bringing with them hopes that were considerably larger than the financial resources they had allocated for outfitting themselves for the trek across the trails.

The Cost of Crossing

Emigrants who crowded the streets of the jumping-off towns were dismayed by the high cost of outfitting. In 1850, California-bound emigrant and diarist Adam Mercer Brown wrote that in St. Joseph "the weather was cold and damp. Prices were high, corn and oats running $1.00 per bushel and horses priced between $40 and $100 a head."[45] William Rothwell flatly accused merchants of engaging in a "general system of extortion."[46]

Without question, greed contributed to the inflated prices that were governed by the "law" of supply and demand, seasonal fluctuations, and frequent shortages. Staples like flour, bacon, rice, beans, sugar, and coffee commanded top dollar, being the nonperishable, easily transported items that constituted the backbone of the trail diet.[47] The controversial guidebook author, Lansford W. Hastings, advised overland travelers to purchase "at least, two hundred pounds of flour, or meal; one hundred and fifty pounds of bacon; ten pounds of coffee; twenty pounds of sugar; and ten pounds of salt."[48] J. L. Campbell's 1864 emigrant guidebook directed travelers to buy twelve sacks of flour, four hundred pounds of bacon, one hundred pounds of coffee, fifty pounds of salt, two hundred pounds of sugar, fifty pounds of rice, and two bushels of beans for a cost of $270. When other necessities, like wagons, oxen, yokes, axles, rope, nails, tents, mining equipment, and cooking utensils, were included, total outfitting costs rose to $570.85.[49]

In addition to staple foods, wagons, animals, yokes, harnesses, and other equipment represented substantial and potentially unaffordable expenses. In 1846, a yoke of two oxen in Independence sold for twenty-five dollars. By the spring of 1849, the price had climbed to between forty-five and sixty-five dollars. Prices for mules ranged from thirty to one hundred dollars a head. These costs could be prohibitive, as a group of Salt Lake City–bound Mormons (most from Liverpool, England) discovered while preparing to depart from Keokuk, Iowa, in 1853. Church emigration agent Isaac C. Haight, in charge of outfitting the group, greatly underestimated the costs of overland travel. His original calculations of $60,000 fell woefully short, and his attempts to borrow money in St. Louis failed. The company was forced to borrow $1,000 from a wealthy Mormon emigrant and received additional assistance from the church's Perpetual Emigrating Fund Company before it could depart.[50]

In at least one overland wagon company, an African American stepped in to bail out several cash-strapped whites in his group. In 1844, George W. Bush, a free black Missourian who left Savannah Landing with his family in Michael Simmons's wagon train headed for the Oregon Country, took the profits from the sale of his Missouri farm with him, carrying some $2,000 in silver coins hidden in the "double or false floor" of his covered wagon.[51] The Bushes were in better economic shape than many of the white families who traveled in the train of eighty-four wagons. John Minto, a twenty-two-year-old English emigrant who became Bush's friend and confidant during the long trip, noted in his journal that "it was understood that Bush was assisting at least two of these [Michael Simmons and Gabriel Jones] to get to Oregon." Bush purchased six wagons for the journey, which cost about $1,000 in total to outfit and were "carefully and thoughtfully stocked with provisions enough to last a year." He then gave four of the fully loaded wagons to financially needy families in his party.[52] By the time they reached Fort Bridger (in the modern state of Wyoming), the company, which had split from the larger Gilliam train, was in dire straits. Many had run out of supplies and clothing. Bush's generosity once again saved the day. He purchased flour "at the wildly inflated price of $60 a barrel, sugar at $1 a pound, and calico at $1 a yard" so that all members of the party were "fed, clothed, and supplied" before they continued.[53]

George W. Bush's financial situation made him an exceptional overlander of any race. The steep financial outlay necessary for the trip was daunting for everyone, but for many African Americans, already living on the economic margins, the costs were insurmountable. Ohioan Rachel Brown, the wife of argonaut David Brown, who left Ohio for California's goldfields, was more typical of the plight would-be emigrants faced. Writing to David in 1853, Rachel, unable to raise the funds needed to join her husband, confessed: "my Dear I don't think It would be profitable for me to come as I think It would Cost so much & you will be home soon. . . . I have not the money to come with. . . . It will cost so much & mother said I could not go with."[54]

In addition to financial problems, African Americans planning to trek west encountered obstacles unknown to their white counterparts—obstaces that complicated, delayed, and sometimes derailed their plans. Slaves, of course, traveled with their owners as chattel property and were accepted into wagon companies much like the mules, oxen, and other cattle that were brought along. Free blacks who took the overland routes usually traveled as members of companies organized by whites, but only after locating one that would accept them. Many wagon company charters expressly excluded African Americans, or wagon masters, acquiescing to the racial antipathy of company members, refused to sign them on.[55] Therefore, would-be black travelers had to invest extra time and effort persuading white outfits to include them.

This was the dilemma confronting former Kentucky slave Clara Brown as she made plans to relocate from Fort Leavenworth, Kansas, to Colorado Territory in the spring of 1859. After spending many days down on the levee in Fort Leavenworth listening to Colorado-bound gold rushers discuss their emigration plans, Brown, a skilled laundress and cook, approached Colonel Wadsworth's wagon company and offered her services in exchange for passage to Colorado. After some debate, she ultimately convinced the group that her value as a cook outweighed their prejudices against traveling with an African American woman of mature years. Brown's biographer, Roger Baker, has noted that the frugal businesswoman likely had the funds to book passage on one of the Concord stagecoaches that regularly made the 687-mile trip from Leavenworth to Denver in a matter of days. But she, like other black travelers, "would not have been welcome as a paying passenger in a public conveyance." Signing on as a cook for Colonel Wadsworth's overland company was "less a matter of economic than of social necessity."[56]

African Americans who managed to find a wagon train in their home state willing to take them could, like white overlanders, contract with the company for a flat fee that covered transportation and board. African American gold seeker David Brown, having contracted with the Sturgeon and Crim Company in his home state of Ohio, set out for California in 1852. His contract required him to pay $150, with $50 payable in advance and the balance due before the scheduled departure date sometime "between the first and fifteenth of April next." The fee entitled him to transportation and board, but company owners were "not bound to furnish clothing or to pay doctor's bills" for him or anyone else in the group.[57] Black travelers who were unable to locate a company that accepted African Americans often waited around in their home states or in the jumping-off towns until they could book one willing to transport them as paying passengers or as laborers in exchange for their passage.[58]

In 1849, Henry Finley, a black freeman, secured a place in an Ohio company bound for the goldfields of California. Finley's journey began in Illinois, where he encountered Maj. John Love's wagon train as it rolled through the state. Offering his services as company cook, Finley was hired.[59] That same year, Harry Withe, a young, unmarried black man, petitioned the seemingly reluctant organizational meeting of a wagon company from Hagerstown, Indiana, to sign him on "to accompany them to California as per agreement hereafter to be entered into." In April 1849, wagon company rosters identified Withe as "Harry With, coloured boy," and listed his position in the company as "cook."[60]

African American emigrants experienced conditions that added another layer of time, effort, and expense to an already costly and stressful venture. The racially based costs of the overland trek increased black overlanders' financial expenditures and heightened their anxieties as well. Thus, for African Americans, the process of outfitting involved more than securing the staple goods and hardware necessary for the trip. It also required them to employ what historian Douglas Daniels has called travelcraft, an "outlook and complex of skills" that "facilitated both long-distance travel and residency" and involved the "determination to succeed, reflectiveness and rationality, and racial consciousness."[61] African American overland emigrants Clara Brown, David Brown, Henry Finley, Harry Withe, George W. Bush, and countless other anonymous black overlanders, free and enslaved, outfitted themselves with an array of travelcraft skills to help them negotiate the treacherous racial terrain before and after jumping off onto the overland trails.

Negotiating the Racial Terrain

Most of the Missouri River outfitting towns were strongholds of slavery that bristled with racial hostility and were overrun by slave hunters who routinely patrolled the Missouri border, preying on vulnerable black people. Charlie Richardson, a former slave in Warrensburg, Missouri, recalled in an interview, "I remember some tough men driving like mad through our place many times, with big chains rattling. We called them slave hunters. They always came in big bunches. Five and six together on horse back."[62] Slave dealers and slaveholders paid a bounty ranging from twenty-five to one hundred dollars for each captive; therefore slave hunters did not hesitate to kidnap free people or steal a slave from his or her owner.[63]

Missouri's black laws, which prohibited freedmen and freedwomen from entering the state and required blacks already residing there to carry a license or risk being jailed as runaway slaves, aided slave hunters in their work.[64] To make matters worse, the Missouri supreme court ruled that "in all slaveholding States *color* raises the presumption of slavery, and until the contrary is shown, a man or woman of color is deemed to be a slave."[65] William Wells Brown, who escaped from slavery in 1834 and became a renowned abolitionist lecturer, writer, and conductor on the Underground Railroad, declared that Missouri, "though a comparatively new state is very much engaged in raising slaves to supply the southern market" in the lower Mississippi region.[66] He warned that black people were in "danger of being arrested" by slave hunters who swarmed into Missouri and nearby free states to kidnap them.[67] African Americans, free or enslaved, in Missouri and surrounding free states were susceptible to slave hunters and kidnappers and being sold at auction to the highest bidder. Black overlanders risked the same fate.[68]

Enslaved overland emigrant Dave Boffman narrowly escaped being captured by slave hunters as he and his master trekked from Missouri to California in 1851. Boffman's journey began in Kentucky, where he was born on the Baughman plantation in Crab Orchard, Lincoln County, around 1820. His original master, Henry Baughman, owned one of the largest cotton plantations in central Kentucky and owned nearly one hundred slaves. In 1837, Dave Boffman (a phonetic spelling of his owner's last name) married sixteen-year-old Matilda, a slave on the same plantation. The couple had six children, three boys and three girls.[69] When Henry Baughman died in 1843, Henry's grandson Newton Baughman inherited Dave, Matilda, and the children.

In the summer of 1848, when news of the gold discovery in California reached Kentucky, Newton Baughman caught gold fever and began to make plans to go west with his wife and daughter. The Baughmans left Kentucky that summer and took Dave and his family with them. They sojourned in northwestern Missouri, where Newton Baughman had purchased a farm in Lafayette Township, Clinton County. Eventually, Baughman prepared to resume his journey to California. To finance the trip, he sold three of Dave and Matilda's children to a slave trader. Baughman, promising Dave a chance to purchase his freedom if he accompanied him to California and worked the diggings with him, set the price of Dave's freedom at $1,000.[70] Boffman readily accepted; like so many other slaves who were taken west, he viewed this as a perfect opportunity to gain freedom for himself and his family.

Boffman and Baughman started out for California in May 1851, planning to follow the Platte River to Fort Kearny and then continue along the California Trail to Sacramento. From the outset, the black man somehow was separated from his owner but pressed on to Fort Kearny alone, keeping a sharp lookout for the slave catchers who lurked around the departure points. Once, as he trudged along the trail by the river, he encountered a party of armed slave hunters with bloodhounds.

Diving into the water and swimming for the other side as bullets pelted the water around him, Boffman managed to elude the gang. Before finally reaching Fort Kearny, he was forced to plunge into the water to avoid capture on two more occasions. Fortunately he found his owner waiting at the fort. After stopping over there for a few days, Boffman and Baughman continued their trip. On the high plains, the unarmed slave was captured by Indians, though his master narrowly escaped. After slipping away from his captors, Boffman continued pushing west to Fort Laramie, where, once more, he met up with Baughman. At the fort the two men joined a wagon company and completed their journey to California without further incident.[71]

Safe passage was not guaranteed to free African Americans, even when they were traveling with white guardians. They still had to contend with slave hunters and other opportunists who, looking to make quick money, took advantage of their vulnerability and fear. In 1853, Charlotta Gordon Pyles, her husband, Harry MacHenry Pyles, and their eighteen-member extended family left Kentucky, escorted by Charlotta's former owner, Frances Gordon, who had manumitted Charlotta earlier that year. Kentucky law forbade manumitted slaves from remaining in the state, so the Pyles family, with Frances Gordon in tow, set out for Minnesota. Fearing that slave catchers might accost them en route, Gordon also persuaded the Reverend Claycome, a sympathetic white minister from Ohio, to accompany them. The interracial entourage made its way to Cincinnati and boarded a steamboat for St. Louis.[72] After arriving in St. Louis, the Pyles, becoming even more alarmed because they were a free black family in a slave state, persuaded Gordon to engage the services of Nathan Stone, a white man, who agreed to guide them to their destination for a fee of one hundred dollars. Before leaving, however, Stone demanded an extra fifty dollars, threatening to "turn them over to slaveholders in Missouri" if Gordon refused. She immediately submitted to his extortion, paid the extra money, and the group resumed their journey.[73]

They departed St. Louis in a "schooner wagon" driven by eldest son, Barney Pyle. They were stopped several times by slave catchers who ultimately "permitted them to go on grudgingly, but unmolested." The Pyles were so unnerved by their experiences that they never made it to Minnesota but settled in Keokuk, Iowa, instead, where Harry found work as a carpenter and Charlotta became active in the abolitionist cause. They used their earnings to buy several family members out of bondage, but were unable to rescue their son Benjamin, who had been kidnapped by Frances Gordon's brothers and sold to Mississippi slave traders before the family left Kentucky. While in Keokuk, Charlotte and Harry learned that their son had been sold once again—this time into "Fayette County" (probably LaFayette County) Missouri, under the name Benjamin Moore. This was the last they heard of their child.[74]

African Americans who were not overland travelers but resided in free states near the jumping-off places were also vulnerable to slave hunters, who kidnapped them to be sold at auction. In 1842, Fanny Wigglesworth, a free black woman who lived with her husband, Vincent, and their four children in Moscow, Ohio (approximately eighteen miles southeast of Cincinnati), was kidnapped by slave hunters who broke into the Wigglesworth home, abducted the mother and children, and spirited them off to Platte County, Missouri, where they were sold into slavery. Vincent Wigglesworth enlisted the help of a prominent Ohio attorney to rescue his family; the attorney succeeded in obtaining an indictment and extradition orders from the state of Ohio against two of the kidnappers. However, the men were never prosecuted.[75]

The fate of Fanny Wigglesworth and her children, like that of Benjamin Pyles and countless other African Americans, remains a mystery. They might have been sold at the slave auctions that were regularly held upriver in St. Louis's five public slave pens, or on the steps of the old courthouse in Independence, or on the auction block in St. Joseph. It was there in St. Joseph that California-bound white overlander and diarist William Lewis Manly witnessed the sale of a "black boy about 18 years old." Manly wrote that after the auctioneer "had told all his good qualities," he then "called for bids" that "started at $500," and "rattled away as if he were selling a steer." But when "Mr. Rubideaux [sic], the founder of St. Jo," made a bid of $800, "he went no higher and the boy was sold."[76]

This was the environment that greeted African American emigrants who arrived in the jumping-off towns along the Missouri River. Some, like the black men who accompanied the Mormon expedition to the Salt Lake basin, found that just getting there exacted a higher toll from them because they were slaves. Those who survived the trek to the jumping-off places soon discovered that their naïve "greenhorn" status put them at risk, even before the real journey began. Newcomers, regardless of race, were overwhelmed and frequently victimized by scams and crimes that ranged from price gouging to robbery, assault, and murder.

For black travelers, the jumping-off places also bristled with racial antipathy, prejudice, kidnappers, and slave hunters, all of which added to the financial and emotional costs of crossing. Despite these challenges, this leg of the journey offered African Americans a preview of freedom's possibilities, exposing them to the accomplishments of African American entrepreneurs like John Berry Meachum, Emily Fisher, Hiram Young, and the energetic black communities that had begun to take root in and around the outfitting towns. Black emigrants carried with them a cautious optimism grounded firmly in these realities and drew on an array of travelcraft skills that helped them negotiate the geographical and social contours of the "providential corridor."

Chapter 4
The Providential Corridor

The journey is not entirely a pleasure trip. It is attended with some hardships and privation—nothing, however, but that can be overcome by those of stout heart and good constitution. . . . The road is a simple wagon trail—part good, and part very bad.

T. H. Jefferson, 1849

A NETWORK OF EXPLORATION, MILITARY, COMMUNICATIONS, trade, stage, and emigration routes developed between the Missouri River and the West Coast during the mid-nineteenth century. Four of these—the Oregon, California, Pony Express, and Mormon emigrant trails—shared a common broad corridor across the central plains and through the Rocky Mountains. While most African Americans and white emigrants traveled these routes, some also trekked west along a complex of lesser-known southern trails—among them the renowned Santa Fe Trail, the Gila Trail, and the Old Spanish Trail. Other ways west included the sea-land route from the Atlantic states to California's coast.

Experiencing the Oregon, California, and Mormon Trails
The intertwining trails across the central plains have been likened to a braided rope that is frayed at both ends.[1] At the eastern end, frayed strands of the rope led from numerous Missouri River settlements into the Platte River valley of today's Nebraska. Several strands carried traffic from the southern jumping-off points of Independence, Westport, Kansas City, Leavenworth, Atchison, St. Joseph, and Savannah Landings (present-day Amazonia). These feeder routes, used heavily in the 1840s, merged to follow the Little Blue River across northeastern Kansas to the Platte River, joining there the main corridor going west toward Fort Kearny.[2]

In 1846, Mormons began establishing new trailheads farther north to accommodate their own parallel emigration to the Great Salt Lake valley in today's Utah. Their initial settlements at Winter Quarters (Omaha), Nebraska, and Council Bluffs, Iowa, soon were joined by the Missouri River towns of Bellevue, Plattsmouth, Old Wyoming, Minersville, and Nebraska City, all in Nebraska. These settlements were located much nearer the Platte River, a tributary of the Missouri, than were the Kansas and Missouri jumping-off places. While commercial and military traffic from St. Joseph and Leavenworth continued to use the Kansas feeder routes to the Platte Valley, by the early 1850s, most emigrants chose to depart from the northern Missouri River towns, eliminating nearly two hundred miles of overland travel across Kansas.

Oregon- and California-bound travelers continued west along the south bank of the Platte, while Mormon emigrants, hoping to avoid conflict, usually followed a church-sanctioned trail along the north side of the river. The "Mormon Trail," which originally had been an Indian and fur trade trail, was not truly segregated, however. Non-Mormon Oregon- and California-bound emigrants who jumped off from the Nebraska settlements north of the Platte River frequently joined the Mormon traffic on the north bank. Historian Merrill Mattes fittingly named this broad, shared corridor "the Great Platte River Road."[3]

Emigrants generally regarded the Great Platte River Road as the easiest part of the trails west. The terrain was gentle, water and fuel (buffalo "chips") were readily available, the prairie provided pasturage for the draft animals, and the ground surface was smooth and hard, well suited for wagon traffic. Sylvia Estes (Stark), an African American girl from Missouri who traveled this road to California in 1851 with her parents, Howard and Hannah Estes, and her brother, Jackson, considered the prairie to be the most agreeable part of the overland trek. Decades after making the trip, Sylvia recalled that she and Jackson "found life on the great plains something new and thrilling." They were captivated by the "little prairie dogs barking and scampering" as people approached them, and were awestruck by the large herds of buffalo "stampeding at the sight of the caravan." Sylvia spent hours gathering bright prairie wildflowers while walking along the trail, "only to throw them away as there was no place to put them."[4] On this stretch of the road, emigrants were seldom out of sight of a wagon: the trains appeared to be an "endless caravan of white-topped wagons," an unrelenting "moving, mooing mob" that extended as far as the eye could see.[5]

At the fork of the river near today's community of North Platte, Nebraska, the trails turned up the North Platte toward Fort Laramie, a major milestone of the emigration. There, at the western edge of the Great Plains, the land begins to rise toward the Rocky Mountains—the prairie schooner's equivalent of a sea change. West of the Continental Divide awaited the most serious challenges of the overland trek. In preparation for the difficulties ahead, emigrants often paused at Fort Laramie to relieve their wagons of unnecessary weight. In fact, the entire Platte River Road became a long, linear dump as travelers abandoned family possessions, equipment, and even foodstuffs along the trail; but many emigrants held on to some of their unneeded goods in hope of selling or exchanging them at Fort Laramie. Usually disappointed in that hope, they purged their wagons to spare their oxen on the hard road ahead as they continued west into the Rockies.[6] Alvin Coffey, a black emigrant who made his first overland trek from Missouri to California in 1849 as the slave of Dr. William Bassett, recalled in his autobiography that his party "got across the plains to Fort Laramie on the 16th of June and the ignorant ox driver broke down a good many oxen on the trains. There were a good many ahead of us who had doubled up their trains and left tons upon tons of bacon and other provisions."[7]

Beyond the fort, the trail corridor followed the arc of the North Platte River into what is now central Wyoming. West of today's city of Casper, the river turns south toward Colorado, but the trail continued west toward the Rocky Mountains. This split marked the terminus of the Great Platte River Road. It also was the end of the separate Mormon Trail. Utah-bound emigrants merged with the Oregon-California traffic here, and all travelers flowed west together, leaving the Platte River lifeline that had conducted them across hundreds of miles of prairie and plain.[8]

After a dry overland stretch of about thirty miles, the combined trail entered the Sweetwater River valley and began the final, gradual climb toward South Pass and the Continental Divide. Along the way, emigrants marveled at the natural landmarks of Independence Rock,

Devil's Gate, Split Rock, and Ice Slough. South Pass itself was visually so unremarkable that many travelers passed through without realizing until hours later that they had crossed the Continental Divide and had entered the Oregon Country.

Yet South Pass was perhaps the most significant milestone of the entire overland journey. The Rocky Mountains were a serious obstacle to wagon travel. Men on horseback could cross in many places by rough routes that wagons could not traverse. Until South Pass was discovered (twice) by mountain men in the 1820s and 1830s—it was, of course, already well known by American Indians—there was no feasible wagon route through the central Rockies. However, wagons could easily negotiate South Pass, with its gradual slope and broad, open summit. African American overlander and cartographer T. H. Jefferson proclaimed in the *Accompaniment* to his 1849 overland map that "the passage of the Rocky Mountains by the South Pass is quite easy, the road being remarkably good."[9] Undoubtedly, South Pass stood as the "Gateway to the West." Without this "accident of geography," overland western expansion might have been curtailed severely.[10]

Here, at the Continental Divide, the western end of the trail "rope" began to fray. The original trunk of the emigrant trail traced a V-shape from South Pass, bending southwest toward Fort Bridger in southwestern Wyoming and then turning northwest to Fort Hall on Idaho's Snake River. Later trail variants, including the Sublette Cutoff, the Kinney Cutoff, and the Lander Road, cut across the top of the "V" to create shorter routes to Fort Hall. Another important strand of the rope, the Hastings Cutoff, split off from the point of the "V" at Fort Bridger and took a southwesterly course through the Wasatch Mountains to the Great Salt Lake valley. Originally blazed by Lansford W. Hastings and the Donner Party in 1846 as an alternate route to California, the Hastings Cutoff became the route used by Mormon pioneers going to the Salt Lake valley, the terminus of the Mormon Trail. Some parties of forty-niners also followed the Hastings route into Salt Lake City in order to resupply before continuing west across the Great Salt Desert and rejoining the main flow of California Trail traffic on the Humboldt River.[11]

From Fort Hall, the primary Oregon-California trail corridor continued westerly along the Snake River. Traveling the Snake River was nothing like traveling along the friendly Platte, for the Snake lies deep between imposing basalt cliffs. Much of the country was dry and littered with sharp volcanic rock, and the water at the bottom of the gorge was difficult, and sometimes impossible, to reach. Emigrants complained about the rough trail and thick dust along the way and worried about raids by Native people and white marauders. Several deadly and highly publicized attacks, not all unprovoked, occurred along the Snake River trails. At the Raft River, west of today's Pocatello, Idaho, the California and Oregon Trails diverged. Oregon travelers continued down the Snake River into present-day Oregon, cut northwest across rugged country to the Columbia River, and floated the river or took an overland alternate south of Mount Hood to the Willamette Valley. However, traffic bound for California, along with some Oregon emigrants taking a long back-route (the Applegate Trail) to their destination, diverged to the southwest and followed the Humboldt River across Nevada.[12]

The Humboldt River trail was misery for the emigrants, who complained of river water contaminated by dead livestock, swarms of biting insects, lack of grass for the mules and oxen, and Indians picking off their cattle. At this point in the journey, too, many had finished off their provisions and now (especially during the initial gold rush years) were reduced to eating lizards, rodents, and the rotting carrion of draft animals that had died along the trail. In western Nevada, the California Trail began to fray wildly, and some emigrants were happy for the chance to leave the "Humbug" River corridor to try their luck on the Lassen or Nobles Trails into northern California, or the notorious Applegate Trail into Oregon.[13]

The Applegate Trail, also known as the Southern Road to Oregon, crossed the fearsome Black Rock Desert of western Nevada, clipped the northeastern corner of California, and turned north along the western foot of the Cascade Mountain range to end at The Dalles, Oregon. Moses "Black" Harris was part of Jesse Applegate's exploration party, which blazed this trail in 1846 to provide a safe land route for emigrants who did not want to raft the dangerous rapids of the Columbia River. Harris, a former mountain man turned wagon guide and emigration promoter, wrote a letter to the *Oregon Spectator* in the fall of 1846 publicly praising the Applegate Trail as a "shorter and in all respects better route than any heretofore known."[14] Nonetheless, the first emigrants to try that "shorter, better route" in the late summer of 1846 began straggling into the Willamette Valley starving, exhausted, and *very* angry in late November of that year. Harris ended up returning to rescue some of the emigrants who were stranded on the trail he had helped blaze. Most who used this difficult route in 1846 denounced it as a scam, although others who tried the "Southern Road" over the next few years found it adequate. The route was only rarely used after 1849.[15]

In 1850, Joseph Alonzo Stuart was one of only a few who chose the Applegate route. Stuart, himself near collapse while trudging through the Black Rock Desert, came upon an enslaved black woman sitting alone on a rock beside the trail. Her master, to spare his teams the weight, had taken a heavy pack of bacon from the wagon and piled it onto her back. He had then driven off to find water, leaving her to catch up if she could. She was a "woman alone and heavily loaded and almost in despair," Stuart wrote. "Cheering her drooping spirits with the hope that the end could not be far ahead, I relieved her of her load and we trudged on with renewed courage." When the two finally caught up with her party, Stuart continued, "we found only the camp of a low-bred Missourian and his family, owner of the female chattel we had assisted and without thanks or even a cup of coffee or morsel of the bacon I had carried, we delivered her over to their clutches."[16]

Unlike Joseph Alonzo Stuart and the slave woman he helped on the Applegate Trail, most emigrants stuck with the main California Trail along the Humboldt River to the Humboldt Sink. These travelers would stop to rest and feed their livestock at Big Meadows, at present-day Lovelock, Nevada, before continuing to the sink and heading into the deadly Forty Mile Desert just ahead. At the brink of the desert, travelers could choose between the Truckee River route on the north side of the desert and the Carson River route on the south side, but the trails were about equally miserable: forty miles of roasting, featureless plain, devoid of vegetation and shade. Emigrants who had tended their cattle well, sparing them weight and the whip, resting and feeding and watering them throughout the journey, might cross safely without mishap or loss. Some travelers started into the desert with wagons and livestock but lost all in the desert and were lucky to escape with their lives. Many emigrants, having lost their draft animals and abandoned their wagons farther east, faced the entire forty-mile crossing on foot—as did slaves and those few confident souls who had set out from Missouri with nothing but a pack or a wheelbarrow to carry their provisions.[17]

Margaret Frink, a white overlander traveling in 1850, observed an unidentified black woman afoot and alone at Big Meadows. She was, wrote Frink, "tramping along through the heat and dust carrying a cast iron bake stove on her head, with her provisions and a blanket piled on top—all she possessed in the world—bravely pushing on for California."[18] Beyond Big Meadows lay the Humboldt Sink and then the formidable Forty Mile Desert, where emigrants sometimes collapsed and died from heat and thirst. The fate of that lone black pioneer, who may have been a free woman reaching for her dreams or a slave left to fend for herself, is unknown. After the Forty Mile Desert, travelers continued toward the elbow of today's state of Nevada, following the Truckee and Carson Rivers. Approaching the Sierra Nevada, those trails forked again and again, sending multiple trail strands through the mountains and on to journey's end: the goldfields and rich farm country of northern California.[19]

Experiencing the Southern Trails to California

Though they did not bear the same amount of traffic found on the California, Oregon, and Mormon Trails, southern trails also carried overlanders west.[20] Many of these routes passed through the important transportation and commercial hub of Santa Fe in present-day New Mexico. Among them were the Santa Fe Trail, which carried emigrant and trade traffic from Independence, Missouri, to Santa Fe; and the Fort Smith–Santa Fe Trail, which took Southern forty-niners from Fort Smith, Arkansas, across Indian Territory (Oklahoma) and the Texas panhandle to Santa Fe. Trails departing Santa Fe for California included the Old Spanish Trail, Beale's Wagon Road, and the Southern Trail, all of which led to Los Angeles.[21] Other routes crossed central Texas and merged with the westerly trails south of Santa Fe.

Travelers starting out from the Old South could cross the Gulf of Mexico to Galveston, then go to El Paso via the Lower Emigrant Road through San Antonio or the Upper Emigrant Road through Austin. From El Paso, travelers continued north up the Rio Grande to join the Southern Trail, the Gila Trail, or Beale's Wagon Road to Southern California.[22] The southern trails were the most direct routes for those starting out from the South, and during the early years of the California gold rush, unknown numbers of black emigrants, many of whom were slaves, traveled these roads as well.

Three black men identified only as Smith (also called Tom in some accounts), Negro Joe, and Little West were members of a Mississippi-Georgia gold-seeking party that became lost in Death Valley while attempting an untested "cutoff" through the Sierra Nevada in December 1849. The suffering of the hapless company gave the valley its somber name; the ultimate fates of the three black forty-niners are not known.[23] Also in 1849, African Americans from Arkansas were part of a trailblazing company that traveled the Cherokee Trail en route to California. On April 24 and 25 of that year, five unnamed slaves and ten unnamed free blacks were part of a forty-wagon company of 130 Cherokees and whites (along with four hundred head of horses, mules, and oxen) that departed Fayetteville, Arkansas, headed for California's goldfields. Under the leadership of Lewis Evans, the group called itself the Washington County Gold Mining Company. Making their "own road, without road, trail or guide through the plains," this multiracial company became the first party to cross the Continental Divide using a route other than South Pass.[24]

Some slave owners from the Deep South and Missouri, slaves in tow, often took the Gila Trail, dipping down into southern New Mexico and southern Arizona to reach California. Los Angeles–bound Benjamin Ignatius Hayes—who in 1856 would sit as the judge in Biddy Mason's freedom suit—took the Gila Trail after leaving Missouri in 1849. While en route, he saw at least three "colored men" (likely slaves) in the two companies with which he traveled. A white overlander and diarist in another Gila Trail group reported that his party included two "negroes named Bob and Jane." New York clockmaker William Lorton crossed the Mojave River in a company that consisted of at least three African Americans, one of whom was an Arkansas slave traveling with his owner. Lorton wrote that as the journey progressed, he even "slept under the same blankets with the black man." Lorton, a talented singer, fondly recalled joining in a "negro concert in [the] New York boys' tent" one evening after his company had set up camp for the night.[25]

In 1849, Jacob Stover was among a party of Iowa gold seekers who were headed for southern California with high hopes of striking it rich. His company started west along the Platte River Road, took the Mormon Road from Salt Lake City to southern Utah, and went from there to southern California via the Old Spanish Trail. On Christmas Day, he and his exhausted companions reached Rancho Cucamonga, a cattle ranch and vineyard owned by Victor Prudomme, a Frenchman who resided in Los Angeles. Stover recalled that the site was called "Pokamongo Ranch in Spanish; in English, Negro Ranch." His group was met by "the owner [who] was a negro." In reality, the black man, whose name was Jackson, was not the owner of the ranch but managed it with his Hispanic wife and several Native American ranch hands. When the worn-out emigrants stumbled in to the ranch, Jackson and his workers were engaged in making wine in "rather a novel way to us." The process involved a beef hide with a hole cut in the center with four forks planted in the ground and four poles "run through holes cut in the edge of the hide which bagged down so it would hold two or three bushels of grapes." On each side of the skin were two forks with a pole tied to both. Stover noted that two "buck Indians, stripped off naked, took hold of this pole with their hands and tramped the grapes. The wine would run." As Jackson looked on, the overlanders first ate the grapes then "went at the wine, caught it in our tin cups, as we all had one apiece." Then they "drank it as fast as the Indians could tramp it for awhile." Jackson encouraged their revelry, saying, "Gentlemen, you have had a hard time of it, I know, but de first ting you know[,] you will know noting. You are welcome to it." The next day, Jackson dispatched two ranch hands to fetch meat for the hungry visitors. Soon the entire party was feasting on beef and cornmeal thanks to Jackson's hospitality. The grateful emigrants "ate what [they] could, thanked him and started for Los Angeles."[26]

Not all travelers experienced such cordial treatment as they made their way. A party of overlanders that included two African Americans started out on the Santa Fe Trail for New Mexico in the fall of 1849, but came under attack by a band of Indians after veering off the main trail. On September 15, 1849, wealthy merchant James M. White left Independence, Missouri, with his wife, Ann, infant daughter, Virginia, and two slaves—Ben Bushman, described as a "mulatto servant," and an unnamed black woman. They traveled in a thirteen-wagon caravan laden with goods for White's far-flung business holdings. Seasoned Santa Fe trader Francis X. Aubry led the company.[27]

The Whites, anxious to get to their destination, split off from the main group in present-day western Kansas and, with their slaves and three armed white men, set out for Santa Fe, taking the faster but more dangerous Cimarron Cutoff, heedless of Aubry's warnings. About seventy miles from Barclay's Fort in New Mexico Territory, at a place known as Point of Rocks, a band of Utes and Jicarillas overtook the party. The attackers killed White, the slave Ben Bushman, and the other men, but took Ann, baby Virginia, and the female slave. The incident made national headlines and ignited public outrage. The army dispatched a team to rescue the captives, with Kit Carson serving as tracker and guide for the expedition. Contemporary accounts disagreed about the fate of Ann and Virginia White; some said they were found murdered, while others claimed she and her child adopted the Jicarilla culture and spent the rest of their days living with the tribe. The fate of the unnamed slave woman, who likely was an involuntary emigrant, aroused little concern at the time and is still a mystery.[28]

Other Ways West

Thousands of overlanders trudged across the California, Oregon, Mormon, and other trails, but there were other passageways to the West as well. California-bound emigrants living in the Atlantic states most often came by sea, sailing around South America and up California's West Coast. Others could choose a combination of sea and land travel through Nicaragua, Panama, or Mexico. About half of all emigrants to the Pacific Coast took the sea-land route.[29]

Escaped slave Barney L. Ford first attempted to go west via the sea-land route, but nearly a decade later, he would trek the overland trail. Ford, born on January 22, 1822, in Stafford, Virginia, grew up on a South Carolina plantation. With help from the Underground Railroad, he escaped his bondage at the age of twenty-six by simply walking off the Mississippi steamboat on which he worked in 1848. Making his way to Chicago, he met Henry O. Wagoner, a well-known barber and leader in Chicago's Underground Railroad. With Wagoner's guidance, Ford also became a barber and immersed himself in Underground Railroad activities.[30]

In 1851, Ford was struck by gold fever so he set out for California with his new wife, Julia Lyoni Ford (Wagoner's sister-in-law) accompanying him. The Fords choose to take the sea-land route through Nicaragua, but fearing re-enslavement if they traveled down the Mississippi River to New Orleans (which would have been the fastest and cheapest way to the Nicaragua crossing), Barney and Julia instead steamed out of New York City on a ship heading to Greytown. Shortly after arriving, however, Barney Ford abandoned his California plans and, hoping to capitalize on the lucrative western emigration traffic, opened a hotel in Greytown. The couple remained there until the outbreak of war threatened their lives and destroyed their property. Returning to Chicago in 1860, the Fords once again headed west, this time taking the overland route to Denver where Barney would become a respected businessman and civil rights activist.[31]

Mapping the Way

No matter what route emigrants took, most were unfamiliar with western geography, and many began the trip without maps to follow. They were, in the words of historian Will Bagley, "naïve sojourners."[32] However, their knowledge of the West grew steadily as publishers, responding to escalating demands, began turning out personal stories, maps, charts, and guides penned by western travelers whose experiences "filled pages of text and drew new lines on well-worn maps."[33] By the mid-1850s, the dissemination of firsthand accounts of early black and white western trailblazers resulted in a flood of increasingly sophisticated and accurate maps and guidebooks.

In the opening years of overland emigration, however, western travelers were, for the most part, left to their own devices. When the Western Emigration Society left Missouri in the spring of 1841, becoming the first overland emigrant wagon train to California, company members were armed with romanticized notions about the West, a few flawed, outdated maps, and virtually no familiarity with the terrain or with the Native peoples they would encounter along the way. John Bidwell, who helped organize the company and served as its secretary, recalled, "We knew that California lay west, and that was the extent of our knowledge." Thirty-four members of the society, known today as the Bidwell-Bartleson Party, later broke away from the main group at present-day Soda Springs, Idaho, to make their own uncharted way to California. When the company elected John Bartleson to lead it, Bidwell noted, "no one knew where to go, not even the captain."[34] This dilemma prompted the Bidwell-Bartleson Party, and other early emigrant companies, to hire, or in some cases, kidnap Native people to point out the trails for them and locate watering and grazing sites.[35]

Most mapping of the West came after a substantial portion of the trail had already been established by use and by explorers seeking better alternate routes and cutoffs. As overland emigration gained momentum and the drama of emigrant exploits and tribulations filtered back east, prospective overlanders clamored for more information about western routes and conditions. Rushing to meet the demand, eastern publishing firms churned out a flurry of personal narratives, maps, and guides, which emigrants scoured for accurate advice. However, some of the early sources depicting the western landscape were of dubious merit, falling woefully short of the mark. Lansford W. Hastings's *The Emigrants' Guide to Oregon and California,* published in early 1845, became the most notorious of the guidebooks. It provided little information about the actual trail between Fort Bridger and California, and was misleading about the difficulty of the journey.[36]

By 1846, however, guidebook quality had improved considerably. Brigham Young's Latter-day Saints produced one of the most reliable and detailed guides of the route from Council Bluffs to the Salt Lake valley. Written by Mormon pioneer William Clayton, it provided accurate mileages, latitudes, longitudes, altitudes, and other useful information. This, and other new works, gave prospective travelers practical and trustworthy information about the physical characteristics of the trail.[37] Edwin Bryant's published description of his trip to California in 1846, *What I Saw in California,* gained enormous success in late

1848 and early 1849 and was widely used as a guidebook. Joseph E. Ware's *The Emigrants' Guide to California*, another highly touted work, was written by a journalist who, before writing the guidebook, had never even set foot on the trail he championed. In 1849, this book was, in the words of overland trails historian John D. Unruh Jr., "the nearly universal recommendation" of newspapers that "warmly endorsed many of the 'instant' guidebooks which appeared with the discovery of gold." Most emigrants, however, routinely damned Ware's work. California-bound overlander Asa Cyrus Call complained that "it hits the truth scarcely as often as the almanacs do the weather . . . his 'guide book' seems to be *all* guess work."[38]

Other publications received more favorable reviews from travelers who also consulted the works of William Gilpin, William Emory, and John C. Frémont. The maps and descriptions published by these explorers of the Intermountain West and the Great Basin region contributed to the area's allure for many emigrants. Beginning in the 1840s, Frémont mounted a series of expeditions for the purpose of exploring and mapping the Great Plains and a path to the Pacific. His "obsession with deciphering" the Intermountain West received valuable assistance from often-overlooked sources, including the Native populations he encountered and Jacob Dodson, a "nearly six feet tall, strong and active" eighteen-year-old free-born African American from Washington, D.C., who accompanied the military man on three of his western missions.[39] Dodson, a member of a free black family in the employ of Frémont's father-in-law, Sen. Thomas Hart Benton of Missouri, joined Frémont's thirty-eight-man party that set out from Westport, Missouri, on May 29, 1843. The group was headed for Fort Vancouver in the Oregon Country via a fur trade route that was becoming known as the Oregon Trail. On the return trip, the company ventured through Utah, Colorado, and Kansas. Although Dodson was officially listed as Frémont's personal servant, he was much more than that. After eleven men quit the company, he stepped up to become one of the most important members of the team. In the winter of 1844, when the group became stranded in the Sierra, exhausted and starving, the black youth rode ahead of the main party with Frémont to scout a path through the mountains.[40]

On his third trip west with Frémont, Dodson was with the band that rode into California in 1847 to participate in the American takeover of the Mexican territory at the outbreak of the Mexican War. During the conflict, Dodson, Frémont, and Don Jesus Pico made an eight-day, 840-mile round-trip from Los Angeles to Monterey to alert the American army about a rumored Mexican attack. For his service in the Frémont expeditions (from May 3, 1843, to September 6, 1844), the federal government granted Dodson a payment of $493.[41] However, Dodson petitioned Congress in 1855 for compensation for his service as a veteran of the Mexican War on the grounds that he, in fact, had served in Richard Owens's company of the California Battalion under Frémont. Sen. John B. Weller of California introduced a bill for the "relief of Jacob Dodson," arguing that the intrepid black explorer had served honorably as a private in Captain Owens's company, but "in consequence of his being a colored man . . . could not be legally mustered." Weller declared that Dodson deserved exactly "what he would have received if he had been of a different color—in other words if he had been a white man." In 1856, both the Senate and the House of Representatives passed the Dodson relief bill without debate. On April 18, 1856, Pres. Franklin Pierce, himself a former general in the Mexican War, signed the bill into law and Congress awarded Dodson "all the pay and allowances of an army private" for his service between July 7, 1846, and April 14, 1847, "as a member of the exploring expedition within this period."[42]

At the outbreak of the Civil War, Dodson, who had returned to Washington in 1848 and now worked as an attendant in the Senate, once again offered his services to his nation. In a letter to Secretary of War Simon Cameron, he urged that the government permit "some three hundred reliable colored free citizens" living in the nation's capital to "enter the service for the defence of the City." Challenging the government policy that banned African Americans from military service, Dodson reminded Cameron that he had traveled "three times across the Rocky Mountains in the service of the Country with Fremont and others." In a terse reply, the secretary of war informed him that "this Department has no intention at present to call into the service of the Government any colored soldiers."[43]

The T. H. Jefferson Map

Jacob Dodson's expeditions across the Rockies with Frémont, the adventures of earlier trailblazers, and the experiences of numerous overland travelers eventually resulted in guidebooks and maps that gained the acceptance and trust of overland travelers. However, African American cartographer T. H. Jefferson's journey to California in 1846 resulted in a map that provided a wealth of precise, reliable, and practical information about the grueling overland trip. Jefferson published his four-part *Map of the Emigrant Road from Independence, Mo., to St. Francisco California* and *Accompaniment* in 1849, after copyrighting and printing it in New York City. His map, in the words of historian Dale Morgan, stands as "one of the great American maps, an extraordinarily original production which will always have a special place in the cartography of the West, and which adds up to a trail document of high importance."[44] Accurate down to the quarter-mile, it provided emigrants with detailed information on the campsites, watering locations, feeding grounds, road hazards, and points of interest along the route. It sold for three dollars. At least one gold seeker, J. Goldsborough Bruff, traveled with a copy of it on his overland trip to California in 1849.[45]

The elegant precision of the T. H. Jefferson map contrasts sharply with the cloudy and contested details of the African American cartographer's life. Many scholars have concluded that Thomas Jefferson, the third president of the United States, fathered several children with his slave Sally Hemings, the "quadroon half-sister of his deceased wife." According to Thomas Jefferson's black descendants and other researchers, T. H. Jefferson was one of the children from that relationship.[46] Constance Moore Richardson, T. H. Jefferson's sixth-generation granddaughter, maintains that the black side of the Jefferson family "always knew" that T. H. Jefferson was the offspring of Sally Hemings and the president, but Richardson recalled in an interview, "There are only a handful of white Jefferson descendants from Jefferson's daughter, Martha, who have accepted what we have said."[47]

T. H. Jefferson, reputedly the eldest son of Sally Hemings and her owner, was born at Monticello in 1790 and was given the name Tom. Thomas Jefferson's political critics, however, derisively referred to the boy as "president Tom" and claimed he bore a "striking though sable resemblance to the president himself."[48] Richardson concedes that her ancestor's background will remain forever wrapped in mystery and debate: "The entire thing has been a controversy since 1802 and it continues to be a controversy."[49]

Although the details of T. H. Jefferson's lineage are ambiguous, there is no dispute that he embarked on his overland journey equipped with a unique set of skills, having been educated in the essentials of reading, writing, carpentry, cartography, music, and nautical crafts. His exposure to the notable visitors who stopped over at Monticello at the invitation of the president undoubtedly contributed to his store of knowledge.[50] Overland trails researcher Rush Spedden has speculated that Tom would have been "a teenager when Meriwether Lewis spent some time as a guest at Monticello before President Jefferson sent the Lewis and Clark expedition to explore the West."[51]

T. H. Jefferson's status as slave or freeman and the circumstances under which he left Monticello are unclear. The oral tradition of the Hemings-Jefferson descendants suggests that a quarrel with Thomas Jefferson in 1802 caused the young man to be exiled to the Virginia plantation (Dover Tract) owned by John Woodson, a relative of Thomas Jefferson's family by marriage. Another Hemings-Jefferson family theory holds that the president gave young Tom money that enabled him to quietly leave the state. He may have traveled to Kentucky in 1805, but by 1806 was back in Virginia, living on a farm owned by planter James Kinkaid in Greenbrier County (now West Virginia). This put him near the residence of his future wife, Jemima Price, her mother Hannah, and sister Fanny, who were relocated to Greenbrier County after their master, Drury Woodson, a planter from Cumberland County, died in 1788. While in Greenbrier County, for reasons unknown, Hannah and Fanny were manumitted—in 1803 and 1805, respectively. Jemima appears to have lived as a free woman in Greenbrier County, although no manumission papers were ever filed for her.[52]

Tom, who now called himself Thomas Woodson, probably met Jemima sometime in 1805 in Greenbrier County. In 1806, he and Jemima Price began living as husband and wife. That same year, Jemima gave birth to their first son, Lewis. The couple and their child settled on land about four miles west of Lewisburg, the county seat, in a section called Brushy Ridge, where Thomas was, according to one of his African American descendants, "more of a cattle grazer than a dirt farmer."[53] In late 1820 or early 1821, Thomas and Jemima Woodson decided to leave Brushy Ridge. Bundling their children and all their possessions into wagons, they set out for Ohio via the Midland Trail. Byron Woodson Sr., a sixth-generation great-grandson of Thomas Woodson, has speculated that part of the trip to Ohio may have been made by water, including a ferry ride across the Ohio River, a flatboat trip down the Kanawha River, or a steamboat trip on the Ohio River to Portsmouth, at the mouth of the Scioto River. Once in Ohio, they settled in Chillicothe where Thomas, using the surname Woodson, rented a farm from Thomas James. The Woodson family remained there for nine years.[54]

In 1830, Thomas Woodson purchased land in nearby Jackson County, Ohio, and by 1830 or 1831, "he and a few others had established Berlin Crossroads," a thriving community in Jackson County.[55] After living there for several years, Thomas Woodson, who now called himself T. H. Jefferson, once again set out on the road, this time for California.[56] Constance Moore Richardson has theorized that he began using the Jefferson surname openly as he moved father west, where his racial lineage could be downplayed: "If he did use the name Jefferson, he may have started to use the name in the West where there is less association with Sally." His African American descendants knew that T. H. Jefferson eventually "went West, but [we] never associated *why* he went out West."[57] In 1846, after outfitting in St. Louis, T. H. Jefferson went to Independence, Missouri, where he jumped off onto the trail, California-bound. The *Missouri Republican* reported, "We notice among those going out to California, Wm. H. Russell, Dr. Snyder, Mr. Grayson, Mr. M'Kinstry, Mr. Newton and others from below; and Messrs. Lippincott and Jefferson from New York; and from about here ex-Gov. Boggs, Judge Morin, Rev. Mr. Dunleavy, and hosts of others."[58]

Shortly after departing but before reaching the Kansas River, T. H. Jefferson broke with his original party, which was led by William Russell, who would later establish the Pony Express. The reason he parted ways with his first group is open to speculation, but Benjamin S. Lippincott, noted businessman, politician, and later signatory to the

1849 California Constitution, who was with Jefferson when he left New York and traveled with him in the company led by Russell, provided an intriguing detail concerning Jefferson's split from the train of sixty-nine wagons. Lippincott, writing to a friend about the trip, noted that families made up most of the company, and Jefferson was one of only six single men in the party. Lippincott recalled that "Edwin Bryant Esqr., cousin of W. C. Bryant, R. T. Jacobs, son of wealthy John J. Jacobs, Louisville, & Col R. formed one mess [a group that shares meals] of the bachelors. Francis Powers Esqr. of Boston, Jefferson with whom I left New York, & myself the other." However, "after three days journey we kicked Jefferson out of the company which I never regretted afterward, although at the time [I] inclined to stay with the man."[59]

Jefferson joined a new wagon train on May 19, 1846, under the leadership of Methodist minister James Dunleavy. The Dunleavy party did not have a chronicler and this perhaps explains why so little is known about the African American mapmaker's overland trek.[60]

Why T. H. Jefferson left his original company is a mystery, but it is clear that as soon as he hit the road, he put his cartographic skills to good use and, with painstaking precision, went about the work of mapping the California Trail. In Part 1 of the map, Jefferson explains that it "represents the emigrant road from Independence, Mo., by the South Pass of the Rocky Mountains to California. The Author was one of a party of emigrants who travelled the road with waggons, in 1846. All the streams of water and springs upon the road are delineated, also daily distances, courses and camps, made by the party." Historian J. Roderic Korns has written that Jefferson was "preparing not a map for a geographical society, but a guide for emigrants" who had little interest in latitude and longitude or the distance to the North Pole but were intensely concerned about the location of the nearest watering hole or safe campground.[61]

The map and its eleven-page *Accompaniment* meticulously calculated distances between points and counseled emigrants on travel modes and provisions. On crossing the formidable Salt Desert, west of Salt Lake City, Jefferson sternly advises, "Take a supply of water and green grass at Hope Wells. Three or four gallons of water per ox is enough. Water is more important than grass. Not more than five wagons should start upon the drive in company. Travel night and day; don't hurry the oxen; make a regular camp about every 20 miles." He addresses the difficulties of overland travel frankly: "The journey is not entirely a pleasure trip. It is attended with some hardships and privation." Yet he reassures the apprehensive travelers that all adversities could be overcome "by those of stout heart and good constitution. A small party (10 or 20 of the *proper* persons *properly* outfitted) might make a pleasure trip of the journey."[62]

Jefferson's map was, according to toponymist and emigration scholar George R. Stewart, "accurate, but in a practical rather than a theoretical way. He was resourceful, and meticulous of detail.... He was independent of judgment. He took hardships as a matter of course."[63] Jefferson was also intimately familiar with the flora and fauna of the West, giving "a name to practically everything which was not already named, and even to some which were, he gave new names." His map was the first to give the Truckee River its present name and preserve the "genuine oral tradition which was to survive against the nomenclature of the official cartographers."[64] Historical cartographer Richard V. Francaviglia has written that in the craft of mapmaking, "names help in the process of claiming places."[65] Accordingly, T. H. Jefferson's work championed western emigration on behalf of national expansion. In the *Accompaniment*, he urged the federal government to "at once dispatch a dozen exploring parties in different directions. The best road should be found speedily." Declaring that "trappers and emigrants with women and babies, have done more towards this object than government," Jefferson demanded, "We want a good wagon trail across this continent and we must have one."[66]

T. H. Jefferson was an advocate of western emigration, but he did not remain in the West. He eventually moved back to Ohio, where he took up farming once again and resumed using the name Thomas Woodson. When he left and whether he took the overland route on his return trip is not known. In 1879, nearly eleven years after Jemima, his wife of sixty-three years had passed away, T. H. Jefferson died in Jackson County, Ohio, surrounded by family and friends.[67]

If, as Francaviglia has suggested, "maps can help us understand the way in which a place becomes recognized as either familiar or exotic," T. H. Jefferson's map served both purposes for emigrants on the overland trail.[68] It was the product of an African American overlander who, like countless other emigrants, irrespective of race, went west seeking to chart new vistas and create new identities. Jefferson memorialized this quest in a remarkable map and guide that balanced the overlanders' need for reassurance and security on the trail with their desire for independence and adventure.[69]

By the mid-nineteenth century, the complex of trails that carried thousands of emigrants west had been charted, expanded, and promoted in maps and guidebooks of varying quality. The major overland routes that eventually became known as the California, Oregon, and Mormon Trails, and the other, less-traveled ones, had evolved from roads that had been discovered and used first by Native peoples, traders, military explorers, and religious pilgrims. The first emigrants who set out on the trails during the initial years of overland migration were generally naïve about, and ill-prepared for, the difficult journey that lay ahead of them. No matter what route they took, overlanders, whether black or white, often had similar responses to the natural wonders they encountered on their trek across the prairies, mountains, and deserts. Most, like Sylvia Stark, were awed and delighted by the beauty of the country through which they passed, but the privations and life-threatening challenges of the road discouraged and frightened even the hardiest travelers at one point or another during the trip. Trail-weary emigrants, like those in Jacob Stover's party, whose flagging spirits were revived by the generosity of Jackson, the African American ranch manager in southern California, were grateful for even a temporary respite from the miseries of the road.

African American emigrants shared the pleasures and hardships of the trail with their white counterparts, but they also shouldered the additional baggage of race prejudice. Joseph Alonzo Stuart's encounter with the dejected slave woman in the sweltering Black Rock Desert underscores the fact that many enslaved overlanders merely served as beasts of burden for their owners. The fates of the slave Ben Bushman and the unnamed slave woman who followed their master over the Cimarron Cutoff to their deaths attests to their ultimate powerlessness over their own lives. They were forced to comply with the decisions of their owners—however foolhardy the decisions might be. In this respect, the African American experience of the overland journey differed sharply from their white trailmates.

However, not all black overlanders were slaves. Some, like Jacob Dodson and T. H. Jefferson, not only traveled the trails but took the lead in establishing, charting, and promoting some of the most important overland routes. Their efforts contributed to the rising numbers of emigrants who followed the complex of trails to the West.

James P. Beckwourth, ca. 1860. BlackPast.org, An Online Reference Guide to African American History.

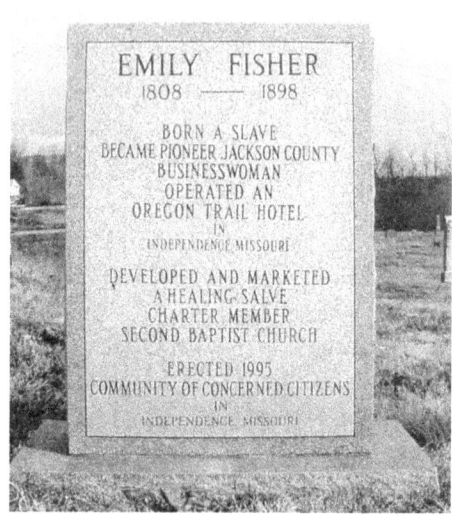

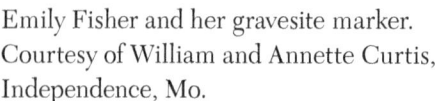

Emily Fisher and her gravesite marker. Courtesy of William and Annette Curtis, Independence, Mo.

Replica of a Hiram Young wagon. Constructed by Joe Louis Moore and members of the community, Sacramento, Calif. Courtesy of the author's personal collection. Photograph by Joe Louis Moore.

Alvin Aaron Coffey, ca. 1887. Courtesy of Jeannette Molson, Davis, Calif.

Mahala Tindall Coffey. Courtesy of Jeannette Molson. Davis, Calif.

Alvin Coffey's descendants. *Left to right:* William Williams, great-grandson; Louis James Williams, great-grandson; Tornelia Williams Smith, great-granddaughter; Lufina Williams Wilcox (seated), great-granddaughter. Courtesy of William Williams and family, Vallejo, Calif. Photograph by Joe Louis Moore.

Peter and Nancy Gooch, portrait taken in San Francisco, 1857. Courtesy of California State Parks, August 7, 2015.

Monroe family in front of the Monroe family house, Coloma, Calif. Andrew, Sarah, Andrew Jr., Pearley, James, Grant, William, Garfield, and Delia. Courtesy of California State Parks, August 7, 2015.

Howard Estes. Courtesy of Salt Spring Island Archives, British Columbia, Canada.

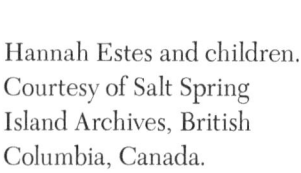

Hannah Estes and children. Courtesy of Salt Spring Island Archives, British Columbia, Canada.

Sylvia Stark. Courtesy of Salt Spring Island Archives, British Columbia, Canada.

Charles and Nancy Alexander. Courtesy of Harold and Gaynelle Alexander, San Jose, Calif.

Charles and Nancy Alexander's descendants. Harold Alexander, great-great grandson (seated left), with wife, Gay Alexander, and their children and grandchildren (standing). Photograph by Joe Louis Moore.

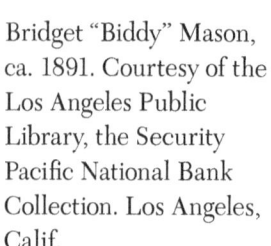

Bridget "Biddy" Mason, ca. 1891. Courtesy of the Los Angeles Public Library, the Security Pacific National Bank Collection. Los Angeles, Calif.

Lewis Southworth and his violin. Courtesy of the Benton County Historical Society and Museum, Philomath, Ore.

Lewis Southworth at his fireplace. Courtesy of the Benton County Historical Society, Horner Collection, Philomath, Ore.

Clara Brown. Courtesy of the Denver Public Library, Western History Collection, call no. Z-275.

Barney Ford. Courtesy of the Denver Public Library, Western History Collection, call no. F-8545.

Sugg family pictures (possibly William, upper right; Mary, lower left). Courtesy of the author's personal collection. Photograph by Joe Louis Moore.

The Sugg family house, Sonora, Calif. Courtesy of the author's personal collection. Photograph by Joe Louis Moore.

Ben Palmer, ca. 1855. Courtesy of Special Collections, University of Nevada, Reno, Libraries (UNRS-P0305 Ben Palmer).

Richard McDonald.
Courtesy of Joanna L.
Nute, Bozeman, Mont.

Mary Harris
McDonald. Courtesy
of Joanna L. Nute,
Bozeman, Mont.

The McDonalds' tin box. Courtesy of Joanna L. Nute, Bozeman, Mont.

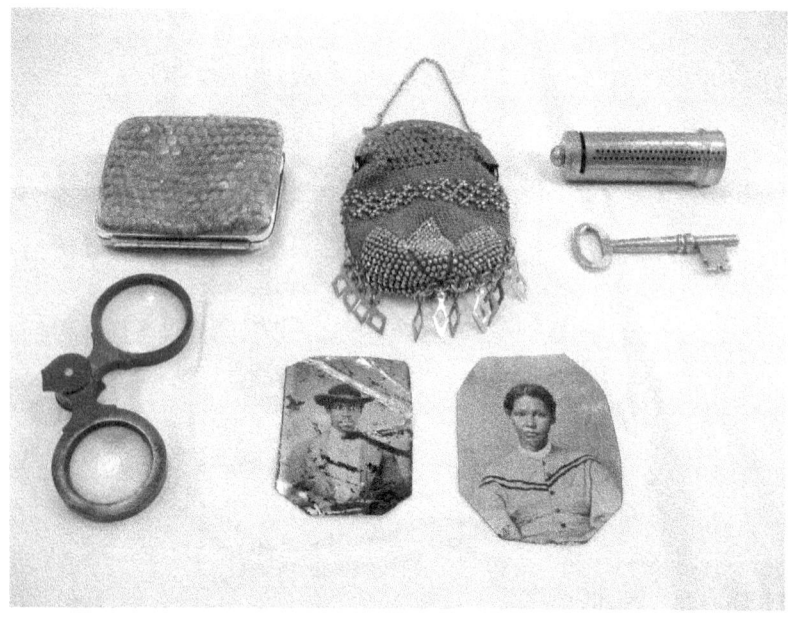

Keepsakes from the McDonalds' tin box. Courtesy of Joanna L. Nute, Bozeman, Mont.

Chapter 5
Community and Work on the Trails

I drove our oxen all the time and I knew about how much an ox could stand.
                        Alvin Coffey, writing of his 1849 trip

There were two stout, healthy looking colored men, supposed to be slaves, with the party who were brought along to do the work, such as cooking, driving teams, pitching tents and everything except guard duty, which it was stipulated, at the time they joined our train, they should not do.
                        Theodore Edgar Potter, 1852

THE MEN AND WOMEN who crossed prairies, mountains, and deserts to the West often started out as a disparate collection of individuals. Gus Blair, a white overlander, observed in 1849: "It is amusing to see what a heterogeneous mass of human beings are going to California, old and young, rich and poor, [C]hristian and infidel, black and white, bond and free, all alike infected with the mania for gold."[1] In a short time, however, this assortment of "greenhorns" would receive a crash course in the geography and work of the trails. Out of necessity, if not affinity, they coalesced into what historian Robert W. Carter has called a "nomadic community of the overland trails." What kept them "alive and moving" was not merely "their will to survive, but their mutual support and willingness to work together as a community."[2]

Working All the Way

Whether emigrants entered into formal contracts that painstakingly specified their obligations or merely assented to a set of loosely framed guidelines, most shouldered their duties with good cheer. Others did so grudgingly, while still others toiled obediently without acknowledgement or compensation.[3] Although the most common relationship of blacks to whites in the trails communities was that of "servant, laborer, or slave," African Americans engaged in every aspect of the work that made up the daily routine of the journey, often in situations requiring skill, reliability, and trust.[4]

Guides: Piloting the Wagons, Pointing the Way

By 1845, the demand for trail guides had begun to fade, but in the initial years of western settlement (even as late as 1849), emigrants placed considerable value on seasoned trail guides, scouts, and interpreters. African Americans sometimes filled these positions.[5] A Virginia company hired the services of an unidentified black guide to take them across the plains to California in 1849. Missouri overlander and diarist, Bennett C. Clark's company happened to be "camped alongside [the] Virginia train" on July 27. Clark noted in his diary that "at dark the negro guide of the Va[.] Company made the valley musical with their chearful voices—Singing the airs of our old mountain home. How rapidly the memory of other days flitted thro ones minds as we sat in the bright moon shine beside our Campfire and listened to this old fashioned musick." During the night, however, "wolves set up a rival melody which made the negroes 'Climb down.'"[6]

Edmund Green, a white Michigan overlander in 1849, recalled that on his way to Fort Hall in Idaho, his group met a black man who was "hunting horses" and was "most familiar with this part of the country and could speak the Indian language." Green's company immediately hired the man "to take them as far as Fort Hall."[7] Dr. Charles Boyle met an experienced and cosmopolitan African American guide and interpreter at Fort Kearny in 1849 who told Boyle that he was born in St. Louis but was "raised among the Indians." The black man was fluent in English, French, and "several other Indian languages," and had even visited Paris. He also let Boyle know that "he received a pension from the government for the share he had in perpetrating an Indian treaty and was also appointed interpreter at a salary of $300 per year."[8]

In the spring of 1849, David Demarest was a member of a company that was making its way to California via the Gila route when his party encountered a black man who approached them just outside of Galveston, Texas. The man offered to guide the travelers to the choicest grazing spots along the way in exchange for a place in the company. They quickly accepted, but shortly after resuming their journey, the group was stopped by a sheriff who threatened to arrest them all for aiding a fugitive slave. Only after paying the sheriff a bribe of seventy dollars in money and goods, were they allowed to continue their trek. What became of the would-be black guide is lost to history.[9]

Drivers: Popping the Whip, Grasping the Reins, and Wrangling the Stock

More than half of all emigrants who made the overland trip used oxen to pull their wagons. Oxen, unlike horses that were guided by bridles, bits, and reigns, were directed by voice commands, hand signals, and prodding by a driver who walked beside the animal, adeptly "popping" the whip to control them. Overland travelers placed a premium on skilled ox drivers who knew when and how to apply the whip. In the outfitting town of Independence, Missouri, some enterprising African Americans made and sold the whips used to drive the oxen. Independence resident W. Z. Hickman wrote in his memoirs that, during the winter, black men would "buy up beef hides and dress them . . . [and] cut them in the proper shape and then plait them into these whips." When the wagon trains began to roll out in the spring, the African American whip makers would take their whips into town and "either sell them to the merchants or to the train men direct" for fifty or seventy-five cents each "according to size and quality." Emigrants dutifully bought the whips to complete their outfitting gear, but few were skilled enough initially to wield the ten- and twelve-feet-long rawhide lashes or to employ the voice and hand commands effectively. Mastery of these arts not only determined the worth of the driver but also improved the chances of making a successful crossing. Therefore, overlanders often competed to secure the services of seasoned drivers and stock handlers.[10]

African Americans, enslaved and free, often filled these positions as well, serving as ox-team drivers, teamsters, wranglers, and herders. They worked independently or alongside their white trailmates in many westbound wagon trains and pack companies. While trudging through the Humboldt Sink in 1849, gold rush diarist Amos Batchelder spotted "a negro teamster on the way whose perspiring face was completely whitewashed with white dust" as he pushed on to California. That same year, a black Kentuckian identified only as John earned passage to California by "cooking, barbering, and caring for the pack animals belonging to a military unit" that was heading west. White Kentuckian William Gill hired Vardaman Buller, a free black Kentuckian, to drive his ox teams to California in 1849.[11]

An African American convert to the Mormon faith named Green Flake proved to be one of the most proficient and resourceful drivers on the overland trail. He was the slave of Mormon converts James and Agnes Flake, who had sold or manumitted most of their slaves shortly after their conversion to Mormonism in 1843. However, they had held on to Green Flake and Elizabeth "Lizzy" Flake—who were not related but individually adopted the surname of their master—whom they took to the Mormon enclave in Nauvoo, Illinois, in 1844 and then to Winter Quarters in Nebraska. When Brigham Young's company started out for what is now Utah, James Flake dispatched his slave Green to go along to assist the expedition. In 1847, Green Flake left Winter Quarters driving his owner's "fine white mountain carriage," tending to Mormon pilgrims, and wrangling a herd of mules, all bound for the Valley of the Great Salt Lake.[12]

In July, the party had arrived at what is now the Utah-Wyoming border, and Green Flake and two other slaves, Hark Lay and Oscar Crosby, joined an advance company to search out the Donner Party's fading 1846 track through the mountains to the Salt Lake valley. This interracial group used shovels, axes, and other tools to improve the Donner trail through Echo Canyon, down Little Mountain, and through Emigration Canyon. On July 21, 1847, the three African American men, along with several other Mormon emigrants (including Mormon elder Orson Pratt), entered the valley. In August of that year, Green drove Brigham Young back to Nebraska but returned to the valley in October 1848, delivering his owner and family to the new log home he had built according to his master's orders.[13] After years of involuntary servitude, Green Flake was manumitted in 1850. He continued to embrace the Mormon faith, despite the restrictions the church placed on its African American members.[14] By 1860, Green and his wife, Martha Crosby

Flake, had acquired property in Union, Utah, where he farmed and raised cattle.[15]

After Martha died in 1885, Green moved farther west to Idaho to be near his children, Lucinda and Abraham. Years later, he was invited to speak at a Pioneer Appreciation Day program in Willow Creek, Idaho, where he was asked a question about his life as a slave. His granddaughter, Bertha Udell, recalled in an interview done many years after the event that her grandfather told the audience: "Sometimes I would work long and hard on a difficult job and no one would even say thanks or tell me and say a few kind words. . . . I drove a team and wagon to the Salt Lake valley for my master . . . and helped build him a home and fit place to live. They moved into the home and I was moved out most of the time to live in a dugout and a shed." He added, "[M]ost everyone don't want to be a slave and be in bondage to another, because you cain't have even your own thoughts and dreams." Green Flake died in Grays Lake, Idaho, in 1903 at the age of seventy-six. His well-attended funeral was held in Union, where he was interred in Union Cemetery beside his wife.[16]

North Carolina-born Elizabeth (Lizzy) Flake, also the slave of James and Agnes Flake, became an expert driver during the Mormon treks to the West as well. In 1848, when her owners departed Winter Quarters, Nebraska, and started for the Salt Lake valley, fifteen-year-old Elizabeth accompanied them on the 1,100-mile journey, leading a team of oxen, herding cattle, and walking all the way. Then in 1851, she and twenty-five other African Americans were part of a five-hundred-member, fifty-wagon Mormon expedition from Utah Territory to Rancho San Bernardino in southern California. On this trip, the young woman drove two yokes of oxen, herded cattle across mountains and desert, and met her future husband, Charles H. Rowan, a freeman who had crossed the plains to Utah and was now driving a team and wagon in the San Bernardino–bound company. Elizabeth Flake became a free woman in California. In 1860, she married Charles Rowan, who continued to work as a teamster while operating a successful barbershop in the Southern Hotel in downtown San Bernardino. Elizabeth worked as a laundress and cared for their three children. The Rowans became leaders of San Bernardino's African American community and were in the forefront of the antislavery movement. Elizabeth Flake Rowan died in 1903 and was buried in San Bernardino's Pioneer Cemetery. Two years later, her husband Charles passed away and was laid to rest beside her.[17]

Alvin Aaron Coffey, one of the best-known of all African American emigrants, became a veteran of the overland trail. He made the first of three round-trips to California in 1849 with his owner, Dr. William Bassett of St. Joseph, Missouri. The Kentucky-born slave performed a number of duties on and off the road in positions requiring skill and reliability. Jeannette Molson noted that her famed ancestor juggled many duties on the trail, "taking care of the oxen. . . . Obviously he tended the stock at night . . . . I would imagine driving a wagon in and of itself had to be tough." Coffey even earned money by repairing shoes for footsore emigrants whose footwear proved to be no match against the rugged terrain of the trail. Molson speculated that "he had to have learned that in Missouri. Yes, but under whose tutelage? That I don't know, so that may have been something he was doing . . . because that isn't a trade that you just automatically pick up. You either know how to sole shoes or you don't."[18]

Although Coffey's services as a trail cobbler were in great demand, his expertise as an ox-team driver was unsurpassed. He recalled in his memoirs that he "drove our oxen all the time and I knew about how much an ox could stand."[19] When his California-bound party was two days out from Honey Lake in northeastern California on the Nobles Trail, they made camp "at a place well known as Rabbit Hole Springs," where the Nobles Trail branched off the Applegate Trail. Here, "an ox had given out and was down, and not able to get up, about one hundred yards from the spring." When the spent animal "commenced bawling pitifully" that evening, Coffey tried to persuade his weary companions to help him "kill the ox for it is too bad to hear him bawl," and the "wolves were eating him alive." However, "none would go with me, so I got two double-barreled shot-guns which were loaded," and approached the dying animal, determined to put it out of its misery. Placing "one of the guns about five or six inches from the ox's head," he "killed him with the first shot." The "wolves were not in sight," but Coffey "could hear them" lurking about. They never "tackled" him, but as a precaution he had "reserved three shots in case they should."[20]

Alvin Coffey, like Green Flake, Elizabeth Flake Rowan, and Charles H. Rowan, started out as a driver on the trail, but for other African American drivers, chance sometimes placed the whip in their hands. This was the situation of a slave who approached Cincinnati diarist John Dalton's wagon company on the trail to California in 1852. Dalton wrote that just before his group came to the Ohio River, "a Darkey calling himself George Berryman came to us and wished to get into our wagon & cross the River." The desperate black man told them that he was "the Slave of another Negro who had brought him & promised him his freedom" in exchange for working for his master for "two years in California." However, the black slaveholder reneged on the deal because "slaves being high [costly], he was about to sell him to go down South." At that point, the despairing slave fled his owner and "he got into the waggon, crossed the river, and the next day commenced driving our team."[21]

Dalton does not mention Berryman's proficiency as an ox-team driver, but many overlanders learned that inexperience with the livestock could result in delays, injuries, and even death. Temperamental animals were a continuing aggravation for newcomers and seasoned travelers alike. African Americans with expertise in this area often were hired, pressed into service, or volunteered to work as "cattle breakers" who habituated the animals to the yoke and the ways of the road. John Johnson Davies, a white overlander on his way to Utah in 1854, observed, "Oh yes, we had a fine time seeing the Negroes breaking the young steers for the company!"[22]

When twenty-year-old Southerner Lavinia Honeyman Porter and her husband outfitted in Missouri for their trek to California in 1860, her greenhorn spouse bought six young oxen that "had never been broken to the yoke." She recalled that the animals were so wild that no one was "brave enough to venture into the corral with them." The Porters "soon concluded that we had six white elephants on our hands." Much to their relief, the problem was solved when her husband "found a Negro man who agreed to break them to yoke and chain." As the couple and their amused neighbors looked on, the anonymous black man succeeded in the "somewhat difficult task of training that bunch of young steers." Under his patient instruction, they eventually "became more amenable to yoke and chain, and sullenly submitted to be harnessed to draw the wagon."[23]

Sometimes black teamsters came to the aid of emigrants who got into other trouble on the trails as well. Edwin Bryant noted that when his wagon bogged down in the mud just outside Independence, it could not be moved until "fortunately a negro man with a well-trained yoke of oxen came down the road . . . and hitching his team to ours the wagon was immediately drawn out of the mud, and, to use a nautical expression, we were 'set afloat' again."[24] However, not all African Americans who handled animals were as skilled or successful. In 1854, white overlander Anna Maria Goodell reported seeing a black man who "got his cattle in a mud hole and had a fine time getting them out."[25]

Wayward animals and inexperienced handlers posed serious problems, but emigrants universally ranked herding as one of the most onerous jobs on the trail.[26] Driving the mules, cattle, and sheep that ambled behind the trains was a tedious, unpleasant chore. The stubborn animals required constant attention, and the job was made even worse by the blinding, choking dust churned up by hundreds of wagon wheels and hoofs. Bridget "Biddy" Mason, who traveled from Mississippi to Nebraska, and then on to the Salt Lake valley in 1848 as a slave with the Mississippi Mormon contingent, was put in charge of herding cattle behind the wagons. In 1851, she joined Elizabeth Flake as a herder on the Mormon trek from Salt Lake City to San Bernardino. She performed this task while caring for her three young daughters, one of whom was still nursing.[27]

A cash-strapped, free black man from Tennessee named Richard G. (Dick) Rapier worked his way west wrangling mules and horses for a Tennessee wagon company in 1850. Rapier, the eldest son of a self-educated former slave and businessman John H. Rapier Sr. and freewoman Susan Rapier, was well educated for an African American man of his time. He had gone to school in Buffalo, New York, where his father had sent him to live under the watchful eye of his paternal uncle

Henry K. Thomas, a fugitive slave and successful barber. While Dick was in his uncle's care, his father continued to monitor his progress, noting in a lettter to Dick written in 1845, that he was "well pleased with your hand writing. . . . [I] hope your studys are as much improved." The father urged his son to apply himself to his education so that he might "grow up an ornament to society."[28]

Dick returned to Tennessee, where he, like many other young men in the state, caught gold fever. Eager to set out for the goldfields, he applied to the Nashville and Clarksville Havilah Mining and Trading Company for passage to California. Twenty-six-year-old Madison Berryman Moorman, one of the organizers of the company and the grandson of a Virginia Quaker and abolitionist, also was impatient to get started. Dick was hired to manage the company's fifty mules and horses on the overland trip and was one of four African Americans (and the only free black man) in a party of about twenty-three Tennesseans. Moorman recorded in his journal that the *"two* negro fellows," identified only as "Walker and John, col'd," were "put in [the company] as *cash stock*," and "Dick Rapier, col'd." had been taken on as one of six "Outsiders." Walker was probably the slave of Dr. E. M. Patterson; John was the slave of J. M. McClelland; and a black man identified only as the "slave boy Ben" was owned by Hugh E. Patterson. Patterson was one of four non-stockholders, "not attached regularly" to the company, who had signed on to work in exchange for food and transportation to the Golden State.[29]

When Dick Rapier and his fellow argonauts left Nashville on the steamboat *Sligo No. 2* headed for St. Louis on April 27, 1850, three of his family members—grandmother Sally Thomas, uncle James Thomas, and younger brother James Thomas Rapier—were on the wharf to bid him farewell. After a layover in St. Louis, where they purchased rifles from the government arsenal (and had to swear before a magistrate that they were indeed California-bound), the group continued to "Kanzas" and arrived in Independence on May 8. They jumped off on the overland trail at Westport on May 14 in a caravan of eleven wagons, eight owned by the Havilah company and three others belonging to smaller Tennessee parties that traveled with them. Upon reaching Fort Kearney, the Havilah company sold three of their wagons and transferred the cargo to the mules, hoping to speed their way across the plains.[30]

Dick Rapier and the other African Americans in the company proved to be capable and resourceful trailmates. Moorman, who "had command of the pack train," drove the mules at the rear of the train with Rapier (and sometimes with the slaves John and Walker), tracked down strays with the black men, and scouted out grazing and watering spots along the route with them as well. Rapier was put in charge of picketing the animals at night. Moorman, who clearly admired Rapier's dependability and perseverance, referred to him as "my colored friend Dick." Working together, the men carried out their duties without incident most of the time, and sometimes enjoyed a bit of camaraderie at the end of a long day. Moorman recalled that on one occasion, after "feasting most bountifully" on a supper of fried catfish and catfish-head soup, "all hands" participated in a "social smoke of *pipe & cigar* . . . with no small degree of cheerfulness around our camp fire."[31]

At other times, however, the job could be treacherous. As they traveled toward the Black Hills beyond Fort Laramie in late June 1850, the company could not locate suitable water and pasturage for their worn-out mules. Moorman was forced to "stay back with the tardy mules," which were "on the eve of giving up the ghost," while the others, in a rush to reach California, "lef[t] me with Dick to bring up the rear." As night fell, the two men made the "best head way we could," scrambling over "hills & through the deep defiles & gorges, through the darkness" to catch up with the rest of the group. Making matters even worse, their colleagues had taken their "blankets and all the edibles," leaving them "almost famished & worn down from fatigue," in charge of "broken down mules, for want of grass & water." Moorman wrote that only the "hope of soon reaching camp led us on, on!" At eleven o'clock that night, the weary mule herders found their companions "encamped near Horse Creek—a stream of clear good water, but no grass worth the name." The entire company "pitied the poor animals" and, Moorman noted, "all regretted not having stopped where I wanted them."[32]

On July 20, Rapier and the other gold seekers reached the "City of the Great Salt Lake," where they enjoyed a brief stopover with the Mormons. Setting out on the trail again, the group, hoping to shorten their trek, took the Hastings Cutoff to the Humboldt route. Before the trip came to an end, they had abandoned more wagons, endured two grueling desert crossings, and survived a skirmish with hostile Indians. By late August 1850, they finally reached the Sierra Nevada. Moorman and four others set out on foot, leaving Rapier and the rest to follow with a single wagon and the mules. After more than four months on the trail, Moorman's party finally reached Placerville (known locally then as Hangtown) on September 8, 1850. Dick Rapier arrived a week later. The boomtown made an unsettling first impression on him with its profusion of businesses, reputable and otherwise, that flourished there and the hard-looking characters who crowded the streets.[33]

Rapier and the other Tennesseans set about the business of "getting gold" as soon as they arrived. However, Moorman reported that they had been "employed in mining: with but poor success." After only six weeks in the goldfields, the end was in sight for the Havilah company. With their capital severely depleted and equipment problems hindering their progress, the company suspended operations and subsequently disbanded, concluding that the "mines [were] too poor to support us."[34]

The record is silent about the slaves Walker and John, but Dick Rapier also gave up on the idea of striking it rich. He remained in California though, eventually settling in the Feather River region of the Sacramento valley, where he purchased land and took up wheat and barley farming. Sometime later, Dick's younger brother Henry Rapier trekked overland to join him, but their reunion was short-lived. The brothers got into a bitter dispute over some unspecified matter and parted company. Their father, John H. Rapier Sr., deeply hurt by the rift between his sons, wrote: "Dick said nothing a Bout his Brother Henry not as much as to call his name. I am Sorry to See Brothers have so littel respect for each other for it is not rite for them to act that way." After his break with Dick, Henry's life seems to have unraveled; he drifted around northern California pursuing card games, whiskey, and women. When his father learned that Henry, following in the footsteps of his younger brother, James Thomas Rapier, had taken up the gambler's life to support himself, he confided to another of his sons: "I am fearful bad company have been thire Ruinnation," and concluded, "I would not be Sirprise to hear of his [Henry's] death."[35]

The father's fears were justified when, in September 1856, the Court of Sessions in Placer County, California, issued an indictment of first-degree murder against Henry and ordered the sheriff to "bring him before the court." Although little is known about the murder and the court proceedings, records indicate that Henry Rapier was again arrested in Marin County, California, in February 1859 on a warrant for murder in the first degree. After this, Henry Rapier seems to have vanished from the historical record.[36]

Dick Rapier fared better in California than his brother Henry, but money problems stalked him as the boom days of the gold rush receded and California's economy changed. In 1865, he had amassed $350 to purchase a building in Auburn, California, where he established a barbershop and bathhouse, and in August 1868, he married Henrietta Stans, who bore him a son whom they named John, in honor of Dick's father.[37] Although Dick Rapier's businesses earned him a passable living, a series of agricultural calamities in the 1850s, which his father called "bad luck farming," kept him tottering perpetually on the brink of financial ruin. Around 1857, fire destroyed a large portion of his crops, costing him about eight hundred dollars; the following season, severe drought ravaged his wheat harvest. Altogether, his losses amounted to almost two thousand dollars.[38] Writing to his uncle James P. Thomas more than two decades after trekking to California, Dick despaired of ever being reunited with his loved ones because "the way things have been running for the past year I don't think that I ever will have money enough again to come and see you all." He added, "to tell you the truth I am poorer to day than I have ever been since I have been in this country."[39]

Dick Rapier suffered a stroke in February 1887 at the age of fifty-six and died in his home three days later. At his death, his estate consisted of a small amount of personal and real property, which was auctioned off to pay his debts. The remaining balance—valued at just over seven hundred dollars—and his personal effects, including clothing and family pictures, went to his half-brothers and sisters who lived in Florence, Alabama. His son John, who resided in Portland, Oregon, made no claim against the estate. The *Placer Argus* obituary for Rapier described him as a "very intelligent and well informed man" who had been a "freeman all his days," and was "well liked by all who knew him."[40]

Hunters: Foraging, Thriving, and Surviving on the Trails

Dick Rapier's experiences as an animal herder attest to the fact that the average wagon company, as historian Will Bagley has written, "spent considerably more time hunting grass or stray oxen than game."[41] Yet, hunting did play an important role in the life of many westbound wagon communities. It could tip the scales in favor of survival in desperate times and provide a welcome break in the monotony of the usual trail fare. African American emigrants, free and enslaved, engaged in hunting on their own or with their white traveling companions. In 1844, George W. Bush put his hunting abilities to good use for himself and his trailmates on several occasions as their large wagon company plodded its way west from Missouri to the Oregon Country. About six hundred miles from their destination, Bush's party straggled into Fort Hall nearly starving. Taking command of the situation, he instructed a small hunting party on the best way to forage for game in the wild terrain, saying, "Boys you are going through a hard country. You have guns and ammunition. Take my advice: anything you see as big as a blackbird, kill it and eat it." John Minto, Bush's friend and confidant, proclaimed that "G. W. Bush [was] one of the most efficient men on the road."[42]

In another wagon company, nine slaves owned by white Kentucky gold rusher C. C. Churchill were entrusted with firearms to hunt antelope as they trekked to California in 1849. That same year, a teenage slave identified only as Alex (or Alek), traveled with his master, Donald Campbell, in a California-bound wagon company from Tennessee. Alex tried his hand at hunting waterfowl when his party set up camp near a river. Company member Hugh Brown Heiskell recorded in his diary that "Mr. Campbell's Alek brought in a large goose, two ducks, & a Cudlien, a bird of the snipe species, large as a summer duck with a bill about 4 inches long, sniped shaped." Thanks to the hunting and fishing efforts, Brown reported, "our train lives high, having ducks, sage hens, & fish daily."[43]

In 1850, the hardworking African American mule drivers Dick Rapier and Walker, who were part of another Tennessee company, participated in an antelope shoot as they worked their way to the California goldfields. Diarist Madison Berryman Moorman, who traveled and worked with the two black men, described the hunt: "I shot an antelope which we put upon a pack mule and drove ahead." Later, the men "divided our antelope and served up a part for dinner; which, well seasoned with pepper, salt and wild onions, or leakes . . . was very palatable and eaten with no little gusto."[44]

Cooks and Other Servants: Preparing the Meals, Bearing the Load

African American men and women, enslaved and free, shouldered the daily work of the trails out of necessity and generally in the spirit of teamwork. They worked with their white counterparts driving, herding, and hunting and also took on the tedious yet critical day-to-day tasks that composed the routine of the trail as well. White overlander Theodore Edgar Potter recalled that his wagon company, which was headed to California in 1852, was joined by a New Orleans group that included "two stout, healthy looking colored men, supposed to be slaves . . . who were brought along to do the work, such as cooking, driving teams, pitching tents and everything except guard duty."[45] These men, and countless other African American overlanders, enslaved or not, routinely performed such tasks and more.

A surprising number of white emigrants from middle-class backgrounds were unfamiliar with basic labor or homemaking duties; back home they had relied on servants to take care of those chores for them. Things were different on the trails.[46] Lavinia Honeyman Porter wrote that she "had been raised South of 'Mason's and Dixon's line.' My parents were well-to-do Southern people, and I had hitherto led the indolent life of the ordinary Southern girl." Her husband, too, "knew nothing of manual labor."[47] Overland diarist Catherine Haun noted that when she and her lawyer husband left Clinton, Iowa, for California in 1849, she "had yet to make [her] first cup of coffee." The Hauns had made arrangements to engage the services of a cook to accompany them, but they "lost the cook in only a few days."[48]

Cooks and servants of all kinds were in high demand in most wagon companies. A skilled cook could make trail life more bearable, if not pleasurable. Benjamin Butler Harris, a Texas lawyer who trekked to California on the Gila Trail in a fifty-two-man saddle horse and pack mule company in 1849, wrote that his party took in "John, a Kentucky

Negro barber" whose owner had left him in El Paso at the end of the Mexican War. Harris's party "mounted and fed" the black man "on condition of his cooking, driving our pack animals, and doing our barbering."⁴⁹ Gold rusher J. Goldsborough Bruff filled his journal with references to the cooking repertoire of his black servant Andy, which delighted and comforted him as they trudged west. On August 3, 1850, he wrote, "Andy, the darkee, is very kind & obliging,—He baked me a nice little loaf of bread to-day." A subsequent entry noted that Andy had prepared a "fine piece of venison" and, though ill, Bruff "drank some of the broth." Later he reported, "Andy made me a peach pie . . . a great luxury for us here." Bruff also recalled sharing a meal with two St. Louis emigrants, "Mr. [Loring] Pickering & lady," who traveled with a "colored man and woman," who cooked and served them a lunch consisting of "a nice white roll of bread, and a cup of good coffee, with *milk*." ⁵⁰

Tennessee argonaut Hugh Brown Heiskell wrote that the young slave "Alleck [Alex] brought us up some clams—common mussels—cooked in excellent sauce. They tasted much like the oyster, but were tough, & we concluded they were no great luxury, notwithstanding Dr. Brown's mess . . . eat them with avidity."⁵¹ Theodore Edgar Potter recounted enjoying a meal with his New Orleans trailmates that was served in "genuine Southern style" by "the two colored men" belonging to the southerners.⁵² An unnamed black New Yorker, headed for California in 1849, joined a party of Germans from New York who were in need of a cook. Historian Rudolph Lapp has speculated that this group was composed of "radical refugees from persecution in Germany . . ." and if so, the "Negro cook was in the most congenial of company."⁵³ In 1850, Bruff reported meeting a California company of "chiefly Germans," who "have a New York Negro for cook; and are well armed and equipped."⁵⁴

Sylvia Estes Stark's mother, Hannah Estes, was employed to cook for her former owner, Charles Leopold, in 1858 when Leopold hired Hannah's husband Howard and their son Jackson to help drive a herd of cattle from Missouri to California. Hannah Estes, Sylvia recalled, cooked for the entire company, often using "Sundried Buffalo Chips," the "only fuel they had." The chips "made their pancakes and bacon taste smoky," but the entire party "ate them with relish."⁵⁵

Despite such congeniality, even the most routine jobs could go awry with serious consequences for African Americans working their way west. In 1849, a fifteen-year-old African American boy named Wash was the subject of a violent confrontation that erupted in his wagon train carrying Tennessee gold prospectors to California. Hugh Brown Heiskell, a member of the party, witnessed the "flare up in camp today" between Wash's owner Mr. Thompson and Mr. Thomas, an Englishman who protested when "Mr. Thompson was whipping Wash." Thomas intervened, arguing that Thompson "should not whip him." The slave owner warned Thomas that "if he interfered he would whip him [Thomas] too, & seizing a hatchet seemed ready to execute this threat." Thomas's wife entered the fray, cautioning Thompson, "If you kill my husband you shall not live." Thomas, "going back to his wagon, now came out with a pistol." Other members of the company attempted to calm the situation, advising the Englishman that "he had no right to say anything to Thompson for whipping his Negro." Finally, Mrs. Thomas relented, reminding her husband, "You are in the States, you are not in England." Unconvinced, Thomas, asked, "Well, but what's the difference? Didn't the Americans all come from England!" With this, Heiskell wrote, "so ended the battle."[56]

Heiskell does not say if Thompson resumed beating Wash when the confrontation ended, but just a month later, Wash found himself in another predicament when his owner ordered him to lug two heavy bundles of provisions across the desert. Heiskell noted, "The poor fellow had more than he could get along with." Jack Johnson, another member of the company, tried to persuade the distraught teenager to leave one of the bundles behind, "but Wash would not." Taking pity on him, Johnson urged Wash to give him one of the packs, but when Wash handed it over, Johnson and another white man proceeded to "eat what they wished & left it." When Wash asked Johnson to return the bundle, "Jack told him to tell Thompson he [Wash] had left it."[57] Two days later, Wash's master angrily dispatched him to take an ox and go back "ten miles on the desert, to where he commenced packing and where he had left divers articles which [he] was to pack back to camp that night." Late the next night, Wash struggled into camp, "carrying a bag of crackers on his back & some other articles."

The black youth had driven "the ox until it gave out then packed the load himself."[58]

Another enslaved black man, known only as Dick, was caught in the middle of a bitter dispute between his owner, Capt. A. Powell and another white man over ownership of a wagon as they all traveled in a westbound Alabama company in 1849. Texas argonaut and diarist Benjamin Butler Harris encountered Powell and Dick on the trail and reported that Powell's adversary retaliated against Powell by whipping Dick when his master was not around. Even though other company members "sternly prevented [the vengeful man] from injuring Dick," who was "a Negro beloved by all," they were not always successful. Dick contemptuously referred to his tormenter as a "nasty, buzzard puke," and alleged that the man's father also had "tortured a Negro by tying him in a yellowjackets' nest." It is not known if Dick ever found relief from this agony; like the teenage slave Wash, Dick's fate is lost to history.[59]

In 1852, the activities of two enslaved black men in Theodore Edgar Potter's company "caused a good deal of discussion among the white men as to the proper place for slaves." Two unnamed black men, who up to that point only had "attended their master," were put to work constructing fishing rafts for the group. Potter wrote that one of the resentful "white boys" who was cooking the evening meal for the group declared that "he didn't propose to work with a 'nigger' on the raft." However, "another replied that these two negroes were good enough to work with him," and added that they were "much better helpers than some white men he knew of." With that, the two cooks "came to blows and grabbing their sizzling frying pans struck each other over the head again and again." The melee was quelled with the intervention of "Uncle Billy," one of the elders in the company who sternly lectured the combatants, threatening them with physical punishment. After that, Potter reported, "the white and colored boys worked together in harmony."[60]

Things did not end as well for an unnamed African American man who had taken a job as servant to a domestically troubled emigrant couple in 1852. The black overlander found himself in an untenable position on the trail and after reaching his destination in California.

While en route, his employer had ordered him, in addition to his other trail duties, to periodically beat his (the white man's) wife. John Doble, a gold seeker who arrived in California via the sea-land route, wrote of his encounter in the gold region with the wife who was "just off the plains" and had lodged a complaint against "a Negro for kicks[,] licks[,] & abuse on the plains and against her husband for . . . encouraging him to do it." The woman had complained to authorities about this abuse but, Doble reported, when they "did not take hold of it . . . the Miners did." They "met[,] heard both sides and gave the Negro 50 lashes." The couple's property was then divided between them, and the miners "ordered the husband to leave the wife which he did immediately," only to rejoin her the next day. Doble noted that, after that, the "Miners say the Negro may do as he pleases now for as much as they care."[61]

Two free African American women faced a similarly desperate situation as they worked their way west via the Gila Trail in August 1849. The women—mother and daughter—had signed on as servants for an army wagon train but were subsequently abandoned on the trail. Robert Eccleston, a California-bound gold seeker from New York who traveled in a nearby train, met the "young colored woman who came near our camp, crying & imploring aid." She told him that "her mother had been beaten, & she was afraid that they would tie her up." The young woman who was "about 18 yrs. old, of middle stature and fine figure," took Eccleston to her mother, who told him that she had "last come from the Sea Willow [perhaps in Texas], but was raised in Albermarle [Albemarle], Va." She explained that "she had talked sassy to Major Henry," but "she could not help it, as she had been used to decent treatment . . . and was as free as Major Henry was." The major had immediately expelled both women from the company. Their "traps were all thrown out in a heap on the campground, and the Army train went on, leaving her & daughter, without provision, to the mercy either of Californians or the savages."[62]

It appears that Eccleston was moved as much by the young woman's looks as by her plight. He wrote, "Her features were not African in the least. She was neatly dressed, her low neck dress showing a breast which in form would eclipse many a belle whose might have been whiter. Her waist was small & exquisite, her color was a shade darker than a mullata & but for the predjudice of color, she would be a charmer." Conversely, he observed that the "old dame," her mother, "was different, being darker and bearing all the marks of the African race." Eccleston noted that one of his trailmates "offered to take one but they would not separate." He "afterwards heard that Mr. Stanmore [another member of Eccleston's party] took them under his protection."[63]

The African Americans who worked their way west—whether as free people or as slaves—were forced to contend with abusive and arbitrary treatment that occasionally threatened their lives and frequently impeded their progress. However, some black travelers found relief from the rigors of the journey at the forts that had been established along the trails to provide protection for travelers. Black emigrants, enslaved and free, undoubtedly stopped over and occasionally ended their journey at these outposts, where some went to work as cooks, laundresses, skilled artisans, and laborers.

Bent's Old Fort was such a place. Established in 1833 in the present-day La Junta region by Charles Bent (who would become New Mexico's first American governor), his brother William Bent, and partner Ceran St. Vrain, this "castle on the plains" was set up to serve the Santa Fe Trail trade between Missouri and the New Mexican settlements. Historian Anne F. Hyde has written that it became a "free trade zone," where Native and other peoples conducted business in a "remarkably dynamic" area, and it served as a liaison point for American government officials and the Native nations of the region.[64] The fort provided explorers, adventurers, traders, and the military a place to replenish supplies and livestock and to repair wagons and equipment. It also offered a welcome rest stop for weary travelers. At least three African Americans—Charlotte Green, her husband, Dick Green, and Dick's brother Andrew Green—were taken there from Missouri as Charles Bent's slaves, and an unknown number of free black people probably worked at the fort as well.[65]

Charlotte Green, commonly called "Black Charlotte," won widespread acclaim for her cooking at Bent's Old Fort; her buffalo stews, assorted vegetables, pastries, and pumpkin pies were renowned throughout the southern Rocky Mountains. In addition to her culinary talents, she was an accomplished dancer in great demand at parties and "fandangos." Charlotte explained that her popularity stemmed from the fact that she was "de only female lady in de whole dam Injun country." Lewis H. Garrard, a white teenager from Ohio who stopped over at the fort en route to Taos, New Mexico, in 1846, described her as "the glib-tongued, sable fort cook," who regaled guests with her "stock of news and surmises," as they dined at tables spread with white linen cloths and decked with fancy castors (decorative condiment containers).[66]

Charlotte's husband, Dick, described as a "large black man," served the fort as a blacksmith, turning out shoes for the mules and horses, equipment for the upkeep of the fort, and supplies for the wagon trains. When Charles Bent was appointed the first American civil governor of New Mexico in 1846, Dick Green spent most of his time in Santa Fe working as the governor's "man servant." Dick's brother Andrew served the fort as a cook, occasional butler, and blacksmith's assistant before gaining his freedom. In 1848, an official license listed Andrew as a "Bent Company Trader."[67]

In 1847, Dick Green fought with the American forces against the Mexicans and Pueblo Indians in the uprising at Taos. He was severely wounded in the fight, and Charles Bent was killed. William Bent, Charles's brother, manumitted Dick and Charlotte in 1848 as a reward for the black man's help in suppressing the rebellion. After being manumitted, the couple once again became overland travelers, setting out across the plains in a wagon caravan headed back to Missouri. According to the census of 1850, Charlotte Green was living in St. Louis without Dick, who likely had succumbed to the injuries he had sustained in the uprising. Andrew Green appears to have faded from the record.[68]

Dick and Charlotte Green were just two of an unknown number of enslaved overlanders who, after trekking to the West and residing there for some time, retraced their footsteps eastward over the trails once they had gained freedom.

Nearly all overland emigrants started out as naïve and untested individuals with little preparation for the road ahead of them. As the journey progressed, this assortment of greenhorns began to coalesce into a community working together for mutual benefit. Black overlanders, whether enslaved or free, worked all the way across, sharing in the hardships and hazards of the trail and taking on responsibilities that demanded perseverance, resourcefulness, and skills that their white trailmates did not possess or chose not to employ. African Americans served as guides, hunters, drivers, cooks, servants, and more, often juggling multiple duties. Sometimes their work placed them in situations that jeopardized their well-being, if not their lives. This was especially true for slaves, who were required to follow their owners' orders, and for African American women, regardless of status, who were vulnerable to harassment and sexual assault by predatory masters, employers, and other men they encountered along the way. African American overlanders were, in theory, confined to the roles of servants, laborers, and slaves in the nomadic communities of the trails. In reality, however, they took on responsibilities that routinely defied these categories.

Chapter 6
Life, Death, and Acts of Kindness

I thot my time had come sure, and my heart almost sank inside of me.
Robert Ball Anderson, 1866

Alone on the great open space with two helpless babes, . . . she saw . . . two colored men with a donkey, and all of their belongings packed on its back. . . . She determined to beg for help. Although in the state where she came from they were not considered reliable. The two men were visibly shocked seeing her plight. . . . Then she heard them say in lowered voice, "[W]hat can we do[?] We haven't enough grub for ourselves, but we can't leave her here."
Sylvia Stark, recollections, 1851

HISTORIAN WILL BAGLEY HAS WRITTEN THAT the "frontier could indeed be a vicious and dangerous place, but popular culture has exaggerated the general level of violence on the trails."[1] This was particularly true concerning violence committed by American Indians. Emigrant diaries and journals brim with stories about encounters with Native people; yet, contrary to the general view of western migration, overlanders were not regularly beset by marauding and murderous bands of Indians. In reality, they often relied on Native peoples to help them negotiate the trails, secure food and supplies, and obtain treatment for illnesses and injuries. Tales of Indian attacks on emigrants most often were fueled by overlanders' general lack of knowledge of Native cultures, by highly embellished pioneer reminiscences, and by lurid newspaper accounts.[2]

Between 1840 and 1860, approximately 250,000 emigrants had, in the words of historian John Unruh Jr., "worn the trails to Oregon and California so deeply that in places the ruts are still visible." Additionally, more than 40,000 Mormons traveled the trails on their way to the Salt Lake valley during the same period. Yet during all those years, 362 emigrants were killed by Natives, and 426 Natives died at the hands of emigrants.[3] (Richard L. Rieck, has revised the number of emigrants slain by Indians slightly downward to 353.[4]) Overland travelers were victimized more frequently by so-called white Indians—bands of white men masquerading as Indians, who robbed, raped, and plundered emigrant companies—and by robbers and outlaws who preyed on them at every opportunity.

African Americans and American Indians
At times, however, Native hostility targeting overlanders did flare up on the trails, and black emigrants who came into contact with indigenous people, voluntarily or otherwise, were not exempt from this violence. However, occasionally they experienced deferential treatment from Native people for a variety of reasons. Some African Americans managed to establish a cultural rapport with them. Stanislaus Lasselle, an Indiana attorney who traveled to the California goldfields via the Santa Fe–Gila Trails, observed a black minister preaching to a group of Natives in their own language at a Baptist mission on the Canadian River and concluded that "Negroes are very popular and have a great deal of influence with the Indians."[5]

Some Native peoples believed that skin color made African Americans harbingers of power and good fortune, and therefore merited special treatment. Sarah Winnemucca, a Northern Paiute born in 1844, recalled that when the wagons began streaming over the plains, scouts reported that "there was something among them [the newcomers] that was burning all in a blaze." Winnemucca said that the mysterious entity "looked like a man; it had legs and hands and a head," but "the head had quit burning and was left quite black." She remembered, "[T]here was the greatest excitement among my people everywhere about the men in a blazing fire." However, she reported, those magical beings ultimately turned out to be "two negroes wearing red shirts."[6]

Dave Boffman, the perseverant slave discussed in a previous chapter, experienced honorific treatment because of his skin color after being captured by Cheyenne raiders during a skirmish on the high plains. As he and his captors "marched with much ceremony" into their camp, the inhabitants constantly touched and rubbed him. He was perhaps the first black man they had ever encountered. Taking Boffman's dark skin to be a good luck omen, they left him unguarded overnight, enabling him to slip away and resume his trek west.[7]

On at least one occasion, a black man's skin color seems to have won safe passage for an entire company of overlanders. The man, identified only as "our good negro comrade," was a member of Joseph Pownall's fifty-one-man gold-seeking expedition en route to California in 1849. Thanks to his presence, the group managed to avoid two conflicts with Native people as they marched west. Setting out from Keachie, Louisiana, on March 28, 1849, Pownall's group traveled trails that took them across Texas and into Mexico. In Mexico, they encountered a band of Apaches, whom they feared had hostile intentions. Much to their surprise, the Indians, whom Pownall claimed were led by Chief "Mangus Colorado," came forward "carrying a white flag & no Sooner was it perceived than answered by the elevation of a Sheepskin, which happened at the time to be the most convenient article."[8]

After both sides were satisfied no violence would erupt, they began to converse. Pownall observed that, "What seemingly interested them the utmost, was our negro comrade as undoubtedly he was the first black man they had seen." After conducting a thorough examination of the man's skin, they allowed the gold seekers to continue on their way. A few days later, Pownall's company saw more Native people and "our negro insisted that we get a large white flag and that he would carry it, which we did, that being a light cream cashmere shawl." From that day forward, the black man carried the makeshift "Indian peace flag" all the way to San Luis Obispo without further incident.[9]

Complexion might arouse curiosity among some Native people, but skin color did not guarantee African Americans protection. Native Americans often regarded blacks as just another kind of white person who was, in the words of archeologist Todd Guenther, "part of the Euro-American culture that was sweeping across the plains despoiling an ancient way of life and destroying everything and everyone that stood in the way."[10]

Moreover, black people often held the same negative attitudes toward the indigenous peoples they encountered and sometimes joined their white counterparts in committing horrific acts against them. Andy, J. Goldsborough Bruff's indispensable black servant, cook, and caregiver, participated in the sexual assault of a Feather River Native woman in California. According to Bruff, "Near sun set, Nicholas, Jas. Marshall, and Andy, rode off, to visit the indian village above. As they purchased whiskey and drink along the route, it is probable that [they] will visit the indians drunk. They returned, at night intoxicated, and tell how that they reached the village and found the males all absent." The men then "caught a Squaw, who offered them roots, willow baskets, &c if they would not molest her," but heedless of her pleas, "they successively, *did molest* her."[11]

In northern California, whites, blacks, and Indians rode in "pursuit-and-vengeance posses" that hunted and killed Native people. A California newspaper described the interracial composition of a Sacramento posse that included "16 whites, two Indians, and a negro." When this group returned to town after a bloody encounter, they "paraded through the streets" with the black man brandishing a "bow and a quiver of arrows," and displaying the "muzzle of his gun decorated with the scalp taken from the enemy." Andy, who had become a fierce and brazen Indian fighter, could have been the man described in the newspaper account.[12]

The Need for Security

Not all African American overlanders shared Andy's anti-Indian zeal, but they frequently stood shoulder-to-shoulder with their white trailmates to protect their trail communities, fending off not only Native Americans but also, and more commonly, the thieves and outlaws who preyed on emigrants. Alvin Coffey, the intrepid African American overlander who crossed the plains three times to California, recalled that when he stood watch for his wagon train the first time, "I was one of three who were on the first night guard. At 12 o'clock three more men took our place and we went to camp. At 6 in the morning there were three more [who] went to relieve those on guard." Coffey's descendant, Jeannette Molson, has concluded that her ancestor's shared night-watch duties suggest "to some degree" that "he was treated pretty much as an equal."[13]

Isaac, the slave of John E. Durivage, who used the pseudonym E. Durivage as a correspondent for the *New Orleans Picayune,* trekked to California with his master in 1849. Isaac also stood guard duty to "prevent thievery by local Mexicans on the Gila Trail to the gold fields." Another African American overlander, identified only as "Black Bob," shared guard duty with white overlander C(ornelius) C. Cox, who reported that Bob, armed with a gun that misfired, nevertheless thwarted an attempted raid (presumably by Native Americans) on the company's horses. When his "watchful eye" detected someone moving toward the animals, Bob "snap[p]ed *old Betsy* [the gun] several times, but finding that she would not *go off,*" the black man's loud calls to Cox scared off the would-be thief.[14]

Jackson Estes, brother of Sylvia Estes Stark, performed night-watch duties for his California-bound train in 1851. According to Sylvia, Jackson was "sitting out in the bright moonlight, gazing at the mounds and shadows" when "something told him to go and sit in the shade of a wagon." He had "scarcely moved from his seat when an arrow whizzed past him and stuck fast in the ground where he had been sitting." After he sounded the alarm, "every man grabbed his gun, but there was not a sound, not even the howl of a coyote." Fearing that the "Indians might plan to raid the camp in the morning when the wagons were loaded and hitched," the group "left before dawn."[15]

Even after arriving safely at their destinations, overlanders, regardless of race, might still be vulnerable to violence from hostile tribes and avaricious bandits. Fourteen-year-old Charles (Charley, sometimes spelled Charlie) Tyler and his eighteen-year-old sister, Anne, accompanied their owner, Edmund Tyler, overland to El Monte in southern California after leaving Arkansas in 1852. Upon reaching California, the black teenagers were freed. In 1860 Charley Tyler was living in Tulare County, and by 1863, he was working as a horse wrangler for two white families that included Mr. and Mrs. Jesse Summers, Alney McGee, and McGee's mother and young niece. Charley and the Summers and McGee families were camped at Owensville near the present site of Laws, on their way from Aurora, Nevada, to Visalia, California, in March of 1863. The whites traveled in at least two wagons, while Charley, on horseback, herded a band of saddle horses and workhorses. On

March 7, Charley and his party were shaken up when they discovered the stripped corpse of a man who had been killed by Indians.

Then, just before the group reached the present-day Tinemaha Dam on the Owens River, they encountered a band of nearly one hundred Indians blocking their path. Charley and company attempted to flee across the river, but the wagons got stuck in the channel. Freeing the horses from the wagons, the families mounted them and made a dash for Fort Independence, about sixteen miles away. Charley surrendered his horse so that the women could escape, assuring the terrified whites that he would catch another one from the ramada and follow them to the fort. When he failed to show up, his companions assumed that he had been captured and killed. It appears, however, that Charley put up a fight. Years later, a gun identified as his was found, chamber emptied, near the site where he had been seen last.[16]

Other African American emigrants, most whose names have been lost, undoubtedly participated in similar life-and-death struggles. One such conflict occurred at Rock Ranch, an abandoned trading post in present-day Wyoming, on the Oregon-California Trail, a "short distance downstream" from Fort Laramie. During the Civil War, a Missouri slave owner, fleeing the turmoil of war and attempting to hold on to his human property, settled at Rock Ranch. Intending to take advantage of the lucrative overland trail trade, the transplanted Missourian put his slaves to work rebuilding the outpost. Wyoming pioneer John Owens recalled in a 1915 interview that the site was rebuilt "by a fellow from Missouri, I don't remember his name. He come up here with seven niggers that he owned and was afraid they would be taken away from him after the war so he came with them to Wyoming."[17]

In 1863, however, most of the occupants of Rock Ranch were killed in a raid by hostile Native people and the ranch was destroyed as an economic site for the overland trail. Few details remain about the black people who lived at Rock Ranch, but the modern-day discovery of "one almost complete skeleton" of a young black man—and other bones also thought to be Rock Ranch slaves—reveals that this group of involuntary black emigrants also waged a desperate fight for survival. The most intact bones found at the site were "those of an adult, black male," of slight build, and "about five feet six and one-half inches in height." At the time of death he was "between 24 and 30 years of age," in "good health," and "only a few minor dental problems were discernable." The man had "died violently; at least three gunshot wounds were discernible, and his corpse had been chopped to pieces with an axe."[18] A .44-caliber bullet was recovered from his spinal column, and it appears that he had been paralyzed and mutilated in the raid. Archeologists surmised that during a lull in the fighting, or under cover of night, two other slaves who had managed to survive the initial onslaught dragged the body of the fallen black man into the building and buried him beneath the floor.[19] Nothing more is known about these enslaved African American emigrants who lived and died in this western outpost of the overland trail.

More than a decade before the African American overlanders at Rock Ranch lost their lives in Wyoming, Amos Kusick, also a Missouri slave, was transported by his owner to California's goldfields, where he met his death. Amos was part of the sixty-seven-wagon contingent that carried white Missourian William J. Pleasants, making the first of two trips to California in 1849 with his father and brother. Pleasants's party, which left from Cass County, included five black men: Amos Kusick, Sam Kusick (probably the slaves of James Kusick), Old Uncle Dick Sloan (probably the slave of Robert Sloan), Emanuel (probably the slave of Middleton Story), and John Arnett (whose status is unknown).[20]

Once in California, Amos, who may have been freed, went to work mining for gold with a partner identified only as "a sailor" (race unknown). According to Pleasants, Amos and his partner met with some success, "having between them about three thousand dollars." The two men had just "left Bidwell's [Bidwell Bar] at noon on their way east." After "going about three miles," they stopped to rest. At that point, they were "attacked by Joaquin Murietta [sic] and his gang of outlaws," who were after their gold. The miners were equally determined to hold on to their hard-earned treasure and put up a ferocious fight, driving off the robbers, who left a "trail of blood leading away from the scene of the crime." Amos Kusick even managed to "come into possession of a knife belonging to one of the robbers, and had used it with deadly effect." Despite their fierce defense, one of the miners was "lassoed and dragged to death," and the other was "killed with a knife."[21]

The experiences of Alvin Coffey, Jackson Estes, Charley Tyler, the Rock Ranch slaves, Amos Kusick, and untold anonymous black emigrants bear witness to the fact that African Americans, regardless of the circumstances that prompted them to head west, like their white counterparts, risked their lives on and off the trails.

Buffalo Soldiers

Security on the trails had been a critical concern since the first wagons rumbled across the plains. But the Civil War transformed the nature and scope of trails security and brought black soldiers out west to help safeguard the overland routes. Before the war, most wagon trains were civilian outfits that provided their own protection without military affiliation, although many companies often organized along a military model, with those in leadership positions adopting martial titles such as captain, major, commander, and general. With the outbreak of war, however, the overland trails increasingly came under military authority as Congress implemented a system of military patrols, escorts, and subposts to quell the Native populations and protect the military, commercial, and communications links between the states east of the Missouri River and the settlements on the Pacific Coast.[22] It was then that African American troops, commonly called Buffalo Soldiers, became important, albeit controversial, guardians of the trails, travelers, and communities on the western frontier.[23]

Between 1866 and 1867, black regiments, comprising two cavalry and four infantry units, were organized by order of Congress. More than 25,000 black men fought in these units. In fact, African American soldiers of the Ninth and Tenth Cavalries made up about 10 percent of the U.S. cavalry in the West.[24] These black units, organized and commanded by white officers, usually followed the direct orders of seasoned black noncommissioned officers in matters pertaining to training and duty details.[25] They crisscrossed the western trails, garrisoning the forts and other military outposts that had been established along these corridors. Historian William Katz has written that they patrolled from the Mississippi "to the Rockies, from the Canadian border to the Rio Grande" and occasionally made forays into Mexico to pursue outlaws and hostile Native groups, frequently accompanied by the legendary frontiersmen Kit Carson and Wild Bill Hickok.[26]

Black infantry units also ranged far and wide, campaigning and burying their dead "the length and breadth of the Great Plains, in Arizona and Colorado."[27] African American soldiers on the western frontier carried out their duties in racially hostile military and (more commonly) civilian environments, but their presence challenged prevailing racial practices and attitudes. Traveling a southern route to California in an eighteen-wagon train with her family from Collin County, Texas, in 1868, nineteen-year-old white overlander Harriet Bunyard was astonished to see "the colored troops [likely the Tenth Cavalry at Fort Concho] standing around among the Yankees, regardless of color or grade."[28]

Black soldiers came from a cross section of African American society. Most were young—in their late teens or early twenties—and joined the military for a variety of reasons. Former slave Reuben Waller enlisted in the Tenth Cavalry in 1867 to fight in the Indian wars that had broken out in Kansas and Colorado. Sgt. Samuel Harris wanted to see the West and believed that military service would be his pathway to steady employment. Some joined to further their educational goals, while others, like Pvt. Charles Creek, "thought there must be a better livin' in this world" and sought in the military relief from the monotony of farm life. Former slaves who had previously served in the army during the Civil War often enlisted in the cavalry or infantry to escape the antiblack violence that swept the South after the war. Others, like Madison Bruin, craved the glamour and adventure a soldier's life seemed to offer. Bruin, a former slave from Kentucky who joined the army as soon as he was old enough, recalled his excitement as a child at seeing Union and Confederate troops march through Fayette County, Kentucky: "What did I think when I seed all dem sojers? I wants to be one, too. I didn't care which side, I jis' wants a gun and a hoss and be a sojer."[29]

Robert Ball Anderson, born a slave in Green County, Kentucky, in 1843, escaped from bondage in 1864, driven by the "idea of owning my own land and being independent." Convinced that military service would get him closer to his goals, Anderson signed up for a three-year stint in the army under the name Robert Ball. He was assigned to the

125th Colored Infantry, Company G, at Louisville, Kentucky. When the war ended approximately six months after his enlistment, Anderson still had nearly two and a half years remaining on his enlistment contract. Staying in the army, he was sent out west. In April 1866, his regiment was transferred from Cairo, Illinois, to Fort Leavenworth, Kansas, where he saw action in several engagements with Native tribes. Anderson and company were transferred to Fort Bliss, Texas, in August 1866. At Fort Bliss, the 125th was assigned to escort a wagon train carrying guns and supplies north to Fort Albuquerque. The route required them to travel across Indian land through a narrow pass known as Hell Gate or Devil's Gap, where wagon trains were most vulnerable to attack. His party moved at night, hoping to get by undetected. As they rolled through the pass, they saw corpses, victims of previous raids, scattered along the trail. Anderson noticed the Indians' campfires on the mountainside above them and recalled being frightened by their yells. He later admitted, "I thot my time had come sure, and my heart almost sank inside of me." However, the company passed through unharmed and finally arrived at Fort Albuquerque. Later, Anderson marched back to Fort Bliss with his unit.[30]

In August 1867, the 125th once again left Fort Bliss, this time headed for Fort Union in New Mexico Territory. Anderson would cross the trails with his unit at least four more times before being mustered out at Jefferson Barracks, Missouri, in late fall of 1867. He received his official discharge papers in Louisville, Kentucky, where he had begun his military career some three years earlier, separating from the military with wages, back pay, and a severance allowance totaling a little more than 250 dollars in cash.[31]

Anderson, like all western soldiers regardless of race, performed grueling, tedious, and often dangerous work. Black units spent countless hours "digging holes in sunbaked soil for telegraph poles," maintaining the telegraph lines that ran between the forts, and securing the wagon roads that connected military posts to the settlements nearby.[32] At Fort Hays, an important military and rail site in northwest Kansas, African American soldiers, most from the Thirty-eighth Infantry and Tenth Cavalry, made up the majority of the enlisted forces there until 1869. Their main responsibility at the fort was to protect stagecoach and rail traffic along the Smoky Hill River to Denver, but they also served as escorts for survey parties, military prisoners, payroll and supply shipments, and performed kitchen, hospital, and sanitation duties.[33]

In the course of their work, all western troops had to contend with diseases ranging from the annoying to the fatal. Deplorable living conditions, poor sanitation, and unhealthy surroundings added to their misery. During the winter of 1866–67, Robert Ball Anderson was one of many soldiers at Fort Bliss who were stricken with a gastrointestinal ailment that temporarily kept them from their work. In 1868, scurvy, another common disorder, broke out at Fort Davis, killing a number of soldiers. It was cholera, however, that periodically wreaked the most havoc on the frontier and on the forts. In 1867, black soldiers caught the worst of it when a deadly cholera epidemic swept through western military posts, striking down civilians and soldiers alike.[34]

African American soldiers on the western frontier made every effort to discharge their duties no matter how unpleasant, but most soldiers who patrolled the western trails, regardless of race, ranked wagon escort duty as their most loathsome responsibility. Gen. George A. Forsyth (sometimes spelled Forsythe), who served in the Southwest after the Civil War, declared that "Escort duty was always distasteful, and of all escort duty, that with a 'Bull' or 'ox train' was the worst." The task required "walking beside a slow plodding wagon train over hundreds of hot and dusty miles." It was a job in which "man was subordinated to the beast, because the distance made, the time of starting, the length of the stops, the situation of camps, everything connected with traveling, depended upon grass, the animal's sole food."[35]

The Twenty-fifth Infantry handled its share of wagon escorts, but this was a chore usually reserved for the cavalry. Occasionally, however, even the cavalry declined an assignment. In 1867, the Tenth Cavalry, led by Capt. Edward Byrnes, refused an escort request from civilian merchant Franz Huning—with disastrous consequences for Huning's overland party. Huning, a German immigrant, held lucrative government contracts and owned stores (with his three brothers) in Las Lunas and Albuquerque, where he lived. A seasoned Santa Fe Trail traveler, Huning set out for Albuquerque from Junction City, Kansas, where he and his party "struck the old Santa Fe trail at Lost Springs" in late spring.³⁶

Huning's train of five mule-drawn wagons carried merchandise for his businesses and also transported his wife's aged mother and younger brother. Unable to coordinate his trip with other wagon parties that were too far ahead or behind him, Huning decided to go it alone until his group reached Fort Zarah or Fort Larned, where they planned to wait "until a regular convoy should be organized as prescribed by the Military." As he wrote in his memoirs many years later, when his group arrived at the Little Arkansas River, they encountered a "full company of cavalry there." He went to see "Capt. Burns [Byrnes] for the purpose of getting an escort," but Byrnes "flatly refused me, using as an excuse his orders that he was there to protect the settlements in that section of the country." The merchant, arguing that there were no nearby settlements, insisted that Byrnes's soldiers could do "a great deal of good, in escorting small trains who happened along that road." Byrnes steadfastly refused, and, Huning recalled, used "harsh and uncivil language and arbitrary acts."³⁷

The merchant's frustration was exacerbated and racialized when, upon leaving the Captain's quarters, he saw two Tenth Cavalry teams approach, "one of the wagons full of negro wenches and the other one with an escort for said wenches besides some horsemen." Huning speculated that the black men and women were "bound for a pleasure excursion to a creek about ten or twelve miles away to hunt plums!!" He angrily concluded that Captain Byrnes had "plenty of men to spare to escort his wenches on a plum hunt, but to protect the lives and property of the travelers he had none." As Huning and company made their way along the trail unescorted, Cheyenne and Kiowa raiders overtook them at a place called Plum Buttes, about fifteen miles from Fort Zarah, between Cow Creek and the Big Bend of the Arkansas River. Several members of the party, including Huning's mother-in-law and his wife's brother, were killed; only Huning and a few teamsters managed to escape. After making burial arrangements for his family and settling his business affairs, Huning continued to Albuquerque by stagecoach.³⁸

The reason the Tenth Cavalry declined to escort the Huning party is unclear, but the incident highlights the multiple and often conflicting realities black western soldiers faced. Their services were needed, but their presence resented. As African Americans, they were subjected to the same attitudes and prejudices that constrained their African American civilian counterparts, yet as members of the military, they were oath-bound to obey orders and carry out government policies, even when those policies meant the destruction of Native peoples. The role of the Buffalo Soldiers has been a subject of continuous debate since their appearance in the West. Historian Jack Forbes has written that black soldiers helped "erect thriving *white* cities, grow fertile *white* fields" on Indian lands.[39] Their legacy is, in the words of historian Quintard Taylor, "enveloped in controversy." But the African American soldiers who served on the western frontier expressed little ambivalence about their role in the settlement of the region and, for the most part, wholeheartedly engaged in the process.[40]

Twenty-one-year old David Turner, a corporal in the Thirty-eighth Infantry, on assignment to secure supplies and guard a surveying party near Fort Wallace, Kansas, participated in a furious battle against a group of Cheyennes led by Chief Roman Nose in June of 1867. Word reached Turner's unit that the nearby Seventh Cavalry, which had been escorting supply wagons, was under attack. Turner and his colleagues left their stations, leaped into a wagon drawn by four mules, and sped off to the conflict, standing up and firing as they advanced into the fray. Elizabeth Custer, wife of Lt. Col. George A. Custer of the Seventh Cavalry, provided a highly embellished eyewitness account of the event, reporting that the black soldier who drove the wagon "lashed the mules with his black snake and roared at them as they ran." When the troopers reached the battle front, the "colored men leaped out and began firing again," eventually repelling their adversaries. Mrs. Custer wrote that "No one had ordered them to leave their picket station, but they were determined that no soldiering should be carried on in which their valor was not proved."[41]

Service on the western frontier appears to have raised few ethical dilemmas for most African American soldiers. Pvt. Henry McCombs of the Tenth Cavalry explained, "We made the West; [we] defeated the hostile tribes of Indians; and made the country safe to live in."[42]

Accidents, Diseases, and Childbirth

The dangers posed to overlanders by the Native populations, bandits, and outlaws paled in comparison to the toll taken by accidents and disease. Although a range of factors make it impossible to determine the exact number of emigrant deaths on the trails, the toll was indisputably substantial.[43] Estimates of trail mortality rates range from a low of 4 percent to 6 percent at the high end. Calculations for the Oregon-California Trail alone show that during the two decades from 1840 to 1860, some 2,540 emigrants perished (out of an estimated total of 20,000).[44] Emigrants reported that the number of graves averaged about ten per mile along the 2,000 miles of trail from the jumping-off places to the end of the Oregon-California Trail. White overlander Cecelia Adams, making her way to Oregon in 1852, reckoned that the 401 graves she counted represented only one-fifth of all the new graves on the trail.[45] Dr. T. McCollum, a California overlander in 1849, a cholera year, declared that the "road from Independence to Fort Laramie is a graveyard."[46] Whatever the actual mortality figures may have been, the reality was that accidents, disease, and complications arising from childbirth were responsible for the majority of overland fatalities.

Accidents

Accidents accounted for a substantial portion of trail deaths, ranking second only to disease in overland mortalities. Journals and diaries are filled with accounts of white emigrants' often fatal encounters with accidents running the gamut from wagon and animal mishaps to gunshot wounds and drownings. But considerably less is known about African American accident victims on the trails. The diary of white overlander John Edwin Banks provides a rare glimpse of a near-fatal wagon accident involving an unnamed, very young enslaved black teamster in 1849. Banks wrote on July 6: "This morning a colored boy some nine or ten years old was driving a team when he was run over by a heavy wagon, one wheeling [sic] passing over his face, the other over his chest. . . . He is expected to recover. . . . I had seen him playing in the morning; such is life." Banks does not say who tended the injured child or what kind of treatment he received, but the next day he reported, "Saw the colored boy; he is better. His master and mistress seem kind."[47]

White Ohio overlander Mary Stuart Bailey wrote that near the Green River in 1852, a "black woman," who was the "slave of an old man who is traveling alone," was the only one hurt when the company's oxen stampeded. The unnamed African American woman was injured when the "wagon she was in was thrown over & pretty badly broken." Bailey made no mention of the extent of the woman's injuries, nor is there any record of treatment she may have received. But, Bailey added, "she was not hurt as bad as she thought."[48]

Alex Campbell, a young white man in a Tennessee wagon train company, suffered a gunshot wound in a hunting accident as he traveled to California with his father, brothers, and "some other young white men" in 1852. His group also included "two young free blacks and a black teenage slave" also named Alex. Hugh Brown Heiskell who traveled in the same party, reported that everyone was "very uneasy about Alex" because his injuries had left him unable to walk. The young man's father was worried that his son would not be able to cross the desert that loomed ahead, but, Heiskell wrote, "We told him that we would haul him, & that he must send Black Alex to wait on him." Alex Campbell resumed his journey under the care of his father's slave who nursed him back to health.[49] He, like many other overlanders, survived his injuries. However, the record is virtually silent about who, if anyone, tended to black overlanders like the child in John Edwin Banks's party, the slave woman in Mary Stuart Bailey's group, and countless others as they recuperated from injuries they sustained while on the trail.

Overland emigrants survived wagon and other mishaps that occurred frequently and were often fatal on the trails, but drowning, the third most common cause of death, claimed the lives of many more overland travelers.[50] Ironically, emigrants who trekked across vast areas of arid terrain were susceptible to perishing in the rivers that stood between them and their western destinations. On at least one occasion, an African American overlander, armed with an impressive set of skills and enormous stamina, saved a member of a wagon train that was attempting to ford the Platte River at the "upper ferry" (present-day Casper, Wyoming). There, travelers were required to ferry their wagons across the river, but most chose to swim their stock. In their eagerness to cross, some of the less seasoned men waded in after their animals, and "many [were] drowned." John Hawkins Clark memorialized the event in his journal after witnessing "one man go down," and another almost drown "had he not been rescued by a negro who, as he heard the cry of 'another man drowning,' jumped upon a big mule, and then, mule and man, [jumped] over a steep bank four feet high into the foaming current." Clark watched as the black man tirelessly fought to save the drowning man and preserve himself. The whirling and shifting current often "prevent[ed] the negro from making a sure grip at the unfortunate man's head. Now he has him, now he has 'lost his grip,' and now he is again reaching for a sure hold, and fortunately, he has it." After a tremendous struggle, the "mule and his rider and the half drowned man land on a sand bar half a mile below." After this extraordinary feat, the black man resumed his business of "strapping his pack upon his mule" and made "busy getting off on his journey." Before he could leave, however, the entire company, in "great appreciation of his heroic conduct," gave the "dusky hero . . . 'three cheers and a tiger,'" after which "with a low bow of his wooly head the negro turned and resumed his journey toward the setting sun."[51]

This Platte River drama represents perhaps hundreds of unrecorded incidents involving African American emigrants who received similar help or who provided it to their fellow overland travelers.

Diseases

The dramatic rescue on the Platte River notwithstanding, the struggle for survival on the trails usually was waged under less spectacular, though no less desperate, circumstances. Despite emigrants' best efforts to combat them, diseases accounted for more trail mortalities than any other factor. The general conditions on the trails, the lack of basic resources, and the limited state of medical knowledge at the time all contributed to the high number of disease-related deaths.[52] Although a range of diseases plagued travelers, cholera was the scourge of the trails. This virulent infection was familiar to most people in the nineteenth century, yet its cause remained a mystery. Transmitted through polluted drinking water and milk, and exacerbated by the lack of proper sanitation, it struck with little warning, spread quickly, and within hours of the first symptoms could be fatal. In some cases, cholera killed entire families and devastated wagon companies.[53]

During the peak emigration years, as thousands gathered in jumping-off places like Independence and St. Joseph, the towns became prime breeding grounds for the disease, which reached epidemic proportions between 1848 and 1855.[54] In 1849, Dr. Leo Twyman of Independence, Jackson County, Missouri, reported, "on the 17th of April occurred the first case of genuine Asiatic cholera in a vigorous and previously healthy negro man." The unnamed black man was the slave of Jabez Smith, the wealthiest man and largest slaveholder—he held more than five hundred slaves—in Jackson County. The following year, Smith lost between one hundred and two hundred slaves to the disease.[55]

Cholera spread rapidly through all the towns along the Missouri River and then spilled out onto the overland trails.[56] Overlanders who, in the words of historian Rudolph Lapp, "plunged west ahead of the crowd" might be able to avoid contact with those already infected, but those who started out late in April or early May "had reduced chances of immunity" because earlier travelers had already contaminated the water sources.[57]

Four of the slaves belonging to Kentuckian C. C. Churchill died "on the plains because of their master's late start." In his autobiography, Alvin Coffey recalled that, when he crossed the Missouri River at Savannah Landing (Caples Landing) the first week in May, a man in his party "had cholera so bad that he was in lots of misery." Despite the care provided by Dr. Bassett and Coffey, "he died at 10 o'clock, and we buried him." Coffey reported, "We got news every day that people were dying by the hundreds in St. Joe and St. Louis. It was alarming. When we hitched up and got ready to move the Dr. said 'Boys, we'll have to drive day and night.'"[58]

In June 1850, Finley McDiarmid, a white Wisconsin emigrant to California, tersely noted in a letter to his wife: "A white woman and a colored one died yesterday of the cholera."[59] In 1851, the California-bound train of twelve-year-old African American emigrant Mary

Elizabeth Snelling had a close call with the disease on the plains.[60] Mary Elizabeth, who traveled from Missouri with her mother and her mother's owner, recollected that "We were told the two trains ahead of us had had trouble with cholera and the wagon boss ordered the route across the plains changed so the people would not come in contact with the infected areas."[61]

Mary Elizabeth's company was spared, but thousands of other overlanders who were stricken by the disease sought relief in a variety of dubious curatives. Treatments for cholera ranged from anal injections and doses of tree bark, to brandy and mustard plasters. The most common therapy consisted of a concoction of calomel, camphor, opium, and cayenne pepper. Laudanum, morphine, and "burnt brandy, burnt rhubarb, and steeped white oak bark" rounded out the emigrants' anticholera arsenal. Preventive measures were equally questionable. Mary Elizabeth Snelling recalled that "everybody in my wagon train had to wear a lump of asafoetida [a foul-smelling herb and common ingredient in many western frontier curatives] in a bag around their necks" as a deterrent against infection.[62] Of course, these cures and precautions had little effect, but when the emigrants boiled their drinking water to rid it of alkaline, saline, insects, and other "wigglies," they inadvertently killed the cholera bacteria which, unknown to them, were the real cause of the disease.[63]

Cholera was not the only life-threatening disease on the trails; a host of other illnesses, including tick-borne diseases, could make the long journey miserable and even deadly. So long after the fact and from the vague descriptions provided in emigrant journals, it is often impossible to determine exactly what caused a particular illness and death. John Lowery Brown, a Cherokee gold seeker, noted in his journal on September 11, 1849, that "Jonas (a black Boy) in my mess very sick." There is no indication of the cause of Jonas's illness or of the type of care he received, but a day later when the company had a "Lay Bye [stopover] on account of Sickness" near the "Peak of the Sier[r]a Nevada Mountains," Brown wrote, "Jonas not expected to live." Finally, on September 14, he reported, "This morning about 10 oclock Jonas died & was buried about 12 oclock."[64]

Whether it was cholera or some other life-threatening disease, African American emigrants, free and enslaved, volunteered or were forced to nurse their trailmates when whites could not or would not do so. Andy, a black member of J. Goldsborough Bruff's gold-mining group, willingly assisted Bruff when he came down with several unspecified illnesses during the trip. On July 30, 1850, Bruff wrote that in his party, "6 of the whites (including myself) are sick, and 2 indians." The next day, he awoke still "sick and weak" somewhere near the Feather River in California, with Andy by his side. A month passed and Bruff, still wracked by chills and fever, reported, "Negro Andy, kindly gave me a skillet and lid, needed much to bake bread in." After regaining his health, Bruff tried to repay Andy's "many little acts of kindness" by presenting him with a "$5 Californian coin."[65]

The stakes were much higher for African Americans who tended emigrants with highly infectious diseases. The performance of their duties, willingly or otherwise, put them at greater risk. Gold rusher and newspaper correspondent George Mifflin Harker explained: "An emigrant who falls sick, unless he has some personal friends, receives scarcely any attention . . . otherwise, he is left to die, gazing on vacancy, after having swallowed a quart or so of medicine, received from the hands of some Negro servant, who hastily throws down the cup and spoon, and rushes away, paying little or no heed to the feeble demands of the sick man."[66]

It is impossible to know how many black overlanders were infected or died because their slave status demanded unquestioning obedience, even at the risk of their own lives. It appears that African Americans, enslaved and free, routinely tended to whites who were stricken by the myriad diseases and other calamities that stalked the trails, but there is little to indicate that their services were reciprocated.

Childbirth

All emigrants were susceptible to accidents and diseases, but childbirth posed a unique hazard for women on the trails. Childbirth is inherently risky, but was more so in the nineteenth century and particularly for those women who went into labor amid the dirt, heat, and physical and emotional stresses of the overland journey. Journal and diaries abound with accounts of women who were left in trailside graves after suffering complications of childbirth.[67] Many likely died from "childbed fever" (puerperal fever), an infection introduced by birth attendants who, ignorant of germ theory, failed to wash their hands after handling livestock, rancid meat, dirty water, "buffalo chips," or other sources of contamination.[68]

In many wagon companies the services of experienced midwives were in great demand. Bridget "Biddy" Mason and Hannah (thought by some to be Mason's younger sister), both the slaves of Mississippi Mormon Robert Smith, were highly skilled midwives who learned and practiced their craft on the Southern plantations where they grew up. Mason and Hannah were undoubtedly called on to put their midwifery skills to use on many occasions in the two Mormon wagon companies in which they traveled in 1848 and 1851. On the trip to Salt Lake with the Mississippi Mormons in 1848, at least three white women and a number of slave women, including Hannah, were pregnant or gave birth en route. Mason and Hannah certainly would have tended to those women and would have taken charge of their deliveries. Mason performed her midwifery duties in addition to herding livestock and caring for her own children (two girls, ages ten and four, and an infant daughter still breastfeeding). After arriving in the Salt Lake basin, Mason and Hannah continued their midwifery practices, serving both black and white women.[69]

Trekking to San Bernardino, California, in 1851 with their master as part of an expedition to establish a Mormon outpost there, Hannah, who had become an "excellent horsewoman," served as the midwife for the San Bernardino colony, where she "responded to calls day or night."[70] After successfully suing for freedom in 1856, Biddy Mason went to work as a "confinement nurse" for Los Angeles physician John Strother Griffin, who paid her "two dollars and fifty cents per day" for her services.[71]

Nearly two decades after Biddy Mason and Hannah traveled west plying their midwifery skills and juggling other responsibilities, Edward Lee Baker Jr. "saw his first light of day from the bed of a freight wagon" on the banks of the North Platte River in present-day Laramie County, Wyoming. Little is known about the circumstances of his birth—if his mother was attended by a midwife, if she survived the birth, or why his parents set out on the trail in the first place—but on December 28, 1865, his mother, an "American colored" woman and his "French father" welcomed him into the world as they trekked the Oregon-California Trail. Baker remained a westerner all his life, spending more than twenty years in the military, where he become a sergeant major in the Tenth Cavalry, served at various western posts, and received the Congressional Medal of Honor for his valor in the Spanish-American War. Edward Lee Baker Jr. passed away on August 26, 1913, and was buried in the Angelus-Rosedale Cemetery in Los Angeles, California.[72]

Acts of Kindness

Even though the long, weary months of overland travel were filled with accidents, diseases, and dangers that tested everyone's endurance and patience, charity and compassion were essential elements of survival in the nomadic communities of the trails. Humane impulses sometimes found expression in reciprocal acts of selflessness and kindness that transcended the racial antipathies of the day. African Americans were occasionally the sources and beneficiaries of benevolent deeds on the trails and at the end of the journey. George W. Bush's generosity financed the trip for at least two families in his wagon train, replenished depleted supplies, came to the aid of several orphans in his company, and supported newcomers who were unprepared for the high prices and harsh winters in the Oregon Country. Bush's traveling companions attempted to repay his kindheartedness by rallying to his aid when the Donation Land Claim Act threatened his claim to the Puget Sound land where he had settled.[73]

George W. Bush was not the only African American to give help to his trailmates, however. Rose Jackson, unlike Bush, went to Oregon as a slave in 1849, yet her generosity saved the day for her master's family. Rose, the slave of Dr. William Allen of Missouri, traveled with her owner and his family to present-day Clackamas County, Oregon. Dr. Allen, wary of Oregon's black exclusion laws, had planned to leave Rose in Missouri, but she somehow convinced him to take her along.

She made the trip in the family's wagon, concealed in a wooden box drilled with air holes. She endured sweltering heat, terrifying river crossings, and steep mountain descents crammed into the box, coming out only at night for fresh air and exercise. Dr. Allen manumitted Rose upon arriving in Oregon, but he died shortly after that, leaving his wife and children nearly destitute. Taking pity on their plight, Rose stayed on with her former owner's family to help them through the first winter. Mrs. Allen went to work as a seamstress, earning about two dollars a day; Rose, working as a laundress, brought home nearly twelve dollars daily, which she shared with the Allen family. Her wages saved the family from economic catastrophe. After the first winter, Mrs. Allen remarried, and Rose struck out on her own, eventually wedding another African American overlander, John Jackson, who worked as a groomer of stagecoach horses in Canemah, Oregon. The couple later moved to Waldo Hills on the outskirts of Salem where they raised two children, Rose and Charles.[74]

The experiences of George W. Bush and Rose Jackson suggest that charity and compassion could continue beyond the journey, but the trail is where these qualities were tested and strained to the limit. Nevertheless, some overlanders, irrespective of race and for a variety of reasons, engaged in acts of good will on the trails that occasionally engendered camaraderie and often made the difference between life and death. Overland diarist Joseph Alonzo Stuart's merciful encounter with an overburdened slave woman trudging through the Black Rock Desert in 1849 is only one of perhaps thousands of such compassionate interactions that took place among blacks, whites, and others on the overland routes.[75]

A runaway slave from Missouri was the beneficiary of some trailside charity when, in 1846, a party of Sioux discovered him "lying exhausted on the ground" and brought him into Francis Parkman's camp near a Sioux village on the plains. With the help of some of the Native people, Parkman and his traveling companions helped revive the black man, who had been wandering the prairie "without shoes, moccasins, or any other clothing than an old jacket and pantaloons." The unnamed black man had signed on with a group of trappers, but became separated from his party while on a hunt for stray horses. For thirty-three days, he had subsisted on crickets, lizards, wild onions, and dove eggs, and was now near death. One of Parkman's trailmates prepared a "bowl of gruel" for him, but he "suffered it to remain untasted before him." Once his appetite returned, however, the man became ravenous, wolfing down the gruel and demanding meat, which the whites were reluctant to give him. They advised him that "his life was in danger if he ate so immoderately at first." He replied that he "knew he was a fool to do so, but he must have meat." When the whites were not watching, several Indian women covertly brought him "dried meat and *pommes blanches*" and "place[d] them on the ground by his side." His hunger still unsatisfied, the man, under cover of night, "crawled over to the Indian village" nearby, where he "fed to his heart's content." When he had regained "tolerable health" the next day, one of the trappers took him by horseback to a fort and left him. Before leaving his benefactors, the black man, who had been on the brink of death, "expressed his firm conviction that nothing could ever kill him."[76]

African Americans also rode to the rescue of emigrants who found themselves in trouble on the trails. John E. Durivage, the correspondent for the *New Orleans Picayune*, and his slave Isaac were on their way to California on the Gila Trail in 1849, when, at some point in the journey, Durivage, dehydrated by the blistering heat, feared he was dying. His "black servant Isaac," saved the entire company by riding ahead fifteen miles to the Gila River and racing back "on horseback, rushing toward us at a headlong gallop," bringing water, "the nectar of the gods," for everyone. Durivage, who usually had little affection for African Americans, wrote that Isaac, in that moment, "Spite his black hide . . . looked like an angel." Another group of overlanders found themselves in a similar situation on the arid trek along the southern route from Salt Lake City. With water supplies gone, these desperate travelers had resorted to slashing their horses' throats to drink the blood. William Lorton reported that one member of the party, identified only as General Blodgett, had collapsed and "then lay down in the valley waiting for his Negro servant to bring him water."[77]

Sometimes relief efforts fell short despite the selflessness of emigrants, white or black, enslaved or free. Bayard Taylor, a well-known Pennsylvania-born poet and gold rush correspondent for the *New York*

Tribune, wrote about a white gold seeker on the Sonora route in 1849 who had taken ill on the trip. The man habitually "rode behind his party," but usually caught up with them at their encampment within an hour or two. However, once, when the ailing overlander still had not arrived after four days, "a negro, traveling alone and on foot" came into camp with news that "many miles behind" a man "lying beside the road" had "begged a little water from him" and urged him to "hurry on and bring assistance." The next day, a "company of Mexicans" approached the campsite and "brought word that the man was dying." When his "old companions hesitated to go to his relief," Taylor wrote, "the humane negro retraced his steps forty miles," and found him "just as the sufferer breathed his last." The anonymous African American "lifted him in his arms," and "in the vain effort to speak, the man expired." His mule, "tied to a cactus by his side," had already died of hunger. It is impossible to know who this black man was, where he was bound, or whether he was a free man or slave. However, the abolitionist poet John Greenleaf Whittier, who learned of this incident while reviewing Taylor's book, remarked, "A picture commemorating such a scene, and the heroic humanity of the Negro, would better adorn a panel of the Capitol, than any battle piece that was ever painted."[78]

Edward Louis, a "colored man from Boston," met with better results in his attempt to rescue emigrants who had become stranded in the desert in 1850. The *Sacramento Transcript* reported that Louis "generously volunteered his services to go out to the valley with Capt. [William] Waldo" to bring relief supplies to emigrants who were suffering in the Humboldt Sink region. Captain Waldo announced that, although "several persons had volunteered their services," only Louis and a few others had followed through on their promise to accompany him. When the rescue party reached the suffering travelers, Louis, an "expert with horses," rode some "400 miles by express" to Sacramento to deliver a letter pleading for more help. He later returned with reinforcements and helped guide the overlanders to safety. His actions were widely reported in eastern newspapers, but southern newspapers failed to mention the African American man and his deeds.[79]

Crises most often served as the catalysts for selflessness on the trails, but friendship also inspired the kindnesses that occasionally flowed between whites and blacks. This was the case with Emanuel, the slave belonging to Middleton Story of Cass County, Missouri, who was part of William J. Pleasants's California-bound company in 1849. As the group rolled along the Platte River valley about six hundred miles into the journey, William Hensley, another member of the party, suddenly died from cholera. Discouraged by this turn of events, Middleton Story decided to go back to Cass County, taking Emanuel with him. Pleasants recalled that the two men "refused to reconsider their determination to return home: so bidding them good-by, we pushed on, leaving their lone wagon standing still surrounded by a few faithful friends, yet pleading with them to remain." Finally the black man, "laying the whip in Story's hand, said, 'Mid, do as you please, but no matter what your decision may be, remember I am with you. If you return, I will go back also; stay, and you will find me by your side.'" Emanuel's unwavering support seems to have caused Story to change his mind and rejoin the group. Pleasants wrote that the "two comrades were once more headed for California, and from that time on until we reached our journey's end swerved neither to the right nor left, but kept their eyes towards the setting sun, and followed where it led until they saw it sink to rest in the mighty waters of the Pacific Ocean."[80]

Occasionally, simple human decency won out over prejudice and suspicion when blacks and whites encountered each other on the trails. African American overlander Hannah Estes, the mother of Sylvia Estes Stark, learned of such an incident from a newly arrived white emigrant woman shortly after the Estes family had settled in California. Sylvia Estes Stark recalled that an unnamed white woman told Hannah that she had "joined a caravan owned by a man she knew and trusted," so she could go to her husband, who was in California. However, when the woman rebuffed the man's sexual advances, he expelled her and her two children from the train, leaving them far from their destination. As night approached, the frantic woman, "alone on the great open space with two helpless babes," saw two figures in the distance advancing toward her. As they drew closer, "she saw that they were two colored men with a donkey, and all of their belongings packed on its back."

The woman "determined to beg for help," but, Stark recounted, she hesitated to ask the black men for assistance because "in the state where she came from, they were not considered reliable." The men, however, were "shocked to see her plight." The woman overheard them say to each other, "What can we do. We haven't enough grub for ourselves, but we can't leave her here." Finally, they asked if she could walk, and told her, "we'll put the children on the donkey." The two men and their accidental traveling companions continued along the trail, and "by stinting themselves they managed to feed the children until they came to a settlement of white people." They then told the woman, "Now you are with your own people, they can look after you." With that, her anonymous black benefactors left her and resumed their journey west.[81]

How often such interracial benevolent exchanges occurred on the overland trails will probably never be known, but at least one group of emigrants, brought together on the trail by chance, temporarily suspended their racially prescribed roles just long enough for compassion to respond to need.

African American overlanders' interaction with their white trailmates and the Native peoples they encountered adds complexity and nuance to the story of western emigration. Even though blacks and whites often held the same negative attitudes about Indians, occasionally African Americans received deferential treatment from Native peoples, whose curiosity about African Americans' color at times benefited black emigrants and their white trailmates. But on the trails or at journey's end, skin color did not automatically exempt African Americans from violence or death. For the most part, Indians regarded blacks and whites as unwelcome interlopers to be driven out of their lands.

However, emigrants were often aided by Native people who posed less a threat to them than did the outlaws, "white Indians," and assorted criminals who plagued the overland routes. Even so, most emigrants, regardless of race, remained wary of, if not hostile to Native people. Emigrant clashes with the Natives and other groups underscored the necessity for security on the trails and bound blacks and whites together in the pursuit of this goal. The outbreak of the Civil War elevated the issue of trail security, as the federal government militarized overland routes and subsequently dispatched African American soldiers west to safeguard them. Black western troops, many only recently freed from slavery and emigrants themselves, were sworn to protect trails, travelers, and settlements, even when carrying out their orders meant the destruction of Native peoples.

Dangers stalked the trails in many forms. Accidents and diseases posed the greatest hazards to overlanders of all races. Unfortunately, trail mortality rates for African Americans defy calculation because of black "invisibility" in the general narrative and official records. Still, it is likely that the subordinate status of blacks may have contributed to making their mortality rates equal to or greater than those of white emigrants.

The types and frequency of the interracial, reciprocal acts of selflessness and kindness that took place on the trails are also difficult to assess. Written and oral sources sometimes offer glimpses into the circumstances surrounding those humane encounters and show that African Americans, enslaved and free, were both sponsors and beneficiaries of such compassionate acts. They also suggest that occasionally, in certain situations, racial antipathies could be transcended, at least momentarily, during the trek west.

Chapter 7
Sweet Freedom's Plains

MANY AFRICAN AMERICANS traveled the routes west and settled in western communities, but their numbers, names, and reasons for making the trip were typically disregarded. Although they sometimes held hopes similar to their white counterparts, black emigrants, known and anonymous, harbored dreams their white trailmates could not share—dreams forged in the context of slavery and antebellum race relations.

From the mid-nineteenth century onward, African Americans were a growing presence in the West.[1] Their rising numbers suggest that slavery, violence, racial discrimination, and other intolerable conditions were likely pushing and pulling them into the West, but just how many African Americans arrived at their new western homes via the overland routes is unknown. Some scholars have calculated that the number of blacks who traveled overland ranged between 7,500 and 15,000. Historian John W. Ravage has estimated that African Americans constituted roughly 1.5 to 3 percent of all nineteenth-century overland emigrants, the majority of whom pushed west via the Platte River route.[2]

African Americans were members of the emigrant companies that trudged along the southern routes as well, but their actual numbers are difficult to determine. They certainly were among the estimated 27,000 argonauts that trails scholar Patricia Etter has calculated traveled a southern route to California in 1849, with the majority arriving in New Mexico via the Fort Smith–Santa Fe Trail. African Americans also made up some of the southern-route travelers who traversed Texas or took to the sea, heading for points along the Rio Grande, then onto the Southern Trail near El Paso or Guadalupe Pass in New Mexico. Blacks also accounted for a portion of the 7,000 emigrants who crossed Mexico to wait for ships at Mazatlán or San Blas, and undoubtedly they composed a portion of the approximately 900 others who trekked the Old Spanish

Trail from Salt Lake, but here too, it is impossible to get an accurate tally of their numbers.[3]

An Invisible Presence

Whatever their numbers and whichever routes they took, African American overlanders were virtually invisible to their white counterparts and official record keepers. Written and oral sources can provide glimpses of these black travelers by confirming their presence and sometimes revealing who they were, why they came, and what they hoped to achieve. For the most part, however, they went unacknowledged by white chroniclers of the overland journey. Emigrant diarists who mentioned them at all usually noted little else than their race, gender, and age; rarely did they include information like surname or place of origin.

Tennessee gold seeker Hugh Brown Heiskell mentioned the slaves Alex and Wash in his party, noting Wash's age and alluding to the presence of "two free Negro boys" and the "Captain's servant" also in the party.[4] California argonaut J. Goldsborough Bruff referred to his devoted black traveling companion only as "Andy," "Negro Andy," and "Andy the darkee." On numerous occasions, his encounters with black people just noted race: "under the shade of some large willows, was a wagon & tent,—and a colored man and woman;" and "three men with packed oxen and a negro;" and a "Danish Captain, 4 Germans, and a negro."[5] Cherokee miner and diarist John Lowery Brown, who departed Stillwater, Oklahoma, in a ten-wagon party of Cherokee gold seekers in 1850, described black overlanders in much the same way: "the Company was joined on a Thursday by five wagons and 21 men which [said] . . . number grew to 105 men 15 Negroes and 12 females all under the command of Clem McNair."[6]

Similarly, a bulletin posted at Fort Smith, Arkansas (from which hundreds of California-bound emigrants departed), announced, "Colonel Bonner's party for California have arrived consisting of 7 whites and 6 blacks." Another white emigrant reported, "Among the wagons that passed us was one train from Georgia, with a carriage or hack containing a man and his wife. That train also had several slaves with them." Yet another merely reported that "big mule teams from Tennessee used black drivers on the way to California." Overland emigrant Anna Maria Goodell's observation in 1854 was also typical: "There is a darkey in the company."[7]

African American emigrants whose names were actually recorded sometimes traveled in companies carrying others who were not identified. Nathaniel Ford's Missouri wagon train, part of a larger Oregon-bound expedition in 1844 that included George W. Bush and family, also transported Ford's slaves Robin, Polly, and Mary Jane Holmes and another black man identified only as "Scott." There may have been other African Americans as well. When Mississippi Mormon slave Bridgett "Biddy" Mason traveled to the Salt Lake basin with her owner, Robert Smith, in 1848, ten slaves made up her immediate party, including her three children, a woman identified only as Hannah, and at least five more unnamed slaves. The larger Mississippi caravan in which Mason's party traveled included fifty-six whites and thirty-four other slaves, including Betsy Flewellen and her daughter Kate, the slaves of John Brown's wife, Elizabeth Crosby Brown.[8]

Although it is impossible to arrive at an exact count of black overlanders, sources suggest that, for each black emigrant noted by name or race in westbound wagon train and pack companies, there were perhaps multiple others who went unacknowledged. Their names, aspirations, and reasons for taking to the trails are lost, but those anonymous black travelers, like those whose names have been recorded, began their journey with great expectations as well.

Who They Were and Why They Went West

African Americans headed west cloaked in invisibility by law and custom, yet most black emigrants, enslaved and free, anticipated that all things might be possible once the trail was struck. The opportunity to escape bondage, to be free of racial persecution, and to prosper economically drove them across the plains, deserts, and mountains to the West. Whether known or anonymous, enslaved or free, the lyrics of a popular abolitionist hymn summed up their purposes: "Behind I leave the whips and chains/Before me spreads sweet Freedom's plains."[9]

Slaves

The trip west became a journey to independence, dignity, and personhood for African Americans.[10] For those who went as slaves, their first steps on the trail seemed to make these goals more attainable. A slave identified only as "Lee, Mr. Thompson's Negro Boy," was emboldened enough to openly declare his intentions shortly after setting off with his master to California on the "St. Joe Road" in 1850. William Dulany, a Missourian who traveled in the same company, wrote to his daughter Susan Dulany that Lee "was heard to say that he would not work for white men much longer." Dulany, commenting on the slave's new attitude, explained that Lee "got too Big for his Britches as soon as he got out of the state." Alarmed by Lee's audacity, Dulany informed his daughter, "I sold him for $700 in gold making our pile most 2000$ after all our expense is paid. A right nice pile to comense with."[11]

Most enslaved overlanders probably were not as outspoken as Lee, but they too anticipated big changes in their lives as well. In the gold rush era, many began the journey sustained by their owners' promises of freedom in exchange for their labor in the goldfields. An unidentified Louisiana slave woman on the road to California with her owner in 1849 confided her hopes to white emigrant Joseph Warren Wood, telling him that although she was not free, she "soon would be if she served her master well on the road to California & 2 or 3 years after she got there." The woman willingly trudged on, envisioning a day when "I shall return & claim my children that they may be free too."[12]

Ohio gold seeker John Edwin Banks noted his encounter with a California-bound slave who nurtured the same dream: "I saw a colored man going to the land of gold prompted by the hope of redeeming his wife and seven children. Success to him. His name is James Taylor." After arriving in the gold fields, Banks also reported, "I have seen a number of slaves here in California, a large majority of whom are struggling for freedom. One of Texas who expects to free himself, wife, and three children; New York or Massachusetts he intends [as] his future home."[13]

Nancy and Peter Gooch, like countless slaves who trekked west anonymously, expected the trip would be transformative for them and for the son they were forced to leave behind in Missouri. The Gooches were slaves when they traveled overland from St. Charles County to California with their owner, William D. Gooch, in 1849. Nancy (Ross) Gooch was probably born free in Maryland around 1811 and may have been enslaved in Missouri. Peter's date of birth is not known, but he may have been a slave in Georgia and brought to Missouri by Gooch. Peter and Nancy probably met on their owner's Missouri plantation, where Nancy gave birth to their first child, Andrew, on January 9, 1846. Three years later, their master, enticed by the gold rush, left for California in a covered wagon with Peter and Nancy in tow. Since three-year-old Andrew was the property of the white Gooches who remained in Missouri and of no use to William D. Gooch in California, Nancy and Peter were forced to leave without him. As soon as they arrived in California, the anguished couple vowed to gain their freedom and then rescue their child. More than twenty years would pass before they could accomplish their ultimate goal.[14]

The Gooches were freed when California joined the union in 1850 and immediately began establishing an independent life for themselves. Working tirelessly to earn the price of their son's liberty, Nancy took in laundry and worked as a cook and domestic servant for miners in the gold regions of Garden Valley and Kelsey, and Peter did construction work, mining, and odd jobs in Garden Valley and Kelsey as well. When Peter and Nancy were freed, they were officially married in a Methodist Episcopal ceremony at the El Dorado County home of their friend Jacob Johnson on January 8, 1857. Josiah Eddy officiated at the ceremony and Louis Booker and Jacob Johnson served as witnesses. The friendship between the Gooches and Johnson and his wife, Sarah, may have been forged by the shared agony of being separated from family members whom they had left still in bondage. Johnson, who had been a slave in St. Louis County, Missouri, like Peter, toiled in the goldfields and other jobs to buy his family's freedom. Delilah Beasley wrote that when Johnson was finally able to send a "large sum of money" back to Missouri to rescue his loved ones, he "never received any word from either his money or family." Despite this tragedy, he continued to build a life in California. A little over a year after Peter and Nancy's wedding, Peter purchased eighty acres of farmland from Jacob and Sarah

Johnson for $1,000 on March 13, 1858. The Gooch holdings eventually grew to 320 acres, including the gold discovery site at Sutter's Mill.[15]

Nancy and Peter Gooch's lives were dramatically changed by their trek west, but their inability to purchase Andrew's freedom remained their biggest disappointment. Peter passed away in 1861, years before his efforts to be reunited with his son bore fruit. In 1868, Nancy finally amassed the seven hundred dollars needed to retrieve their child, but by that time, slavery had been abolished and Andrew was now a grown man with a family of his own. Nancy used her hard-earned money to bring Andrew (who had adopted the surname Monroe), his wife, Sarah Ellen, and their sons Pearly (often spelled Pearley) and Grant to Coloma in 1870. Nancy Gooch, now reunited with her family, continued to live in Coloma as a successful businesswoman and the matriarch of a family that spanned several generations. Some five decades after crossing the plains as a slave, Nancy Gooch died a free and prosperous woman on September 17, 1901. She was interred in the Coloma Pioneer Cemetery beside her husband, Peter.[16]

The opportunity to break the chains of bondage sustained unknown numbers of enslaved men and women as they trekked west. Some, like Howard Estes, a perseverant Missouri slave, had in-demand skills that could be used as their path to freedom, even though the path might take many unexpected twists and turns. Howard Estes, an expert livestock handler, persuaded his owner, Tom Estes to allow him to take charge of driving a herd of cattle from Missouri to the booming California goldfields in 1849. Tom Estes agreed and in the bargain offered Howard his freedom papers in exchange for $1,000. In the spring of 1849, Howard left his wife, Hannah, and their three children, Sylvia, Jackson, and Agnes, who were slaves on a different Missouri plantation, and set out, with his owner's two inexperienced sons, driving a large herd of cattle to California.[17]

Once in California, Howard went to work in the goldfields, eventually earning the price of his freedom papers. He sent his master the $1,000 as promised, but Tom Estes reneged on the deal after receiving the money, forcing Howard to remain in California to eke out another $1,000 as a miner. Howard amassed the additional money but, now distrustful of his master's promises, sent it directly to his wife's owner,

Charles Leopold. Howard's daughter, Sylvia, recounted in an interview done many years later that, when Tom Estes heard about this, "he claimed that money too, on the grounds that Howard was his slave." However, Charles Leopold, who owned Howard's wife and children, contended that "Howard was in a free state, and therefore a free man." The two slave owners became embroiled in a legal battle that culminated in Tom Estes being awarded $800, and being ordered to turn over the freedom papers to Howard. Officially free, Howard Estes remained in California, now working to earn the purchase price of his wife and children.[18]

Sylvia Estes Stark recalled that "the time seemed long while waiting for [his] return." Her older sister Agnes never lost faith in Howard's return and dreamed of his homecoming so vividly that she described exactly what he would be wearing when he came back to claim them. Agnes died from a mysterious fever before Howard could return, plunging her mother, Hannah, into deep mourning. Sylvia recalled seeing Hannah steal away "alone to the seclusion of an old shed" where she would fall "on her knees praying for the safe return of Howard, and that her children would be blessed and free."[19]

In 1851, when Howard Estes had earned enough money to rescue his family, he made plans to return home via Panama, booking passage on the *Grace Darling*, a steamer that ran between San Francisco and the port of Colombo. However, a bout of malaria caused him to miss his departure date. Sylvia later recalled that her father's illness turned out to be a stroke of luck because the "boat was rammed amidship" and all on board, except for the cook, were lost. A year after Agnes's death, Howard returned to his family, and Sylvia remembered him "coming through the pasture, wearing a new grey suit, a new white panama and tie of many colors," carrying "a carpet bag and had a soldier's coat thrown over his arm," just as Agnes's dream had foretold. He had "returned a free man, happy that he had been spared to return home, though he felt very sad for the loss of . . . Agnes." He paid Charles Leopold $1,000 each for Hannah and their son Jackson; Sylvia's freedom cost $900.[20]

Once they were free and back together again, the Estes family left Missouri, heading out to California. Hannah's former owner, Charles

Leopold, anxious to take a herd of six hundred cattle to the lucrative California market, now hired Howard and Jackson as herders and employed Hannah to cook for the entire company which Sylvia described as "a large caravan." On April 1, 1851, Howard, Hannah, Sylvia, and Jackson Estes clattered out of Missouri in a refurbished covered wagon given to them by Charles Leopold. Sylvia recalled that they "made a jolly start by making April fool jokes, etc." As they rolled through Missouri, Hannah "gathered wild greens . . . and they had one last good feed of good old Missouri wild greens." Like other emigrant children, Sylvia and her brother amused themselves by "playing tag" with each other, running between the wagons, and admiring the abundant buffalo herds and the wildflowers that flourished on the prairie.[21]

Sylvia also remembered the swarms of mosquitoes that occasionally tormented their company and the locusts that "darkened the sky and fell about the wagons, creeping inside the canvas, getting into the cooking utensils, and other paraphernalia." They considered these things routine annoyances, but when the party was camped at "Humbolt Creek" [Humboldt River], Hannah and Sylvia were frightened by a story told by two white women they encountered there. The women, "who as children had witnessed the slaying of their parents, a sister and a brother" by Indians, had been taken captive, but "in time they were rescued." They now were married and "still living in the same isolated district where stalked the ghost in memory of that dark tragedy." Their tale caused Hannah and Sylvia some "apprehension for the future on the long trail that lay ahead," but, Sylvia noted, her family was determined to push ahead despite "the dangers attending the journey."[22]

The group arrived in Salt Lake City "sometime during the harvest," and Sylvia reported that all were treated with "the greatest hospitality by the Latter Day Saints." She claimed that Brigham Young visited them and invited them to stay for the winter and pasture their cattle in "a place called Mountain Meadows." However, Howard Estes declined the invitation, "having passed through that country before and hearing strange tales about Indians robbing and killing the immigrants in that locality, [but] suspected that the real source of the crimes had never been divulged." Howard decided to leave the Salt Lake City area with his family, preferring to "continue the journey alone in his own wagon rather than take the risk, even if the rest of the caravan wanted to stay."[23]

It is not known if any other company members accepted the invitation to stay over, but according to Sylvia, the Estes family pushed on to the Golden State. After a "long and tiresome journey across the desert they arrived in California," having spent "exactly six months less three days on the journey." The wagon company disbanded, and the Estes family moved to Placerville, where they "found an empty miner's cabin which [made] a comfortable home."[24]

Perseverance also played an important role in Daniel Rodgers's bid for freedom as he traveled overland. His persistence epitomized the spirit of most overland slaves and gives insight into their expectations of the journey. Like Howard Estes, Daniel Rodgers's ability and tenacity overcame deception and theft. Rodgers, who grew up a slave on plantations in North Carolina and Tennessee, expected that his initial attempt to go west would be the start of his life as a free man, but he was mistaken.[25] Rodgers was the slave of Redmond Rodgers, a planter who took his slaves from Tennessee to a cotton farm in Johnson Valley, Arkansas. Before moving to Arkansas, Daniel married Artimisa Penwright, a "free mulatto woman," and the couple had ten children: John, Martin, Sam, James, Carrol, Redmond, Jessie, Julia-Ann, Martha and Sallie.[26]

The family remained together on the Arkansas plantation for nearly a decade, until gold fever gripped Redmond Rodgers, who quickly set out for California with his slave Daniel, traveling overland from Little Rock in 1849. The slaveholder expected to strike it rich in the California goldfields, and Daniel, driven by his master's promise of emancipation in exchange for his labor and a fee of $1,100, was just as eager to get there. After arriving in California, the two men took a brief tour, stopping in Pajaro Valley in present-day Santa Cruz County, where they worked on the Mexican land-grant ranch owned by Don José Amesti (*Rancho Los Corralitos*). Daniel and Redmond moved again to nearby Soquel Valley, where they built a small cabin and worked in the surrounding mountains logging redwood timber to sell to the government.[27]

Daniel left Santa Cruz County with his owner in 1850, relocating to Sonora, where they worked a nearby mining claim. Daniel mined for gold for his master by day; after sundown, he spent his "spare time" washing and ironing for the other miners to earn enough to pay for his freedom.[28] Daniel paid his master in full in 1852, after toiling for two long years. Redmond presented the black man with the promised papers, but Daniel, who could not read or write, had no way to verify the documents and relied on his former owner's word. Daniel and Redmond returned to Arkansas in 1854, and Daniel prepared to depart for California with his family. He built an ox wagon, bought a team of oxen, and outfitted himself with supplies for the journey. His enthusiasm persuaded John Derrick and Robert Johnson, two former slaves from neighboring plantations who also had purchased their freedom, to move west as well. Derrick and Johnson made the move first, setting out in 1858. They settled in Pajaro Valley and sent word back to Daniel that they were delighted with their new home.[29]

Shortly after receiving the encouraging report from his two friends, Daniel, Artimisa, and the children packed up and began the long trip to California. Just as they reached the county line, slave patrollers stopped them and demanded their papers. Artimisa's documents stated that "Artimisa Penwright was the daughter of her mistress by a negro man, and neither she nor any of her children were to ever be slaves."[30] Daniel, however, was shocked to learn that Redmond Rodgers had taken his hard-earned money and had given him, not manumission papers, but a note authorizing any white person who read it to "sell the slave, Dan Rodgers" at auction to the highest bidder and transmit the proceeds of his sale to Redmond Rodgers.[31]

Finding himself in bondage and on the auction block once again, Daniel attempted to repurchase his liberty. This time he received help from an unexpected source. Fifteen prominent slaveholders from nearby Dardanelle, Yell County, Arkansas, outraged by the unscrupulous treatment Daniel had received at the hands of his owner, came together to buy him at auction and presented him with legal manumission documents. To ensure his unhampered passage, the group also furnished him with a certificate attesting to his personal character and free status. The slaveholders declared in the document that they, "having been personally acquainted with the bearer, Daniel Rodgers, a free man of color for many years past and up to the present time, take pleasure in certifying to his character for honesty, industry and integrity; also as a temperate and peaceful man; and one worthy of trust and confidence of all philanthropic and good men wherever he may go."[32]

With this, Daniel and his family got ready once again to hit the trail west. The Rodgers family traveled alone but encountered Natives with whom they traded some of their supplies in exchange for lodging and information about the best routes to take. Historian Sue Bailey Thurman has written that the Indians they met seemed "particularly concerned for the welfare of a colored man, making his way alone with wife and small children across the plains." Be that as it may, in the spring of 1860, more than a decade since his first trip to California, and after a year-long journey, Daniel Rodgers, his wife, and children, all rolled into the Pajaro Valley in an ox-drawn wagon. They finally ended the trip in the town of Watsonville, Santa Cruz County, where their old friends John Derrick and Robert Johnson greeted them. Their welcoming party also included a crowd of white abolitionist well-wishers, who had learned of Daniel's ordeal. Daniel, in turn, brought the assembled crowd the news that other black Arkansans would be following him to Santa Cruz County.[33]

The Rodgers family settled on eighty acres near Watsonville and developed their homestead into a prosperous farm. Not content to rest on his economic success, Daniel Rodgers involved himself in community affairs, quickly rising to leadership of the small black community. The Rodgers family, which increased considerably when John Derrick and Robert Johnson married two of Daniel and Artimisa's daughters, was in the forefront of the fight for black enfranchisement. Daniel worked tirelessly for that cause, circulating petitions, raising funds, and organizing meetings and rallies to challenge California's discriminatory laws.[34]

Education, however, became his main focus. He and his sons-in-law engaged in a long battle with the school board to allow black children to attend the local school, which, in 1860, barred African

American students. Yielding a bit to the pressure, the board established a separate school for black children and hired a teacher for them. This was the beginning of the first "public schools" for the education of black children in the state. The Rodgers, Derrick, and Johnson children attended the school and were taught by a Miss Knowlton, described by Delilah Beasley as a "young white girl of northern parentage" who was an abolitionist and a strong influence on her black students. Black children finally were permitted to attend local schools with white students in 1878. Rodgers dedicated himself to the task of getting the best education for his grandchildren as well; he helped three grandsons graduate from the University of California and saw most of his offspring go on to have productive careers in public service, journalism, and the military.[35]

Shortly before his death in 1903, when asked to recall his years of enslavement and his fight to establish himself as a free man in the West, Daniel admitted, "Sometimes it seems that I can look back upon forever." Being more accustomed to self-reliance than nostalgia, however, he added that he would not have anyone "coddling and making a lot of fuss over [me]."[36] Until the day he died at the age of 103, he had no need for glasses and refused to use a cane. In the winter of 1903, while visiting a daughter in Oakland, he was struck by a trolley car and succumbed to his injuries on January 21, 1903.[37] Daniel Rodgers died scarcely realizing that he was, in the words of historian Sue Bailey Thurman, "a hero whose daring journey across the continent to California . . . was prophetic not only of the great trek of his people to the West," but was a true "indication of the high hopes and creative adventures which characterize their spirit."[38]

Kentucky-born slave Alvin Aaron Coffey is perhaps the best-known black overlander whose journey to the West took many unexpected turns. Coffey's determination to become a free man eventually triumphed over his master's deception and greed, but not before he had made three round-trips overland to California. His first occurred in 1849 and the next two in 1854 and 1857. Coffey, described as a "bright mulatto . . . heavyset [with] grey eyes," and "a full head of hair, about five feet nine inches in height," traveled to the gold diggings in Shasta County, California. He did so "in hopes of making enough money to purchase his own freedom," and that of his children and pregnant wife, whom he referred to as "my pretty Mahala."[39]

When he started out on the trail the first time, he was the slave of Dr. William Bassett of St. Joseph, Missouri. Coffey's reason for trekking west was to save his family, but Bassett had other plans. When they arrived in California, Coffey worked as a miner for Bassett and also did laundry for the other miners, earning about $700 for this "side work."[40] In addition, he plied his skills as a cobbler, just as he had done for the emigrants in his wagon company. His great-great-granddaughter Jeannette Molson has written that his customers at the diggings paid him, "$18 for half-soling a pair of boots and the miners even furnished the leather." Coffey carefully separated his earnings from the money he made for his owner, keeping "the gold he made for Dr. Bassett in one sack and the gold he received for his after-hours work in another sack," but all his precautions were in vain. The first "money he was able to save, which was somewhere in the neighborhood of around $600 to $616, his master swept into his own pile and kept," and then decided to return home with the money and his slave.[41]

Coffey explained in his autobiography that Bassett robbed him after he had earned $5,500 in "gold dust" for him and had saved "$616 of my own money in gold dust." As master and slave traveled back home in 1851 "by the way of New Orleans," Bassett decided to "go to the mint and have our gold coined." But, as Coffey relates in his autobiography, Bassett kept Coffey's money, and "when we got up to Missouri, he sold me for $1,000." Coffey calculated that "in this way" his owner had raked in "$6,876 clear profit."[42] Molson noted that the cheated slave "thought about running away from Dr. Bassett because he knew that there were people who would protect him," but he "just acted peaceably and helped him about getting ready to go away."[43] She also stated that "Alvin was afraid that if they went back to Missouri, via New Orleans, he might end up on the auction block. So Alvin kept his mouth shut about the fact that this man had duped him out of his money, and as it turns out when he did get back to Missouri, Dr. Bassett did sell him to Mary Tindell."[44]

When Alvin Coffey set out across the plains for the second time in 1854, he was now the property of a new owner, Mary Tindall, whose son Nelson Tindall handled most of the transactions concerning her newly acquired slave. Nelson's brother Ben, who had just returned from California himself, asked Nelson to let Coffey go back to California to try to earn his freedom. Coffey recalled years later that Nelson at first was reluctant to do this, but "I reasoned with him, and I expect I talked pow'ful strong, with my liberty and my wife's and children's at stake." Finally, he struck a deal for a manumission fee of $1,000 to be paid to his owner.[45]

Then he and Ben Tindall headed west again. As they made their way, Coffey, now a veteran of the trail, earned extra money by hiring himself out. He remained in California from 1854 to 1857, working for his new master and for himself in the Shasta and Sutter mines. By 1857, he had made enough to buy himself out of slavery and had earned about $5,000 in gold from his mining, more than enough to buy his wife and children out of bondage.[46] He then traveled back to Missouri, where Mahala and the children were waiting for him, and, he recalled, "you'd better believe they were glad to see me and I to find them well and sound." He had to wait more than two months to retrieve his family, however, because, as his descendant explained, "it seems as if there were only two days per year when slaves could be freed legally in Missouri." Coffey "first went to an attorney [by the name of Coombs] to make sure that everything was copacetic" and that the transaction would withstand any legal challenge.[47]

With that completed, the Coffey family "left Missouri forever" in mid-1857. Deciding to leave their two younger children—Mary J. Coffey and Lavinia Bassett Coffey—in the care of their grandmother in Ontario, Canada, Alvin and Mahala headed west with their three sons, John, Alvin Jr., and Stephen. Back in Shasta County, the family began a new life. Alvin Coffey, a firm believer in education, cofounded a school for African American and American Indian children in 1858. The family then moved to Red Bluff, Tehama County. In 1860, Alvin Coffey traveled to Canada (via the Isthmus of Panama) to bring his daughters to the family homestead in Red Bluff. Finally, after more than a decade of toil and three grueling trips across the plains, Alvin Coffey and his family were reunited and were free residents of the West. The former slave became a respected member of his community, prospering as a farmer, turkey rancher, and laundry operator. The Society of California Pioneers inducted him into their ranks in 1887—the only African American to earn this distinction. Alvin Coffey died on October 28, 1902, in Beulah, Alameda County, California, in the Beulah Home for Aged and Infirm Colored People, an institution he had helped to establish. In his obituary, the Society of California Pioneers wrote, "Alvin Coffey was a noble man, ever generous to his unfortunate neighbor. Perfectly honest, he paid every debt he owed and was brave."[48]

Alvin Coffey's perseverance and hard work eventually won out over treachery and greed, but some enslaved African American overlanders had their hopes crushed, no matter how resolute or industrious they were. This was the case for Dave Boffman, the resourceful slave from Missouri (discussed in a previous chapter) who accompanied his owner west in order to buy himself, his wife, and his children out of slavery. Boffman's arrival at the northern mines near Mokelumne Hill in October 1851 initially appeared to bring him closer to his goals. His work at the diggings produced gold enough to pay in full the $1,000 freedom fee his master demanded.[49]

When he obtained his freedom, he stayed on at the site long enough to amass another stake, before moving southwest to the Santa Cruz region. In Santa Cruz, Boffman purchased a small house on an acre of land and, in partnership with a white man named Samuel McAdams, leased a sawmill and began cutting redwood timber that they planned to sell in San Francisco for one hundred dollars per thousand feet. Boffman intended to use his proceeds to buy freedom for his family, whom he had not seen in more than a year. Unfortunately, the schooner transporting their timber up the coast sank, and Boffman's expected profits vanished. Subsequently, he parted company with McAdams and hired himself out as a laborer in the Santa Cruz area. His hard work and frugality allowed him to purchase a forty-five-acre ranch in the Rodeo Gulch area of Santa Cruz in February 1860. There, in partnership with German emigrant Herman Siegmann, he planted an orchard and a crop of wheat and oats. With his prospects looking better, Boffman now planned to locate his family, buy their freedom, and bring them to his ranch. However, a dispute with the powerful county sheriff John T. Porter concerning ownership of livestock, once again placed his plans on hold.⁵⁰

Porter, claiming that a mare and colt that had been pasturing on Boffman's property belonged to him and that the black man had sold them illegally—a charge that Boffman denied—demanded two hundred dollars in compensation and threatened Boffman with imprisonment. Knowing that African Americans had no right to testify in court against whites, Boffman acquiesced to the sheriff's demand. However, on October 9, 1860, a local businessman George Otto, a German emigrant and friend of Boffman's business partner Seigmann, intervened, offering Porter one hundred dollars to end the matter once and for all. Porter accepted the money but still initiated a lawsuit against Boffman on January 3, 1861, for the full two hundred dollars and won. The court directed Boffman to pay the sheriff the money plus interest. Unable to satisfy the judgment against him, Boffman watched the county auction off his land and livestock for eight hundred dollars at a constable's sale on March 16, 1861. He received nothing from the sale.⁵¹

Destitute and disheartened by the loss of everything for which he had toiled so long and hard, Boffman once again went to work as a laborer and farmhand. In 1864, local merchant and Methodist minister Elihu Anthony befriended him, moving him onto a section of land owned by the school in the Vine Hill district of Santa Cruz County. Over time, Boffman cleared the land, built a small wooden dwelling, and planted an orchard and a forty-acre vineyard. As the years slipped by, however, he gave up hope of ever being reunited with his wife and children. Elihu Anthony did not, though, and continued to search for them, eventually locating Boffman's granddaughter, Annie Drisdom, the child of his oldest daughter, Matilda, his wife's namesake. Annie had been living in Colusa County in northern California. The minister sent her money for a train ticket to Santa Cruz and was with Boffman when she arrived at the depot. Annie informed her grandfather that his wife, Matilda, thinking him dead, had remarried and moved to Kansas, where she had died several years earlier. Boffman's only remaining child, George, who had been an infant when his father trekked to California in 1851 and had no memory of him, was now living in

Topeka. Annie stayed on in Santa Cruz to look after her grandfather for six months before returning home to Colusa County.[52]

Dave Boffman lived on in the Vine Hill district for thirty years. He became known as an eccentric figure in the area. He never owned a pair of shoes in his life, and when he came into town on supply trips, he could often be seen walking barefoot beside his old plow horse. The *Santa Cruz Sentinel* once reported that he had been spotted "carrying on his back a heavy plow from a Santa Cruz blacksmith shop to his farm, a distance of fully eight miles, performing this great task to save the strain on his old horse." On September 23, 1893, Dave Boffman died in his sleep. He was taken back to the city of Santa Cruz to be buried in Elihu Anthony's family plot in the Odd Fellows Cemetery. The *Santa Cruz Sentinel* remembered him as "honest, confiding, simple, industrious, and without a vice."[53]

For Dave Boffman, the trek across the plains ultimately resulted in his freedom and, after some severe setbacks, provided him with a degree of economic independence. Yet it proved to be bittersweet as well. Despite his best efforts, the overland journey permanently separated him from his loved ones and dramatically altered his plans for a new life in the West.

The overland trek proved to be transformative for Lewis (also mistakenly spelled Louis) Alexander Southworth, another slave who accompanied his master on the western trails with the expectation of buying himself and his mother out of slavery. Lewis Southworth—his original surname was Hunter—was born a slave in Tennessee on July 4, 1830, to slave parents, Lewis and Pauline Hunter. From the age of two, Lewis lived on the plantation of James Southworth in Franklin County, Missouri, where his father died of smallpox when Lewis was a boy. James Southworth set out for Oregon in 1853, taking young Lewis and Pauline with him. Mother and son traveled in a company that included at least two other slaves: Amanda Johnson, whose owner was Nancy Wilhite, and Benjamin Johnson, who later became Amanda's husband.[54]

During the journey, Lewis, an accomplished violinist, entertained the company with his playing. Upon arriving in Oregon, his owner allowed him to settle on an abandoned Oregon Donation Land claim near Monroe, in Lane County, despite the fact that blacks were barred from occupying Donation Land. His master, feeling the pinch of hard times, moved in with his slaves for a while. Around 1855, Lewis left the Donation Land residence for a stint in southern Oregon's goldfields near Jacksonville, where he managed to earn three hundred dollars from mining and fiddle playing in the local gold camps. While making his way back from Jacksonville in March or April of 1856, Lewis was stopped by soldiers from Col. John Kelsey's Second Regiment who had been fighting in the Rogue Valley Indian wars. The soldiers demanded that he turn over his rifle. Rather than relinquish his firearm, for which he had paid fifty dollars, Lewis chose to sign on with them because, as he would later explain, "Feeling as if I could not part with my gun, which was the only means of defense I had, I joined the company."[55]

While with Kelsey's regiment, Southworth sustained an injury in a skirmish with Indians, but eventually made his way back home with three hundred dollars, which he presented to his master as a down payment on his freedom. After his seventy-year-old mother died in the fall of 1858, Lewis accompanied his owner farther south to California. He tried mining there but quickly discovered that he could earn more money "playing the violin for dancing schools." He began teaching violin and playing for dance schools in Yreka, California, and Virginia City, Nevada. A Benton County, Oregon, resident who had seen Southworth perform at local dances recalled in a 1915 interview: "Oh, boy, could he play the fiddle! He would sing . . . and he would get out there and dance with it."[56]

Lewis Southworth explained in an interview with the *Corvallis Daily Gazette* why he relished playing in the gold camps for the "boys who were far away from home for the first time," saying he wanted them to remember his fiddling and "talk over the days when there was not society for men like us out West; when . . . men didn't go by their right names and didn't care what they did." He hoped they would think back to the times they heard him play and ask themselves, "Where'd we all been and what'd we all done in the mines, but for Uncle Lou's fiddle which was the most like church of anything we had?" The African American overlander described himself as an "old man who's done some mighty hard work in eighty-five years," but added, "I forget the work I've done and the years I've lived when my bow comes down soft and gentle-like and the fiddle seems to sing the songs of slavery days till the air grows mellow with music and the old-time feelin' comes back, and I can hear familiar voices that are no more."[57]

In 1859, Lewis completed the last four hundred dollar installment on his freedom claim, paying his master a total of $1,000. Although now a free man, he never received formal emancipation papers from his owner. However, it seems the slaveholder suffered some misgivings about letting his slave go. Shortly after freeing Lewis, James Southworth signed and circulated a petition in Lane County, calling on the Oregon territorial government to grant the "recognition of the right of legislative protection of slave property."[58]

By 1868, Lewis Southworth had moved to Buena Vista, Polk County, Oregon, where he learned to read and write. He also purchased land, opened a blacksmith and livery stable, married Mary (or Maria) Cooper, and joined the Victoria Lodge of Masons. He eventually relocated to Tidewater, Oregon, near Waldport, where he farmed and operated a ferry business on the Alsea River. He also devoted himself to education, donating land for a schoolhouse and serving as chair of the school board. After Mary's death in 1901, Lewis bought a home in Corvallis, where he hung his violin and a portrait of Abraham Lincoln over the fireplace. Years later he reported that leaders in his Baptist congregation disapproved of his fiddling and threatened to expel him unless he gave it up: "I told them to keep me in the church with my fiddle if they could, but to turn me out if they must; for I could not think of parting with the fiddle. I reckon my name isn't written in their books here anymore; but I somehow hope it's written in the big book up yonder, where they aren't so particular about fiddles."[59]

Lewis Southworth died on June 28, 1917, at the age of eighty-eight and was buried next to Mary in an unmarked grave in Crystal Lake Cemetery in Corvallis.[60]

Although enslaved overland emigrants like Lewis Southworth, Dave Boffman, and Alvin Coffey toiled incessantly to gain freedom, others were willing to use more direct means to escape the chains of slavery after setting out on the trails. Twenty-year-old Marinda Redd, who trekked to Spanish Fork, Utah, from North Carolina in 1850 with five other slaves owned by John Hardison Redd, seized the opportunity to break away from her captors en route. Marinda, described as "slim, happy and attractive," recounted in an 1899 interview for the Salt Lake City newspaper, the *Broad Ax*, that when her group reached Kansas, "during the dark hours of the night, the majority . . . made good their escape, which was a great loss to their owner." But she was "not so successful in that direction." Marinda was recaptured and forced to complete her march to the Salt Lake valley, where she became the property of a physician in Salem. Sometime later, she married Alexander (Alex) Bankhead, a Mormon slave who had arrived in Utah from Alabama in 1848 as the property of George Bankhead. Marinda and Alexander would have to wait until the Civil War to be emancipated. Decades later they still remembered the "joyful expressions which were upon the faces of all the slaves when they ascertained that they had acquired their freedom through the fortunes of war." Once freed, Alexander and Matilda bought some farmland and a small adobe cottage in Spanish Fork, where they raised their son, Billy. Alexander earned a living as a farmer and also worked as a blacksmith's assistant in the off-season. Marinda, a superb cook, sold baked goods, cared for their son, and tended to their home, which was her great pride. Marinda and Alexander continued to reside in Spanish Fork, remaining devout Mormons for the rest of their lives, despite the church's racist policies. Alexander Bankhead died on January 10, 1902, and five years later, Marinda passed away on January 20, 1907. Both were buried in the Spanish Fork Cemetery.[61]

Marinda Redd Bankhead's attempted escape on the trail ended in failure, but some fourteen years later, a Virginia-born slave, thirty-eight-year-old Henry C. Bruce, from Chariton County, Missouri, made good on his bid for freedom when he and his fiancée, a slave on a neighboring plantation, fled westward. Bruce, the brother of the first black U.S. senator, Blanche K. Bruce, recalled in his autobiography that he had been "engaged to a girl belonging to a man named Allen Farmer, who was opposed" to his relationship with his female slave "on the ground . . . that he did not want a Negro to visit his farm who could read, because he would spoil" the other slaves on his plantation. When Farmer learned Bruce was "courting the girl, he would not allow me to visit his farm or any of his slaves to visit ours." However, Bruce recollected, the slaves "did visit notwithstanding this order, nearly every Sunday." His fiancée's aunt got involved, becoming the couple's "mutual friend and made all arrangements" for the young lovers' clandestine meetings. At one of those rendezvous they decided to "elope," setting March 30, 1864, "at nine o'clock, P.M. sharp, as the date for starting."[62]

His future wife "met [him] at the appointed time and place with her entire worldly effects tied up in a handkerchief." Seeing that everything was in order, "I took her up on the horse behind me," and then "in great haste we started for Lacled [Laclede, Missouri]," the "nearest point reached by the Hannibal and St. Joe Railroad," where a squad of occupying Union troops was stationed. With his fiancée's master leading a posse in hot pursuit, Bruce was prepared to kill or be killed: "I had carefully weighted the cost before starting, had nerved myself for action and would have sold my life very dearly had they overtaken us in our flight." He added, "I was a good shot and knew it, and intended to commence shooting as soon as my pursuers showed up . . . surrender meant death to me. I had buckled around my waist a pair of Colt's revolvers and plenty of ammunition." Bruce explained that he "could not have done otherwise in the presence of the girl I loved, one who had forsaken mother, sister and brothers, and had placed herself entirely under my care and protection." Fortunately, his "almost perfect knowledge" of the surrounding countryside helped the two runaway slaves evade detection as they fled along the "by-paths" on horseback. They "avoided the main road, and made the entire trip without touching the traveled road at any point and without meeting any one and reached Laclede in safety." From there they took a train to "St. Joe, thence to Weston."[63]

After crossing the Missouri River by ferry to Fort Leavenworth, Kansas, Bruce declared, "I then felt myself a free man." Once in Kansas, the couple was married in the home of the Rev. John Turner, pastor of the local African Methodist Episcopal Church. They initially settled in Fort Leavenworth, but later moved to Atchison, Kansas, where Bruce worked as a bricklayer, tried his hand at running his own businesses, made an unsuccessful bid for public office, and served for a term as an elected doorkeeper for the Kansas state senate.[64]

In the spring of 1865 Henry Clay Bruce met another runaway slave named Bluford "on the street in Fort Leavenworth, Kansas." Bruce had known the man when Bluford was a slave on a hemp plantation in Saline County, Missouri. He, like Bruce had been prepared to use deadly force to gain his freedom. Bluford confided to Bruce that, in July 1855, his "overseer got angry at [him] for some offence or neglect and attempted to flog him, but instead got flogged himself" when Bluford, turning the tables, "flogged his master and then ran away." With a mob of angry whites on his trail, the defiant slave, who "could read quite well . . . and had paid attention to the maps and rivers of the state of Missouri," managed to cross the Missouri River into another county and slip away. He hid in a wheat field awaiting nightfall, but a white farmer discovered him, grabbed him "in the collar, and refused to let go after being warned." Bluford then slashed the white man with a "butcher's knife" and left him to die on the road. He pushed on, "[following] Grand River to its head water, which was in Iowa, then [making] his way to Des Moines, where he remained until the war." Enlisting in the Union army, Bluford "served to the close of the war," after which he again employed his knowledge of maps to make his way on foot back to Kansas.[65]

It is not known if Bluford traveled any farther west, but Henry Clay Bruce's westward journey ended in Kansas. In 1881, he reversed his course and relocated to Washington, D.C., where his politically connected brother had secured a job for him in the Department of the Post Office. Henry C. Bruce remained in Washington with his family until his death in 1902.

Free People

Not all African Americans entered the West as slaves, but like their enslaved counterparts, they brought with them great expectations for the journey. Peter Brown, a free man and gold seeker in 1851, optimistically wrote to his wife, Alley, in St. Genevieve City, Missouri, about conditions in California, where he was "now mining on the Cosumnes River about 25 miles from Sacramento City," and, "doing very well." He wrote that he had been "working for myself the last two months by paying 80 dollars a month and cleared three hundred dollars since I have been in this country." Brown reported that "wages are four dollars a day and some diggings more. The company that I came out with are doing well and have been all summer." He declared that California was the "best country in the world to make money. This is the best place for black folks on the globe. All a man has to do, is to work, and he will make money." Brown concluded his letter with a poignant plea to his wife that revealed the most important reason for all his hard work: "I wish you to tell Peter [probably their son] to be industrious. . . . I am trying to make enough money to buy him when I get home, and not to let my mother suffer for anything." Whether Peter Brown accomplished his objectives is not known.[66]

Nelson Ray, another free black Missourian, came to California at the age of thirty-six, determined to liberate his family as well. Ray had been the slave of a prominent white Lexington, Missouri, family, but was manumitted in 1846 after his owner's death. He remained in Missouri to work as a miner and stockman in order to purchase freedom for his wife, Lucinda, and three of their four children—George, seven; Nelson, three; and Sara, two months. The couple's five-year-old-son, Francis Marion Ray, had been sold in probate proceedings and taken to Texas to satisfy the debts of Lucinda's master. Nelson Ray trudged overland to the California goldfields in 1852 for the sole purpose of earning enough money to free his wife and children still in Missouri. Within a year he had accumulated $3,700 working as a miner and at other jobs.[67]

In 1853, at the age of thirty-seven, Ray returned to Lexington, where he found work as a drover, teamster, and freight handler for W. B. Waddell (one of the founders of the Pony Express), who at that time owned a freighting company that hauled goods west to Fort Bridger in present-day Wyoming, Fort Kearny in Nebraska, and all along the Santa Fe Trail. While in Waddell's employ, Ray made several trips to California, working as a drover for other outfits as well. By 1854, Ray finally had the funds to free his entire family, and he returned to Missouri. Being wary of Missouri's slave codes and predatory slave hunters, he sought legal assurance that his wife and children were free and could not be re-enslaved. He secured the services of attorney Jonathan P. Bowman, who, on June 9, 1854, submitted a writ of emancipation to the Missouri courts that legally and permanently guaranteed their freedom. When that was settled, the Rays set out for the West as free people, and as Nelson Ray's great-great-grandson George Jenkins noted in an interview, W. B. Waddell became their "ticket back to the Golden State." They "returned to California [with Nelson] driving a herd of 600 cattle as part of [a] small freight train." The family stopped for a time in Sacramento, then pushed on to Placerville, where they ended their journey. In 1855, Lucinda and Nelson were legally wed; they became property owners that same year. In 1877, a chance encounter reunited them with their son Francis Marion Ray, who had been sold away from them more than thirty years earlier.[68]

The Rays, like most African American emigrants, remained in California, but some free black people who were pulled west by the desire to live as they saw fit, unrestricted by racial laws, were prepared to push beyond geographic and other boundaries to pursue their goals. Charles and Nancy Alexander traveled from Missouri to California in 1857 as free people, but eventually headed to Canada. The Alexanders, according to their fourth-generation grandson Harold Alexander, "were never slaves," and were "of mixed blood"—Nancy being the daughter of a black mother and a father described as an "Irishman," and Charles the son of an Indian father and black mother. Charles and Nancy were married sometime in the early 1840s on Christmas Day in Springfield, Illinois. The newlyweds settled in St. Louis, Missouri, where for sixteen years Charles operated a grist mill.[69]

Charles and Nancy were "farmers for the most part," but Charles also worked as a carpenter and was a minister as well. According to British Columbia scholar James William Pilton, "when the gold mines of California proved too powerful an attraction," Charles, Nancy, and their two children packed up and started out on the trail to California. Doug Hudlin, Charles Alexander's great-great-grandson, recounted in an interview that the family traveled in a "van pulled by a four-yoke bullock team," and were accompanied by "four friends and a guide, Mr. Hullinback." The group followed the established California Trail (possibly from Plattsmouth, where the Platte meets the Missouri River) through Nebraska to South Pass and on to Fort Bridger, and then took the Hastings Cutoff to Salt Lake City. From there they likely took the Salt Lake Cutoff north to join the California Trail at City of Rocks. They followed the Humboldt to its sink south of Lovelock and then split off onto the Carson River Route through the Forty Mile Desert. At Fort Churchill, the Alexanders continued on the Carson Route through the Sierra, south of Lake Tahoe to Sacramento, and from there made their way to San Francisco.[70]

Harold Alexander recalled hearing stories as a child about his pioneer ancestors "fighting Indians" as they rolled westward and encountering Native people who were "occasionally a menace, stealing the cattle and other possessions carried by the party."[71] Raids by Shoshones and Paiutes were common occurrences along the Humboldt River route and were a source of complaints from other overlanders. But, great-great-grandson Doug Hudlin recalled that Charles Alexander was confident that he and his family would "make the trip safely as he had faith in his Bible, his compass, and his log book."[72]

Once they reached their destination in San Francisco however, Charles "was not long satisfied in California, arriving as he did when there was so much discontent among the coloured people when rumours of new discoveries were beginning to come down from the north." Harold Alexander explained their departure more bluntly: "They left San Francisco because of discrimination."[73]

The Alexander family moved on to Victoria, British Columbia in 1858. Shortly after arriving, Charles, still in the grip of gold fever, left Nancy and the children in Victoria and headed for the Fraser River. After meeting with modest success as a miner, he returned to his family in Victoria, where he "worked at his trade as a carpenter at $6.00 per day." In the fall of 1858, the Alexanders relocated to Saanich, north of Victoria, and there Charles and Nancy spent thirty-three years engaged in farming. The family moved for the last time, in 1894, into a home they christened "Rockabella Gardens" in the Swan Lake district, later called the Lake Hill district. There, at the age of seventy-eight, Nancy Alexander passed away on March 23, 1912. A little less than a year later, eighty-nine-year-old Charles died on January 13, 1913. Both were buried in the Shady Creek Cemetery in Saanich, Vancouver Island, British Columbia.[74]

Gay Alexander, Harold Alexander's wife, noted that "when they left California, those people . . . must have had some sense of individuality, knowing they had to work the land." They were "hardworking ... there was no idleness. . . . He built the church [Shady Creek Church], he built his home. . . . They had to [multitask] because that is what pioneers had to do." Harold Alexander recalled that as a boy, he had resented the "work, work, work" ethic that had been instilled in the Alexander family for generations, but later in life he "came to realize that [for] those people, that's how they survived."[75]

Charles and Nancy Alexander's efforts influenced many generations. Great-great-grandson Doug Hudlin charted the Alexander family tree in 1992 and counted four hundred descendants of the couple whose journey began on the overland trail to California and ended in western Canada.[76]

Howard and Hanna Estes—parents of Sylvia Estes Stark and Jackson Estes—were imbued with the same work ethic that motivated the Alexanders. Like the Alexanders, the Estes family was determined to realize their goals, even if it meant moving beyond the borders of the United States. In 1851, when Howard, Hannah, and their children arrived in California and began setting up their household, Hannah Estes cautioned her children, "We'll have to work hard . . . but we are working for ourselves now." Hannah worked as a laundress in her home and Sylvia assisted her; Howard farmed the land he had purchased and also worked as a miner. Sylvia, now a young woman, married Louis Stark, a free black man from Kentucky who also farmed his own land. But Sylvia reported in an interview years later that her husband and parents, like many other black Californians, were "becoming alarmed over general agitation under southern pressure to make California a slave state." Therefore, the Estes and Stark families prepared to leave their "comfortable home" in California and "go in search of greater freedom." They had heard about "New Caledonia as B.C, was then called," and "longed for the freedom of B.C.'s fir covered hills." Howard Estes and Louis Stark sold their farms, and in 1858, the two families left San Francisco on the *Brother Johnathan*, steaming up to British Columbia. They arrived in Vancouver, where they lived for a while. Eventually, however, Sylvia, Louis, and their children settled on Salt Spring Island, where Sylvia and Louis homesteaded for many years. After Louis's death, Sylvia continued to live there, running the family farm with her son, Willis, until her death in 1944 at the age of 106.[77]

The Civil War provided the backdrop for Richard and Mary McDonald's trek across the plains in 1864 as newly freed people. Richard and Mary had been born into slavery, were manumitted by their owners, and were married in Missouri in 1861, at the outbreak of the Civil War. They found themselves in a tenuous position. They were free, but like all other African Americans, had no citizenship rights. They could not vote, testify in court, or file a homestead claim. The war had all but destroyed the institution of slavery in Missouri; thousands of slave owners had fled the state, taking their human property with them, and thousands of slaves were escaping to nearby free states. The tumult of war pushed the McDonalds, and countless other free (and enslaved) black people, onto the overland trails. Three years after they were wed, thirty-year-old Richard and twenty-two-year-old Mary piled their six-month-old son, Robert, and their meager belongings into a wagon drawn by six oxen, and with several other families, jumped off onto the trail in St. Joseph, bound for the newly designated Montana Territory. Among their most prized possessions was a rawhide whip that Richard had made especially for the trip and a "green glass bottle" that contained camphor and whiskey that "served as their all-purpose medicine on the journey." They also carried a little tin box that held all their money and keepsakes, including a photo of Mary's mother from whom she had been separated as a child. The box was soldered shut for the duration of the trip, and the couple buried it "every night when they came from St. Joseph, Missouri."[78]

The trip took a high toll on the couple; their infant son, Robert, became ill and died en route. Richard and Mary's granddaughter Belle Fisher stated in an interview years later that the grieving parents had to bury their child "beside the dusty trail" and keep moving west. After nearly five months on the road, the McDonalds arrived in the boomtown of Virginia City, Montana Territory, where their second son, Eddy, was born. But this child, too, lived only a few months. Shortly after Eddy's death, they relocated to Bozeman, where Richard bought a small tract of land on Sourdough Creek and built a one-room cabin. With his ox team and wagon, he went to work freighting goods from

Bozeman to Virginia City, and occasionally to Fort Benton, farther north.[79]

By the end of the decade, the McDonalds were thriving in their new western home. Mary, described by her granddaughter Belle Fisher as a "little, short, heavyset woman, but always so jolly," had a full life that "centered around her home and family" and the First Methodist Church in Bozeman. For a time, Richard and Mary also worked at Fort Ellis, east of Bozeman and so impressed an officer there that he tried to persuade them to accompany him back east, where he was to be transferred. They declined his offer, saying that they had "had enough of being servants." Richard McDonald died in 1898 at the age of sixty-five, and Mary lived to be one hundred years old. The two-story house that Richard built from scrap materials still stands.[80]

Nancy Lewis was a free woman when she began her overland trek. Born on December 25, 1841, in Platte County, Missouri, Lewis arrived in Fort Leavenworth, Kansas, in 1865, when she was, according to historian William Loren Katz, "an attractive and vivacious teenager." She married a black Union army veteran at Fort Leavenworth, and in 1866, the newlyweds joined the "wagon train of Sisler and Saur" and made their way in a covered wagon to Central City, Colorado. Nancy "took a job as a cook" shortly after arriving, while her husband "search[ed] for gold in the nearby hills." Little else is known about these African American overlanders, but in 1888, Nancy moved to Denver (probably after her husband had passed away) and became a "household employee" of the flamboyant silver miner and politician, Horace Austin Warner Tabor. When she was ninety-eight years old, Lewis expressed only one regret: "I can't read nor write, and it's my own fault." Nancy Lewis died in 1944 at the age of 102, and was buried in Fairmount Cemetery.[81]

Those Who Stayed Behind

When Lancaster, Ohio, resident David Brown was lured across the plains to California by gold in 1852, he too traveled west as a free person, but Brown's trip permanently separated him from his family and altered the course of his and other lives. David Brown's wife, Rachel, chose to remain in Ohio but carried on a lively correspondence with her husband. Unfortunately, none of David's letters to Rachel have been discovered, but this extraordinary collection of her letters offers a rare glimpse into the hopes and fears that accompanied African American overlanders, provides intimate evidence of the journey's impact on free family members who were left behind, and challenges the race, gender, and class nexus that stigmatized African American women in the nineteenth century.

David Brown, born in Hampshire County, Virginia (now West Virginia), in 1812, carried documents that declared he was "aged twenty-two years, five feet, eight inches high, with pleasant countenance, a scar on the forefinger of the left hand, a scar on the shin of each leg, and born free."[82] Historian John Mark Lambertson has written, "nothing else is known about his background," but a bit more about him can be gleaned from existing records.[83] In 1834, before his departure from Hampshire County, fifteen of his white neighbors with whom he had a "life long acquaintance" signed and presented him with a document attesting to his "rectitude and propriety, honesty and industry."[84] In 1848, after leaving Hampshire County, Brown eventually settled in Lancaster, Ohio, a small community thirty-three miles southeast of Columbus, and married free black Ohioan Rachel Ann Johnson on Christmas Eve, 1848. Rachel was born about 1825 to free parents, Samuel and Sarah Johnson. Samuel Johnson, a farmer and shoemaker, died when Rachel was only five years old, and Sarah later married Scipio Smith, who worked as a "tinner" and was prominent in Lancaster's African American church community. As newlyweds, David and Rachel lived with Sarah and Scipio Smith in Lancaster.[85]

Despite Ohio's free-state status and the active abolitionist community that developed in the area, an intractable minority of the state's white population from the South staunchly supported slavery, a fact that caused some apprehension in Lancaster's small African American community (187 blacks and 3,296 whites in 1850).[86] In 1853, Rachel, in a letter to David, who had been in California for about a year, hinted at her anxiety over these conditions, writing, "I don't like this place [Lancaster] to think of buying here nor I don't think that you will likt It any more. I would like to go some place where you Could do well. you know that you can do nothing In this place." Imploring her husband to "come home so we can get a place for house keeping. I don't want to stay here unless you do," her words suggest that striking it rich was not the only factor that contributed to David's decision to go west. She reminded him, "You know penlty well all about the Buisness of this place."[87]

Rachel, a literate and fairly well educated African American woman for her time, was not ignorant of, or isolated from, the issues facing black people in her state and around the country. In April 1853, she told David of her interest in emigration to Canada, writing, "they was going to hold a convention a[t] Cleveland to take In consideration of Emagration." A month later, she informed him, "I would like to visit Canada with you to see It & to Cleaveland to[o] when you returned."[88]

By then, however, David was living the life of a gold miner in California, where he hoped his wife would eventually join him. How he managed to financed his trip is unknown, but after spending $150 to outfit himself, he had signed on with Thomas Sturgeon and Samuel Crim's California-bound company of "forty-two men, . . . six wagons and 65 horses" on February 28, 1852.[89] There is no indication of other African Americans in Brown's party.[90] The group traveled overland from Lancaster to Cincinnati, then by steamboat to St. Louis, where they unsuccessfully attempted to book passage up the Missouri River. They were able to ship the "wagons, harness, provisions, and 24 mules they had bought to St. Joseph, MO," but experienced a setback when the steamboat carrying their cargo sank, resulting in the loss of a large number of animals and provisions. Undeterred, Brown and twenty-eight other men trudged on across Missouri with the remaining horses and supplies. Upon reaching St. Joseph, the group jumped off for California in April 1852, traveling through Salt Lake City and finally arriving in Downieville, California, just sixty miles from Marysville, in September 1852.[91]

David Brown quickly settled into his new life as a miner. According to a receipt from a local merchant, Jackson's Jo. Wright & Co., one of his first purchases in Downieville was a pair of boots for eight dollars and two pairs of socks for two dollars. He was able to reduce his ten-dollar tab "by Sawing wood" for the shop, which credited him four dollars for his work.[92] Later that year, he purchased a "Silver Hunting watch" for twenty dollars from a Downieville resident, Ernest Zoller.[93] In July 1853, he bought "two [mining] claims of thirty full front" for the sum of fifty dollars. The claims also came with "one half wheel-Barrow, one Rocker, two Picks, & two Shovels" and "one-half of the Cabin, Stove, Cooking utensils[,] dishes[,] Y&C."⁹⁴

By 1854, Brown had formed a partnership (one of several he would enter over the next decade) with George M. Rollin (race unknown). The two men purchased for $440 the "Hydraulic & drifting Claims situated South of Downieville on the Hillside and known as the Teibbe, Brown & Co Claims."⁹⁵ In June 1855, he paid $150 for a quarter-interest in the William Berryman & Co. sluicing claims located at "Coiotoville [Coyoteville] on the Bank of the Yuba River."⁹⁶ He and a business partner, Stephen Campbell (race unknown), jointly owned a ranch located "North West of Cayotoville [Coyoteville]," where they cut oak and pine timber and sold it in Downieville in 1857.⁹⁷

Despite his ceaseless efforts, David Brown was only nominally successful as a miner, but over the next decade he proved to be a much better businessman, buying and selling mining claims, equipment, and property. Within five years of arriving in California, he had established himself as a respected member of the community, earning a reputation for reliability and trustworthiness. It appears he had little trouble securing credit and loans for his mining and other business dealings. By December 1855, he had made the final payment of $180 on the Coyoteville property that he had purchased in June of that year. This represented payment "in full for a Claim and in full of all demands against him up to this date." Then, in February 1857, Brown entered into a land transaction with his then-mining partner Charles Thomas Millard (race unknown), in which Brown agreed to pay $225 in installments over a period of nine months.⁹⁸

David Brown's creditworthiness also was in good standing at William Wilkerson's Downieville saloon, where he ran a bar tab. Receipts show that from December 3, 1856, through January, 5, 1857, Brown imbibed nine "cocktails" and "1 glass [of] Porter" at that establishment, for a total of $2.50. On January 5, 1857, Wilkerson "received payment of the above a/c [account] in full up to this date."⁹⁹ On at least one occasion, David Brown loaned money to a business associate, Richard James (race unknown). A note addressed to Brown from another business partner, Charles Millard, in June 1855 indicates that Brown authorized Millard to collect from James a debt of $18.52. Millard succeeded in collecting $12 that James owed Millard himself, but he could not secure Brown's money, even though Millard wrote that he had "tried my best to collect it for you." Millard reported to Brown that James promised "he will pay [you] the first time he comes up."[100]

David Brown and other black miners formed the Colored American Joint Stock Quartz Mining Company in 1866, and Brown served as secretary of the organization. Eventually, David Brown bought a house in Downieville, where he also owned some city water rights.[101]

Back in Ohio, Rachel continued with her life, which had been changed profoundly since her husband's departure. Her letters tell a story of economic and emotional stress as she struggled to keep up the responsibilities of maintaining a household, providing for her family, and caring for her sickly mother, who worked as a laundress to help make ends meet while David was busy with his new life in California. Rachel admitted, in a letter dated January 1853, that with her mother being ill most of the winter, "I had a hard time of It then. [H]er to waite on & all the work to do & all the Burtchen to do myself.... I had a dull Christmass I working all day & New years day the same. It appears to me that I work harder now then ever[.]"[102] She worried constantly about the family's financial situation, sprinkling her correspondence with references to the high cost of living. She wrote in January 1853, "Every thing Is so Dearder then it has ever been before. [F]louer is $400 a barrel poark 9 cts Beef 6 &7 Butter 15 Eggs 15 Appels 44 Candles 15 [W]ages Is no more then when you left so you see how hard I have to work to get any thing to Eat or wear Wood $200 a Cord I have saw & split the most of It until Woodruff Came home [W]e could not affoard to hire It done [M]y hoges Cost me a great deal to fatten them & to get them Bucherd." She pleaded, "I wish that you Could send some money soon to me."[103]

David responded to her dire situation, mailing money and gifts to her, including a ring that "raised a great talke they Envy It much[.] It most kills them for you to send me any thing."[104] However, the haphazard transportation and communication systems of the day caused agonizing delays, and mail sometimes simply disappeared. In March 1853, Rachel acknowledged, "I recived you letter with the Check & was pleased with It. It rendered me great satisfaction." She fretted about the delay in receiving her husband's letters, concluding, "I know the reason why I don't recived your letters more regular [T]hey have been so many accidents by steamers latey none of them get there letters any sooner."[105] She wrote in another letter, "I expect that some of my letters to you was lost as I have not here form them yet."[106]

Although money was the major topic of discussion, Rachel's letters also covered a range of concerns and were steeped in the routine of daily life, which she affectionately chronicled for her husband in faraway California. She updated him on the weather, the progress of the family vegetable garden, her spring-cleaning efforts, church activities, and even the state of her teeth—which, she wrote, were "very bad & are decaying. [T]hey have began to decay on the other side. I thought of getting then pluged but It Is a $1.00 for one now." In a May 1853 letter, she declared, "I told you all the knewes in my other letters. . . . I wrote you a few days go all the particular newes."[107] In her last known letter to David, Rachel informed him, "I thought that I would learn musich & strive to Improve my mind but It will cost me something to learn. I thought I would learn the gaitear first. It will cast 6$ per quearter & the gaitear some 8 or 12. Piano Is Dearder yet but just as you say about It."[108]

She, in turn, was eager to learn about David's business in California and about conditions there, reminding him, "O you never told me how yours mining turned out. I hope that you will write In your next about prohibiting the Emigration of Colored people the state that did not pass." She requested in another letter: "I want you to tell me what you have made & what your prospects are & you think that Country would suit me I win [will] so too."[109]

In one of many tender moments captured in the correspondence, Rachel assured her husband of her sincere appreciation of his efforts to provide for her, writing, "my Dear you are excuseabl for not leaveing me any money as I know that you Done the best you could as I know you always do the best you can for me & I belived that you always will."[110] Her love for David is palpable, even in the opening salutations of the letters that begin, "My Dear Husband" and "My Dear & very affectionate husband," and her closing endearments that simply say, "I remain you[r] wife until Death."[111] Although his letters to her were slow in arriving and her economic situation was fragile, she tried to reassure him of her love and trust, writing, "you must not think that I have lost confidence In you by no menes I have not I think that we ought to live affectionate to gether as they are but us two."[112] Insisting that she was up to the task of running the household in his absence, she urged David not to "weary yourself about me as I am getting more us[ed] to being a lone I don't think It so hard as I did at first."[113]

However, their long separation seems to have overwhelmed her at times, as she confided, "I am very lonely without your company I would much rather be writing to you then sleeping to night so you m[a]y judge that I have not forgotten you by no means." In another letter she admitted, "I know that you can not content youself to sleep alone for I know I can not." Rachel declared, "I know thayt If I should see you come home I don't think I would consent fore you to go again without taken me along."[114]

Rachel, in fact, steadfastly refused to make the journey west. A year after David's arrival in California, she wrote, "I hope that you will be able to come home this fall as I have no desire to [go] there to live."[115] She repeatedly urged him to "write and tell me what time you will be at home," and hoped that his return "will not be long[.]" In a letter dated October 14, 1853, she demanded, "as soon as you make two thousand you must come home."[116] Although it appears that David tried, he could not persuade her to travel west. She worried that it would be too expensive and admitted that "mother Is not willing for me to go." However, she finally confessed that the primary reason for not joining him in California was that she "would be afraid to Cross the waters."[117]

Rachel and David Brown had their own reasons for following different paths. Life in the West, with its greater economic and social freedom, contributed to David's decision to remain in California. His mining business and community activities in Downieville undoubtedly were more attractive than his old life in Ohio. But, by 1892, he was in failing health and was forced to deed his Downieville house over to friends, who promised to give him a "decent burial through the Methodist Church" when his time came. His condition continued to deteriorate, and he was transported to the local hospital, but he left shortly after being admitted. He was moved to the insane asylum in Napa, California, and died there at the age of eighty. Although one of the executors of his property had given the hospital twenty dollars to pay for burial expenses, David was laid to rest in an unmarked grave in the hospital's "potters field."[118]

At the time of his death, Rachel had been separated from David for nearly forty years. She had long since ended their marriage and had gone on to create a new life for herself in Ohio. After six years of living apart from her husband, she successfully petitioned for divorce in May 1858, citing desertion, and resumed using her maiden name. She remarried twice, but after 1884, Rachel and her last husband, Silas Smith, an African Methodist Episcopal preacher, disappear from the historic records. Her mother, Sara Smith—the putative reason Rachel could not go west—lived to be one hundred years old.[119]

Rachel Brown never traveled on the overland trail, but overland emigration affected every part of her life. David's decision to head west and remain there eventually opened up new options for both of them. For these two African Americans, and countless others who remain anonymous, western emigration was both a signal of, and catalyst for, change.

Although law and custom attempted to strip African Americans, both slave and free, of their humanity, black people nonetheless headed west conscious of their self-worth and character. Most were motivated by the desire to free themselves from slavery's shackles, oppressive black codes, and riotous mobs; all looked forward to the opportunity for economic progress; and many risked their lives and livelihoods to achieve their goals. Their expectations were fulfilled, disappointed, or transformed, but often the outcome of the journey and life in the West was a mixture of all these things. For some African American overlanders, the promise of the West rang hollow when, despite their best efforts, their hopes were diminished or crushed altogether.

In all cases, the journey changed the black men and women who trekked the trails to the West. Whether they set out as slaves or free people, the trip literally and figuratively placed them on new paths, sometimes redirecting them beyond the borders of the United States and altering the course of their lives and those of future generations. Reaching the end of the complex of trails did not signal the end of the journey, nor did it end their fight to establish themselves as free people—a fight that would be much longer and infinitely more difficult than their trek across sweet freedom's plains.

Chapter 8
Place of Promise

I want it to come out right. I don't want to go back to Mississippi.
Archy Lee, 1858

In California, Oregon and Washington Territory we seldom hear of the outrages that were constantly perpetrated upon our defenseless race.
Pacific Appeal, 1862

THE WEST BECKONED AFRICAN AMERICANS as a place of promise, and for most black overlanders, freedom lay at the heart of its promise. Wherever the trail ended for them, black people confronted the difficult tasks of establishing themselves as free people, which for some meant mounting legal challenges to slavery. They had to carve out a place for themselves in the emerging economies of the West, establish communities, and dismantle the barriers that prevented them from achieving their goals. Foundational to all of this was overturning the racial status quo—a battle that represented the opening rounds of a fight that would continue long after the last wagons rolled across the plains and would be waged in courtrooms across the West. Launched from institutions established by African Americans, the fight would often spill into the streets, where the court of public opinion sometimes played a decisive role.

Establishing Themselves as Free People:
Courts, Streets, Community of Saints

Robin Holmes

The experiences of Robin Holmes illustrate the difficulties individual African American emigrants faced as they attempted to remove the chains of slavery and make a place for themselves on the "free soil" of the West without a support system or the resources to aid them in the work. The Holmes family, like untold numbers of black overlanders, entered the West as slaves, only to discover that their master had no intention of fulfilling his promise to free them. Robin Holmes waged a courtroom battle to redeem that promise for himself, his wife, Polly, and their children. In so doing, he became the principal player in a case that struck a major legal blow to slavery in Oregon and challenged its presence throughout the Pacific Northwest.

In 1844, Robin and Polly Holmes and their three-year-old daughter, Mary Jane, accompanied their owner, Nathaniel Ford, to Oregon from Missouri. Ford, the former sheriff of Howard County, Missouri, headed west to escape financial problems. Their group was part of the wagon train led by Moses "Black" Harris, and it included a slave identified only as Scott, also owned by Ford. George W. Bush and family were members of this company as well. After arriving in the Willamette Valley, Ford moved the Holmeses into a small cabin he built for them, and permitted them (and Scott) to travel to the local market to sell the produce they raised on the property. Ford had promised to emancipate his slaves once they arrived but now refused to let them go.[1]

Robin and Polly had four more children in Oregon: James, born in 1845; Roxanna, in 1847; Harriet, birth date unknown; and a son, Lon, born in 1850. Robin again asked his master to make good on his promise, but Ford demanded that he go down to California and mine for gold with Ford's son, Mark, and the slave Scott, this time promising to free the Holmeses when Robin returned with gold. Robin traveled to California, where he hired on as a mining camp cook and prospected for gold. After working there for a while, he started back to Oregon with Mark Ford and Scott—and with the nine hundred dollars he had earned. Mark and Scott were drowned en route, but Robin made it back safely and handed over the money to his master, as agreed. Ford manumitted Robin, Polly, and baby Lon in 1850, and the family immediately moved to a house near Nesmith's Mills, and later to Salem, where Robin and Polly operated a small commercial fruit tree and shrub nursery. Ford still refused to relinquish the other Holmes children because he planned to sell them.[2]

Harriet Holmes, still the slave of Nathaniel Ford, died while visiting her parents in 1851. Although the circumstances of her death are unknown, Robin blamed his former master for his child's death. Robin, realizing that Ford would never free his other children, brought a custody suit against him a year later. Though unable to read or write, Robin Holmes was aware that Oregon Territory banned slavery. Even so, at the initial hearing, Ford claimed to be the legal owner of the children and their parents as well. He declared that Roxanna, Mary Jane, and James were his wards until the girls reached the age of eighteen and until James turned twenty-one, according to an agreement he claimed to have made with Robin on his return from California. Ford also maintained that he had expended considerable funds on the children and was entitled to recoup his money by selling them in Missouri. Finally, he asserted that the Holmes children would suffer should they be returned to their parents, who were poor, illiterate, and unfit to care for them.[3]

In his testimony, Robin Holmes rejected Ford's accusations and denied entering into any custody arrangement with his former owner. Given the hotly contested facts of the case, Judge Cyrus Olney ordered Nathaniel Ford to bring the children to court, where they would be held until the matter was settled. Ford refused to comply, and instead pledged to pay Holmes a $3,000 bond to ensure that the children would not be removed from the territory. After a two-month delay in getting a key witness to testify, Robin, fearing his children were being mistreated, renewed his petition to the court. Judge Olney then directed Ford to relinquish the children to the court or to the local sheriff. Ford ignored this order as well. Despite Ford's blatant flouting of court orders, the judge ruled that Mary Jane Holmes could stay with Ford if she chose, or go with her parents, and awarded temporary custody of Roxanna to Ford and custody of James to his father. In addition, both men were required to post a $1,000 bond to guarantee the children's appearance in court.[4] Unable to pay the bond, Robin grew increasingly frustrated by the slow pace of the hearing. After eleven months of inaction, he took the case of *Holmes v. Ford* before Judge George A. Williams in 1853. Williams, a newly arrived justice of the Oregon territorial supreme court, and a free-soil Democrat from

Iowa, quickly found in Holmes's favor, ruling that slavery could not exist in Oregon without specific legislation to support it. He declared that since these "colored children are in Oregon, where slavery does not legally exist, they are free."[5]

Robin and Polly Holmes were at last awarded full custody of their children. Their legal victory represents the last attempt of proslavery emigrants in Oregon to secure their slave property through judicial means. Nathaniel Ford, lamenting ever having brought his human property to the West, wrote his friend James A. Shirley, back in Missouri: "You know I brought some negroes with me to this country which has proved a curse to me. . . . Robin and his wife done verry well until the spring of '50 when the abolitionists interfered—and the country is full of them—the interference was so great that I had to let them go." In a scheme to get Shirley to buy the Holmeses from him and return them to Missouri under the fugitive slave law, Holmes proposed, "If the case of the negroes can be attended to it will releave me and my fambly of much trouble and you may be benefitted by it."[6]

Though the Holmeses celebrated their hard-fought freedom, Robin and Polly suffered from severe financial difficulties. The Polk County, Oregon, tax roll listed the total value of Robin's personal property at $655 in 1854. Their dire economic circumstances prompted their eldest daughter, Mary Jane, now also free, to remain voluntarily with Nathaniel Ford and work as his paid household servant in order to provide a source of income for her impoverished parents. She did so for a while, but by 1857, sixteen-year-old Mary Jane was making plans to marry Reuben Shipley, a former Kentucky slave who had been brought to Oregon by his owner, Robert Shipley. Reuben, too, had been promised freedom in the West when he left his wife and two sons, who were slaves on another plantation. Working as a farmhand in Oregon, Reuben had been able to buy himself out of bondage in the mid-1850s, paying his owner $1,500 in full. When his wife passed away back in Missouri, her master refused to let Reuben purchase his sons' freedom. In 1857, before he could wed Mary Jane, Nathaniel Ford insisted that Reuben pay him $750, even though the young woman had been free for four years. Fearing a protracted legal battle whose outcome was uncertain, Reuben paid the ransom and the couple was wed.[7]

Reuben and Mary Jane Holmes Shipley subsequently purchased eighty acres of farmland located between Corvallis and Philomath, where they settled and raised six children—three girls and three boys. The community-minded Shipleys deeded two acres of their land to the county to be used as a cemetery where African American burials would be permitted, and in 1861 the land became Mount Union Cemetery in Benton County, Oregon. Twelve years after the cemetery was dedicated, Reuben and one of his daughters died from smallpox and were buried there.[8]

Mary Jane married R. G. Drake in 1875 and lived in Corvallis until his death, then moved to East Salem to live with her children, Nettie and Charles Shipley. She later relocated to Portland, where she died in 1925. The woman, who, as an infant, had crossed the plains as a slave and had become the centerpiece of her father's fight for freedom in a western court, was taken back to Corvallis to be buried beside her two husbands and children in Mount Union Cemetery.[9]

Biddy Mason

Bridget "Biddy" Mason, who had been taken as a slave to California in 1851 by her Mormon owners, fought her way to freedom by way of the courts in California, a state with the largest African American population in the West. Unlike the Holmeses, Mason carried out her fight with the help of an organized, alert, and supportive African American community. Before Mason trekked to the Golden State with her owner, Robert Smith, Brigham Young had warned Mormon slaveholders, "there is little doubt but [the slaves] will all be free as soon as they arrive in California." Mason, who traveled from Salt Lake City to southern California with her extended family of thirteen people, undoubtedly found in his words reason to be hopeful about the journey.[10]

While on the trail, Mason had the opportunity to discuss these matters with Charles H. Rowan, a free black teamster in the company (and future husband of Elizabeth "Lizzy" Flake), who urged her to claim her freedom once she set foot on California's "free soil." After arriving in southern California, Mason also became acquainted with members of the free black community there, who also encouraged her to contest her status. Los Angeles residents and former Texas slaves

Robert and Minnie Owens had a profound impact on Mason's decision to sue for freedom. Robert Owens, a horse and mule trader, had come to Los Angeles overland by ox team in 1850 and owned a thriving corral business, where he and his crew of ten Mexican vaqueros broke wild horses and mules from the surrounding ranchos, which supplied the settlers with animals.[11] His son's romantic involvement with Mason's seventeen-year-old daughter, Ellen, gave Owens a personal stake in the Mason family's future. Moreover, Manuel Pepper, an African American cowboy and Owens's good friend, was also in love with seventeen-year-old Ann, the daughter of Mason's purported sister, Hannah. Ann and Hannah, like Mason, were the slaves of Robert Smith.[12]

Mason confided to Owens that Smith was preparing to take her and the rest of his slaves to Texas, where there would be no question about their status. In late 1855, Smith had already moved his household, including Mason, Hannah (who was pregnant), and his other slaves, to a remote encampment in the Santa Monica Mountains, where he was readying for departure to Texas. Owens and Rowan, hoping to thwart Smith's plans, alerted the Los Angeles County sheriff that slaves were being held illegally in the vicinity. A posse consisting of the sheriff, Robert Owens, Charles Owens, Manuel Pepper, and several of the vaqueros who worked at Owens's corral was quickly assembled. The group made a daring surprise raid on the camp, rescuing Mason, her family, and the other slaves, who were then placed under the protective custody of the sheriff until the matter could be sorted out.[13]

After suffering five years of enslavement in a "free state," Biddy Mason petitioned the court for freedom on behalf of herself and her family on January 19, 1856. The case was heard in the Los Angeles district court, with Judge Benjamin Hayes (who was also an overlander) presiding. The hearing lasted three days. Because California law barred African Americans from testifying in cases against whites, none of the black people could speak in open court. However, when questioned in the judge's chambers, Mason admitted that she would not willingly go to Texas, explaining, "I have always done what I have been told to do; I always feared this trip to Texas, since I first heard of it. Mr. Smith told me I would be just as free in Texas as here." Hannah, however, was reluctant to speak because, the judge speculated, she and others may have been threatened by Smith. Therefore, Hayes announced that the court would pay attention to the "speaking silence of the petitioners." Later in the proceedings, however, Hannah summoned up the courage to admit that she "never wished to leave, and prays for protection."[14]

Just one year before the infamous *Dred Scott* ruling, Judge Hayes handed down his decision on January 21, 1856. Citing California's constitutional prohibition of slavery and involuntary servitude, he declared, "all of the said persons of color are entitled to their freedom and are free forever," adding that all that "remained was . . . for the petitioners to become settled and go to work for themselves in peace and without fear."[15]

Biddy Mason did just that. When the trial ended, Robert and Minnie Owens welcomed Mason and her daughters into their home as temporary guests. Mason purchased a house (located in present-day downtown Los Angeles) in 1866, and her home became a gathering place for her family and many friends. Distancing herself from her Mormon past, Mason and Charles Owens founded the Los Angeles branch of the First African Methodist Episcopal Church, which was officially organized in her home. Using her own funds, she paid the church's property taxes and the minister's salary at the AME church but continued to attend the predominately white Fort Street M. E. (Methodist Episcopal) Church, which was located across the street from her home. Mason became a respected businesswoman, midwife, philanthropist, and leader of the African American and general Los Angeles community. Her great-granddaughter, Gladys Owens Smith, recalled that Mason often reminded her that, "If you hold your hand closed . . . nothing good can come in. The open hand is blessed, for it gives in abundance, even as it receives." Bridget "Biddy" Mason died in Los Angeles on January 15, 1891, and was buried in Evergreen Cemetery in the Boyle Heights district.[16]

Archy Lee

Archy Lee, an eighteen-year-old Mississippi slave, who had traveled overland to California with his owner, benefited from a highly organized network of black and white abolitionists who fought for his freedom in the courtroom, in their churches, and on the streets. Lee's owner, Charles Stovall, who claimed he went west "for the benefit of his health" and never intended to make California his permanent home, was blindsided by this politically connected united front and ultimately lost his bid to keep Archy Lee as his slave.[17]

The circumstances under which Stovall and Lee began their trip across the plains together are unclear. The most plausible explanation comes from an 1858 interview with Lee, published in the *Alta California* newspaper, in which he recounted that he had stabbed a white man who tried to kidnap him as he worked at Stovall's mill in Choctaw County, Mississippi. After his encounter with the would-be kidnapper, Lee went into hiding near the mill until Charles Stovall "appeared with a buggy and took him and drove away with him."[18] The two men ferried across the Mississippi River at Memphis and made their way to the plantation of John Carnes in Cape Girardeau County, Missouri. Stovall left his slave there for several months. In court documents, Lee claimed that Stovall's brother William took him from Missouri to Kansas, and then on to the "crossing of the Platte," where they met up with Charles in a Missouri wagon train bound for California. Lee and the Stovall brothers continued with the wagon company, with Lee driving the ox team and cooking for the party.[19] When they reached Carson Valley on Nevada's western border, the exhausted oxen were unable to cross the Sierra. Stovall purchased a 160-acre ranch and remained there with Lee for several months, then pushed on to Sacramento, arriving in October 1857.[20]

Stovall testified in court that he had always planned to return to Mississippi immediately, yet he opened a private school in Sacramento where he taught for several months and hired out Archy Lee for wages, which made up a significant portion of the slaveholder's income. When Lee became ill and could no longer work, Stovall, also in poor health, decided to return to Mississippi and prepared to depart from San Francisco. However, Lee had learned of his rights through his acquaintance with black Sacramentans Charles Hackett and Charles W. Parker, owners of the Hackett House Hotel in downtown Sacramento, and other members of the statewide Colored Convention organization. He resolved to claim his freedom, escaped from Stovall, and went into hiding at the Hackett House. Discovered by police on January 6, 1858, he was arrested for violating the national Fugitive Slave Law that had been in place since 1850.[21]

The next day, Charles Parker obtained a writ of habeas corpus, demanding Lee's release from city prison on the grounds that he had been illegally detained. County Judge Robert Robinson, having received the writ, began the proceedings on January 7, with abolitionists Edwin B. Crocker (brother of railroad magnate Charles Crocker), John H. McKune, and eventually Joseph W. Winans serving as Lee's defense team. The hearing began on January 8, with black and white spectators—many of whom had provided legal and financial assistance for Lee's defense—crowding the courtroom. Stovall's attorney, James H. Hardy, an outspoken proponent of slavery, argued that Lee was property worth $1,500 in Mississippi, and Stovall had every right to his slave. Lee, who could not read or write, was silent during most of his appearances in court, but on January 23, when Judge Robinson once again asked him what his wishes were, he replied, "I don't understand what you are speaking of but I want it to come out right. I *don't* want to go back to Mississippi."[22]

After all the evidence had been presented, on January 26, Judge Robinson ruled that Lee should be freed. No sooner than this decision had been rendered, however, Lee was re-arrested and whisked back to jail because Stovall's lawyers, after a series of complex legal maneuvers, had managed to have the case transferred to the state supreme court. The California supreme court heard lengthy arguments from both sides on February 5, 1858, and six days later, the three justices, two of whom were proslavery, announced their decision. The court held that the state's Fugitive Slave Law applied if the slave owner was only temporarily residing in California. In other words, they considered Stovall a temporary resident and Lee an escaped slave who was not protected under California law. Despite Stovall's lengthy residency in California, the court had ruled in his favor, noting that his youth, poor health, and inexperience with the legal process should not be grounds for forfeiture of his human property. The court ordered Lee to be returned to his master. As several policemen escorted him back to jail, surrounded by an angry crowd, the desperate black man attempted to escape three times.[23]

Stovall made preparations to steam out of San Francisco Bay back to Mississippi via Panama. In the meantime, Archy Lee was taken from Sacramento and placed in the city jail in Stockton. Stovall and Lee left Stockton on March 1, traveling to San Francisco where patrols set up by Negro Convention members were on the wharves, ready to rescue the captive. All "classes of Negroes were involved" in the rescue effort, and the "eyes and ears" of the Negro Convention organization included maritime workers and black businessmen, who closed their offices to participate in the patrols. James Riker, a ship steward and prominent figure in San Francisco's African American community, obtained a writ of habeas corpus, demanding Lee's release from Stovall's control. He also filed a complaint for the slaveholder's arrest on kidnapping charges. As Stovall and Lee were in a rowboat, just about to board the *Orizaba*, black and white antislavery protesters blockaded the steamship and a melee ensued. When Lee was taken into custody and sent to the San Francisco County jail to await trial, his supporters rallied around him once again. San Francisco's Zion AME Church organized a statewide fund-raising campaign that spread across the country to abolitionist centers on the East Coast. After weeks of intense legal arguments in various courts, Lee was freed, then re-arrested and jailed. But finally, on April 6, 1858, U.S. Commissioner George Pen Johnston handed down the final decision: Archy Lee was free. California's last fugitive slave case came to an end on April 14, 1858.[24]

Archy Lee quickly moved out of the country, joining an estimated four hundred African Americans (almost 10 percent of the state's black population) who left California for British Columbia when gold was discovered along the Fraser River in 1858. While in Victoria, Lee ran a successful drayage business and became a property owner. By 1862, after the outbreak of the Civil War, he was back in the United States, working as a barber in Washoe, Nevada, according to the black-owned *Pacific Appeal*. After that, little else is known about his activities. In 1873, newspapers around the state reported that Archy Lee had been found buried up to his neck in the sands along the banks of the American River, seriously ill but refusing help. He was taken to the county hospital in Sacramento where he died.[25]

Jane Elizabeth Manning James

Jane Elizabeth Manning James's struggle to make a place for herself as a free woman in the West did not take place in a courtroom but within a religious community whose teachings sanctioned her subordination solely because of her race, irrespective of her character, conduct, and free status. She, like Biddy Mason, was regarded highly by all who knew her, but unlike Mason, James remained committed to the Mormon Church, even though its doctrines doomed her efforts to secure full inclusion in the faith she had embraced for nearly five decades.

Although her story is one of perseverance, adaptability, and accomplishment, ultimately race and religious dogma prevented her from fulfilling what became her highest aspiration as a black member of a distinctive religious community in the West. Historian Ronald G. Coleman has written that Jane Elizabeth's story "embodies the intersection of religion, race, and gender in the nineteenth century, as well as its implications for the western frontier region." James's western pilgrimage and involvement in the community of Latter-day Saints reveal the unique dilemma confronting many of Utah's black settlers, free and enslaved.[26]

In the fall of 1847, Jane Elizabeth, her husband, Isaac James, and two sons began their trek across the plains from Nauvoo, Illinois, to the Salt Lake valley. They traveled as free people and devout Mormons. Jane Elizabeth Manning, born in 1813 in Wilton, Connecticut, to free parents, Isaac and Phillis Manning, had gone to work as a young girl as a servant in the household of well-to-do Wilton farmer Joseph Flitch. While in Flitch's employ, Jane Elizabeth became pregnant and gave birth to a son, Sylvester, in 1838.[27]

Jane Elizabeth had joined the Presbyterian Church at the age of fourteen, but recalled many years later, "[I]t seemed to me there was something more that I was looking for." Her spiritual void was filled in 1842, when she attended a Mormon missionary service in her area. Convinced that she had heard the "true gospel," she was subsequently baptized and confirmed as a member of the Church of Jesus Christ of Latter-day Saints. In 1843, the newly converted black Saint and several members of her family joined a band of white Mormons who were departing Wilton, bound for the Mormon enclave in Nauvoo, Illinois. The interracial group traveled together via the canals to Buffalo, New York, where the black members ran out of money. When the white members of the party did not come to their aid, the African Americans walked the remaining eight hundred miles of their journey. Once in Nauvoo, Jane Elizabeth was introduced to Mormon prophet Joseph Smith, who asked her to stay on as a servant in his home. Her piety so impressed the family that Smith's wife offered to adopt her. Jane Elizabeth declined, but she regretted her decision years later, saying, "I did not understand or know what it meant. . . . I did not know my own mind. I did not comprehend."[28]

After Joseph Smith was murdered in 1844, Jane Elizabeth worked in Brigham Young's household as a servant. In February 1846, she married Isaac James, a free black Mormon who also lived in Nauvoo. As violence between the Mormons and their non-Mormon neighbors escalated, Jane Elizabeth and Isaac joined the phased exodus of the Latter-day Saints from Nauvoo to the Salt Lake valley. When they started out on the first leg of the trip in the spring of 1846, Jane Elizabeth was pregnant and in June 1846, she gave birth to their son Silas at the James's temporary homesite in Hog Creek (identified in some accounts as Keg Creek), Iowa. One year later, the James family gathered with other Mormon emigrants at a church-directed outfitting post west of Winter Quarters to prepare for the second half of the journey, from the Missouri River to the Salt Lake valley. Isaac, Jane Elizabeth, and the two children joined a Mormon company made up of seventy-six wagons led by Daniel Spencer and Ira Eldredge. The group departed on June 17, 1847, and arrived at their destination on September 19, 1847, the first free African Americans to enter the valley.[29] Jane Elizabeth's autobiography, written in 1893, tended to "minimize the hardships" of the overland trek—the ones that other "Mormon emigrants vividly recall." Ronald Coleman has theorized that she downplayed these things out of a growing concern about how her fellow Mormons would view her and out of concern for her "place in the afterlife."[30]

Jane Elizabeth and Isaac quickly immersed themselves in the routine of setting up a household and caring for their family. In the spring of 1848, they welcomed a daughter, MaryAnn, the first black child born in Utah. By 1860, Jane Elizabeth had given birth to five more children. She and Isaac were also, in the words of Ronald Coleman, "intimately involved in the network of mutuality and reciprocity that characterized the Mormon settlement during the early years in Utah." In difficult times, she received assistance from, and offered it to, her neighbors.[31] No matter how little she had, she could be counted on to share in times of need. Eliza Lyman recalled a particularly hard time when she [Lyman] did not have enough flour to make bread for her family and had "no prospect of getting more till after harvest." Lyman went on to note in her journal that "Jane James, the colored woman let me have two pounds of flour, it being half of what she had."[32]

The James family's circumstances had improved by 1865, however. They now owned land, a home, household items, and some livestock. Isaac's occupation was listed in the Utah federal census as farmer, but from 1849 to 1851 he also worked as a coachman for Brigham Young. Sylvester, the oldest son, was a member of the Nauvoo Legion (the Utah Territorial Militia); in 1865, he owned a musket and ten pounds of ammunition. Jane Elizabeth and Isaac divorced in 1870. Four years later, she entered into a short-lived marriage. Ultimately, these events and the considerable financial demands of her children left her nearly destitute.[33]

Through it all, Jane Elizabeth clung to her religion and continued to ask for the rituals of her faith that would make her eligible to attain the "highest level of the celestial kingdom in the afterlife." The temple ordinances Jane Elizabeth yearned for—and were denied her on account of her race—included the rites of "endowment" that promise faithful Mormons "access to God's presence in the next life," and the ritual "sealing" that binds family members together for eternity. She believed that without these rights, she would be relegated to a lower tier of heaven, away from God, and would have no certainty of sharing the afterlife with her children.[34] For more than a decade, she requested her endowments with the poignant query, "Is there no blessing for me?" In response, church officials extolled her piety, exemplary character, and service to the community, but continued to deny her appeals.[35]

Jane Elizabeth Manning James died in Salt Lake City in 1908 at the age of ninety-five, without ever having fulfilled her most important goal. Seven decades later, when the ban on black men in the Mormon priesthood was lifted, an interracial group of Saints performed the rites that finally bestowed on her the endowments she had sought most of her life. Like Robin Holmes, Biddy Mason, and Archy Lee, she had fought to establish herself as a full and equal member of her western community, but her prolonged and quiet struggle took place in a religious rather than a legal arena, without the support of the community she had helped sustain most of her life.[36]

For Jane Elizabeth Manning James, an African American living in the unique corner of the West known as Utah, and for African Americans residing elsewhere in the West, neither piety, character, hard work, nor perseverance was enough to overcome the prejudices and racial restrictions that plagued black men and women across the country.

Making a Place for Themselves

As African American overlanders fought to establish themselves as free people in the West, they worked to make a place for themselves in western economic, social, and political arenas as well. For most black emigrants, economic stability was the building block for social and political progress, but these three things were inextricably linked. Black westerners therefore battled on three fronts to overturn the obstacles that kept them from these goals.

George W. Bush

George W. Bush, an ardent proponent of American settlement in the contested Oregon Country, believed that western emigration was an act of patriotism, but his primary reason for going west was his desire to escape the racial restrictions that he encountered on a daily basis in his home state of Missouri. Bush's great-granddaughter Emma Belle Bush Twohy stated, "I am not sure why George came west in 1844. As far as I know, he was having a hard time in Missouri. People would not sell him anything because they said he was a Negro. That is probably one reason why he wanted to leave there." He was also, she said, "the roving type of person."[37] Bush, his white wife Isabella, and their five sons traveled as free people, but his trailmate John Minto observed, "it was not in the nature of things that he should be permitted to forget his color."[38]

No place was that more evident than in the Oregon Country, where the Black Exclusion Law had been put in place six months before Bush's arrival. When Bush's company reached The Dalles, on the lower Columbia River, everyone in the party was welcomed—except the Bushes. Undeterred, George decided to bypass the rich Willamette Valley, where most of the whites had settled, and push farther north to Puget Sound, where the exclusion law (which was limited to American settlements south of the Columbia River) did not apply. In October 1845, the Bushes, along with five white families and six single white men, arrived at the Deschutes River falls. Here they established the town of New Market (later renamed Tumwater), the first permanent American settlement on the Puget Sound. Bush built the first gristmill in 1846, and a sawmill in 1847. He also established a thriving farm on 640 acres of land now called "Bush Prairie" at the southernmost tip of Puget Sound.[39]

From the beginning, Bush prospered, but the first years in the new country were hard and left many of his friends and neighbors nearly destitute when the wheat harvest fell short. Renowned for his openheartedness, Bush once again came to their aid, just as he had done on the trail. When speculators offered him an exorbitant price for his entire crop of wheat, he rejected their offer, declaring, "I'll just keep my grain to let my neighbors who have had failures have enough to live on and for seeding their fields in the spring. They have no money to pay your fancy prices and I don't intend to see them want for anything in my power to provide them with."[40]

George and Isabella Bush's friends and neighbors tried to repay their many kindnesses in 1850, when Bush's right to homestead was threatened by the Donation Land Claim Act, which reserved free land exclusively to white settlers. Rallying to his aid, they enlisted the help of the newly established Washington territorial legislature. Members of that body voted on March 18, 1854, to send a petition to Congress, demanding that Bush's land claim be validated. In their petition, the territorial lawmakers noted that the black man had "contributed much towards the settlement of this territory, the suffering and the needy never having applied to him in vain for succor and assistance."[41]

On February 10, 1855, Congress passed "An Act for the Relief of George Bush, of Thurston County, Washington Territory," confirming his right to the land he had homesteaded for nearly a decade. George W. Bush became the beneficiary of special legislation that allowed him to live the life he had crossed the plains to have, but he, like other African Americans, still was not permitted to vote. Overland emigrant Ezra Meeker, whom Bush had befriended when he arrived in the territory in 1853, wrote that "George Bush was an outlaw but not a criminal; he was a true American and yet was without a country; he owned allegiance to the flag and yet the flag would not own him."[42]

George W. Bush died in 1863 at the age of seventy-four, and Isabella passed away three years later. If success can be measured by the "possession of material comfort, economic security and the love and respect of one's family, neighbors and contemporaries," historian Darrell Millner has written, then George W. Bush was a "most successful pioneer." Just as the African American overlander had managed to overcome the "physical, emotional and environmental challenges presented by the trail and the western farming frontier," he also was able "to defeat the additional societal impediments created by racism."[43]

George Washington

Six years after George W. Bush had entered the Oregon Country, George Washington arrived in 1850. Like Bush, his efforts to make a place for himself as a free man in the West were both thwarted and aided by white people.

Washington was born in Frederick County, Virginia, on August 15, 1817, to a slave father and a mother who was "of English descent."[44] He never knew his father, who was sold soon after he was born, and his mother gave him as an infant to James and Anna Cochrane (sometimes spelled Cochran), a white couple who adopted him and raised him as their child. The Cochranes took their adopted son to Ohio and then to Missouri, where as an adult, Washington attempted to go into business for himself. Frustrated by Missouri's black laws, he resolved to head west, and on March 15, 1850, he rolled out of Missouri in a wagon train heading for the Oregon Country, accompanied by James and Anna Cochrane. In a few months, they arrived in Oregon City, where George found employment as a timber cutter. After some time in Oregon City, he pushed across the Columbia River into what would soon become Washington Territory. In 1852, Washington staked a claim, built a cabin, and fenced off and cleared a twelve-acre farm on land situated at the confluence of the Skookumchuck and Chehalis Rivers. Washington was only the fourth settler in the area, but Oregon's black laws prevented African American settlement anywhere in the territory.[45]

Maneuvering around this obstacle, he enlisted the help of his adoptive parents, who filed a claim for 640 acres under the Donation Land Claim Act. Their claim included the twelve acres that Washington had already staked out. When the Cochranes' claim was validated after four years of living on the land, and Washington Territory, which did not ban black land ownership, had been established, the Cochranes deeded the property over to their adopted son. James and Anna Cochrane died several years after that, and George Washington, now an established farmer, married Mary Jane Cooness (perhaps Cornie), a widow who was of African American and Jewish descent. In the 1870s, George and Mary Jane's financial situation was given a boost when the Northern Pacific Railroad, advancing from the Columbia River to Puget Sound, slated the line to cross the Washingtons' land. Seizing the opportunity, George immediately plotted out the town of Centerville on the site, which would become a key point on the railroad between the Columbia River and Puget Sound.[46]

Centerville—its name later changed to Centralia—grew rapidly, and the Washingtons became active and charitable residents of the town they had helped create. The couple donated land to build their Baptist church, established a cemetery, offered no-interest loans to their neighbors, and reserved land for a public square, now called George Washington Park. After Mary Jane's death in 1888, Washington continued his civic involvement. When economic crises devastated the nation in the last decades of the nineteenth century, he organized a private relief program for needy Centralia residents and refused to foreclose on the mortgages he held.[47]

George Washington, who took to the overland trail in search of freedom and opportunity, passed away on August 26, 1905, eleven days after his eighty-eighth birthday. His well-attended funeral was held at the Baptist church he helped build, and he was buried in the cemetery located on the land where he had staked a claim some fifty years earlier.[48]

The Suggs

African American overland emigrants Mary Elizabeth Snelling and William Sugg became civic-minded residents of their gold rush community in Sonora, California, after arriving in the state in 1852. They trekked overland in separate companies, but the two met during a stopover in present-day Merced, California.

Mary Elizabeth Snelling was born in Johnson County, Missouri, on February 4, 1839, but the circumstances of her birth are unclear. Her mother, Julia Snelling, was the slave of William Snelling, and Julia maintained that a member of the Snelling family had fathered her daughter. The white Snellings (and their descendants) denied this account. When twelve-year-old Mary Elizabeth and her mother set out in the Snelling family wagon as part of a California-bound train, they did so as free people.[49]

Mary Elizabeth's grandson, Vernon Sugg McDonald, noted in an interview that his grandmother told him that her trip was difficult. She recalled that the Native people who stopped to trade with the wagon company often mistook her for an Indian child who had been kidnapped by the whites, and they would try to rescue her. The wagon train boss, afraid that Mary Elizabeth's presence would incite violence, ordered Julia to hide the girl when Indians were nearby. Thereafter, an empty sugar barrel roped to the side of the wagon became her hiding place for the rest of the journey. The girl would squat inside the barrel in agony for hours as the wagon jostled over the trail. Understandably, Mary Elizabeth recalled that "I always hated being put in the barrel."[50]

Mary Elizabeth claimed that her company was "never attacked by the Indians, but the two wagon trains just ahead of us had been." She noted that the Natives did not try to steal the horses or oxen, since the livestock was always "kept inside the circle of wagons every night and a heavy guard of armed men was set up each night around the camp." She stated that her party was "more worried while travelling through Utah," since "the Mormons made two attempts to stampede the horses because they were short of these animals. . . . There was a lot of shouting and shooting on two different nights, but the raids were stopped. No one was shot or injured and the horses were saved."[51]

Mary Elizabeth's future husband, William Sugg, had a very different experience on his overland trek to California. His journey began in Raleigh, North Carolina, where he was born a slave on the estate of Francis Trale. When Trale was struck by gold fever, he and his slave set out for Mariposa County. Sugg handled various duties on the trail. In addition to tending to his owner's needs, he worked as a muleteer and bullwhacker, driving his master's wagon. Trale had promised Sugg freedom in exchange for his faithful labor when they arrived in gold country, but unlike the enormous payments slave owners usually demanded from their slaves, Sugg was inexplicably permitted to buy his way out of bondage for just one dollar. His deed of manumission, witnessed and recorded in Tuolumne County, noted that Trale—who signed his name with an X—relinquished ownership of his slave "as an act of benevolence." No mention was made of the fact that California was a free state and did not legally permit slavery.[52]

When William Sugg and fifteen-year-old Mary Elizabeth Snelling met in Merced, Mary Elizabeth and her mother were living on the Snelling ranch there. William and Mary Elizabeth enjoyed a yearlong courtship while attending church and social activities, then moved on to Sonora, where they were married on January 20, 1855. The newlyweds bought a lot on Theall Street and lived in a small cabin on the northeast corner, adjacent to a stable and barnyard owned by the City Hotel.[53] William, a harness maker by trade, opened a business repairing and restoring leather harnesses. He also supported his family by operating a livery stable and a donkey and cart rental business run by the city of Sonora's street-cleaning department. Mary Elizabeth, an accomplished seamstress, contributed to the family income by sewing and giving sewing and quilting lessons to the young women in the community. The Suggs also arranged with the Victoria Hotel and City Hotel to rent out rooms in their house when those hotels were filled. According to Vernon Sugg McDonald, despite the tight quarters in the house, "the matter of economics" made it an absolute necessity. The Sugg House, as it became known, was a particular favorite of the "drummers [traveling salesmen]" who passed through the area. When fire destroyed the house next door to their property, William and Mary Elizabeth purchased the lot and began enlarging their house. The Suggs' home expanded considerably between 1855 and 1876 to accommodate the eleven children who were born there. It was crammed with books, paintings, literary works, and musical instruments.[54]

The Suggs were active in their community, participating in church, social, and political events in the area. William proudly posed for a photograph wearing the regalia of his fraternal organization, the Lion Chapel Sonora Tribe of the G.O.R., of which he was a trustee in the 1850s.[55] William and Mary Elizabeth also fought for equal rights, joining other African Americans to overthrow California's black laws. They backed the Franchise League's spirited but unsuccessful campaign for equal rights and supported the Convention of Colored Citizens of the State of California, which met for the first time in 1855 at Sacramento's St. Andrews AME Church to plan their attack on the state's antitestimony and fugitive slave laws.[56]

The Suggs very likely attended the spectacular antiblack laws political rally, banquet, and fancy-dress ball fund-raiser that took place in the nearby town of Columbia. However, as with so many other African American emigrants, education became the flashpoint in their fight for equal rights, and they joined friends and neighbors who pushed to eliminate segregated public schools. William wrote to the state legislature, protesting the fact that California law barred his children from attending the white school in Sonora, even though the local school board would not establish a school for African American students. William and Mary Elizabeth were also among the signers of a petition to the school board demanding the equalization of the school term for black and white students. The battle for equal education was ongoing in California, but by 1877, the Sugg children were attending the public school in Sonora along with white students.[57]

For reasons unknown, William left his family in 1877, after his last child was born, and moved to Merced, though he continued to operate the harness business for another twenty-two years. He died in 1889 at the age of seventy-one. Mary Elizabeth continued her sewing and quilting lessons and converted the family's three-story, seven-bedroom residence into a boardinghouse, which she operated for the next forty years. Vernon Sugg McDonald recalled that his grandmother was a "strict adherent to the old maxim, 'Church on Sunday, washing on Monday, etc.'" However, her exhausting work routine took its toll when, on a cold fall day, she contracted pneumonia and died on November 19, 1915.[58]

Ben Palmer

The Suggs managed to create an economic and social niche for themselves in the heart of California's gold-mining region, but some black overlanders ended their journey before reaching the western boomtowns. Ben Palmer, who could neither read nor write, became one of the wealthiest men in Nevada's Carson Valley because his overland trek ended before he could get to the goldfields in California. He became a permanent resident of Genoa, Douglas County, near present-day Carson City, and began paving the way for more black settlement in the area.

Ben Palmer, his sister Charlotte, and her white husband, David (D. H.) Barber arrived in Nevada in 1853. Before that, much about him is a mystery. Palmer, whose birthday, birthplace, and early life are in dispute, may have been born in South Carolina in 1817 or in Illinois in the 1820s. Carson Valley historian and anthropologist Grace Dangberg has suggested that he and his sister were Missouri slaves who purchased their freedom. The 1875 Nevada state census identified him as a forty-six-year-old farmer born in Illinois, and Charlotte as a fifty-year-old South Carolina–born woman.[59]

All accounts agree that, in 1853, Ben Palmer joined the ranks of the argonauts who trudged overland to California. He probably departed from Missouri, and his trip across the plains appears to have been a family affair. He may have traveled with Charlotte and David, or the two men may have set out together, with Charlotte joining them later. When they reached the verdant Carson Valley—which was at that time in western Utah Territory—Palmer and David decided to settle there and raise cattle and feed to supply the lucrative market created by the steady stream of emigrants tramping across the Carson Trail. A skilled cattleman and drover, Palmer was the first-known African

American to settle in the valley, and one of a small group of black ranchers residing in Nevada in the nineteenth century.[60]

Palmer staked out 320 acres of choice grassland just south of Genoa, and Charlotte and David Barber settled on 400 acres of equally desirable land adjacent to Palmer's spread. Palmer claimed water rights for his property, and he and David constructed ditches and dams to control the water in the area. The two men employed African American, Native, and white ranch hands to help them run their operations. They did a brisk business selling grazing privileges to the emigrants who drove oxen, horses, mules, and other livestock through the area during the spring and early autumn. Palmer, an accomplished horseman, also raised horses and introduced a rare breed known as the Bonner horse to the area. By 1857, business was booming, and Palmer, needing to replenish his severely depleted livestock herd, drove 1,500 head of cattle from Seattle down to his ranch in Carson Valley. The next year, he was on the trail again, this time driving a large herd north. The local newspaper reported, "Ben Parmer's [sic] cattle—450 head—passed through Genoa last Tuesday on their way to Goose Lake, Oregon."[61] Tax records for 1857 listed Ben Palmer as one of the forty-seven largest taxpayers in Douglas County, with assessed valuations of $5,000 or more, and ranked him tenth in terms of property value. In 1867, the *Virginia City Territorial Enterprise* called him "one of the heaviest taxpayers in Douglas County." Over the next five years, his personal and real estate worth rose considerably.[62]

David Barber's ranch was not as profitable as his brother-in-law's spread, but it continued to yield handsome profits each year. David and Charlotte Barber raised their children on the ranch and enjoyed a close-knit family life. Charlotte, well-known for her hospitality and inquisitive nature, earned the reputation as a "prophetess" in the area. A contemporary recalled that if anyone were to "come by [the Barber ranch] anywhere near noon, you didn't get by. You had to stop and have dinner and they'd find out everything you knew." When David died in 1873, their son Benjamin kept the ranch going for the next three decades.[63]

Ben Palmer's achievements are all the more remarkable given the racist laws legislators put in place for the benefit of "white men."[64] The Nevada territorial legislature ensured that African Americans could not vote, hold office, serve on juries, testify against whites, or join the militia. Schools were restricted to white children, and interracial marriages were outlawed. When Nevada entered the Union in 1864, not much changed; black children were still constitutionally excluded from attending white public schools. But in 1865, African Americans were allowed to give testimony in court under limited conditions. Despite Palmer's economic success, the law prevented him, and all other African Americans—men and women—from voting. This changed in 1870 with the ratification of the Fifteenth Amendment, which gave the franchise to all male citizens of the United States. Palmer's white neighbors held him in such high regard that they invited him to register and vote in the Mottsville precinct, even before the Fifteenth Amendment was ratified. He became, and remained, an officially registered voter from 1876 through 1906. He even entered the political arena in 1878 as a member of the Douglas County central committee, representing the Mottsville precinct for the short-lived Greenback and Workingmen's Party. Palmer also served on the county grand jury and was appointed to the panel of trial jurors for that year's term of the district court.[65]

Charlotte Barber died in 1887; her brother Ben passed away in 1908 at the age of eighty-two. The *Record-Courier*'s eulogy noted that Palmer "met success in every meaning of the word and leaves one of the finest farms in Carson Valley as a monument. He bore a man's part in the battle of life, bore it bravely, gently and without ostentation." He was buried in the Mottsville Cemetery, just south of Genoa, where David and Charlotte Barber and their seven children were also interred.[66]

Ben Palmer blazed the trail for African American settlement in the Carson Valley. By 1860, at least two other black families had joined him there. Sophia Miller, a forty-one-year old Tennessee-born woman, her husband Winfield Miller (also a gifted horseman), and their children homesteaded a ranch in Genoa adjacent to Palmer and Barber. After Winfield passed away in the 1860s, Sophia continued to operate the ranch for many years. The 1870 census valued her real estate holdings at $4,000 and set her personal estate at $1,000. With the Palmers, Barbers, and Millers leading the way, the number of black Nevadans continued to grow through the end of the century.[67]

Clara Brown

Virginia-born Clara Brown (discussed in a previous chapter) could not read or write, but was undaunted by the prospect of trekking west. Family ties played a part in her story of overland emigration as well. Born on January 1, 1800, near Fredericksburg, Virginia, Brown grew up as a slave in Logan County, Kentucky. When her owner, Ambrose Smith, died, thirty-six-year-old Brown, her husband, two daughters, and a son were sold off to settle his estate. Brown herself was sold to a series of owners, including George Brown, who would be her last master. When he died in 1856, Clara was manumitted. She was fifty-six years of age. Forbidden by law to remain in Kentucky as a free woman, she packed her belongings and boarded a flatboat headed for St. Louis, where the heirs of her former owner had arranged for her employment as a servant in the household of Jacob Brunner, a hardware merchant, and his wife, Sarah. Thus began Clara Brown's nearly three-decades-long search for her daughter, Eliza Jane.[68]

The Brunners relocated to Leavenworth, Kansas, in 1857, taking Clara with them. The following year, when the Brunners made plans to go to California, Brown declined to accompany them. She remained in Leavenworth, where she started a successful laundry business. Her plan was to save enough money to travel to newly created Arapahoe County in Colorado, where gold had been discovered in the Pike's Peak area, and where she believed her daughter might be. In the spring of 1859, she packed up everything—including her laundry pots—and, at the age of fifty-nine, she became part of a sixty-person caravan crossing the plains to Denver. She served as the company's laundress and cooked for twenty-six men in the company. For most of the seven-hundred-mile trek, she, like the other overlanders, walked alongside the wagons. The company arrived in Denver (then called Cherry Creek) in June 1859.[69]

By 1860, Clara Brown had established herself as a successful businesswoman in the Denver-area community. Her business skills and investment saavy provided her with an economic independence unknown to most African American women at the time. Six months after arriving in Denver, she relocated to the goldfields in Central

City (Mountain City). There, in 1860, in the Gregory Gulch area, she set up her laundry, purchased a lot, and built a house, paying fifty dollars cash for the property, the first of many she would buy.[70]

Although illiterate, Brown was bright, talented, and always alert for business opportunities. She honed her business skills under the tutelage of two African American overlanders who had arrived in Colorado some time before she had. Lorenzo Bowman, who had been a slave in Missouri and worked in the lead mines there, and Jeremiah Lee, who was probably a free-born Virginian who had lived in Missouri for a time, became her friends and business mentors. Bowman and Lee had become experts in the mining and ore-smelting industry from having worked in Missouri's lead mines. The two had subsequently traveled overland separately to Colorado, where they met and became partners in several real estate and mining enterprises. In 1867, they built and operated the Red, White and Blue Smelting Company in Central City's Leavenworth Gulch district. This venture met with moderate success; that same year, they also started the Red, White and Blue Mining Company, a group of African American miners who operated in nearby Georgetown. Bowman and Lee constructed, owned, and operated the first road over Burrell Hill, the primary road used for many years to transport millions of dollars' worth of ore. Bowman, who died in 1870, and Lee, who died in 1904, were among the wealthiest men in the territory.[71]

Clara Brown's association with the two men was friendly and profitable. It was from them that she learned how to invest her money in mining claims and residential real estate and was able to sell most of her holdings at a profit before the mining and property boom went bust in 1864. By 1865, Brown's business acumen had allowed her to accumulate $10,000, and though she could have led a self-indulgent life of relative ease, she instead chose to invest her efforts on behalf of the community in which she lived. Her home and businesses in Central City became hubs of activity. Her home served as an unofficial hospital where the ill and infirm of all races could recuperate under her care, and she put her midwifery skills at the service of pregnant women in the region. Brown also opened her doors to homeless miners and others seeking a safe, clean place to stay. All of these things were provided free of charge. Her compassion and good will earned her the title "Angel of the Rockies."[72]

Brown, a devout and ecumenical Christian, contributed time, effort, and money to the construction and maintenance of at least four different churches in the Denver and Central City areas. She established a Sunday school in Denver, and after moving to Central City, helped establish the Presbyterian Union Sunday school there. She also donated one hundred dollars to the building fund for the Congregational church in Central City, and contributed fifty dollars when the church was rededicated after being destroyed by fire several years later. She also gave money to the town's only Catholic church, and her two-room log cabin on Lawrence Street, which had once housed her laundry operation, became the first home of Central City's Methodist church. In 1860, she opened her home to weekly Methodist services and became a founding member of the congregation. Her largest financial contribution went to the St. James Methodist Church in Central City.[73]

Clara Brown's philanthropy also extended to former slaves, some of whom were relatives, others friends, but most strangers in need of help. Her efforts helped more than a dozen black families settle in the Denver area. She brought them out of the South by train or wagon caravans at her own expense and boarded many in her own home. During her decades-long search for her daughter, Brown managed to locate twenty-six of her relatives and friends, paying $4,000 to transport them by rail to Leavenworth, Kansas, then overland by wagon train to Colorado.[74]

Eliza Smith Gilmore, a black overlander who was on the trail at the same time, witnessed one of Brown's caravans making its way across the plains. Gilmore, the "daughter of free colored parents of Cleveland, Ohio," recounted in an interview years later that she and her mother had traveled from Kansas City to a "small freighting town in Kansas," where her mother purchased outfitting supplies and hired a driver for their overland trek. Gilmore's mother learned that another wagon train was just ahead of them on the road but was assured that she could overtake them easily since the other wagons "were drawn by oxen" and the Gilmores' wagon used mules. Gilmore recalled the moment her party caught up with the other wagon train on the plains: "It was there we met Aunt Clara Brown, who was bringing her covered wagon with emancipated slaves, at her own expense, from Leavenworth Kansas, back to Central City, Colorado. They brought twenty or thirty people at a time."[75]

This was the first of several black wagon trains that Clara Brown would sponsor. Once the newcomers were settled, Brown assisted them with finding jobs and, in some cases, paid for their education. She and Jackson Smith, a black man whom she had brought from Kentucky in one of her caravans, contributed money for the support of several African American women enrolled at Oberlin College in Ohio. Many of these students had been members of Clara Brown's wagon trains that transported former slaves to Colorado.[76]

Clara Brown's most important quest, however, was to find Eliza Jane, the daughter who had been sold away from her in slavery. In 1879, Brown moved from Central City, which had been her home for twenty years, back to Denver, where she continued her search, offering a reward of $10,000 to anyone who could bring her news of Eliza. The *Denver Republican* reported in 1882 that Brown had received a letter from a "colored woman" in Council Bluffs, Iowa, informing her that her daughter, now Mrs. Eliza Jane Brewer, was living there. Brown was "almost overwhelmed with joy," and telegraphed Eliza that she would meet her in Council Bluffs as soon as she could arrange transportation. By now, Brown's lifelong search, her charitable work, several devastating fires, and financially draining legal problems had taken a heavy toll on her finances, and she was forced to rely on the fund-raising efforts of friends and neighbors to raise the hundred dollars for her train fare.[77]

Clara Brown, eighty-two years old, boarded the train in Denver and once again crossed the plains, arriving in Council Bluffs to be reunited with her fifty-seven-year-old daughter, Eliza Jane, who introduced Clara to a granddaughter she had never met. The *Council Bluffs Nonpareil* reported that when Brown finally saw her "long-lost child," she leapt from the seat of the streetcar in which she had been riding, ran down the sidewalk, and there on the muddy streets, "in an ecstasy of joy mother and child were collapsed in each other's arms." As the two women shared a long, tearful embrace, the "joys and sorrows of a life-time were forgotten, and only the present thought of."[78]

Clara, Eliza, and at least one granddaughter traveled back to Denver. In 1885, three years after their reunion, a reporter from the *Denver Tribune Republican* asked Brown when she had last seen her husband. She replied, "I don't remember just when. He was sold nearly thirty years ago. I don't know where they took him. I had four children, too, darlin.' They sold them too." Eliza Jane was the only child she ever found.[79]

Clara Brown died in her home at 607 Arapahoe Street in Denver in October 1885, surrounded by friends and family members, some of whom she had personally escorted across the plains to freedom in the West.[80]

Barney Ford

When Barney Launcelot Ford arrived in Denver in 1860, Clara Brown was there to give him a hand. Ford made his first attempt to go west in 1851 by the sea-land route during the California gold rush, but after a stay in Nicaragua, he returned to Chicago. In 1860 he set out for the West once more, this time training his sights on Colorado. Selling his Chicago livery business for $2,200, he divided the profits equally with his wife, Julia—who would remain temporarily in Chicago with their two children, Lewis Napoleon and Sadie—and, at the age of thirty-eight, boarded a train bound for the Missouri River. He had intended to take a stagecoach from Fort Leavenworth to Denver, but the stage line refused to transport black passengers, no matter how much money they had. Therefore, Ford waited in Fort Leavenworth to find a Denver-bound wagon company that would accept him. In April 1860, he signed on as a cook in a train of twenty-two wagons, in exchange for transportation to Denver. The majority of the group consisted of pro-slavery white Southerners with whom Ford sometimes clashed. Guiding the train, according to western author Forbes Parkhill, was an experienced frontiersman named Sorepaw Beck, who had led a dozen companies across the plains as far as Oregon. En route, however, Beck suffered a rattlesnake bite and had to be left at Fort Kearny. Thereafter, Ford's company made their way without a guide, until Uriah Coventry was elected wagon boss and the group continued its slow journey over the trail.[81]

When he arrived in Denver on May 18, 1860, Ford found it to be little more than a frontier boomtown filled with log huts and tents, and he quickly moved on to the gold region of Mountain City, where he joined thousands of other gold seekers. Unable to rent a room in any of the makeshift hotels that had sprung up there because he was African American, he sought out Clara Brown, who allowed him to sleep in her woodshed until he could make other arrangements. Ford immediately began prospecting in the Gregory Gulch region, all the while encountering hostility from white miners. Colorado law did not permit African Americans to file mining claims, so Ford hired a white attorney to file on his behalf in exchange for twenty percent of the profits. Instead of honoring the deal, the attorney served Ford with eviction papers and siezed the black man's claim for himself. Ford, who had no legal recourse when his claim was jumped and white miners chased him away from the diggings, moved on to nearby Breckenridge and tried again to prospect at French Gulch, where he met with similar problems.[82]

Undeterred, Ford revised his plans, moving back to Denver—with his wife and children, who had now joined him—where he launched his new career as a businessman, hoping to capitalize on the gold rush boom. Colorado law prohibited African Americans from owning claims, but nothing prevented them from owning real estate. Returning to the skill he had learned in Chicago, Ford bought a building in downtown Denver and opened his first barbershop in 1862. The shop catered to some of the area's leading citizens, who were impressed with Ford's "eloquent speech and worldly knowledge."[83] Barbering offered Ford, and other African Americans, financial independence, and a certain amount of status. By the end of the decade, many other black Denverites had followed in Ford's entrepreneurial footsteps; the 1870 census showed that Denver-area black barbers made up 65 percent of the territory's barbers.[84]

In April 1863, Ford's barbershop was consumed in the great fire that swept through much of Denver, destroying lives and property. But he started over after securing a loan of $9,000 from local banker Luther Kountze, who charged him 25 percent interest. Four months after the fire, Ford opened a new and grander establishment, the People's Restaurant, at 1514 Blake Street in downtown Denver. His new venture included a saloon upstairs and a shaving and hairdressing salon in the basement. It was an immediate hit, and he was able to repay the loan in ninety days. He advertised that his restaurant and other shops would offer customers "the most choice and delicate luxuries of Colorado and the East."[85]

In 1867, Ford traveled to Cheyenne, the capital of Wyoming Territory, to build another restaurant there. The place thrived because of the increased traffic brought to the area by the extension of the railroad. However, in 1870, that restaurant was destroyed by fire. Barney shut down operations and returned to Denver, where he opened several new businesses, including the luxurious Inter-Ocean Hotel, located on the corner of Sixteenth and Blake Streets. A contemporary described the place as the "aristocratic hostelry of Denver." During the last three decades of the nineteenth century, he opened several more businesses, including barbershops, restaurants, and hotels in San Francisco, Breckenridge, and again in Wyoming. Unlike his earlier successes, most of these floundered and folded because of the economic turbulence of the boom-and-bust cycles that wracked the last half of the century. The Inter-Ocean Hotel in Denver and his Restaurant and Chop House in Breckenridge were the most consistently successful of his ventures, earning Ford the nickname "the Black Baron of Colorado."[86]

Barney Ford clearly made an economic place for himself in the West, but he did not rest on economic achievement alone. Ford, like other African Americans, knew that economic success and independence were inextricably linked to civil rights; he therefore joined a group of black Coloradans who led a protracted campaign against Colorado's black laws, which had rapidly begun to replace the territory's earlier race-neutral laws. The most egregious of the racist laws, which limited voting to white males, was enacted in 1864 by the territorial legislature. This was a reversal of the territory's first election law of 1861, which had given the franchise to all males twenty-one or older and extended the franchise to American Indians, who were declared citizens by treaty.[87]

Outraged over the erosion of their rights, black Coloradans initiated an intense petitioning and lobbying effort from 1864 to 1867 that targeted territorial and national politicians. Ford, along with other prominent African Americans, including his brother-in-law and antislavery veteran Henry O. Wagoner, businessman and rancher Edward Sanderlin, and Kentucky-born former slave and orator William Jefferson Hardin, pressed the issue of suffrage. Under their leadership, African Americans in Colorado waged a relentless campaign to block Colorado's admission to statehood until territorial lawmakers constitutionally guaranteed black voting rights. The territorial legislature and the U.S. Congress steadfastly ignored their efforts until January 1867, when Congress passed the Territorial Suffrage Act, which regulated voting in the territories and gave all male residents—excluding Native Americans—the right to vote. As a result, some eight hundred African American men in the West gained the right to vote. For the first time in six years, black men in Colorado cast their ballots in the 1867 municipal elections in Denver and Central City.[88]

With the ratification of the Fourteenth Amendment in 1868, African Americans became citizens with constitutionally recognized rights—in theory at least. Two years later, the ratification of the Fifteenth Amendment ensured voting rights for all male citizens of the United States. When Colorado entered the Union in 1876, its constitution contained no racial restrictions, thanks in large measure to the efforts of African Americans like Ford, Wagoner, Sanderlin, and Hardin.

A little more than a decade after his arrival in Colorado, Barney Ford (and Wagoner, Sanderlin, and Hardin) had become a political force in the state. The Colorado Republican Party's Central Committee selected him to run for a seat in the territorial House of Representatives. His bid, though unsuccessful, was notable; he became the first African American to run for elected office in Colorado. He also had the distinction of being the first black man to serve on a grand jury in the state. Henry O. Wagoner, Ford's brother-in-law and mentor, served as deputy sheriff of Arapaho County, becoming the only one of the group to hold a political office in Colorado. William J. Hardin, a masterful but often intemperate speaker, managed to anger whites with his militancy on the issue of suffrage and other civil rights issues; he also alienated many African Americans with his abrasive and often condescending attitude toward the black community. Moreover, problems in

Hardin's personal life called his character into question. In the late 1870s, as Hardin's political and economic prospects declined and Ford's continued to rise, Hardin left Colorado for Wyoming, where he was elected to the territorial legislature. The first African American to be elected to a legislature in the trans-Missouri West, Hardin served from 1879 to 1882.[89]

Ford continued to be politically connected, but he also immersed himself in the tasks of community building. He and Julia were founding members of the Zion Baptist Church, which opened its doors in the Five Points area of Denver on November 15, 1865. Because he never forgot his years of bondage, the fear of being a fugitive slave, and his work on the Underground Railroad, Ford joined with other members of the community to assist hundreds of former slaves who streamed into Colorado during the Civil War. He cofounded an adult education program that taught freedmen and freedwomen to read and write. This literacy program, the first of its kind in Colorado Territory, undoubtedly held special meaning for Ford, who secretly learned to read when his mother, Phoebe, took a dictionary from her master's home and enlisted the help of a self-taught slave on a neighboring plantation to teach her young son to read. A tireless campaigner for education, Ford was also in the forefront of the campaign to abolish segregated schools.[90]

Barney and Julia Ford relocated to Breckenridge in 1879, but they returned to Denver in 1890. Julia Ford died there of pneumonia nine years later. Three years after his wife's passing, Barney suffered a stroke and died. He was laid to rest in Denver's Riverside Cemetery beside Julia. Barney Ford escaped slavery, trekked the overland trails to the West, and became one of the most powerful and politically active African American men in Colorado. For him, the West became a place where he could, as a free man, build a life for himself and his family as he saw fit. He fought for the rights to which all free people are entitled, and he eased the way for others, just as so many, including black overlander Clara Brown, had done for him. His experiences and activism suggest that, for some African Americans, the West's potential for freedom and opportunity could be unlocked only by remembering the past and building on it. Barney Ford, reflecting on his long, eventful life, declared, "We shall not fail our future by losing our past."[91]

Imagined Possibilities

Black westerners, driven by the desire for economic, political, and social freedom, fought vigorously for suffrage and civil rights. These were the primary goals of all African Americans who traveled the overland trails and were fundamental to their expectations of life in the West. The *Pacific Appeal* championed and reinforced these basic expectations in an editorial that proclaimed: "In California, Oregon and Washington Territory we seldom hear of the outrages that were constantly perpetrated upon our defenseless race."[92]

This is what all African American overlanders sought as they set out on the journey. However, some black emigrants imagined that the West might hold other possibilities as well, possibilities that were rooted in the region's aesthetic qualities, intangible elements that offered their own unique rewards.

Thomas Detter, an African American barber, writer, and correspondent for two black-owned newspapers, the *San Francisco Elevator* and the *Pacific Appeal,* traveled to California from Washington, D.C., in 1852. There he became active in the Colored Convention movement and the fight for equal rights. In 1857, he left California and eventually settled in Elko, Nevada. His reasons for leaving the Golden State are unclear, but the failure of African Americans to overturn the state's antiblack laws after mounting a hard-fought campaign likely contributed to his decision. Detter expressed his disappointment in 1870, writing, "Little did many of us contemplate the reverses and misfortunes California had in reserve for us." After this setback, he traveled throughout California, Nevada, Washington, and Idaho Territory, reporting on the quality of life black people seemed to enjoy in those areas. His reports overflowed with praise for the gains he believed they had made. Reporting on the Idaho boomtown of Bannock City (near Boise), he wrote, "I entertain a very flattering opinion of this country." His dispatches also tended to romanticize the climate and other natural phenomena of the regions he visited, linking these things to black economic success. In May 1868, during a tour of mining communities after a particularly harsh winter, he reported to the *Elevator* from Idaho City that "mountain life" was "romantic" because of the "many sudden changes requiring fortitude and strength," and added, "He who would succeed must not surrender, but fight the battles of life."[93]

African American emigrant Jennie Carter, probably arrived in Nevada County, California, from Louisiana with her first husband, the Reverend Correll (or Corrall), around 1860. She, like Detter, became a popular correspondent for the *San Francisco Elevator*. Writing under the pseudonyms "Ann J. Trask" and "Semper Fidelis," she turned out a series of eclectic letters covering family dynamics, community life, personal observations, politics, and race. Carter's work not only presents a unique gendered analysis of the black western experience but also challenged her readers to view California, the West, and America as, in the words of literary scholar Eric Gardner, "a space inhabited by blackness"—a blackness centered on self-definition.[94]

Carter's writings acknowledge the opportunities that African Americans enjoyed in the West, but also criticized the limitations that denied them equality. She urged her western readers to live by the motto: "civility to all, servility to none." Like Detter, she grounded her racial consciousness in the natural aesthetics of the West, championing its bounty and beauty. In early 1869, reporting on Sacramento's recovery from one of the many floods that periodically devastated the town, she reflected, "Some of the company (thinking of our Granite mountains left behind,) said 'What a sea of mud.' Not so thought I." Urging hard-hit black Sacramentans to "labor on through all discouragements, being weak, yet fainting not by the way," she promised that ultimately they would "have their reward, a beautiful city above the floods. And how it would gladden the hearts of their ancestors in Eastern homes to see the beautiful gardens as I saw them on the 1st day of January, 1869, filled with rose bushes in full bloom."[95]

Carter and Detter used words to extol the West's aesthetic allures, but lithographer and painter Grafton Tyler Brown created visual confirmation of the region's appeal. Brown, who was the first successful African American western artist, rose to fame as a lithographer and landscape painter, yet even his "day-to-day job work" of stock certificates, billheads, and maps, celebrated the area's natural beauty.[96] Although Brown himself was not an overlander, his artistic representations of the West contributed to its attraction for many overlanders, irrespective of race. Curator and Grafton Tyler Brown scholar, Lizzetta LeFalle-Collins, has noted that his art "produced images that illuminate key aspects of the lure of California for African Americans and of the broader dream of the last frontier for all."[97]

Brown was born in 1841 in Harrisburg, Pennsylvania, to free black parents, Thomas and Wilhemina Brown, who were originally from Maryland. Primarily a self-taught artist, he studied with German-born lithographer C. C. Kuchel, who had worked in the lithographic business of noted Philadelphia lithographer P. S. Duval. In 1858, anxious to begin his own career, seventeen-year-old Brown traveled steerage class on a Panama steamer to California, where he hoped to work as a lithographer and cartographer "in the booming economy based on the profits from the gold and silver mines."[98] When the nearly destitute young man arrived in Sacramento, he found a job as a waiter in the restaurant of a local hotel, but continued to refine his artistic skills. When he was twenty, he left Sacramento for San Francisco, armed with a portfolio of his work and found employment as an errand boy in the San Francisco lithography firm of his old mentor, C. C. Kuchel. From 1861 to 1867, Brown was employed by the firm of Kuchel and Dresel, where he quickly advanced to become a sought-after lithographer, producing maps of claims, city boundaries in Nevada Territory, and views of towns and ranches in the San Francisco Bay Area. During this period, his art was "as much a part of the enterprise to develop the Pacific Northwest as any other surveyor or developer." His works both documented and encouraged western settlement and commercialization. In 1867, Brown bought the business where he was employed, renaming it G. T. Brown & Company, and enjoyed considerable success, counting large mining firms and western businessmen among his clientele.[99]

Brown's commercial success as a lithographer provided him the opportunity and means to begin another career as a traveling landscape artist. In the late 1870s or early 1880s, he sold his business, left San Francisco and headed north. His travels took him to Oregon, Washington's Mount Rainier, Yellowstone's Lower Falls, Yosemite, and other parts of the West. His paintings of majestic vistas, towering trees, broad waterways, and exotic flora, portrayed the region as an unspoiled wilderness worthy of preservation, and, as Lizzetta LeFalle-Collins has noted, served the dual purpose of "sharing his experiences in the wilderness and preserving the scenes for future generations."[100]

Grafton Tyler Brown eventually moved on to St. Paul, Minnesota, where he married and worked as a draughtsman for the U.S. Army Engineer's Office. He lived in Minnesota until his death in 1918. His work expressed the "spirit of renewal" and evoked the West's "promise of new beginnings"—themes that undoubtedly resonated deeply with African American emigrants who trekked the overland trails.[101]

African American westerners fought to establish themselves as free people, make economic, political, and social places for themselves, and build communities with institutions that reflected the personhood and self-worth that law and custom tried to erase. They accomplished some of these objectives, but not unconditionally and not without struggle. They battled in courtrooms and in the court of public opinion in every sector of the West in pursuit of these goals. As both slaves and free people, African Americans resolutely challenged laws that denied them freedom and rights. In doing so, they relied on their own individual efforts, on support from their own communities, and often on rallying allies in the white community. Their fight, carried out on multiple fronts, was incremental, generational, and influenced by notions of race, class, and gender. Freedom and opportunity were the principal magnets that pulled them over the trails. But less tangible, sometimes romanticized, and often unquantifiable factors contributed to their expectations of life in the West as well. Enslaved and free, African American men and women undertook the journey filled with imagined possibilities of living in what historian Quintard Taylor has described as the "free air" of the West—a climate capable of nurturing both material well-being and aesthetic fulfillment.[102]

Epilogue

The prospects for our oppressed race is a glorious future. It is for colored men to show themselves equal to the emergency—to fearlessly meet the opponents of justice, and contend for rights and privileges which might withholds from them.
                              Dr. W. H. C. Stephenson, 1866

AFRICAN AMERICANS WHO TRAVELED the overland trails, like their white counterparts, carried with them hopes and fears for the journey, but for reasons rooted in the racial caste system that regulated every aspect of life in nineteenth-century America, blacks and whites diverged significantly in their expectations. The color line in the United States was entrenched, intractable, and pervasive—even on the overland trails—and black men and women, whether enslaved or free, began and ended their trek mindful of the line.

As I discuss earlier, negotiating the trails in pursuit of their goals required African Americans to implement an array of abilities and assume an outlook or consciousness that historian Douglas Daniels has summarized as "travelcraft."[1] The story of African Americans on the overland trails is a study in travelcraft, but it is also a study in perseverance, flexibility, and improvisation. The map and narrative of the California Trail created by African American overlander and cartographer T. H. Jefferson epitomize the notion of travelcraft. Not only did Jefferson apply his knowledge and expertise to accomplish his personal overland trek, but he also meticulously charted, interpreted, and helped demystify the route so that others would be better prepared and more confident about their journey. The map is precise in its calculations and measurements, and the *Accompaniment,* with its warnings and reassurances, underscores the determination and resourcefulness the journey required of all overlanders, irrespective of race.

The black men and women who trekked overland on the California-Oregon Trail, and other routes, assumed a vigilant but hopeful outlook about the journey and employed an array of skills that helped them negotiate a physically and racially treacherous terrain. They began and ended their trip with a self-awareness centered on personhood and value, despite an environment that attempted to strip them of such things. That attitude and skill set are reflected in the work of entrepreneurs like wagon maker Hiram Young and hotel owner Emily Fisher, neither of whom traveled west themselves but who made it possible for others to do so, thus challenging racism in slavery's stronghold. It can be seen in George W. Bush's proficiency on and off the trail, and in the bids for freedom made by the slaves Henry C. Bruce and Bluford, who carefully planned the time and method of their escapes and utilized their knowledge of the landscape to get to "free soil." It is seen as well in the stories of Alvin Coffey, Howard Estes, Daniel Rodgers, Dave Boffman, and the many anonymous black overlanders who willingly trudged west for the opportunity to free themselves and their loved ones—and yet were compelled to create alternate strategies in negotiating the obstacles placed in their paths by greedy and deceitful slave owners.

Although common themes and circumstances are frequently woven through the experiences of African Americans on the trails and in their western communities, black emigrants pursued their goals and confronted obstacles in ways that were unique to their own personal objectives and situations. That is, travelcraft for black overlanders rested on individual effort and individual creativity.[2] Like white travelers, blacks consulted maps, compasses, and guidebooks. But compared with that of their white trailmates, the black overland journey was more open-ended. The desire for opportunity, independence, and security weighed heavily in determining when and where the trail ended for them. Harold Estes, Charles and Nancy Alexander, and George W. Bush represent many other African American overlanders who were determined to push beyond national boundaries if, in the words of Bush, "the rights of a free man" could not be obtained in the United States.[3] The 1858 exodus from California to Victoria, British Columbia, that included Archy Lee emphasized the willingness of African Americans to, as Albert Broussard has written, "swap one western community where they had become dissatisfied for another."[4]

Most African Americans did not leave the country, but channeled their dissatisfaction into political action. In black communities across the West, churches, schools, and voluntary associations served as the staging grounds for these campaigns; African Americans pressed the case for equality in every way they could. In Virginia City, Nevada, Dr. W. H. C. Stephenson, one of a handful of black professionals in the region and an outspoken leader in the campaign for black suffrage, decried the situation in an address to a predominantly white audience at an Emancipation Day program in 1866: "It is for colored men to show themselves equal to the emergency," he said, "to fearlessly meet the opponents of justice, and contend for rights and privileges which might withholds from them." As unrelenting as his words were, they also conveyed optimism about the future of black westerners. Stephenson declared that "the prospects for our oppressed race is a glorious future." But it could not be achieved without concerted, unceasing struggle.[5]

The black men and women who took to the overland trails were long-term optimists. Despite encountering oppression, exploitation, and crushing setbacks, they endured unbearable conditions for themselves, their children, and future generations. But they were neither martyrs nor saints. They were determined pragmatists, willing to adapt or change completely in the pursuit of their geographic and personal goals. Irrespective of race, emigrants perceived the West as both a place and an ideal, but for the African Americans who crossed sweet freedom's plains, scaled mountains, and trudged through deserts, the West also represented a testing ground where it would be determined if they could have a stake in the American dream.[6] Some had their expectations fulfilled, others were disappointed, but all were transformed as soon as they stepped out onto the trail to begin the journey.

The saga of western expansion and settlement has been a touchstone in the history of the United States, reverberating throughout American society and culture. In the standard narrative, African American participation has been minimized and black voices muted for myriad reasons, some of which can be attributed to nineteenth-century racial attitudes and others to the mistaken notion that their small numbers made them peripheral to the story. The accounts examined in this book provide compelling evidence for the centrality of African Americans in the story of overland emigration and western settlement. Their involvement in virtually every phase of this nationally transformative movement, from the bustling jumping-off places to the foundation of western communities, is indisputable. Their experiences and perspectives clarify and enrich our understanding of this tumultuous period in the nation's history.

Notes

Introduction

1. For total emigration numbers of 500,000, see Merrill J. Mattes, *Platte River Road Narratives: A Descriptive Bibliography of Travel over the Great Central Overland Route to Oregon, California, Utah, Colorado, Montana, and Other Western States and Territories, 1812–1866* (Urbana: University of Illinois Press, 1988), 5. Mattes explains his reasons for revising his earlier estimate of 350,000 for the period 1841–66, which was included in his earlier work, *The Great Platte River Road: The Covered Wagon Mainline via Fort Kearny to Fort Laramie*, 2nd ed. (1979; repr., Lincoln: University of Nebraska Press, 1987), especially 22–23. A number of factors contributed to his revision of the 350,000 figure, including broader coverage of emigrant accounts that indicate higher totals, going beyond the numbers shown in the Fort Kearny and Fort Laramie registers to include all probable nonregistrants on both sides of the Platte, and allowing for the probability of higher figures for 1859–66 migrations to Colorado, Nevada, Idaho, and Montana as well as California, Oregon, and Utah. For a more conservative estimate of just over 300,000, see John D. Unruh Jr., *The Plains Across: The Overland Emigrants and the Trans-Mississippi West, 1840–60* (Urbana: University of Illinois Press, 1979), especially table 1 (119), in which Unruh sets the 1848, pre–gold rush emigration subtotals at 18,847; and table 2 (120), in which he sets the 1840–60 grand total at 296,259. He places the total number of overlanders who emigrated to Oregon, California, and Utah from 1840 to 1860 at 315,106. Todd Guenther, in "'Could These Bones Be from a Negro?': Some African American Experiences on the Oregon-California Trail," *Overland Journal* 19, no. 2 (Summer 2001): 45, also uses the 350,000 figure.

2. Archeologist Todd Guenther has stated that the last documented wagon trains rolled through South Pass in present-day Wyoming in 1912. Guenther, "Could These Bones Be from a Negro?" 45.

3. Ibid., 53.

4. Anne F. Hyde, *Empires, Nations, and Families: A History of the North American West, 1800–1860* (Lincoln: University of Nebraska Press, 2011), 1; Albert L. Hurtado, "When Strangers Met: Sex and Gender on Three Frontiers," in Elizabeth Jameson and Susan Armitage, eds., *Writing the Range: Race, Class and Culture in the Women's West* (Norman: University of Oklahoma Press, 1997), 123.

5. See Quintard Taylor, *In Search of the Racial Frontier: African Americans in the American West, 1528–1990* (New York: W. W. Norton, 1998); Albert S. Broussard, *Expectations of Equality: A History of Black Westerners* (Wheeling, Ill.: Harlan Davidson, 2012); Albert S. Broussard, *African American Odyssey: The Stewarts, 1853–1963* (Lawrence: University Press of Kansas, 1998); Quintard Taylor and Shirley Ann Wilson Moore, eds., *African American Women Confront the West, 1600–2000* (Norman: University of Oklahoma Press, 2003); Douglas Flamming, *African Americans in the West* (Santa Barbara, Calif.: ABC-CLIO, 2009); John W. Ravage, *Black Pioneers: Images of the Black Experiences on the North American Frontier* (Salt Lake City: University of Utah Press, 1997); William Loren Katz, *The Black West: A Pictorial History*, 3rd ed. (Seattle: Open Hand, 1987); Douglas Daniels, *Pioneer Urbanites: A Social and Cultural History of Black San Francisco* (Philadelphia: Temple University Press, 1980); Rudolph M. Lapp, *Blacks in Gold Rush California* (New Haven: Yale University Press, 1977); Jack Forbes, *African Americans in the Far West: A Handbook for Educators* (Berkeley, Calif.: Far West Laboratory for Educational Research and Development, 1970).

6. The location of the American West has been a subject of intense debate among historians who have attempted to define it as a process of the movement of the frontier, a clearly defined region, or a combination of the two. The West, as a target of settlement, has moved across the continent for more than three hundred years, starting from "just outside the stockades of colonial villages to the flatboats and steamboats of the Ohio and Mississippi valleys to the great cities of the Pacific Coast." All of these areas had their moment as the "frontier." However, the West and frontier are not synonymous, and not all westbound emigrants started out from the East. Long before the great migrations of the mid-nineteenth century, Spanish explorers and settlers moved northward from Mexico, and French settlers and fur traders traveled southward from Canada to reach the West. See Hyde, *Empires, Nations, and Families,* especially 11–15. For the ongoing debate about the American West as region or process, see Patricia Nelson Limerick, *The Legacy of Conquest: The Unbroken Past of the American West* (New York: W. W. Norton, 1987); Richard White, *It's Your Misfortune and None of My Own: A New History of the American West* (Norman: University of Oklahoma Press, 1991); Walter Nugent, "Western History, New and Not So New," *OAH Magazine of History* 9, no. 1 (Fall 1994): 5–9; Donald Worster, "New West, True West: Interpreting the Region's History," *Western Historical Quarterly Quarterly* 18, no. 2 (April 1987): 141–56; Gerald Thompson, "Another Look at Frontier versus Western Historiography," *Montana The Magazine of Western History* 40, no. 3 (Summer 1990): 68–71. For the quote regarding the American West, see Walter Nugent, *Dictionary of American History,* s.v. "West, American," *Encyclopedia.com*, http://www.encyclopedia.com (accessed February 8, 2013). See also Walter Nugent, *Into the West: The Story of Its People* (New York: Vintage Books, 1999), 8–9; Taylor, *In Search of the Racial Frontier,* 53.

7. For examples of numbers of unidentified African American overlanders, see Stanley B. Kimball, *Historic Resource Study: Mormon Pioneer National Historic Trail* (Denver: Denver Service Center, National Park Service, 1991), 6; Lapp, *Blacks in Gold Rush California*, 25–26; Taylor, *In Search of the Racial Frontier,* 83.

8. Daniels, *Pioneer Urbanites*, 59, 62–74.

9. Delilah Beasley, *The Negro Trail Blazers of California* (Los Angeles: University of California Press, 1919); Kenneth Wiggins Porter, ed., *The Negro on the American Frontier* (New York: Arno Press and the *New York Times,* 1971); W. Sherman Savage, "The Negro in the Westward Movement," *Journal of Negro History* 24, no. 4 (October 1940): 531–39, and "The Negro in the History of the Pacific Northwest," *Journal of Negro History* 13, no. 3 (July 1928): 255–64; Sue Bailey Thurman, *Pioneers of Negro Origin in California* (1949; repr., San Francisco: A and E Research Associates, 1971).

10. Forbes, *African Americans in the Far West*; Katz, *The Black West*; Lapp, *Blacks in Gold Rush California;* James Fisher, "A History of the Political and Social Development of the Black Community in California, 1850–1950" (Ph.D. diss., State University of New York, Stony Brook, 1971); John W. Ravage, *Black Pioneers: Images of the Black Experiences on the North American Frontier* (Salt Lake City: University of Utah Press, 1997); Lawrence B. de Graaf, "Recognition, Racism, and Reflections on the Writing of Western Black History," *Pacific Historical Review* 44, no. 1 (February 1975): 22–51; and Taylor, *In Search of the Racial Frontier.* See also Taylor and Moore, *African American Women Confront the West*; Hyde, *Empires, Nations, and Families*; Unruh, *The Plains Across*; Mattes, *Platte River Road Narratives*; Dale L. Morgan, ed., *Overland in 1846: Diaries and Letters of the California-Oregon Trail,* 2 vols. (Lincoln: University of Nebraska Press, 1963); Will Bagley, *So Rugged and Mountainous: Blazing the Trails to Oregon and California, 1812–1848* (Norman: University of Oklahoma, 2010); Will Bagley, *With Golden Visions Bright before Them: Trails to the Mining West, 1849–1852* (Norman: University of Oklahoma Press, 2012); William H. Leckie and Shirley A. Leckie, *The Buffalo Soldiers: A Narrative of the Black Cavalry in the West* (Norman: University of Oklahoma Press, 2003); Richard V. Francaviglia, *Mapping and Imagination in the Great Basin: A Cartographic History* (Reno: University of Nevada Press, 2005).

Chapter 1

Epigraph 1. Pedro de Castañeda, *The Narrative of the Expedition of Coronado,* quoted in Carroll L. Riley, "Blacks in the Early Southwest," *Ethnohistory* 19, no. 3 (Summer 1972): 251.

Epigraph 2. James P. Beckwourth, *The Life and Adventures of James P. Beckwourth, As Told to Thomas D. Bonner* (1856; repr., Lincoln: University of Nebraska Press, 1972), 51–52.

1. For an overview of the early African presence, see Taylor, *In Search of the Racial Frontier,* 27–37; Katz, *The Black West,* 1–34; Broussard, *Expectations of Equality,* 1–8.

2. Hyde, *Empires, Nations, and Families,* 17 (for quote), 97–132, 270–75.

3. Taylor, *In Search of the Racial Frontier,* 28–29. Esteban, a native of Azamor, on the Atlantic shore of Morocco, was also known as Estevanico, Estevan, Estebanico, Black Stephen, and Stephen the Moor. See Donald E. Chipman, "Estevanico," *Handbook of Texas Online,* published by the Texas State Historical Association, http://www.tshaonline.org/handbook/online/articles/fes08 (accessed January 3, 2012).

4. A. D. F. Bandelier, ed., *The Journey of Álvar Núñez Cabeza de Vaca* (New York: A. S. Barnes, 1905), 52–54, 65; Taylor, *In Search of the Racial Frontier,* 27–28; Broussard, *Expectations of Equality,* 1–2; Richard Flint and Shirley Cushing Flint, "Dorantes, Esteban de," New Mexico Office of the State Historian, http://www.newmexicohistory.org/filedetails.php?fileID=464 (accessed March 2, 2013).

5. Ramón A. Gutiérrez, *When Jesus Came, the Corn Mothers Went Away: Marriage, Sexuality, and Power in New Mexico, 1500–1846* (Stanford, Calif: Stanford University Press 1991), 39–40. See also Riley, "Blacks in the Early Southwest," 247–52; Flint and Flint, "Dorantes, Esteban de"; Taylor, *In Search of the Racial Frontier,* 28–29.

6. Taylor, *In Search of the Racial Frontier,* 27–43; George P. Morehouse, "Padilla and the Old Monument near Council Grove," *Kansas Historical Collections* 10 (1908): 472–79; Riley, "Blacks in the Early Southwest," 253–58. See also "Isabel de Olvera Arrives in New Mexico," in Taylor and Moore, eds., *African American Women Confront the West,* 31; Dedra S. McDonald, "To Be Black and Female," in Taylor and Moore, eds., *African American Women Confront the West,* 32–52; Rick Moss, "Not Quite Paradise: The Development of the African American Community in Los Angeles through 1950," *California History* 75, no. 3 (Fall 1996): 222–24.

7. McDonald, "To Be Black and Female," 35. See Lonnie Bunch III, *Black Angelenos: The Afro-American in Los Angeles, 1850–1950* (Los Angeles: Afro-American Museum, 1988), 10–12.

8. For a discussion of the 1781 expedition, see McDonald, "To Be Black and Female," 40–41; Moss, "Not Quite Paradise," 223. The twelve families who participated included forty-year-old *mulata* Maria Petra Rubio and her husband, Luis Quintero, a fifty-five-year-old black tailor and their five children; Maria Guadalupe Gertrudis, nineteen, and her husband, José Moreno, twenty-two, who were *mulatos*; *mulato* newlyweds Maria Tomasa, twenty-four, and her husband, Manuel Camero, thirty; Ana Gertrudis Lopez, the twenty-seven-year-old *mulata* wife of Antonio Mesa, thirty-eight, a "*negro*," and their two children; Maria Manuela

Calixtra, a forty-three-year-old *mulata* mother of six and her Indian husband, Basilia Rosas, sixty-seven; and Maria Rufina Dorotea, a forty-five-year-old *mulata* mother of three and her *mestizo* husband, José Antonio Navarro, age forty-two. See Bunch, *Black Angelenos*, 10–12.

9. Broussard, *Expectations of Equality*, 2.

10. McDonald, "To Be Black and Female," 32. McDonald notes that de Olvera was not the only African-descended woman from New Spain to petition the courts for legal rights. See especially, 50n 2.

11. Ibid., 43–48.

12. For the quote, see Darrell Millner, "York," The Black Past: An Online Reference Guide to African American History, BlackPast.org, http://www.blackpast.org/?q=aaw/york (accessed September 18, 2010); Darrell Millner, "York of the Corps of Discovery: Interpretations of York's Character and His Role in the Lewis and Clark Expedition," *Oregon Historical Quarterly* (Fall 2003): 2–25, http://www.historycooperative.org/journals/ohq/104.3/millner.html (accessed September 18, 2010).

13. Millner, "York"; Millner, "York of the Corps of Discovery," 2–25; Taylor, *In Search of the Racial Frontier*, 48–49. Ethnologist John C. Ewers has written that the black man Leonard met in the Crow village was not York, but Edward Rose, a black trapper and mountain man who was a member of Manuel Lisa's 1807 expedition to the West. Rose was a trapper, explorer, and interpreter who became a "leader of influence" among the Crows. See Zenas Leonard, *The Adventures of Zenas Leonard Fur Trader*, John C. Ewers, ed. (Norman: University of Oklahoma Press, 1959), 52.

14. For a discussion of the mixed lineages of fur traders and trappers, see Hyde, *Empires, Nations and Families*, especially 100–104; Robert M. Utley, *A Life Wild and Perilous: Mountain Men and the Paths to the Pacific* (New York: Henry Holt, 1997), xiv, 12–20, 86–89; Harvey Lewis Carter and Marcia Carpenter Spencer, "Stereotypes of the Mountain Men," *Western Historical Quarterly* 6, no. 1 (January 1975): 17–32. See also LeRoy R. Hafen, ed., *Trappers of the Far West: Sixteen Biographical Sketches* (Lincoln: University of Nebraska Press, rev. 1983), xiv–xv.

15. Taylor, *In Search of the Racial Frontier*, 48–52; Katz, *The Black West*, 26–28; Donald Grinde Jr., "Rose, Edward (c. 1780–c. 1833)," The Black Past, An Online Reference Guide to African American History, BlackPast.org, http://www.blackpast.org/?q=aaw/rose-edward-c1780-c-1833 (accessed March 8, 2013).

16. Utley, *A Life Wild and Perilous*, 27.

17. Keemle is quoted in Utley, *A Life Wild and Perilous*, 59.

18. Taylor, *In Search of the Racial Frontier*, 49–50. See also Leonard, *The Adventures of Zenas Leonard*, 51–52, 139. Leonard wrote that the black man he met in the Crow village claimed to have accompanied the Lewis and Clark

Expedition, spoke the Crow language, and served as an interpreter in business transactions. He noted that the man lived in "perfect peace and satisfaction, and has everything that he desires at his own command." See also Kerry R. Oman, "Winter in the Rockies: Winter Quarters of the Mountain Men," *Montana The Magazine of Western History* 52, no. 1 (Spring 2002): 43.

19. See Taylor, *In Search of the Racial Frontier,* 49–50, for an account of Rose's encounter with the 1811 overland Astorian Expedition that entered the Absaroka camp on the Powder River in present-day Wyoming. See also Utley, *A Life Wild and Perilous,* 27; Katz, *The Black West,* 26–28; Grinde, "Rose, Edward."

20. Grinde, "Rose, Edward."

21. Ronald Coleman, "A History of Blacks in Utah" (Ph.D. diss., University of Utah, 1980), 28–29; Peter Ranne's surname is sometimes written Raney. See Lapp, *Blacks in Gold Rush* California, 6; Broussard, *Expectations of Equality,* 18. John Reid, "Peter Ranne of the Jedediah Strong Smith Party," *One: The Online Nevada Encyclopedia,* http://www.onlinenevada.org/peter_ranne_of_the_jedediah_strong_smith_party (accessed March 7, 2013); Maurice Isserman, *Exploring North America, 1800–1900* (New York: Chelsea House, 2010), 56–58.

22. Coleman, "A History of Blacks in Utah" 29; Utley, *A Life Wild and Perilous,* 94–96; Reid, "Peter Ranne of the Jedediah Strong Smith Party."

23. James Beckwourth adopted a variation of his father's surname, but also used Beckwith and Beckwoth.

24. Delmont R. Oswald, "James P. Beckwourth," *Trappers of the Far West,* ed. LeRoy R. Hafen (Lincoln: University of Nebraska Press, 1983), 162–64; National Park Service, "James P. Beckwourth, Black Mountain Man," Stories of Exploration, Stories to Be Told: African American History in Your National Parks, http://www.nps.gov/untold/banners_and_backgrounds/adventurbanner/adventurestories/beckwourth.htm (accessed December 19, 2008).

25. National Park Service "James Beckwourth," 1; Taylor, *In Search of the Racial Frontier,* 50; Savage, *Black Pioneers,* 11–13.

26. National Park Service, "James Beckwourth"; Bagley, *So Rugged and Mountainous,* 51.

27. Taylor, *In Search of the Racial Frontier,* 50.

28. Elinor Wilson, *Jim Beckwourth: Black Mountain Man and War Chief of the Crows* (Norman: University of Oklahoma Press, repr. 1988), 3–10.

29. Beckwourth, *The Life and Adventures of James P. Beckwourth*; Taylor, *In Search of the Racial Frontier,* 51. Broussard, *Expectations of Equality,* 18; Flamming, *African Americans in the West,* 31–34.

30. Established in 1851, the Beckwourth Trail split off from the Truckee Route at today's Sparks, Nevada, and continued into California through present-day Lassen, Plumas, Butte, and Yuba Counties. See the National Park Service, "James P. Beckwourth"; Andrew Hammond and Joanne Hammond, "Mapping the

Beckwourth Trail," *Overland Journal* 12, no. 3 (1994): 15; Andrew Hammond and Joanne Hammond, *Following the Beckwourth Trail: A Guide to the 1851 Emigrant Trail and to the Route Markers Placed by Trails West, Inc.* (1994; repr., self-published, 1999).

31. National Park Service, "James P. Beckwourth," 1; Oswald, "James P. Beckwourth," 181; Wilson, *Jim Beckwourth*, 134–35.

32. For Beckwourth's recollections of his ranch, see Beckwourth, *Life and Adventures of James P. Beckwourth*, 519–23. See also Wilson, *Jim Beckwourth*, 147.

33. Beckwourth, *Life and Adventures of James P. Beckwourth*, 226.

34. Henry Taylor, quoted in Hammond and Hammond, "Mapping the Beckwourth Trail," 10.

35. Taylor, *In Search of the Racial Frontier*, 51; Broussard, *Expectations of Equality*, 18; National Park Service, "James P. Beckwourth," 2.

36. Dale Morgan, *Jedediah Smith and the Opening of the West* (1953; repr., Lincoln: University of Nebraska Press, 1964), 218; Elizabeth McLagan, *A Peculiar Paradise: A History of Blacks in Oregon, 1788–1940* (Portland, Ore.: Georgian Press, 1980), 14–15; Vern Bright, "Black Harris, Mountain Man, Teller of Tales," *Oregon Historical Quarterly* 52, no. 1 (March 1951): 7.

37. James Clyman, "James Clyman: His Diaries and Reminiscences (continued from Vol. IV, No. 2)," ed. Charles Camp, *California Historical Society Quarterly* 4, no. 3 (September 1925): 279. In his autobiography, Beckwourth describes meeting "'two white men,' Black Harris and my old friend Portuleuse" on a hunting and trapping expedition to the Sage River. See Beckwourth, *Life and Adventures of James P. Beckwourth*, 100. W. H. Gray is quoted in Bright, "Black Harris," 7.

38. For Alfred Jacob Miller's description of Harris, see Marvin C. Ross, ed., *The West of Alfred Jacob Miller (1837), From the Notes and Water Colors of the Walters Art Gallery* (Norman: University of Oklahoma Press, 1951), 67. Miller's painting of Harris was part of the artist's "Trappers" series, watercolor works done in 1837, which now hang in the Walters Art Gallery, Baltimore, Maryland. Also see Morgan, *Jedediah Smith*, 218; and Bernard J. Reid, *Overland to California with the Pioneer Line: The Gold Rush Diary of Bernard J. Reid*, ed. Mary McDougall Gordon (Stanford: Stanford University Press, 1983), 195, for a brief discussion of the painting. British-born adventurer and writer George Frederick Ruxton wrote a series of highly romanticized and fanciful articles about life in the American West for *Blackwood's Magazine* in the 1840s. In one of the articles, a contemporary of Harris's claims that the mountain man, who was known for spinning tall tales, says of himself, "this niggur's no traveler. I ar'a trapper, marm, a mountain-man." He also refers to himself as a "coon." Ruxton's crude depiction of Harris as an uncouth, unlettered buffoon sharply contrasts with the literacy and

eloquence demonstrated in Harris's letter to the *Oregon Spectator* in 1846. See George Frederick Ruxton, *Life in the Far West*, ed. LeRoy R. Hafen (Norman: University of Oklahoma Press, 1951), 7; Jerome Peltier, "Moses 'Black' Harris," 106, in *The Mountain Men and the Fur Trade of the Far West*, vol. 4, LeRoy R. Hafen, ed. (Glendale, Calif.: Arthur Clark, 1966), 103–17.

It is possible that some black frontiersmen may have identified themselves as "white" to differentiate between Natives and non-Natives. This seems to have been the case of noted black fur trader, Native language specialist, and prosperous Minnesota businessman George Bonga. Bonga, the son of a black father and Ojibwe mother, was born in 1802 near the present-day city of Duluth. He is believed to have been the first African American born in Minnesota. He was educated in Montreal, Canada, and returned to Minnesota to work in the family fur business. He served as an interpreter during Indian-U.S. treaty negotiations in 1820 and 1868, worked for the American Fur Company before establishing his own trading post, and enjoyed a prosperous life in Minnesota. In 1858, Judge Charles E. Flandreau (who later served on the Minnesota supreme court) spent two weeks as Bonga's houseguest. Flandreau described him as "the blackest man I ever saw," but reported that Bonga astonished his guests by proclaiming, "Gentlemen, I assure you that John Banfil [member of Minnesota's first state legislature] and myself were the first two white men that ever came into this country [Minnesota]." See Katz, *The Black West*, 28–30.

39. Clyman's tribute to Harris reads, "Here lies the bones of old Black Harris/who often traveled beyond the far west/and for the freedom of Equal rights/he crossed the snowy mountain Hights/was free and easy kind of soul/Especially with a Belly full." See Clyman, "James Clyman," 283.

40. Trekking back to St. Louis in January 1827, Harris and fellow trapper William Sublette are reported to have carved their names on the striking geological formation that became known as Independence Rock. In fact, he was likely one of the trappers in Sublette's company who, on July 4, 1830, bestowed the name on that iconic overland trail landmark. Morgan, *Jedediah Smith*, 219; Barton H. Barbour, *Jedediah Smith: No Ordinary Mountain Man* (Norman: University of Oklahoma Press, 2009), 91; Oregon-California Trails Association, "Virtual Tour, Independence Rock," http://www.octa-trails.org/learn/virtual_trail/virtual_tour/independence_rock/index.php (accessed August 19, 2010); Clackamas Heritage Partners, Historic Oregon City Presents: End of the Oregon Trail Interpretive Center, "Black Pioneers and Settlers—Moses 'Black' Harris,'" http://www.historicoregoncity.org/HOC/index.php?option=com_content&view=article&i (accessed December 29, 2008); Moses Mountain Man website, "Moses 'Black' Harris," http://home.att.net/~mman/HarrisMoses.htm (accessed December 19, 2008); McLagan, *Peculiar Paradise*, 15; Mattes, *The Great Platte River Road*, 502.

41. Clyman, "James Clyman," 279; Reid, *Overland to California*, 195; Thornton Grimsley to "Honorable John Bell, Secty. Of War, 16 April 1841," in "Colonel Grimsley's Proposed Expedition to Oregon, in 1841," ed. T. C. Elliott, *Quarterly of the Oregon Historical Society* 24, no. 4 (December 1923): 434–35; Grimsley to Bell, June 16, 1841, "Colonel Grimsley's Proposed Expedition," 438.

42. For the Bush-Simmons party joining Gilliam, see David Dary, *The Oregon Trail: An American Saga* (New York: Oxford University Press, 2004), 111–15, 120; National Park Service, "George Washington Bush and the Human Spirit." For the African American members of the party, see McLaglan, *Peculiar Paradise*, 15.

43. Clyman, "James Clyman," 281–82; McLaglan, *Peculiar Paradise*, 15–16. In June 1847, a Utah-bound advance party of Mormon emigrants (George A. Smith, John Brown, Heber C. Kimball, and Orson Pratt) encountered Harris guiding an eight-man pack party from Oregon, just west of South Pass on the Dry Sandy River. The Mormons consulted Harris about their destination in the Valley of the Great Salt Lake, inquiring about the suitability of the area. To their dismay, he informed them that the region was barren, sandy, and devoid of timber and usable vegetation. See Kimball, *Historic Resource Study*, chapter 5.

44. Kimball, *Historic Resource Study*, 17; Mary McDougall Gordon, "Overland to California in 1849: A Neglected Commercial Enterprise," *Pacific Historical Review* 52, no. 1 (February 1983): 17–36. See especially 22 for Moses "Black" Harris serving as the pilot for the expedition. The $200 fee charged by the Pioneer Lines is the 2014 equivalent of $6,390. "Measuring Worth," based on the 2014 Consumer Price Index (CPI). The comparative prices are based on the CPI, which calculates the cost of things that the average household buys, such as food, housing, transportation, medical services, etc., for the historic year in question as compared with the CPI in the present day. The CPI is the most useful measure when comparing the historical costs of consumer goods and services, etc., with those of today. The present-day money equivalencies given in this book are approximations based on the most recent (2014) calculations. See "Measuring Worth: Purchasing Power of Money in the United States, 1774 to Present," http://www.measuringworth.com/ppowerus/ (accessed September 7, 2015). Hereafter referred to as "Measuring Worth," CPI 2014.

45. For the "Gerald" letter, see Reid, *Overland to California*, 195. A reprint of the "Gerald" letter is also found in Hafen, *The Mountain Men and the Fur Trade of the Far West*, vol. 4, 117.

46. Hyde, *Empires, Nations, and Families*, 167.

47. In contrast to the United States, the territories held by Spain and Mexico constructed an elaborate system of racial classification.The Spanish "*Sistema de Castas*" (System of Castes) was a hierarchy of more than forty racial classifications (*castizo, morisco, mestizo, mulatto, indio, negro,* etc.) designed to delineate

degrees of whiteness. For social and political purposes *negro* (black) was the least desirable, while *español* (Spanish) was the most desirable. Under this system, people of African ancestry were vulnerable to enslavement, exploitation, and marginalization, but still might achieve a measure of social and economic mobility. African American history curator Rick Moss has observed that the type of rigid social discrimination based on race that had emerged in the United States "failed to take root in the complex multiracial society" of the Spanish and Mexican territories of the West. With the American takeover of the Mexican holdings in the mid-nineteenth century, however, the relative social fluidity enjoyed by people of color ended. See Herbert G. Ruffin II, "*Sistema de Castas* (1500s–ca. 1829)," The Black Past: An Online Reference Guide to African American History, BlackPast.org, http://www.blackpast.org/?q=aaw/sistema-de-castas-1500s-ca-1829 (accessed July 4, 2011); Taylor, *In Search of the Racial Frontier*, 37–48; McDonald, "To Be Black and Female," 35–49; Moss, "Not Quite Paradise," 225.

Chapter 2

Epigraph 1. *African Observer* newspaper editorial quoted in Carol Wilson, *Freedom at Risk: The Kidnapping of Free Blacks in America, 1780–1865* (Lexington: University Press of Kentucky, 1994), 118.

Epigraph 2. John Malvin, *Autobiography of John Malvin: A Narrative Containing an Authentic Account of His Fifty Years' Struggle in the State of Ohio in Behalf of the American Slave, and the Equal Rights of All Men before the Law without Reference to Race or Color; Forty-Seven Years of Said Time Being Expended in the City of Cleveland* (Cleveland: Leader Printing Company, 146 Superior Street, 1879), 11–12.

Epigraph 3. Clarke's remarks published in *The Anti-Slavery Standard*, October 20 and 27, 1842, ed. Lydia Maria Francis Child, reprinted in "Documenting the American South," University of North Carolina, Chapel Hill, online library, http://docsouth.unc.edu/neh/clarke/support1.html (accessed March 25, 2013). See also John W. Blassingame, *Slave Testimony: Two Centuries of Letters, Speeches, Interviews, and Autobiographies* (Baton Rouge: Louisiana State University Press, 1977), 152.

1. For a detailed discussion of the distinctions white American colonists drew between themselves as "*Englishe*" and blacks as "Negroes," see Winthrop D. Jordan, "Modern Tensions and the Origins of American Slavery," *Journal of Southern History* 28, no. 1 (February 1962): 22.

2. Jordan, "Modern Tensions," 22–23. Jordan notes that the John Punch incident of 1640 was the first "definite indication of outright enslavement" in any English colony. In this case, the General Court of Virginia punished an interracial group of indentured servants who had run away and were recaptured. The

two white men were ordered to serve their masters for an additional year, and the colony for three more. John Punch, the black runaway in the group, was sentenced to "serve his said master or his assigns for the time of his natural life." Later that same year in Virginia, a band of seven runaways was apprehended. This time, six white men in the group were sentenced to additional years of service, but the lone black man in the party received none. Jordan speculates this was because he was already serving for life. See Winthrop Jordan, *White over Black: American Attitudes toward the Negro, 1550–1812* (Chapel Hill: University of North Carolina Press: 1968), 75. For the status of blacks in the early British colonies, see Darlene Clark Hine, William C. Hine, and Stanley Harrold, *The African American Odyssey*, combined vol., 4th ed. (Upper Saddle River, N.J.: Pearson, 2008), 53–54 and 59, for the account of John Punch and the treatment of black and white runaways. Also see John Hope Franklin and Alfred A. Moss Jr., *From Slavery to Freedom: A History of African Americans,* 7th ed. (New York: McGraw Hill, 1994), 56–61; Russell R. Menard, *Migrants, Servants and Slaves: Unfree Labor in Colonial British America* (Aldershot, U.K.: Ashgate, 2001); Warren M. Billings, "The Case of Fernando and Elizabeth Key: A Note on the Status of Blacks in Seventeenth-Century Virginia," *William and Mary Quarterly,* 3d Series, 30, no. 3 (July 1973):467–74.

3. Theresa Zackodnik, "Fixing the Color Line: The Mulatto, Southern Courts, and Racial Identity," *American Quarterly* 53, no. 3 (September 2001): 420–51, especially 420–30, 432, 433 (for quote), and 448n26.

4. Victoria E. Bynum, "'White Negroes' in Segregated Mississippi: Miscegenation, Racial Identity, and the Law," *Journal of Southern History* 64, no. 2 (May 1998): 247–76, especially 266; and Walter Johnson, "The Slave Trader, the White Slave, and the Politics of Racial Determination in the 1850s," *Journal of American History* 87, no. 1 (June 2000): 21–25; David A. Hollinger, "Amalgamation and Hypodescent: The Question of Ethnoracial Mixture in the History of the United States," *American Historical Review* 108, no. 5 (December 2003): 1363–90, see especially, 1368–70.

5. Jordan, *White over Black,* 248–59; Nicholas Hudson, "Nation to 'Race': The Origin of Racial Classification in Eighteenth-Century Thought," *American Society for Eighteenth Century Studies* 29, no. 3 (Spring 1996): 247–64, especially 252–58; Johnson, "Slave Trader," 13–38, especially 16–17; Ruffin II, "*Sistema de Castas* (1500s–ca. 1829)."

6. Lydia Maria Francis Child, ed. "Lewis Clark[e], Leaves from a Slave's Journal of Life," *Anti-Slavery Standard,* October 20 and 27, 1842, 78–79, 83, http://docsouth.unc.edu/neh/clarke/support1.html (accessed March 25, 2013).

7. Jordan, *White over Black,* 44–98; Hudson, "Nation to Race," 248–53; and Zackodnik, "Fixing the Color Line, 420–30, 432–33, 448n26, 451n90. See also Bynum, "White Negroes," 266; Johnson, "The Slave Trader, the White Slave," 21–25.

8. Kenneth M. Stampp, *The Peculiar Institution: Slavery in the Ante-Bellum South* (New York: Vintage Books, 1956), especially 34–85; Eugene

Genovese, *Roll, Jordan, Roll: The World the Slaves Made* (New York: Vintage Books, 1976), see especially 295–324; Deborah Gray White, *Ar'n't I a Woman?: Female Slaves in the Plantation South* (New York: W. W. Norton, 1985), especially 262–90; Shirley Ann Moore, "African American Women," in *Encyclopedia of Social History*, ed. Peter N. Stearns (New York: Garland, 1994), 9–10; Gavin Wright, "Slavery and American Agricultural History," *Agricultural History* 77, no. 4 (Autumn, 2003): 527–52; James Oakes, *The Ruling Race: A History of American Slaveholders* (New York: W.W. Norton, 1998), 153–91; Randall M. Miller, "The Fabric of Control: Slavery in Antebellum Southern Textile Mills," *Business History Review* 55, no. 4 (Winter 1981): 471–90; Ira Berlin and Herbert G. Gutman, "Natives and Immigrants, Free Men and Slaves: Urban Workingmen in the Antebellum American South," *American Historical Review* 88, no. 5 (December 1983): 1175–1200.

9. *Encyclopedia of Black America*, ed. W. Augustus Low and Virgil Clift (New York: Da Capo Press, 1981), s.v. "Slavery."

10. Missouri field hands planted and processed tobacco and hemp, Missouri's primary crops, until the cotton gin made cotton a lucrative commodity in the early 1800s and landowners in southern Missouri began to use slave labor to cultivate that crop. In addition to performing agricultural work, slaves in Missouri often served as crew on riverboats or as blacksmiths and engineers in the iron industry. A considerable number toiled in lead and salt mines—hired out by owners who collected their pay. See Harrison Anthony Trexler, *Slavery in Missouri, 1804–1865* (Baltimore: Johns Hopkins Press, 1914), 20–26, http://www.dinsdoc.com/trexler-1-0b.htm (accessed April 12, 2011). By 1810, 3,011 slaves and 607 free blacks lived in Missouri Territory; the 1820 census recorded 97,797 "bondsmen" and 376 black freemen residing there. U.S. Bureau of the Census, *Eighth Census of the United States, 1860.* The 1810 data is from Washington, D.C.: Government Printing Office, 1864, 601, and 1820 data is from the Fourth Census for the United States, 40, as reported in Trexler, *Slavery in Missouri*, 9.

11. Trexler, *Slavery in Missouri*, 58; *Laws of the State of Missouri, Revised and Digested by Authority of the General Assembly in Two Volumes with Appendix*, vol. 2, 1825 (St. Louis: E. Charles for the State) 600, hereafter cited as "*Laws of Missouri*, 1825"; Missouri State Archives, "Missouri's Early Slave Laws: A History in Documents," published by the Missouri Office of the Secretary of State, Missouri Digital Heritage, 2014, http://sl.sos.mo.gov/archives/education/aahi/earlyslavelaws/slavelaws (accessed September 11, 2015), hereafter cited as Missouri Digital Heritage, "Missouri's Early Slave Laws." For the tension between slave "personhood" and property status, see David Thomas Konig, "The Long Road to *Dred Scott:* Personhood and the Rule of Law in the Trial Court Records of St. Louis Slave Freedom Suits," originally published in the *University of Missouri, Kansas City, Law Review* 75, no. 1 (Fall 2006): 54–79, http://www.s1.sos

.mo.gov/CMSImages/MDH/TheLongRoadtoDredScott.pdf (accessed September 13, 2015)

12. All quotes in "*Laws of Missouri*, 1825," 600, 741–42, 746, 747–48. See also Dennis K. Bowman, "The Dred Scott Case Reconsidered: The Legal and Political Context in Missouri," *American Journal of Legal History* 44, no. 4 (October 2000): 405–28, especially 406–7; "Missouri's Early Slave Laws." For the arbitrary nature of court decisions regarding transactions between African Americans and whites in Missouri, see *Redmond (colored) v. Murray et al., 30 Mo.* The *Redmond* case, 1860, involved a Missouri slave who had been sold by his master *after* having purchased his own freedom and despite holding a receipt proving payment in full. The court denied the black man the right to sue his owner and refused to enforce any contract between master and slave "even where there might be complete fulfillment on the part of the slave." For the *Redmond* case quote, see Trexler, *Slavery in Missouri*, 64. The year the *Redmond* case was heard, Missouri was home to 114,931 slaves (about 10 percent of the state's total population) and 3,572 free blacks, a relatively low number compared with the slave population of the lower South. See 1860 census numbers as reported in Trexler, *Slavery in Missouri*, 9.

13. All quotes from *Laws of Missouri*, 1825, 600.

14. *The Revised Statutes of the State of Missouri, Revised and Digested by the Thirteenth General Assembly, to Which Are Affixed the Constitutions of the United States and of the State of Missouri, and the Act of Congress Authorizing the People of Missouri Territory to Form a State Government, and the Ordinance of the Convention of the People of Missouri, by Their Representatives, Declaring the Assent of the People of Missouri to the Conditions and Provisions of the Said Act of Congress, with an Appendix* (St. Louis: J. W. Dougherty for the State, 1845), hereafter cited as "Revised Missouri Statutes, 1845."

15. Between 1814 and 1860, more than 300 "people of color," including people of American Indian and African American ancestry, filed freedom suits in St. Louis courts; a little less than half were successful. See National Park Service, "Freedom Suits, St. Louis, 1804–1865," and Jefferson National Expansion Memorial, http://www.nps.gov/jeff/learn/historyculture/freedom-suits.htm (accessed September 12, 2015), hereafter cited as NPS, "Freedom Suits"; St. Louis Circuit Court Historical Records Project, "History of Freedom Suits in Missouri," http://stlcourtrecords.wustl.edu/about-freedom-suits-history.php (accessed September 15, 2015). For the "once free, always free" principle, see Konig, "The Long Road to *Dred Scott*, especially 75 n79. Bowman, "The Dred Scott Case Reconsidered," 406–13, see especially 410–11; Eric Gardner, "'You Have No Business to Whip Me': The Freedom Suits of Polly Wash and Lucy Ann Delaney," *African American Review* 41, no. 1 (Spring, 2007): 33–50, especially 34–38; Helen Tunnieliff Catterall, "Some Antecedents of the Dred Scott Case," *American Historical Review* 30, no. 1 (October 1924): 56–71, see especially 59–62.

16. As early as 1807, according to Missouri territorial law, persons held in "wrongful servitude" could sue for freedom. The *Winny v. Whitesides* case of 1824 was the first to be filed under Missouri state law, and established the "once free, always free" precedence. See St. Louis Circuit Court Historical Records Project, "History of Freedom Suits in Missouri," hereafter cited as "History of Freedom Suits in Missouri," http://stlcourtrecords.wustl.edu/about-freedom-suits-history.php (accessed September 12, 2015); Konig, "The Long Road to Dred Scott." Although Pierre was unsuccessful, Charlotte's bid for freedom was eventually granted after three decades of litigation. See *Charlotte v. Chouteau* and *Chouteau v. Pierre,* quoted in Trexler, *Slavery in Missouri,* 58–64, especially 59n9, and 215n30. Also see Bowman, "The Dred Scott Case Reconsidered," 410–11, 418–20; Catterall, "Some Antecedents of the Dred Scott Case," 60–61, 65–66.

17. The quote is from John E. Kleber, "Kentucky, A Historical Overview," *The Kentucky Encyclopedia,* ed. John, E. Kleber (Lexington: University Press of Kentucky, 1992), xxiii; Marion B. Lucas, *A History of Blacks in Kentucky: From Slavery to Segregation, 1760–1891,* 2d ed., vol. 1 (Lexington: University Press of Kentucky, 2003), 49–50.

18. George C. Wright, s.v. "Afro-Americans," in *Kentucky Encyclopedia,* 4. Wright notes that in 1860, 11,000 free blacks resided in Kentucky compared with 211,000 slaves. Lacy Ford, "Reconfiguring the Old South: 'Solving' the Race Problem of Slavery, 1787–1838," *Journal of American History* 95, no. 1(June 2008): 105–9, 117–18; See also Lucas, *History of Blacks in Kentucky,* especially figure 1, "Kentucky's Free Black Population, 1790–1860," 108. Unlike other slaveholding states, Kentucky law did not prevent the education of slaves and free blacks; however, black Kentuckians were allowed limited educational opportunities. See H. Blaine Hudson, s.v. "Education, Afro-American," in *Kentucky Encyclopedia,* 285.

19. The soaring demand for hemp induced many Kentucky planters (and some from Virginia, Tennessee, and North Carolina) to flood into Missouri with their slaves and begin planting the crop in places where cotton could not be grown. In fact, so many planters from Kentucky and elsewhere took their slaves and settled on the high-value Missouri farmland located along the Missouri River that it became known as "Little Dixie." See George C. Wright, "Oral History and the Search for the Black Past in Kentucky," *Oral History Review* 10 (1982): 76; Gavin Wright, "Slavery and American Agricultural History," *Agricultural History* 77, no. 4 (Autumn 2003): 527–52, especially 535; Kleber, "Kentucky," xiii; Wright, s.v. "Afro-Americans," *Kentucky Encyclopedia,* 3–4. See also Lucas, *A History of Blacks in Kentucky,* 107–14, 115–17.

20. Wright, "Oral History," 76; Wright, "Slavery and American Agricultural History," 535; Wright, s.v. "Afro-Americans," 3–4; Kleber, "Kentucky," xiii. See Lucas, *A History of Blacks in Kentucky,* 107–14, 115–17.

21. Jordan, *White over Black*, 319–21; Walter Johnson, *Soul By Soul: Life inside the Antebellum Slave Market* (Cambridge, Mass.: Harvard University Press, 2001) 22–30, 33–37, 41–44, 48–51; Daina Ramey Berry, "'In Pressing Need of Cash': Gender, Skill, and Family Persistence in the Domestic Slave Trade," *Journal of African American History* 92, no. 1 (Winter 2007): 22–36; Robert H. Gudmestad, "The Troubled Legacy of Isaac Franklin: The Enterprise of Slave Trading," *Tennessee Historical Quarterly* 62, no. 3 (Fall 2003): 193–217, especially 193–95, 204–206; "Quantitative Estimates of the United States Interregional Slave Trade, 1820–1860," *Journal of Economic History* 61, no. 2 (June 2001): 467–75, see especially 467–68. Despite the involuntary migration of African Americans from Virginia in the antebellum era, the census of 1860 showed that 490,865 slaves and 58,042 free blacks still resided in the Old Dominion, making its black population the largest in the country. See 1860 federal census figures for Virginia slaves and free blacks, reported in *Encyclopedia of Black America*, s.v. "Slavery: Slavery in Selected States/Virginia"; Daniel W. Crofts, "Late Antebellum Virginia Reconsidered," *Virginia Magazine of History and Biography* 107, no. 3 (Summer 1999): 260–61.

22. Wright, "Slavery and American Agricultural History," especially 541–44; Berlin and Gutman, "Natives and Immigrants," 1179, 1181, 1182–83, 1185, 1196.

23. Crofts, "Late Antebellum Virginia Reconsidered," 257–60; Hine, et al., *African American Odyssey*, 150–51.

24. *Encyclopedia of Black America*, s.v. "Slavery: Restrictions on African Americans," s.v. "Slavery: Slavery in Selected States/Introduction," s.v. "Slavery: Slavery in Selected States/Virginia"; Loren Schweninger, "The Vass Slaves: County Courts, State Laws, and Slavery in Virginia, 1831–1861," *Virginia Magazine of History and Biography* 114, no. 4 (2006): 464–97; see especially 477–88.

25. Taylor, *In Search of the Racial Frontier*, 37–41 Flamming, *African Americans in the West*, 34–35; Broussard, *Expectations of Equality*, 11–17; Alwyn Barr, *Black Texas: A History of African Americans in Texas, 1528–1995* (Norman: University of Oklahoma Press, 2d ed., 1996), 17.

26. Barr, *Black Texas*, 17.

27. Ibid., 8.

28. 1860 census, reported in Taylor, *In Search of the Racial Frontier*, 76.

29. Ibid., 62–72 (quote, 62), 114.

30. For the treaty with the Confederate States, see Emmet Starr, *History of the Cherokee Indians and Their Legends and Folk Lore* (Oklahoma City: Warden Company, 1921), 155–58. Also see *Declaration by the People of the Cherokee Nation of the Causes Which Have Impelled Them to Unite Their Fortunes with Those of the Confederate States of America*, Tahlequah, Cherokee Nation, October 28, 186, digital repr., n.d., http://www.unitednativeamerica.com/cherokee.html (accessed April 12, 2011).

31. Hine, et al., *African American Odyssey,* combined vol., 5th ed. (Upper Saddle River, N.J.: Pearson, 2011), 172–77; Leon F. Litwack, *North of Slavery: The Negro in the Free States, 1790–1860* (Chicago: University of Chicago Press, 1961), 15–16, 104–12, 126–39. New York's property requirement of $250 is the modern-day equivalent of $5,400, "Measuring Worth," CPI 2014.

32. Katz, *The Black West,* 54–55, 57. Indiana's three dollar tax for all black men is the present-day equivalent of $64.80; the $500 bond required in Ohio is the present-day equivalent of $10,800, "Measuring Worth," CPI 2014.

33. Litwack, *North of Slavery,* 15. The term "unfreedom" was used in an influential article by historians Oscar and Mary F. Handlin, "Origins of the Southern Labor System," *William and Mary Quarterly* 7, no. 2 (April 1950): 199–222. See especially 200, 204, 206.

34. Katz, *The Black West,* 54–55, 57.

35. Taylor, *In Search of the Racial Frontier,* 104. For the Doolittle quote, see "The African American Population in Western States and Territories, 1860," regarding Montana's black population of 183 (total population of 20,592), 121.

36. For a discussion of the creation of New Mexico Territory and the Compromise of 1850, see B. Sacks, "The Creation of the Territory of Arizona," *Arizona and the West* 5, no. 1 (Spring 1963): 29–62, part 1 of 2 parts. In 1860, New Mexico's black population was only 85 (in a total population of 93,516). By 1870, that number had increased to 172 (in a total population of 91,874). In 1870 Arizona Territory, blacks numbered 26 (in a total population 9,658). For population figures, see Taylor, *In Search of the Racial Frontier,* 74–76, 104, especially the charts "Black Population in Western States and Territories, 1860," 76, and "The African American Population in Western United States and Territories, 1860–70," 104. Taylor's figures for blacks in New Mexico, Arizona, and Nevada Territories are based on the 1860 Census, *iv.* See also U.S. Bureau of the Census, *Negro Population in the United States, 1790–1915* (Washington, D.C.: Government Printing Office, 1918), 43, 44; U.S. Bureau of the Census, *Statistics of the Population of the United States, 1870* (Washington, D.C.: Government Printing Office, 1872), 3; and Michael F. Doran, "Population Statistics of Nineteenth Century Indian Territory," *Chronicles of Oklahoma* 53, no. 4 (Winter 1975): 501.

37. Taylor, *In Search of the Racial Frontier,* 74–75; Barret Kaubisch, "New Mexico Territory Slave Code (1859–1867)," The Black Past: An Online Reference Guide to African American History, BlackPast.org, http://www.blackpast.org/?q=aaw/new-mexico-terriory-slave-code-1859-1867 (accessed April 14, 2011).

38. Taylor, *In Search of the Racial Frontier,* 75; Kaubisch, "New Mexico Territory Slave Code." For a discussion of Arizona Territory, the Confederate Territory of Arizona, and pro-Southern sentiments, see Martin Hardwick Hall, "The *Mesilla Times:* A Journal of Confederate Arizona," *Arizona and the West* 5 no. 4 (Winter 1963): 337–51; Sacks, "Creation of the Arizona Territory," part 1,

especially 58–59, and part 2, 109–48. For a discussion of the battle of Glorieta Pass, see National Park Service, CWSAC Battle Summaries, "Glorieta Pass," A Project of the American Battlefield Protection Program, http://www.nps.gov/hps/abpp/battles/nm002.htm (accessed April 26, 2011); Robert G. Athearn, "West of Appomattox: Civil War beyond the Great River: A Stage-Setting Interpretation," *Montana The Magazine of Western History* 12, no. 2 (Spring 1962): 2–11; Lewis D. W. Hall, "A Summation of Events," *Montana The Magazine of Western History* 12, no. 2 (Spring 1962): 12–15.

39. For black Nevada population figures, see Elmer R. Rusco, *"Good Time Coming?" Black Nevadans in the Nineteenth Century* (Westport, Conn.: Greenwood Press, 1975), 14–16, 124, especially table 1, "Black Population of Nevada, 1860–1870." Rusco's population figures are based on Daniel O. Price, *Changing Characteristics of the Negro Population* (Washington, D.C.: U.S. Government Printing Office, 1969), 9, 13.

40. Rusco, *"Good Time Coming?"* 22. This statement was made by territorial assemblyman Abraham Curry, who was objecting to a House resolution that proposed banning the sale of firearms and ammunition to Indians. Curry opposed the provision, observing that Indians relied on these resources for their livelihood. He conceded that territorial representatives had met "to legislate for white men, but that was no reason for starving the Indians." Curry's remarks are quoted in Andrew J. Marsh, *Letters from Nevada Territory, 1861–1862*, ed. William C. Miller, Russell W. McDonald, and Ann Rollins (Carson City, Nev.: Legislative Counsel Bureau, 1972), 553. Marsh was the official reporter of the Nevada legislative sessions for the *Sacramento Daily Union* newspaper.

41. For a detailed discussion of territorial and state antiblack legislation in Nevada, see Rusco, *"Good Time Coming?"* especially 21–38.

42. U.S. Slave, "Oregon Black Exclusion Laws," http://usslave.blogspot.com/2011/04/oregon-black-exclusion-laws.html (accessed August 29, 2011); State of Oregon, "Oregon Racial Laws and Events, 1844–1959," http://www.ode.state.or.us/opportunities/grants/saelp/orraciallaws.pdf (accessed August 29, 2011). The $1,000 fine is the modern-day equivalent of $32,700, "Measuring Worth, CPI 2014.

43. Oregon's black exclusion stipulation of 1849 remained in the state constitution until 1926. The outdated clause banning black suffrage was removed the following year. Quintard Taylor, "Freedmen and Slaves in Oregon Territory, 1840–1860," *Peoples of Color in the American West*, ed. Sucheng Chan, Douglas Henry Daniels, Mario T. Garcia, and Terry P. Wilson (Lexington, Mass.: D. C. Heath, 1994), 77–79.

44. Taylor, *In Search of the Racial Frontier*, 78.

45. Shirley Ann Wilson Moore, "'We Feel the Want of Protection:' The Politics of Law and Race in California, 1848–1878," *Taming the Elephant: Politics, Government, and Law in Pioneer California*, ed. John F. Burns and Richard J. Orsi

(Berkeley: University of California Press with the California Historical Society, 2003), 108–9. For a detailed account of California's black laws, also see Eugene Berwanger, "The Black Law Question in Ante-bellum California," *Journal of the West* 6, no. 2 (April 1967): 205–20.

46. Unlike the weakly enforced Fugitive Slave Law of 1793, the federal Fugitive Slave Act of 1850 was harsher and more comprehensive. It required all U.S. marshals, their deputies, and even ordinary citizens to help arrest suspected runaways. Those refusing to comply with the law could be fined or imprisoned. The new act made it virtually impossible for African Americans to prove they were free, but slave owners or their agents merely had to provide legal documentation from their home state or have a white witness testify to a federal commissioner that the captured black person was a slave. Federal commissioners received payment of ten dollars for every captive returned to slavery and only five dollars for those declared free. See Hine, et al., *African American Odyssey*, 141, 238–44.

47. Moore, "We Feel the Want of Protection," 109. Katz notes that, in California, slavery had "powerful defenders" who, by 1852, had "convinced the legislature to pass a broad and arbitrary fugitive slave law" that permitted slave owners to remain in the state for an indefinite time, thus institutionalizing slavery, despite its being constitutionally outlawed. See Katz, *The Black West*, 134; Berwanger, "The Black Law Question in Ante-bellum California," 214. The $500 fine imposed by California's Fugitive Slave Law is equivalent to the modern-day $15,800, "Measuring Worth," CPI 2014.

48. Taylor, *In Search of the Racial Frontier*, 71; Jack Beller, "Negro Slaves in Utah," *Utah Historical Quarterly* 2 (October 1929): 122–23; Dennis L. Lythgoe, "Negro Slavery in Utah," *Utah Historical Quarterly* 39 (Winter 1977): 41–42; William E. Parrish, "The Mississippi Saints," *The Historian* 50, no. 4 (August 1988): 492; Coleman, "A History of Blacks in Utah, 1825–1910," 30–36; Ronald G. Coleman, "Blacks in Utah History: An Unknown Legacy," Utah History to Go, an online project, http://historytogo.utah.gov/people/ethnic_cultures/the_peoples_of_utah/blacksinutahhistory (accessed January 2, 2011), hereafter cited as Coleman, "Blacks in Utah History." At the close of 1847, ten more African Americans had arrived in the territory with other Mormon groups. These black overlanders represented only a fraction of the blacks who eventually settled in territorial Utah. Within the first four years of Mormon settlement, between 110 and 119 slaves and free black men and women were brought, or freely immigrated, to the Great Basin. The peak years of black immigration to the region occurred between 1847 and 1850. See Newell G. Bringhurst, *Saints, Slaves and Blacks: The Changing Place of Black People within Mormonism* (Westport, Conn.: Greenwood, 1981), 218, and especially table 9, "Number of Blacks (Slave and Free) Who Apparently Migrated to Utah during the Period 1847–1850," 224. In 1848, some 50 black

people lived in the Salt Lake Valley among a general population of 1,700. The federal census of 1850 reported 24 free persons of color in Utah, and 26 slaves. The 1860 census counted 59 African Americans living in Utah Territory—30 free and 29 slaves. For the black population of Utah, see Taylor, *In Search of the Racial Frontier*, 72; U.S. Bureau of the Census, "Historical Census Statistics on Population Totals by Race, 1790 to 1990, and By Hispanic Origin, 1790 to 1990, for the United States, Regions, Divisions, and States," table 59, Utah—Race and Hispanic Origin: 1850 to 1990, online project of the Population Division, U. S. Bureau of the Census, Washington, D. C., Working Paper Series, no. 56, September 2002, http://www.census.gov/population/wwwdocumentation/twps0056/twps0056.html (accessed May 19, 20011); U.S. Bureau of the Census, *Seventh Census of the United States*, 1850 (Washington, D.C.: Government Printing Office), 993. See also 1860 Census; and Coleman, "Blacks in Utah History"; Nathaniel R. Ricks, "A Peculiar Place for the Peculiar Institution: Slavery and Sovereignty in Early Territorial Utah" (master's thesis, Brigham Young University, 2007), especially 18–49, 99–124.

49. For the Mormon position on African Americans and slavery, see Newell G. Bringhurst, "The Mormons and Slavery: A Closer Look," *Pacific Historical Review* 50, no. 3 (August, 1981): 337–38; Bringhurst, *Saints, Slaves and Blacks;* D. Michael Quinn, *The Mormon Hierarchy: Extensions of Power* (Salt Lake City: Signature Books, 1997), 286–87; Lester E. Bush, Jr., "Mormonism's Negro Doctrine: An Historical Overview," *Dialogue* 8 (1973): 11–68; Ronald G. Coleman, "'Is There No Blessing for Me?': Jane Elizabeth Manning James, a Mormon African American Woman," in Taylor and Moore, *African American Women Confront the West*, 144–62; James B. Christensen, "Negro Slavery in the Utah Territory" *Phylon Quarterly* 18 (third quarter 1957): 298–305, especially 299 for black population; and Ricks, "A Peculiar Place," 18–49, 99–124; D. Michael Quinn, *The Mormon Hierarchy: Origins of Power* (Salt Lake City: Signature Books) 659; Ronald G. Coleman, "Blacks in Utah History: An Unknown Legacy," Utah History to Go, an online project, http://historytogo.utah.gov/people/ethnic_cultures/the_peoples_of_utah/blacksinutahhistory (accessed January 2, 2011), hereafter cited as Coleman, "Blacks in Utah History"; Coleman, "A History of Blacks in Utah, 1825–1910," 32–36; Coleman, "History of Blacks in Utah, 1825–1910," 32–36.

50. Some accounts claim that in 1836 in Kirtland, Ohio, church founder Joseph Smith had personally ordained Elijah Abel, a former slave and Mormon convert, into the Mormon priesthood. Mormon newspapers like the *Nauvoo Neighbor* and the *Latter Day Saints Millennial Star* condemned the "slaveholder who deprives his fellow-beings of liberty," and proclaimed that the institution of slavery had turned the United States into "an asylum for the oppressed." See *Nauvoo Neighbor*, September 10, 1845, and *Latter Day Saints Millennial Star* (published in Liverpool, England), September 1843, both quoted in Bringhurst, "The

Mormons and Slavery," 332; Bringhurst, *Saints, Slaves, and Blacks,* 37–39; Newell Bringhurst, "'The Missouri Thesis' Revisited: Early Mormonism, Slavery, and the Status of Black People," in *Black and Mormon,* ed. Newell G. Bringhurst and Darron T. Smith (Urbana: University of Illinois Press: 2006), 13–33; Margaret Blair Young, "Abel, Elijah (1810–1884)," The Black Past: An Online Reference Guide to African American History, BlackPast.org, http://www.blackpast.org/?q=aaw/abel-elijah-1810-1884 (accessed July 7, 2011).

51. See Joseph Smith's published presidential campaign platform of 1844, *General Smith's Views on the Government and Policies of the United States* (Nauvoo: John Taylor, 1844), online at the Joseph Smith Home Page, The Church of Jesus Christ of Latter-day Saints, from the L. Tom Perry Special Collections at Brigham Young University, http://contentdm.lib.byu.edu/cdm4/document.php?CISOROOT=/NCMP1820–1846&CISOPTR=2836 (accessed May 10, 2011). See also Bringhurst, "The Mormons and Slavery," 3, 332; Quinn, *Mormon Hierarchy: Origins of Power,* 119; Timothy L. Wood: "The Prophet and the Presidency: Mormonism and Politics in Joseph Smith's 1844 Presidential Campaign," *Journal of the Illinois State Historical Society* 93, no. 2 (Summer 2000): 167–93, especially 180–82; and Bush, "Mormonism's Negro Doctrine," especially 13–22.

52. For a discussion of Mormon persecution, anti-Mormon violence, and general nineteenth-century perceptions of Mormons, see Bagley, *So Rugged and Mountainous,* 291–93, 370–72, 82–141; Quinn, *Mormon Hierarchy: Extensions of Power,* 241–61; Kenneth N. Owens, *Gold Rush Saints: California Mormons and the Great Rush for Riches* (Norman: University of Oklahoma Press, 2004), 23, 31–32.

53. The text was originally published in the *Latter Day Saints Messenger and Advocate,* August 1835; Timothy L. Wood: "The Prophet and the Presidency," 180–81; Bringhurst, "The Mormons and Slavery," 331.

54. Quinn, *Mormon Hierarchy: Origins of Power,* 659 (appendix 7, July 24, 1847).

55. For Young's position on slavery and the inferior position of blacks, see "Speech by Governor Young in Joint Session of the Legislature, Giving Counsel on a Bill in Relation to African Slavery, Given at Salt Lake City on Friday, January 23rd, 1852 (reported by George D. Watt; BPP, HDC)," in *The Teachings of President Brigham Young,* vol. 3, 1852–1854, ed. Fred C. Collier (Salt Lake City: Collier's, 1987), 26, 27 (hereafter cited as Collier, "Governor Young's Speech, January 23, 1852"); Collier, *The Teachings of President Brigham Young,* "Governor Young's Speech, February 5th, 1852" (hereafter cited as Collier, "Governor Young's Speech, February 5, 1852"), 44, 45; "The Message of Governor Brigham Young, delivered to the Council, and House of Representatives of the Legislature of Utah Territory, at Salt Lake City, on Monday, January 5, 1852 (reported and prepared

for delivery by Thomas Bullock and Thomas W. Ellerbeck; DN, vol. 2:18–25, 1/10/52), 16. See also Brigham Young interview by Horace Greeley, July 13, 1859, reprinted in the *Salt Lake Tribune,* August 15, 1993, http://www.utlm.org/onlineresources/sermons_talks_interviews/brighamgreeleyinterview_july131859.htm (accessed May 12, 2011); Bush, "Mormonism's Negro Doctrine," 22–27; and Bringhurst, "Mormons and Slavery," 336.

56. For accounts of the creation of Utah, see Bagley, *So Rugged and Mountainous,* 370–72, and Quinn, *Mormon Hierarchy: Extensions of Power,* 236–40. Young was virulently antiblack. Citing theological reasons, he opposed intermarriage between blacks and whites, even within the Mormon faith, but condoned intermarriage between Mormon men and Indian women. For example, when informed that a black Mormon man had married a white Mormon woman in Boston, Young stated that he would have both of them killed "if they were far away from the Gentiles," instead of in Boston. By contrast, Young urged Mormon elders to marry Indian women as part of God's plan to make Indians "a White and delightsome people" and to "learn them the [Mormon] gospel." Young's statement about the marriage of a black Mormon man and a white Mormon woman is quoted in Quinn, *Mormon Hierarchy: Origins of Power,* 478. For Young's comment about Mormon elders and Indian women intermarrying, see Scott G. Kenney, ed., *Wilford Woodruff's Journal,* vol. 3 (Midvale, Utah: Signature Books, 1983), 241, as quoted in David L. Bigler and Will Bagley, *The Mormon Rebellion: America's First Civil War, 1857–1858* (Norman: University of Oklahoma Press, 2011), 29. For the quotes regarding Young's support of slavery, see Collier, "Governor Young's Speech, January 23rd, 1852," 28, 218

57. "Collier, "Governor Young's Speech, February 5th, 1852," 218. For a succinct summary of the act, see Taylor, *In Search of the Racial Frontier,"* 73–74. For a more detailed account of the act, see Bringhurst, "Mormons and Slavery," 332–38.

58. Collier, "Governor Young's Speech, February 5, 1852," 45. See also Bringhurst, "Mormons and Slavery," 336, and Lythgoe, "Negro Slavery in Utah," 52.

59. Original quotes from "An Act in Relation to Service," in *Acts, Resolutions, and Memorials of the Legislative Assembly of the Territory of Utah* (Salt Lake City, 1855), 160–62, quoted in Bringhurst, "Mormons and Slavery," 335. See also Taylor, *In Search of the Racial Frontier,* 73–74.

60. In Nauvoo, Mormon leaders had begun to restrict African Americans' political and civil rights by legally preventing them from voting, holding municipal office, marrying whites, and joining the militia. Bringhurst, "Mormons and Slavery," 336–37.

61. Taylor, *In Search of the Racial Frontier,"* 73; Bringhurst, "Mormons and Slavery," 337; Lythgoe, "Negro Slavery in Utah," 51–54; Ricks, "A Peculiar Place," 121–30; Coleman, "Blacks in Utah History."

62. For a discussion of "amalgamation," or racial intermixture, see Jordan, *White over Black*, 577–82; Hollinger, "Amalgamation and Hypodescent," 1365–67. For an overview of white mob violence against free blacks in the antebellum era, see Leonard P. Curry, *The Free Black in Urban America, 1800–1850: The Shadow of the Dream* (Chicago: University of Chicago Press, 1986), especially 96–98.

63. Malvin, *Autobiography of John Malvin*, 11–12.

64. Nikki Taylor, "Reconsidering the 'Forced' Exodus of 1829: Free Black Emigration from Cincinnati, Ohio, to Wilberforce, Canada," *Journal of African American History* 87 (Summer 2002): 283–302, especially 290–91. For population numbers, see especially 285.

65. Thomas Crissup had come to Cincinnati prior to 1820, and Israel Lewis settled there after escaping slavery with his wife. See Taylor, "Reconsidering the 'Forced' Exodus," 286–87 for a discussion of black laws and oppression of African Americans in the city. For a discussion of immigration plans to Canada before the 1829 riot, see 287–93. The present-day equivalent of the cost of the land purchased by the group is $157,600, "Measuring Worth," CPI 2014.

66. Taylor, "Reconsidering the 'Forced' Exodus," 283–302.

67. Ibid., 291; Curry, *The Free Black in Urban America*, 105, 107.

68. Taylor, "Reconsidering the 'Forced' Exodus," 289, 292. The number of African Americans who left Cincinnati as a result of the 1829 riot is a matter of dispute. See Curry, *The Free Black in Urban America*, 104–5, especially 305n22; J. Stephen Ellingson, "Understanding the Dialectic of Discourse and Collective Action: Public Debate and Rioting in Antebellum Cincinnati," *American Journal of Sociology* 1, no. 1 (July 1995): 100–144, especially 116–17.

69. Ellingson, "Understanding the Dialectic," 100–144, especially 116–17; Joan E. Cashin, "Black Families in the Old Northwest," *Journal of the Early Republic* 15, no. 3 (Autumn 1995): 449–75, especially 451–52; J. Reuben Sheeler, "The Struggle of the Negro in Ohio for Freedom," *Journal of Negro History* 31, no. 2 (April 1946): 208–26, see especially 212–14. For an account of Randolph's former slaves and their heirs' legal battle to reclaim their land, see Frank F. Mathias, "John Randolph's Freedmen: The Thwarting of a Will," *Journal of Southern History* 39 no. 2 (May 1973): 263–72.

70. For a detailed account of the Philadelphia riots, see Curry, *The Free Black in Urban America*, 103–8.

71. For a detailed account of antiblack violence in northern cities, see James M. McPherson, *The Negro's Civil War: How American Blacks Felt and Acted during the War for the Union* (New York: Ballantine Books, 1991), 69–78; Leonard R. Riforgiato, "Bishop Timon, Buffalo, and the Civil War," *Catholic Historical Review* 73, no. 1 (January 1987): 62–80; Michael P. McCarthy, "The Philadelphia Consolidation of 1854: A Reappraisal," *Pennsylvania Magazine of*

History and Biography 110, no. 4 (October 1986): 531–48, especially 533–35; Carl E. Prince, "The Great 'Riot Year': Jacksonian Democracy and Patterns of Violence in 1834," *Journal of the Early Republic* 5, no. 1 (Spring 1985): 1–19; John A. Williams, "The Long Hot Summers of Yesteryear," *History Teacher* 1, no. 3 (March 1968): 9–23.

72. For a summary of the free black convention movement emerging in the aftermath of the Cincinnati riot and the public dialogue among African Americans about emigration to Canada, see Taylor, "Reconsidering the 'Forced' Exodus of 1829," especially 295–97. Also see Shirley Yee, "National Negro Convention Movement (1831–1834)," The Black Past: An Online Reference Guide to African American History, BlackPast.org, http://www.blackpast.org/aah/national-negro-convention-movement-1831-1864 (accessed September 19, 2015).

73. Kansas State Historical Society and the Kansas Collection of the University of Kansas, "Immigration and Early Settlement," Online 1854–1861, A Virtual Repository for Territorial Kansas History http://www.territorialkansasonline.org/~imlskto/cgi-bin/index.php?SCREEN=immigration (accessed April 12, 2011).

74. For an account of a free-born, Northern African American who was kidnapped and enslaved, see Solomon Northup, *Twelve Years a Slave*, ed. Sue Eakin and Joseph Logsdon (1853; repr., Baton Rouge: Louisiana State University Press, 1979). For vulnerability of escaped slaves in the North, see Harriet Jacobs, *Incidents in the Life of a Slave Girl*, ed. Nellie Y. McKay and Frances Smith Foster (New York: W. W. Norton, 2001), especially 138–42; Jean Fagan Yellin, *Harriet Jacobs: A Life* (Cambridge, Mass.: Basic Civitas, 2004), especially 41, 49, and 109–11.

75. Missouri State Archives, "Missouri's Dred Scott Case, 1846–1857," the Missouri Digital Heritage Collections, African American History Initiative, http://www.sos.mo.gov/archives/resources/africanamerican/scott/scott.asp (accessed May 19, 2011); Lea VanderVelde, "The *Dred Scott* Case as an American Family Saga," OAH Magazine of History 25, no. 2 (April 2011): 24–28.

76. Harriet's suit was set aside, pending the outcome of Dred's claim. Missouri law held that slaves who were taken to free states or territories were freed, even if they returned to the slave state of Missouri. Missouri's judicial standard maintained that once the bonds of slavery had been broken, they did not reattach. See Missouri State Archives, "Missouri's Dred Scott Case"; VanderVelde, "The *Dred Scott* Case," 28.

77. For Taney's opinion, see Taney, Opinion of the Court, U.S. Supreme Court, *Scott v. Sandford,* 60 U.S. 393, Cornell University Law School, Legal Information Institute, http://www.law.cornell.edu/supct/html/historics/USSC_CR_0060_0393_ZO.html (accessed May 20, 2011); U.S. Supreme Court, *Dred Scott v. Sanford,* 60, U.S. 393 (December Term 1856), Westlaw, http://laws.findlaw.com/us/60/393.html (accessed May 19, 2011).

78. Missouri State Archives, "Missouri's Dred Scott Case"; VanderVelde, "The *Dred Scott* Case," 28.

79. For an examination of the Dred Scott case and its legal, social, cultural, and political implications, see David Thomas Konig, Paul Finkelman, and Christopher Alan Bracey, eds., *The Dred Scott Case: Historical and Contemporary Perspectives on Race and Law* (Athens: Ohio University Press, 2010). For a comprehensive examination of the Dred Scott decision, see Don E. Fehrenbacher, *The Dred Scott Case: Its Significance in American Law and Politics* (New York: Oxford University Press, 1979).

80. *The African Observer: Illustrative of the General Character, and Moral and Political Effects of Negro Slavery* 1, no. 13 (seventh month, 1827): 103. Also quoted in Wilson, *Freedom at Risk*, 118.

Chapter 3

Epigraph 1. J. Quinn Thornton, *Oregon and California in 1848*, quoted in McLagan, *Peculiar Paradise*, 14.

Epigraph 2. Edward H. N. Patterson, journal entry dated Friday, April 19, 1850. Patterson's journal entries were published in the *Oquawka Spectator*, Summer and Fall, 1850, in a series titled, "Overland Journal, Impressions by E. H. N. Patterson." The entire series is located in the *Oquawka Spectator* microfilm holdings of the Abraham Lincoln Presidential Library, Springfield, Illinois. See also University of Illinois at Urbana-Champaign, Illinois, Newspaper Project, *Oquawka Spectator* (Henderson County), oclc no. 11347317, 1848–1908, Record Set Name: Henderson County Quill, Notes: filed under Stronghurst.

1. Mattes, *Great Platte River Road*, 103.

2. Ibid.,104.

3. In 1847, Hark Lay and Oscar Crosby joined Green Flake, another slave (euphemistically called "servants" by their Mormon owners), to become the only African Americans in the first contingent of 143 Latter-day Saints to arrive in what would become present-day Utah. Green Flake and Hark Lay had converted to Mormonism before jumping off on the trail, and Oscar Crosby was baptized into the faith two weeks after arriving in the Salt Lake valley in July 1847. See Coleman, "A History of Blacks in Utah," 30–33; Coleman, "Blacks in Utah History"; Parrish, "The Mississippi Saints," 490–99; Beller, "Negro Slaves in Utah," 122–24; Lythgoe, "Negro Slavery in Utah," 40–42. See also Miriam B. Murphy, "Those Pioneering African Americans," in Utah History to Go, http://historytogo.utah.gov/utah_chapters/pioneers_and_cowboys/thosepioneeringafricanamericans (accessed March 24, 2011)]. In the early stages of Mormon western immigration, most of the "Saints" had only a hazy understanding of their final destination, "Utah." Historian Kenneth N. Owens has written that "Along with the Bear Lake

and Salt Lake Valley regions in the Great Basin and possibly Texas or Oregon or Vancouver Island, California ranked high on the short list of alternatives." See Owens, *Gold Rush Saints,* 32n3.

4. Coleman, "A History of Blacks in Utah," 32–33; Parrish, "The Mississippi Saints," 493–98; Lythgoe, "Negro Slavery in Utah," 40–43; Beller, "Negro Slaves in Utah," 122; John Brown, *Autobiography of Pioneer John Brown, 1820–1896,* ed. John Zimmerman Brown (Salt Lake City: Stevens and Walls, 1941), 72.

5. Brown, *Autobiography of Pioneer John Brown,* 72. See also Kate B. Carter, *The Story of the Negro Pioneer* (Salt Lake City: Daughters of Utah Pioneers, 1965), 7–8; Parrish, "The Mississippi Saints," 499; Beller, "Negro Slaves in Utah," 123; Lythgoe, "Negro Slavery in Utah," 43–44.

6. For an 1849 account of an overland slave carrying additional supplies at the behest of her owners, see the journal of Joseph Alonzo Stuart, "Notes on a Trip to California, and Life in the Mines," 1849, 14–16, WA MSS S-619, Western Americana Collection, Beinecke Library, Yale University. Also described in Lapp, *Blacks in Gold Rush California,* 30.

7. For a discussion of slave health and susceptibility to diseases, see Eugene D. Genovese, "The Medical and Insurance Costs of Slaveholding in the Cotton Belt," *Journal of Negro History* 45, no. 3 (July 1960): 141–55, especially 150–51 for the quotes.

8. This statement is from the Medical Society of the State of North Carolina, *Transactions at the Third Annual Meeting,* May, 1852, 77, as quoted in Genovese, "Medical and Insurance Costs," 150.

9. Coleman notes that when Brown's party arrived at Winter Quarters, at least six or seven other African Americans were already there. These included Isaac and Jane Manning James and their sons, Sylvester and Silas, a free black family who had converted to Mormonism, and two slaves, Elizabeth (Lizzie) Flake and Green Flake (no relation), who were owned by James and Agnes Flake. See Coleman, "A History of Blacks in Utah," 31–35. See also Brown, *Autobiography of Pioneer John Brown,* 72; Parrish, "The Mississippi Saints," 499–500; and Lythgoe, "Negro Slavery in Utah," 43–44.

10. For a comprehensive discussion of the jumping-off towns, see Unruh, *The Plains Across,* 111–17; Mattes, *Great Platte River Road,* 103–35; and Bagley, *So Rugged and Mountainous,* 171–76.

11. Francis Parkman, *The Oregon Trail: Sketches of Prairie and Rocky Mountain Life,* 6th ed. (Boston: Little, Brown, 1877), 6.

12. Emigrant Silas Newcomb in 1850, quoted in the Federal Writers' Project of the Works Progress Administration, *The Oregon Trail: The Missouri River to the Pacific Ocean* (Washington, D.C.: Oregon Trails Memorial Association, 1939), 49.

13. "Circular to California Emigrants," *Daily Missouri Republican*, St. Louis, Missouri, March 27, 1850. Many thanks to Hiram Young scholar Annette W. Curtis of Independence, Missouri, for making this available to me. The 1850 price for the $80–$100 wagons and carriages is the present-day equivalent of $2,500–$3,130, "Measuring Worth," CPI 2014.

14. Unruh, *The Plains Across*, 68–74; Walker D. Wyman, "The Outfitting Posts," *Pacific Historical Review* 18, no. 1 (February 1949): 14–23, especially 16–23; "Circular to California Emigrants," in the *Daily Missouri Republican*, March 27, 1850; "Independence, California Outfits, &c.," a letter signed by "Justice," in the *Daily Missouri Republican*, n.d., courtesy of Bill and Annette Curtis, Independence, Missouri.

15. Parkman, *The Oregon Trail*, 8.

16. Lucius Fairchild to J. C. Fairchild and family, May 5, 1849, quoted in Unruh, *The Plains Across*, 114; Gail Schontzler, "McDonald House Holds History of Freed Slaves Who Helped Settle Bozeman," *Bozeman Daily Chronicle*, February 13, 2011.

17. Patterson, "Overland Journal," entry Friday, April 19, 1850.

18. Hyde, *Empires, Nations, and Families*, 412.

19. Betti Vanepps-Taylor, *Forgotten Lives: African Americans in South Dakota* (Pierre: South Dakota State Historical Society Press, 2008), 32; Herbert T. Hoover, "The Arrival of Capitalism on the Northern Great Plains: Pierre Choteau Jr., and Company," in *South Dakota Leaders: From Pierre Choteau, Jr. to Oscar Howe*, ed. Herbert T. Hoover and Larry J. Zimmerman (Vermillion: University of South Dakota Press, 1989), 6–10.

20. For Manuel Alvarez, see U.S. Department of the Interior, National Park Service, National Register of Historic Places, Multiple Property Documentation Form, "Historic Resources of the Santa Fe Trail, 1821–1880," 7, hereafter cited as National Park Service, "Historic Resources of the Santa Fe Trail." For Manuel X. Harmony, see Mark L. Gardner and Mark Simmons, eds., *The Mexican War Correspondence of Richard Smith Elliott* (Norman: University of Oklahoma Press, 1997), 239n42; Susan Shelby Magoffin, *Down the Santa Fe Trail and into Mexico: The Diary of Susan Shelby Magoffin, 1846–1847*, ed. Stella Drumm (1926; repr, Lincoln: University of Nebraska Press, 1982), 50–51, see especially n 14; U.S. Department of Education, "A Tale of Two Trails: The History of the Oregon Trail," by Amy Trenkle, Teacher-to-Teacher Workshops, Online Report, National Park Service, 2005, 5; National Park Service, "Santa Fe Stories" http://www.nps.gov/safe/historyculture/stories.htm (accessed March 31, 2013). For Doña Gertrudis Barceló, see Richard W. Etulain, *Western Lives: A Biographical History of the American West* (Albuquerque: Center for the Southwest, University of New Mexico, 2005), 74–83; Sophia Truneh, "The Ilfelds: A Family Story of Jewish Pioneers in New Mexico," *Southwest Jewish History* 3, no. 2 (Winter 1995), http://parentseyes

.arizona.edu/bloom/sjhilfeld.htm (accessed May 3, 2011). For more about Jewish merchants in the Santa Fe trade, also see William Patrick O'Brien, "Olam Katan" (Small World): Jewish Traders on the Santa Fe Trail," *Journal of the Southwest* 48, no. 2 (Summer 2006): 211–31.

21. J. Quinn Thornton, quoted in McLagan, *Peculiar Paradise*, 14.

22. Thomas concluded that these towns were perfectly situated for trade because "all freight for the west, overland, was shipped by boat to Kansas City, Leavenworth, and St. Jo, there unloaded to be sent by wagons drawn by Oxin [sic] to New Mexico, California, or any place away from the river. James Thomas, *From Tennessee Slave to St. Louis Entrepreneur: The Autobiography of James Thomas*, ed. Loren Schweninger (Columbia: University of Missouri Press, 1984), 148–49.

23. James Thomas noted that racial and ethnic friction was not uncommon in these towns. He wrote of watching an ox train, newly arrived in Westport from New Mexico or Arizona, being unloaded and overhearing "one man, looking on while the Jews were drumming up trade, sa[lying] to his pal, O, Fred, I killed one of them fellows in Salt Lake last winter." See James, *From Tennessee Slave to St. Louis Entrepreneur*, 149.

24. Lorenzo J. Greene, Gary R. Kremer, Antonio F. Holland, *Missouri's Black Heritage* (Columbia: University of Missouri Press, rev. ed., 1993), 71–73. The combined wealth of $360,000 is equivalent today to $10,600,000, "Measuring Worth," CPI 2014.

25. Greene, et al., *Missouri's Black Heritage*, 67; Donnie D. Bellamy, "The Education of Blacks in Missouri prior to 1861," *Journal of Negro History* 59, no. 2 (April 1974): 149. See also The First Baptist Church of St. Louis, "Our History: The First Baptist Church Story," http://firstbaptistchurchstlouis.org/history (accessed March 31, 2013); Willie Brenc, "Meachum, John Berry (1789–1854)," The Black Past Remembered: An Online Reference Guide to African American History, BlackPast.org, http://www.blackpast.org/aah/meachum-john-berry-1789-1854 (accessed September 23, 2015).

26. Meachum quoted in Bellamy, "The Education of Blacks in Missouri," 149; Green, et al., *Missouri's Black Heritage*, 68–69; Jessie Carnie Smith, Millicent Lownes Jackson, Linda T. Wynn, ed., *Encyclopedia of African American Business* (Westport, Conn: Greenwood Press, 2006), s.v. "Black Business Development in Missouri," 58; "St. Louis Historic Preservation, "Mound City on the Mississippi: A St. Louis History—People, John Berry Meachum," n.d., http://stlcin.missouri.org/history/peopledetail.cfm?Master_ID=1126 (accessed August 5, 2010). See also *Dictionary of Missouri Biography*, ed. Lawrence O. Christensen, William E. Foley, Gary R. Kremer, and Kenneth H. Winn (Columbia: University of Missouri Press, 1999), s.v. "Meachum, John Berry." For reference to "Candle Tallow Schools," see First Baptist Church of St. Louis, "Our History"; Brenc, "Meachum, John Berry (1789–1854)."

27. Joe Louis Mattox, "Taking Steps to Record Steptoe, Westport's Vanishing African American Neighborhood," *Journal of the Jackson County Historical Society* (Autumn 2004), online http://jchs.org/Journal/Autumn%202004/steptoe.htm (accessed March 31, 2013). Also see David W. Jackson, "African American Neighborhood of Steptoe Vanishing," in *Kansas City Chronicles: An Up-to-Date History* (Charleston, S.C.: History Press, 2010), not paginated.

28. Unruh claims that prior to the gold rush, "at least through 1846," Independence had the best reputation as an outfitting town. By 1849, St. Joseph was vying for that title, and by 1852, Kanesville (Council Bluffs) "had become the dominant jumping-off point." See Unruh, *The Plains Across,* 68–74.

29. Ibid., 97–100, 115; Vanepps-Taylor, *Forgotten Lives,* 32. For reference to slaves helping to build towns and roads in Missouri, see William J. Curtis, *A Rich Heritage: A Black History of Independence, Missouri* (Kansas City, Mo.: Better Impressions, 1985), 1; Ted Stillwell, "Sam Shepherd and the Broadaxe," *Independence Examiner,* January 3, 2002; Michael Dickey, "George Caleb Bingham's Missouri," *Friends of Arrow Rock, Summer Newsletter,* 2007, http://www.friendsar.org/binghamsomo2.lhtml (accessed August 8, 2010); and The City of Independence Heritage Commission, "Independence Historic Survey," ca. 1976, 11.1.

30. William J. Curtis, "Emily Fisher: First Independence Black Business Woman," *Kansas City Genealogist* 36, no. 2 (Fall 1995): 76–77; Tricia Martineau Wagner, *It Happened on the Oregon Trail* (Guilford, Conn.: Morris Book, 2005), 115–17; Adrianne DeWeese, "Top 10: The People and Places Who Made Up a Rich Black History in Independence," *Independence Examiner,* February 19, 2010; *Encyclopedia of African American Business,* ed. Jessie Carnie Smith, Millicent Lownes Jackson, and Linda T. Wynn (Westport, Conn.: Greenwood Press, 2006), s.v. "Black Business Development in Missouri," 58.

31. Curtis, *A Rich Heritage,* 1; Wagner, *It Happened on the Oregon Trail,* 117.

32. By 1860, few people started their journey to the West from Independence; instead they headed out from Kansas City or other more westward points. See Unruh, *The Plains Across,* 97–100, 115; Ted Stillwell, "Emily Fisher and Her Healing Salve," unpublished manuscript in the personal collection of Bill and Annette Curtis; *Encyclopedia of African American Business,* "Black Business Development in Missouri" 58; DeWeese, "Top 10."

33. Savage, "The Negro in the Westward Movement," 534–35.

34. Young's description is from his friend, fellow businessman, and former slave, James Thomas. See Thomas, *From Tennessee Slave,* 99; Mark L. Gardner, *Wagons for the Santa Fe Trade: Wheeled Vehicles and Their Makers, 1822–1880* (Albuquerque: University of New Mexico Press, 2000), 34–35; Bagley, *So Rugged and Mountainous,* 335; and William P. O'Brien, "Hiram Young: Black Entrepreneur on the Santa Fe Trail," *Best of Wagon Tracks* 4, no. 1 (November 1989): 1–4,

http://www.santafetrail.org/the-trail/history/best-of-wagon-tracks/Hiram_Young.pdf (accessed May 30, 2011).

35. O'Brien, "Hiram Young," 1.

36. Ibid.

37. Ibid., 2.

38. Thomas, *From Tennessee Slave*, 99.

39. O'Brien, "Hiram Young," 1–2; Thomas, *From Tennessee Slave*, 99; Bagley, *So Rugged and Mountainous*, 335. For original source of "colored man of means," see Affidavit of Hiram Young, 1881, *Estate of Hiram Young, Deceased v. The United States* [No. 7320 Cong.], National Archives. Calculated at present-day value, his real estate holdings would be $1,060,000 and his personal property would be $587,000. See "Measuring Worth," CPI 2014.

40. Annette W. Curtis, *Jackson County, Missouri in Black and White: Jabez Smith, His Slaves, Plantations, Estate and Heirs*, vol. 1 (Independence: Two Trails, 1998), 67–68, 87, 95, 105–6. Many thanks to Bill and Annette Curtis for making Hiram Young's business and probate records available to me. See Hiram Young Business in Jabez Smith Probate, October 17, 1856, voucher no. 41, regarding the slave named Sam hired out to Hiram Young; also January 5, 1856, voucher no. 7, regarding Hiram Young's hiring a slave named William from the estate of Jabez Smith.

41. O'Brien, "Hiram Young, Black Entrepreneur," 2. The quotes about wages and training are from William Curtis, telephone conversation with the author, August 29, 2009. Hereafter cited as Curtis interview, August 29, 2009; Thomas, *From Tennessee Slave*, 99.

42. O'Brien, "Hiram Young, Black Entrepreneur," 2; Curtis interview, August 29, 2009, for the "rank and file" quote; Thomas, *From Tennessee Slave*, 99.

43. For 1970s interview with Josephine Flanagan Randall, see William and Annette Curtis, "Searching for the Real Hiram Young," 5–7, unpublished manuscript in the personal collections of William and Annette Curtis, Independence, Missouri; Curtis interview, August 29, 2009; see also Union Historical Company, "Daniel Flanagan," *The History of Jackson County, Missouri: Containing a History of the County, Its Cities, Towns, Etc.* (Kansas City, Mo.: Union Historical Company; Birdsall, Williams & Co., 1881), 888.

44. O'Brien, "Hiram Young: Black Entrepreneur," 1–2; Curtis and Curtis, "Searching for the Real Hiram Young," 3.

45. Adam Mercer Brown, "Over Barren Plains and Rock-Bound Mountains," *Montana The Magazine of Western History* 22, no. 4 (Autumn 1972): 18. Dollar equivalencies in today's money varied over the three decades of the overland emigration. In present-day prices: corn and oats, $31.30 per bushel, horses, $1,250–$3,130 per head, "Measuring Worth," CPI 2014.

46. Unruh, *The Plains Across*, 111–17, especially 112 for the quote from William Rothwell's letter to his parents, May 5, 1850. The original is in William

Renfro Rothwell, "Journal and Letters, 1850," a typescript archived at the Beinecke Rare Book and Manuscript Library, Yale University. See also Bagley, *So Rugged and Mountainous,* 130, 171–73.

47. National Park Service, *National Historic Trails Auto Tour Route Interpretive Guide: Western Missouri through Northeastern Kansas,* by Lee Kreutzer (Salt Lake City: National Trails System–Intermountain Region, September 2005), 5.

48. Lansford W. Hastings, *The Emigrants' Guide to Oregon and California: The 1845 Pioneers' Guide for the Westward Traveler* (1845; repr., Bedford, Mass.: Applewood Books, 1994), 143.

49. J. L. Campbell, *Idaho: Six Months in the New Gold Diggings, The Emigrant's Guide Overland* (Chicago: John R. Walsh, 1864). Microfiche copy in the California State Library, Sacramento. See also a reproduction of Campbell's section on "Provisions and Equipment Recommended," Wyoming State Historic Preservation Office, the Bridger Trail, http://wyoshpo.state.wy.us/btrail/images/big/pg/119.jpg (accessed July 19, 2010). Present-day price equivalents would be $4,200 and $8,870, "Measuring Worth," CPI 2014.

50. For fluctuating oxen prices, see Unruh, *The Plains Across,* 114. For mule prices, see Wyman, "The Outfitting Posts," 17. For the story of Isaac C. Haight and the Keokuk, Iowa, Mormon party, see William G. Hartley, "LDS Emigration in 1853: The Keokuk Encampment and Outfitting Ten Wagon Trains for Utah," *Mormon Historical Studies* (Fall 2003): 49–51.That yoke of two oxen with an 1846 value of $25 would cost $799 today; its 1849 value would have an equivalent cost of between $1,440 and $2,080 today, and mules would cost between $958 and $3,190. Today, the Mormons' budget of $60,000 would be $1.9 million. Today, the $1,000 they were forced to borrow would be $31,600. See "Measuring Worth," CPI 2014.

51. George W. Bush has also been called George Washington Bush. His middle name, or lack thereof, has sometimes caused him to be confused with George Washington, another African American who, in 1850, crossed the plains and founded Centralia, Washington. John Minto traveled with Bush to Oregon Country and referred to him as G. W. Bush in his journal. There is no indication that the middle initial stood for the name Washington. In order to avoid confusion, I have used the name George W. Bush in this book as referring to the African American man who went to Oregon Country in 1844 in the Simmons-Gilliam party. See John Minto, "Reminiscences of Experiences on the Oregon Trail in 1844," II, *Quarterly of the Oregon Historical Society* 2, no. 3 (September 1901): 212, 219, 241; Clackamas Heritage Partners, Historic Oregon City Presents: End of the Oregon Trail Interpretive Center, "Black Pioneers and Settlers—George Washington Bush," http://www.historicoregoncity.org/HOC/index.php?option=com_content&view=article&i (accessed December 29, 2008); and National Park

Service, "George Washington Bush and the Human Spirit of Westward Expansion," *The Museum Gazette* (February 1999), http://www.nps.gov/untold/banners _and_backgrounds/expansionbanner/gwbush.htm (accessed July 29, 2010). Bush's $2,000 today would be $65,300, "Measuring Worth," CPI 2014.

52. For the number of wagons in Bush's party, see Oregon-California Trails Association, Census of Overland Emigrant Documents, Document ID #44 MIN01, Minto, "Journey Description," 2. For Bush assisting others in the party, see Minto, "Reminiscences of Experiences on the Oregon Trail," II, 212; and Bagley, *So Rugged and Mountainous,* 336. See also Katz, *The Black West,* 73–77; Savage, "The Negro in the History of the Pacific Northwest," 259; "A Negro Pioneer in the West," the *Advertiser Journal* [Kent, Washington] (December 23, 1920; repr., *Journal of Negro History* 8, no. 3 (July 1923): 334; Taylor, *In Search of the Racial Frontier,* 82. For Bush providing carefully stocked wagons, see Clackamas Heritage Partners, "Black Pioneers and Settlers—George Washington Bush," and National Park Service, "George Washington Bush and the Human Spirit." According to present-day prices, Bush paid $32,700 to outfit wagons for his trailmates. See "Measuring Worth," CPI 2014.

53. National Park Service, "George Washington Bush and the Human Spirit." Present-day flour: $1,960 per barrel; sugar: $32.70 per pound, calico: $32.71 per yard. See "Measuring Worth," CPI 2014.

54. Rachel Brown's letter is from the exhibition "I Remain Your Affectionate Wife, Until Death . . . Seven letters written to David Brown, a Colored Man (in Downieville, California) From his wife and mother-in-law Rachel Ann Brown and Sarah Smith (in Lancaster, Fairfield County, Ohio)." See letter "To Mr David Brown from Rachel A Brown," dated October 14, 1853. The original letters, discovered and collected by John Mark Lambertson, are in the National Frontier Trails Museum in Independence, Missouri (hereafter cited as "Brown Letters"). Thanks to John Mark Lambertson for providing me with copies of these remarkable documents.

55. Free blacks usually traveled as members of companies organized by whites. Rudolph Lapp has speculated that "no record of any overland company organized solely by and for blacks" exists because the money necessary for such an undertaking would have been extremely difficult for most African Americans to obtain. Lapp, *Blacks in Gold Rush California,* 25. For a discussion of racially exclusive wagon train charters, see Guenther, "Could These Bones Be from a Negro?" 46. For wagon company members' racial hostility toward an African American in the group, see Forbes Parkhill's heavily fictionalized account of Colorado pioneer Barney Ford, *Mister Barney Ford: A Portrait in Bistre* (Denver: Sage Books, 1963), 79–89.

56. Kathleen Bruyn, *"Aunt" Clara Brown: Story of a Black Pioneer* (Boulder, Colo.: Pruett, 1970), 24–25; Roger Baker, *Clara: An Ex-slave in Gold Rush*

Colorado (Central City, Colo.: Black Hawk, 2003), 14–15, 21. The Leavenworth & Pikes Peak Express Company began running Concord coaches to Denver in April 1859. Baker notes that Brown's arrival in Denver on June 6, 1859, suggests her departure date from Leavenworth was sometime in mid-April 1859. For the "color line" drawn by the stage coach company, also see Forbes, *Barney Ford,* 90.

57. Contract for transportation from Lancaster, Ohio, to Marysville, Ohio, Thomas Sturgeon, Samuel Crim, David Brown, February, 1852, in Beasley, *Negro Trail Blazers,* 87–88. In present-day money, David Brown contracted to pay $4,740 for his trip, with a down payment being the equivalent of $1,580, "Measuring Worth," CPI 2014.

58. For a detailed discussion of overland transportation contracts, see John Phillip Reid, "Binding the Elephant: Contracts and Legal Obligations on the Overland Trail," *American Journal of Legal History* 21, no. 4 (October 1977): 285–315, especially 293–310.

59. Lapp, *Blacks in Gold Rush California,* 26. For a brief discussion of Maj. John Love, see William Henry Perry, J. H. Battle, and Weston Arthur Goodspeed, *The History of Medina County and Ohio* (1881; repr., Evansville, Ind.: Unigraphic, 1972), 132.

60. Lapp, *Blacks in Gold Rush California,* 27.

61. Daniels was writing specifically about the African Americans who settled in San Francisco. See Daniels, *Pioneer Urbanites,* 59, 62–74.

62. Charlie Richardson, "Slave Narratives: A Folk History of Slavery in the United States from Interviews with Former Slaves, 1936–1938: Volume X, Missouri Narratives," Federal Writers Project (Washington, D.C.: Library of Congress, 1941), released by Project Gutenberg, February 23, 2011; Missouri State Museum, "Slavery's Echoes: Interviews with Former Missouri Slaves, Quotes from Exhibit Panels, Panel 6: A-Freedom and B-Selling," http://www.mostateparks.com/sites/default/files/se_panels%5B1%5D.pdf (accessed July 21, 2010).

63. For slave catchers patrolling the Missouri border, see James L. Hill, "Migration of Blacks to Iowa, 1820–1960," *Journal of Negro History* 66, no. 4 (Winter 1981–82): 291–92. Missouri State Archives, Missouri Digital Heritage, "Missouri's Early Slave Laws: A History in Documents, Laws concerning Slavery in Missouri Territorial to 1850s," http://www.sos.mo.gov/archives/education/aahi/earlyslavelaws/slavelaws.asp (accessed August 1, 2010).

64. Donnie D. Bellamy, "Free Blacks in Antebellum Missouri, 1820–1860," *Missouri Historical Review* 67 (January 1973): 205. In 1849, these bounties would be the equivalent of $799–$3,190 in present-day dollars. See "Measuring Worth," CPI 2014.

65. Judge William B. Napton ruling for the Missouri supreme court, quoted in Bellamy, "Free Blacks in Antebellum Missouri," 207 (italics in original).

66. Brown, *Narrative of William W. Brown*, 95. For slave hunters overrunning free states, see Hill, "Migration of Blacks to Iowa," especially, 290–92. For accounts of the vulnerability of fugitive and free blacks to slave hunters, also see Stanley W. Campbell, *The Slave Catchers: Enforcement of the Fugitive Slave Law, 1850–1860* (New York: W. W. Norton, 1970); Wilson, *Freedom at Risk*, especially 75–82, 113–20; Northup, *Twelve Years a Slave*.

67. William Wells Brown, *The Travels of William Wells Brown, a Fugitive Slave and the American Fugitive in Europe. Sketches of Places and People Abroad* (1847, 1853; repr., ed. Paul Jefferson, New York: Marcus Weiner, 1991), http://books.google.com/books?id=02IVODKxz7KC&pg=PA238&lpg=PA238&dq=William+Wells+Brown+Narrative+of+a+Fugitive+Slave (accessed July 26, 2011), 57; William Wells Brown, *Narrative of William W. Brown, A Fugitive Slave. Written by Himself* (1847; digital repr., Chapel Hill: University of North Carolina Press, 2001), 81, http://docsouth.unc.edu/neh/brown47/brown47.html (accessed August 4, 2010).

68. Bellamy, "Free Blacks in Antebellum Missouri," 206–7. See also Kenneth MacKenzie to Gabriel S. Chouteau, letter dated St. Louis, May 3, 1843, regarding MacKenzie's refusal to pay for a "negro woman and children bid off by me at the Court House" because they "claim that they are free and that a suit has been instituted for the purpose of obtaining their freedom." This letter is located in Missouri Historical Society, A1518 Slaves and Slavery Collection, 1772–1950, Folder 4, dated 1843 May 3.

69. Phil Reader, "Uncle Dave's Story: The Life of Ex-slave Dave Boffman," Parts 1–2. Santa Cruz Public Library, http://www/santacruzpl.org/history/articles/207/ (accessed July 21, 2010).

70. Reader, "Uncle Dave's Story," Part 1. His sale price would be the present-day equivalent of $30,900, "Measuring Worth," CPI 2014.

71. Reader, "Uncle Dave's Story," Part 1.

72. Margaret Ann Reid, "Charlotta Gordon Pyles," *Notable Black American Women,* Book II, ed. Jessie Carney Smith (Detroit: Gale Research, Thomson, 1996), 535.

73. Hallie Q. Brown, *Homespun Heroines and Other Women of Distinction* (Xenia, Ohio: Aldine, 1926), 38. The original fee for safe passage is the present-day equivalent of $3,160; the extortion demand amounts to an extra $1,580 in present-day currency, "Measuring Worth," CPI 2014.

74. Brown, *Homespun Heroines,* 39, 40; Reid, "Charlotta Gordon Pyles," 536. Brown and Reid both state that Benjamin "was sold into Fayette County," this was probably LaFayette County (county seat, Lexington) located in west-central Missouri, east of Kansas City. LaFayette County was one of several counties settled mostly by Southerners to the north and south of the Missouri River who brought their slaves and slaveholding traditions with them. This area became

known as "Little Dixie." See "LaFayette County, Missouri History," http://www.lcmogov.com/P-100/History.aspx (accessed January 8, 2012).

75. For a summary of the Fanny Wigglesworth incident, see Stanley Harrold, *Border War: Fighting Over Slavery before the Civil War* (Chapel Hill: University of North Carolina Press, 2010), 61. Also see Tom Calarco, Cynthia Vogel, Kathryn Grover, Rae Hallstrom, Sharron L. Pope, and Melissa Waddy-Thibodeaux, *Places of the Underground Railroad: A Geographical Guide* (Santa Barbara, Calif.: Greenwood, 2011), 73; National Underground Railroad Network to Freedom, The Clermont County, Ohio, Freedom Trail, Moscow Underground Railroad and Abolitionist Sites, "The Wigglesworth Kidnapping," http://www.firstohio.com/maps/tours_pdf/Underground_Railroad_Tour.pdf (accessed July 27, 2011); Ann Hagedorn, *Beyond the River: The Untold Story of the Heroes of the Underground Railroad* (New York: Simon & Schuster Paperbacks, 2002), 223–24. Hagedorn's account of the Wigglesworth kidnapping mistakenly concludes that Ohio abolitionist Robert Fee "found the wife and children somewhere near Independence, Missouri and brought them home." See Hagendorn, *Beyond the River,* 224. In fact, Fee made two unsuccessful attempts to rescue Fanny Wigglesworth and her children.

76. For discussion of slave auctions in Independence, see "Black History in Independence: Black History Month Celebrates Historic Sites and Attractions," *Road and Travel Magazine,* 2006. For John Hudson's description of a slave auction, see John Hudson, *A Forty-niner in Utah with the Stansbury Expedition of Great Salt Lake: Letters and Journal of John Hudson, 1848–50,* ed. Brigham D. Madsen (Salt Lake City: University of Utah Tanner Trust Fund: Salt Lake City, 1981), digital transcription by Kay Threlkeld, National Park Service, January, 2008, 25, 42 (note 64); William Lewis Manly, *Death Valley in '49: The Autobiography of a Pioneer, Detailing His Life from a Humble Home in the Green Mountains to the Gold Mines of California; and Particularly Reciting the Sufferings of the Band of Men, Women, and Children Who Gave "Death Valley" Its Name* (1849; digital repr., Project Gutenberg, 2004), http://www.gutenberg.org/files/12236/12236-h/12236-h.htm (accessed December 12, 2008). In the Manly quote, the spelling of the name of one of the founders of present-day St. Joseph is incorrect. The correct spelling is "Robidoux."

Chapter 4

Epigraph. T. H. Jefferson, *Map of the Emigrant Road from Independence, Mo., to St. Francisco, California, and Accompaniment* (1849; repr., San Francisco: California Historical Society, with an introduction and notes by George R. Stewart, 1945), 1, 2, hereafter cited as *Jefferson Map and Accompaniment.*

1. See Unruh, *The Plains Across,* map 4, 238; Mattes, *Great Platte River Road,* 5–6.

2. Unruh, *The Plains Across,* 68–73, 97–98; Mattes, *Platte River Road Narratives,* 5–7, and *Great Platte River Road,* 103–35.

3. Mattes, *Platte River Road Narratives,* xi–xii, and *Great Platte River Road,* 7–8.

4. Marie Albertina (Stark) Wallace, "Recollections of Sylvia Stark, Part 2," http://www.canadianmysteries.ca/sites/robinson/archives/diaryjournalreminiscence/3109en (accessed July 14, 2009), hereafter cited as Sylvia Stark interview, part 2. Mary Albertina Stark Wallace was the daughter of Sylvia Estes Stark and Louis Stark. The original Sylvia Stark interviews, parts 1–2, are located in Salt Spring Island Historical Society Archives, Add. Mss. 91, Salt Spring Island, British Columbia.

5. For a description of the course of the road see, Mattes, *Platte River Road Narratives,* 5–7, and *Great Platte River Road,* especially, 103–39; Bagley, *So Rugged and Mountainous,* 89–91; and Unruh, *The Plains Across,* 119–22. See also National Park Service, *National Historic Trails Auto Tour Route Interpretive Guide: Nebraska and Northeastern Colorado,* by Lee Kreutzer (Salt Lake City: National Trails System-Intermountain Region, August 2006), 3; National Park Service, *National Historic Trails Auto Tour Route Interpretive Guide across Wyoming* (Salt Lake City: National Trails System-Intermountain Region, July 2007), 7–11, and individual National Park Service map brochures for each trail. I am indebted to Lee Kreutzer for orienting me to the complex of overland trails.

6. Mattes, *Great Platte River Road,* 50–52; Unruh, *The Plains Across,* 149–55.

7. Alvin Coffey, *The Autobiography of Alvin A. Coffey* (1891; repr., *The Pioneer* 23 no. 1, December 2000), 11. See also LeRoy R. Hafen and Francis Marion Young, *Fort Laramie and the Pageant of the West, 1834–1890* (1938; repr., Lincoln: University of Nebraska Press, 1984), 150–54.

8. This description of the route is derived from National Park Service, *Across Wyoming,* 7–11.

9. *Jefferson Map and Accompaniment,* 21.

10. Quotes from Lee Kreutzer, NPS Cultural Resource Specialist, in National Park Service, "South Pass, Fremont County, Wyoming," California National Historic Trail, http://www.nps.gov/cali/planyour visit/site7.htm (accessed June 1, 2011); National Park Service, *Across Wyoming,* 4.

11. Unruh, *The Plains Across,* 50, 149, 274, 354; Bagley, *With Golden Visions,* 101–3, 174–80, 202–4, 278–85, 354–55.

12. Unruh, *The Plains Across,* 185; Richard K Brock, ed., *Emigrant Trails West: A Guide to the California Trail Featuring the Trails West Markers Located along the California Trail from the Raft River to the Humboldt Sink and the Greenhorn Cutoff* (Reno, Nev.: Trails West, 2000), 5; Michael E. LaSalle, *Emigrants on the Overland Trail: The Wagon Trains of 1848* (Kirksville, Mo.: Truman

State University Press, 2011), 268–74; Bagley, *With Golden Visions*, 114–16, 152–56, 211–12.

13. LaSalle, *Emigrants on the Overland Trail*, 420–23; Bagley, *With Golden Visions*, 217–22, 285–88, 420–23.

14. For a biographical sketch of Harris, see Jerome Peltier, "Moses 'Black' Harris," in *The Mountain Men and the Fur Trade of the Far West*, vol. 4, ed. LeRoy R. Hafen (Glendale, Calif.: Arthur H. Clark, 1966), 103–17; Moses Harris, letter to the editor, *Oregon Spectator*, November 26, 1846, quoted in Ross A. Smith, "The Southern Route Revisited," *Oregon Historical Quarterly* 105, no. 2 (Summer 2004): 14, http://www.historycooperative.org/journals/ohq/105.2/smith.html (accessed August 12, 2010); Stafford Hazelett, "Let Us Honor Those to Whom Honor Is Due," *Oregon Historical Quarterly* 111, no. 2 (Summer 2010): 2–3, 24, http://www.historycooperative.org/journals/ohq/111.2/hazelett.html (accessed August 12, 2010).

15. Unruh, *The Plains Across*, 348–50; Bagley, *So Rugged and Mountainous*, 296–304.

16. Stuart, "Notes on a Trip to California," quoted in Lapp, *Blacks in Gold Rush California*, 30.

17. Kenneth N. Owens, "The Mormon-Carson Emigrant Trail in Western History," *Montana The Magazine of Western History* 42, no. 1 (Winter 1991): 14–27; Brock, *Emigrant Trails West*, 111–59; Unruh, *The Plains Across*, 106–7, 369–70; Bagley, *With Golden Visions*, 155–67, 259–63, 365–66; LaSalle, *Emigrants on the Overland Trail*, 423–27.

18. Margaret Frink, quoted in Lapp, *Blacks in Gold Rush California*, 30.

19. Brock, *Emigrant Trails West*, 190–99; Bagley, *So Rugged and Mountainous*, 56, 211–13, 308–9; Bagley, *With Golden Visions*, 157–60.

20. For more detail on the lesser-known southern routes, see Gregory Franzwa, "Covered Wagon Roads to the American West" (Tucson: Patrice Press, 1998), a map prepared in cooperation with the Long Distance Trails Office, National Park Service, Department of the Interior, Salt Lake City, Utah, hereafter cited as Franzwa, "Covered Wagon Roads." See also The TNGenNet, "Trails West: A Map of Early Western Migration Trails," http://www.tngenweb.org/tnletters/usa-west.htm (accessed June 26, 2011); Oregon-California Trails Association, Southern Trails Chapter, "Proposal for a New Southern National Historic Trail" (n.d.),http://southern-trails.org/PDF/Proposal_for_a_%20New_Southern_National_Historic_Trail.pdf (accessed June 26, 2011); National Park Service, *Comprehensive Management and Use Plan/Final Environmental Impact Statement, California National Historic Trail, Pony Express National Historic Trail; Management and Use Plan Update/Final Environmental Impact Statement, Oregon National Historic Trail, Mormon Pioneer National Historic Trail* (Salt Lake City: National Park Service, 1999), especially "Additional Routes for the California National

Historic Trail," 71, 73, 75. See also Blaine P. Lamb, "Travelers on the California Leg of the Southern Route 1849–1852," a publication of California State Parks, http://www.parks.ca.gov/?page_id=24680 (accessed September 4, 2010).

21. Franzwa, "Covered Wagon Roads"; National Park Service, *Comprehensive Management Plan*, 75; Oregon-California Trails Association, "Proposal for a New Southern National Historic Trail"; Lamb, "Travelers on the California Leg," 3; Stanislaus Lasselle, "The 1849 Diary of Stanislaus Lasselle," ed. Patricia A. Etter, *Overland Journal* 9, no. 2 (1991): 27n3.

22. Franzwa, "Covered Wagon Roads"; Lamb, "Travelers on the California Leg," 3; Harlan Hague, "The Search for a Southern Overland Route to California," http://www.softadventure.net/roadcal.htm, 6–7 (accessed September 4, 2010); Phil Brigandi, "The Southern Emigrant Trail," *Overland Journal* 28, no. 3 (Fall 2010): 103–4; Bagley, *So Rugged and Mountainous*, 110–11, 386–87; U.S. Department of the Interior, Bureau of Land Management, "Old Spanish Trail/Mormon Road Historic District," *National Register of Historic Places Registration Form*, prepared by Terri McBride, Nevada State Historic Preservation Office, in collaboration with Stanton D. Rolf, Las Vegas Field Office (Washington, D.C.: National Park Service, 2001). See especially sec. 7, 1, sec. 8, 1–6.

23. "Black Forty-niners," Death Valley National Park, History and Culture: People, http://www.nps.gov/deva/historyculture/people.htm (accessed August 29, 2011); Carl I. Wheat, "The Forty-Niners in Death Valley: A Tentative Census," *Historical Society of Southern California Quarterly* 21(December 1939): 112, reprinted online, http://www.scvhistory.com/scvhistory/wheat-49ers.htm (accessed January 10, 2012). Wheat lists "Tom (Negro)," "Joe (Negro)," and " 'Little West' (Negro)" as members of "The Mississippi Boys," which was part of a larger group of Mississippians who broke away from the Jayhawkers and Briers parties near Towne's Pass. Wheat notes that "only the names of these three Negro slaves have apparently been recorded." Rudolph Lapp refers to "Tom" as one of the three slaves who were in the Death Valley group. See Lapp, *Blacks in Gold Rush California*, 31.

24. Ivan Denton, *Old Brands and Lost Trails: Arkansas and the Great Cattle Drives* (Fayetteville: University of Arkansas Press, 1992), 63–69; Bagley, *With Golden Visions*, 186–90.

25. Benjamin Hayes, *Pioneer Notes from the Diaries of Judge Benjamin Hayes, 1849–1875*, ed. Marjorie Tisdale Wolcott (Los Angeles: McBride Printing, 1929), 34–35, reprinted online by Library of Congress American Memory Project, "California as I Saw It: First-Person Narratives of California's Early Years, 1849–1900," https://memory.loc.gov/ammem/cbhtml/ (accessed February 10, 2016). For the mention of "Bob and Jane" and sharing a blanket with the black man, see Lapp, *Blacks in Gold Rush California*, 31. For Lorton's comment about the "negro concert," see Edward Leo Lyman, *The Overland Journey from Utah*

to California: Wagon Travel from the City of Saints to the City of Angeles (Reno: University of Nevada Press, 2004), 58–59.

26. Jacob Stover, "The Jacob Y. Stover Narrative: History of the Sacramento Mining Company of 1849, Written by One of Its Number Jacob Y. Stover," ed. John Walton Caughey, *Pacific Historical Review* 6, no. 2 (June 1937): 176–77. See, especially, 177n25 regarding Jackson, the African American manager who was in charge of Prudhomme's Rancho Cucamonga. Although Stover does not state that the grapes being pressed by the Indians were fermented, his description indicates that the men became intoxicated after drinking the juice and "began to tumble over and the wine came up as fast as it went down." He wrote that Jackson "got a spade and gave it to me, told me to dig holes at their mouths. So I did." At the end of the night, Stover and one other man in his party "were the only ones left on our feet," 177. For a bit more about Rancho Cucamonga and Jackson, see also Lyman, *Overland Journey from Utah to California*, 57.

27. Gregory Michno and Susan Michno, *A Fate Worse Than Death: Indian Captives in the West, 1830–1885* (Caldwell, Idaho: Caxton Press, 2007), 99–100.

28. Michno and Michno, *A Fate Worse Than Death*, 100; Maria E. Montoya, *Translating Property: The Maxwell Land Grant and the Conflict over Land in the American West, 1840–1900* (Berkeley: University of California Press, 2002), 41. For differing accounts of the fate of the white captives, see Montoya, *Translating Property*, 228n60; Hampton Sides, *Blood and Thunder: An Epic of the American West* (New York: Doubleday, 2006), 241, 252; Jay W. Sharp, "Desert Trails: Kit Carson and the Santa Fe Trail," *Desert USA*, http://www.desertusa.com/mag03/trails/trails08.html (accessed August 9, 2010).

29. Mattes, *Platte River Road Narratives*, xii. See also Unruh, *The Plains Across*, 66–68, for a brief discussion of land-sea emigrants.

30. Moya Hansen, "Ford, Barney L. 1822–1902," The Black Past: An Online Reference Guide to African American History, BlackPast.org, http://www.blackpast.org/?q-aaw/ford-barney-1-1822-1902 (accessed August 7, 2010); Brooke Cleary, "Barney L. Ford: Runaway Slave, Denver Pioneer," Colorado Historical Society, 2001, adapted from "Barney Ford—From Plantation Slave to Denver Leader" by David F. Halass, *Colorado History NOW*, October 2000, www.docstoc.cdom/docs/44329510/BARNEY-FORD (accessed September 23, 2010); National Park Service, "Barney L. Ford Building," Aboard the Underground Railroad: A National Register Travel Itinerary," http://www.cr.nps.gov/nr/travel/underground/co1.htm (accessed June 25, 2011).

31. Parkhill, *Mister Barney Ford*, especially 38–67, 78–89; Cleary, "Barney L. Ford"; National Park Service, "Barney L. Ford Building"; Taylor, *In Search of the Racial Frontier*, 202–3.

32. Bagley, *So Rugged and Mountainous*, 88.

33. Francaviglia quoted in *Mapping and Imagination*, 97.

34. Bidwell, quoted in Bagley, *So Rugged and Mountainous*, 87–88, 106–10. See also Unruh, *The Plains Across*, 110, 118; Morgan, *Overland in 1846*, 15–16.

35. Unruh, *The Plains Across*, 157.

36. Bagley, *So Rugged and Mountainous*, 133; Bagley, *With Golden Visions*, 27–28.

37. William Clayton, *The Latter-Day Saints' Emigrants Guide* (1848; repr., Gerald, Mo.: Patrice Press, 1983); Richard T. Stillson, *Spreading the Word: A History of Information in the California Gold Rush* (Lincoln: University of Nebraska Press, 2006), 45, 47; Bagley, *So Rugged and Mountainous*, 132–34.

38. Unruh, *The Plains Across*, 74–75, 160. Call quoted in Bagley, *With Golden Visions*, 28.

39. Unruh, *The Plains Across*, 74–75. See also Stillson, *Spreading the Word*, 45, 47. For an intimate perspective of some of Frémont's exploits and the popularity of his works, see Pamela Herr and Mary Lee Spence, eds., "'I Really Had Something Like the Blues': Letters from Jessie Benton Frémont to Elizabeth Blair Lee, 1847–1883," *Montana The Magazine of Western History* 41, no. 2 (Spring 1991): 16–31, especially 17–18. The 1845 Frémont-Preuss maps were some of the earliest attempts to accurately map the Great Basin region of the West. Frémont is credited with coining the name "Great Basin." See Francaviglia, *Mapping and Imagination*, 82–90, 97, 105. For the quote about Frémont's overlooked sources, see Francaviglia, *Mapping and Imagination*, 82–83. Jacob Dodson's description is in G. M. Bergman, "The Negro Who Rode with Frémont in 1847," *The Negro History Bulletin* 28, no. 2 (November 1964): 32. For a brief biographical sketch of Jacob Dodson, see Shaun Michael Mars, "Jacob Dodson (1825–?)," The Black Past: An Online Reference Guide to African American History, BlackPast.org, http://www.blackpast.org/?q=aaw/dodson (accessed September 18, 2010).

40. Mars, "Jacob Dodson (1825–?)"; Taylor, *In Search of the Western Frontier*, 49; Bergman, "The Negro Who Rode with Frémont in 1847," 31–32.

41. Mars, "Jacob Dodson (1825–?)"; Bergman, "The Negro Who Rode with Frémont in 1847"; Taylor, *In Search of the Western Frontier*, 49. Dodson's payment of $493 would be the present-day equivalent of $16,100. See "Measuring Worth," CPI 2014.

42. See Weller's remarks in the *Congressional Globe*, 33d Cong., 2d Sess. (January 31, 1855), 493, 34th Cong., 1st Sess. (February 21, 1856), 482, 34th Cong., 1st Sess. (April 17, 1856), 916. See also Robert E. May, "Invisible Men" Blacks and the U.S. Army in the Mexican War," *The Historian*, 49 (1987): 475–76, especially note 24. Congress deducted $281 from Dodson's compensation because that had already been paid to him by Frémont.

43. See Jacob Dodson (colored) to Simon Cameron, Secretary of War, letter dated April 23, 1861; Simon Cameron, Secretary of War to Jacob Dodson

(colored), April 29, 1861. Both letters are in Sheldon Moody, Calvin Duvall Cowell, Frederick Clayton Ainsworth, Robert N. Scott, Henry Martyn Lazelle, George Breckridge Davis, Leslie J. Perry, and Josephy William Kirkley, eds. *The War of the Rebellion: A Compilation of the Official Records of the Union and Confederate Armies,* series 3, vol. 1 (Washington, D.C.: Government Printing Office 1880–1901), 107, 133, from the Cornell University Library Digital Collections, http://ebooks.library.cornell.edu/cgi/text/pageviewer-idx?c=moawar;cc=moawar;1l=Jacob (accessed July 2, 2013). See also James M. McPherson, *The Negro's Civil War: How American Blacks Felt and Acted during the War for the Union* (New York: Pantheon Books, 1965), 19.

44. T. H. Jefferson, *Map of the Emigrant Road from Independence, Mo., to St. Francisco, California, and Accompaniment* (1846; repr., San Francisco: California Historical Society, 1945); Morgan, *Overland in 1846,* vol. 1, 237. For more on the significance of the T. H. Jefferson map, see also J. Roderic Korns, "West from Fort Bridger: The Pioneering of the Immigrant Trails across Utah, 1846–1850," *Utah Historical Quarterly* 19 (1951): 177–85, and *West from Fort Bridger: The Pioneering of the Immigrant Trails across Utah, 1846–1850, Original Diaries and Journals* (1951; repr., Logan: Utah State University Press, 1994).

45. Morgan, *Overland in 1846,* vol. 1, 237. The three-dollar map would be the present-day equivalent of $95.80, "Measuring Worth," CPI, 2014.

46. Byron W. Woodson Sr., *A President in the Family: Thomas Jefferson, Sally Hemings, and Thomas Woodson* (Westport, Conn.: Praeger, 2001), especially 61–66, 72, 119–20, 183–88; Rush Spedden, "Who Was T. H. Jefferson?" *Overland Journal* 8, no. 3 (1990): 2–8; Fawn M. Brodie, *Thomas Jefferson: An Intimate History* (New York: Bantam, 1974), especially 22–27, 393–94 , 478 730–31n20; Annette Gordon-Reed, *The Hemingses of Monticello: An American Family* (New York: W. W. Norton, 2008); Fawn M. Brodie, "The Great Jefferson Taboo," *American Heritage Magazine* 23, no. 4 (June 1972): 48–57, 97–100, http://www.americanheritage.com/print/52886 (accessed July 3, 2013); Fawn M. Brodie, "Thomas Jefferson's Unknown Grandchildren," *American Heritage Magazine* 27, no. 6 (October 1976): 23–33, 94–99, http://www.americaheritage.com/print/53472 (accessed July 3, 2013); Will Bagley, "Pioneer Map Leads Jefferson Scandal to West," *Salt Lake Tribune,* May 6, 2001. For a discussion of DNA evidence of Jefferson and his children with Hemings, see Jennifer Jensen Wallach, "The Vindication of Fawn Brodie," *Massachusetts Review* 43, no. 2 (Summer 2002): 277–95; Jan Lewis, "Introduction: Thomas Jefferson and Sally Hemings Redux," *William and Mary Quarterly,* 3d series, 57, no. 1 (January 2000): 121–24; Joseph J. Ellis, "Jefferson: Post-DNA," *William and Mary Quarterly,* 3d series 57, no. 1 (January 2000): 125–38; Peter S. Onuf, "Every Generation Is an 'Independant Nation': Colonization, Miscegenation, and the Fate of Jefferson's Children," *William and Mary Quarterly,* 3d series, 57, no. 1 (January 2000):

153–70; Frontline Documentary Films, "Interview with Dr. Eugene Foster: Jefferson's Blood," Public Broadcasting System documentary film and related transcripts and documentary materials available at the PBS website, http://www.pbs.org/wgbh/pages/frontline/shows/jefferson/true/ (accessed September 18, 2010).

47. Constance Moore Richardson, telephone interview with Shirley Ann Wilson Moore, September 11, 2009, hereafter cited as Richardson interview, September 11, 2009.

48. James T. Callender, the *Richmond Recorder,* September 1, 1802 as quoted in Brodie, "Thomas Jefferson's Unknown Grandchildren," 23–24. See also Brodie, *Thomas Jefferson,* 464.

49. Woodson, *A President in the Family,* 40–41; Richardson interview, September 11, 2001. For the continuing controversy surrounding T. H. Jefferson's background, see Robert F. Turner, ed., *The Jefferson-Hemings Controversy: Report of the Scholars Commission* (Durham, N.C.: Carolina Academic Press, 2011), especially 12; Gordon-Reed, *The Hemingses of Monticello,* 718–19n52; Wallach, "Vindication of Fawn Brodie," 283–90; Dumas Malone and Steven H. Hochman, "A Note on Evidence: The Personal History of Madison Hemings," *Journal of Southern History,* 41, no. 4 (November 1975): 523–28; Ellis, "Jefferson: Post-DNA," especially 127–30; Lewis, "Thomas Jefferson and Sally Hemings Redux," 121–24.

50. Woodson, *A President in the Family,* 32, 40; Spedden, "Who Was T. H. Jefferson?" 2; Brodie, *Thomas Jefferson,* especially 322, 384–85, 478–79, 602–3, 730–31n20. For speculation on T. H. Jefferson's nautical background, see Korns, "West from Fort Bridger," 177.

51. Spedden, "Who Was T. H. Jefferson?" 7.

52. Woodson, *A President in the Family,* 61–66, 72. See also Brodie, "Thomas Jefferson's Unknown Grandchildren," especially 27–33.

53. Woodson, *A President in the Family,* 66–67, 72, 82–83; Brodie, "Thomas Jefferson's Unknown Grandchildren," especially 27–33.

54. Woodson, *A President in the Family,* 87–88, 101–4.

55. Richardson interview, September 11, 2011; Woodson, *A President in the Family,* 119–20.

56. Richardson interview, September 11, 2011. For departure of T. H. Jefferson from Missouri, see *Jefferson Inquirer* (Jefferson City, Missouri), May 13, 1846, which quotes a late issue of the Independence *Western Expositor* that lists T. H. Jefferson among "those going out" West. See also Korns, "West from Fort Bridger," 177–78.

57. Richardson interview, September 11, 2011.

58. The *Missouri Republican* reprinted the departure notice that first appeared in a late issue of the Independence *Western Expositor.* Quoted in Morgan, *Overland in 1846,* vol. 2, 518.

59. Benjamin S. Lippincott to John L. Stephens, Esqr., Feby. 6, 1847, *Ciudad de los Angelos.*" The letter is in the online archive "Familytales," http://www.familytales.org/dbDisplay.php?id=ltr_bs1838&person=bsl (accessed July 4, 2011). For the original letter, see Benjamin S. Lippincott letters: ALS, 1847–1851, BANC MSS 95/15c, Bancroft Library, University of California, Berkeley (hereafter Bancroft Library). Also see Bill Coate, "Jim Savage Revisited," *The Madera* (California) *Tribune,* Tuesday, March 30, 2004, http://www.maderatribune.com/life/lifeview.asp?c=102108 (accessed July 4, 2011).

60. Morgan, *Overland in 1846,* vol. 1, 238; Korns, "West from Fort Bridger," 181.

61. T. H. Jefferson, *Map and Accompaniment;* Korns, "West from Fort Bridger, 178.

62. All quotes from T. H. Jefferson, *Map and Accompaniment.* See also Morgan, *Overland in 1846,* vol. 1, 240–42; Korns, "West from Fort Bridger," 182.

63. George R. Stewart, "An Introduction to Maps of the Emigrant Road," in Jefferson, *Maps of the Emigrant Road* (1846; repr., California Historical Society: San Francisco, 1945*)*, 7; Korns, "West from Fort Bridger," 178.

64. Stewart, "An Introduction," viii.

65. Francaviglia, *Mapping and Imagination,* 116.

66. T. H. Jefferson, *Map and Accompaniment.* See also Morgan, *Overland in 1846,* vol. 1, 244.

67. Woodson, *A President in the Family,* 126, 139; Beverly J. Gray, "The Hemings Family of Monticello," *Recorder,* Ross County Historical Society Magazine, February 1994 (updated 1998). Reprinted on the Thomas Woodson Family website, http://www.woodson.org/Hemingshistory.shtml (accessed January 1, 2016).

68. Francaviglia, *Mapping and Imagination,* xvi.

69. Woodson, *A President in the Family,* 126–27, 139.

Chapter 5

Epigraph 1. Coffey, "Autobiography and Reminiscence of Alvin Coffey," 47.
Epigraph 2. Theodore Edgar Potter, *The Autobiography of Theodore Edgar Potter* (Concord, N.H.: Rumford Press, 1913), 28, digitized version from the HathiTrust Yale University, http:/hdl.handle.net/2027/yale.39002028259050 (accessed April 13, 2014).

1. Gus Blair to Dr. Sir, July 13, 1849. Blair's letter was published in the *Fort Des Moines Star,* November 2, 1849. Thanks to Will Bagley for sharing this with me. For the quote about the "heterogeneous mass" of emigrants, see Reid, *Overland to California,* 50.

2. Robert W. Carter, "'Sometimes When I Hear the Winds Sigh': Mortality on the Overland Trail," *California History* 74, no. 2 (Summer 1995): 146.

3. Reid, "Binding the Elephant," especially 287–300. See also Walter T. Durham, *Volunteer Forty-Niners: Tennesseans and the California Gold Rush* (Nashville: Vanderbilt University Press, 1997), 5.

4. See especially Unruh, *The Plains Across*, 140–49. Lapp quoted in *Blacks in Gold Rush California*, 33, 36.

5. Unruh, *The Plains Across*, 108–11.

6. Bennett C. Clark, "Diary of a Journey from Missouri to California in 1849," ed. Ralph P. Bieber, in *Missouri Historical Review* 23 (1928): 35.

7. Edmund Green, "Reminiscences of a Pioneer," 17. Original at the Bancroft Library, quoted in Lapp, *Blacks in Gold Rush California*," 34.

8. See "Dr. Charles Elisha Boyle Diary," reprinted in the *Columbus* (Ohio) *Dispatch*, May 14, 1849. Also see Lapp, *Blacks in Gold Rush California*, 34. The man's annual salary would be the present-day equivalent of $9,580, "Measuring Worth," CPI 2014.

9. David Demarest, "Diary: and Related Material of Trip in Bark, Norumbega to Galveston, Texas, Then Overland to California, Experiences in the Mines, etc.," diary entries for April 29, 1849, and April 30, 1849. The original is in the Bancroft Library. See also Lapp, *Blacks in Gold Rush California*, 33. Lapp speculated that this was a ruse concocted by the Texas "sheriff" and his black cohort to extort money from the gullible travelers. The $70 extorted from the group is the present-day equivalent of $2,240, "Measuring Worth," CPI, 2014.

10. Unruh, *The Plains Across*, 108; Walker D. Wyman, "Bullwhacking: A Prosaic Profession Peculiar to the Great Plains," *New Mexico Historical Review* 7, no. 4 (October 1932): 300–301; Floyd Edgar Bresee, "Overland Freighting in the Platte Valley, 1850–1870" (master's thesis, University of Nebraska, 1937), 29; Alexander Majors, *Seventy Years on the Frontier: Alexander Majors' Memoirs of a Lifetime on the Border* (Chicago: Rand, McNally, 1893), 103; John Johnson Davies, "Historical Sketch of My Life," *Utah Historical Quarterly* 9, nos. 3–4 (July–October 1941): 155–67, especially 160 regarding the "circus" that ensued when trail novices attempted to use the whip and direct oxen by voice commands. See also Gardner, *Wagons for the Santa Fe Trade*, 9–10; Hal Schindler, "Bullwhacking Was No Snap: Occupied Lowest Rung on the Social Ladder," *Salt Lake Tribune*, October 29, 1995. See also Madison Berryman Moorman, *Journal of Madison Berryman Moorman, 1850–1851*, ed. Irene D. Paden (San Francisco: Westgate Press, 1948), especially entries, May 19 (1850), 10, May 30, 16, June 16, 22–23, July 1, 34–35, July 10–July 11, 40–41. For the quote from W. Z. Hickman, see Curtis, *A Rich Heritage*, 12. The present-day equivalent of the whips made by the black men in Independence is $16–$24, "Measuring Worth," CPI, 2014.

11. For the quote about the black Kentuckian named John and the quote from Amos Batchelder, see Lapp, *Blacks in Gold Rush California*, 29, 30; Eva

Turner Clark, ed., *California Letters of William Gill* (New York: Downs Printing, 1922), 34. See also Davies, "Historical Sketch of My Life," 160; Guy Washington, "California Pioneers of African Descent," compiled for the National Park Service, http://home.nps.gov/subjects/ugrr/discover_history/upload/California-Pioneers-of-African-Descent.pdf (accessed July 15, 2011), 73, 139–41.

12. Jane McBride Choate, "Heroes and Heroines: Green Flake—Black Pioneer," *Liahona,* June 1989, http://www.lds.org/ldsorg/v/index.jsp?vgnextoid=f31811 8dd536c010VgnVCM1000004d8 (accessed August 23, 2008); Miriam B. Murphy, "Those Pioneering African Americans," *Beehive History* 22, in Utah History to Go, http://historytogo.utah.gov/utah_chapters/pioneers_and_cowboys/thosepioneer ingafricana (accessed August 23, 2008); Coleman, "Blacks in Utah History"; Margaret Blair Young, "Flake, Green (1828–1903)," The Black Past: An Online Reference Guide to African American History, BlackPast.org, http://www.blackpast .org/?q=aaw/flake-green-1828-1903 (accessed July 24, 2008); Washington, "California Pioneers of African Descent," 1, 52, 73, 126.

13. Carter, *Story of the Negro Pioneer,* 4–6; Murphy, "Those Pioneering African Americans."

14. Carter, *Story of the Negro Pioneer,* 6.

15. Ibid., 5; Coleman, "Blacks in Utah History"; Clark, *California Letters of William Gill,* 34; Choate, "Heroes and Heroines"; Murphy, "Those Pioneering African Americans."

16. Carter, *Story of the Negro Pioneer,* 6–7. Green Flake's remarks about slavery are quoted in Ron Freeman, "James Madison Flake, 1815–1850," 41, online website, https://familysearch.org/patron/v2/TH-300-41879-6-92/dist.pdf?ctx =ArtCtxPublic (accessed January 16, 2016); Margaret Blair Young, "Green Flake: Who Can Tell His Story?," Patheos Mormon: Hosting the Conversation on Faith, online website, http://www.patheos.com/Mormon/Green-Flake-Margaret-Blair -Young (accessed January 14, 2016). The interview with Bertha Udell was conducted by family historian John Fretwell, "Miscellaneous Family Papers, 9," unpublished, Fresno, Calif. 1997.

17. Carter, Story of the Negro Pioneer, 18–19; Will Bagley, "Black Youths Helped Blaze Mormon Trail," Utah History to Go, *Salt Lake Tribune,* August 27, 2000, http://www.historytogo.utah.gov/salt_lake_tribune/history_matters/082700 .html (accessed August 22, 2010). Jequetta Bellard, "For Many Enslaved San Bernardino Was the First Stop," *The Black Voice News: The California Connection to the Underground Railroad,* March 23, 2006, 11–12. See also Nicholas R. Cataldo, "Lizzy Flake Rowan," San Bernardino: Where History and the Future Meet (City of San Bernardino, 1998), http://www.ci.san-bernardino.ca.us/about /history/lizzy_flake_rowan_slave.asp (accessed August 22, 2010); San Bernardino Historical and Pioneer Society, "The Area's First Black College Graduate: Alice Rowan Johnson," 1983. Online reprint by the City of San Bernardino, California,

http://www.sbcity.org/about/history/pioneer_women/alice_rowan_johnson.asp (accessed August 2, 2013).

18. Interview with Jeannette Molson, conducted by Shirley Ann Wilson Moore, June 24, 2009. Hereafter cited as Molson interview.

19. Coffey, "Autobiography and Reminiscence of Alvin Aaron Coffee," 47.

20. Thurman, *Pioneers of Negro Origin,* 12. See also Coffey, "Autobiography," *The Pioneer,* 10–13; Alvin A. Coffey, "The Autobiography of Alvin A. Coffey," *Overland Journal* 20, no. 2 (Summer 2002): 64–73. Robert Clark, Don Buck, and Tom Hunt, who wrote an introduction and notes for this version of Coffey's autobiography, point out that Coffey was mistaken about some dates, geographic details, and place-names, perhaps confusing his 1849 crossing with subsequent trips.

21. John Dalton, "Diary of John Dalton," October 23, 1926, entry for May 14, 1852, typescript, digital copy, unnumbered. Original is in the State Historical Society of Wisconsin, Madison. Dalton's diary entry is also reprinted in Reid, "Binding the Elephant," 292n30.

22. Davies, "Historical Sketch of My Life," 160.

23. Lavinia Honeyman Porter, *By Ox Team to California: A Narrative of Crossing the Plains in 1860* (Oakland, Calif.: *Oakland Enquirer,* 1910), 2–3.

24. Edwin Bryant, *What I Saw in California: Being the Journal of a Tour; by the Emigrant Route and South Pass of the Rocky Mountains, Across the Continent of North America, the Great Basin and through California, 1846, 1847* (1849, repr. Minneapolis: Ross & Haines, 1967), 20.

25. Anna Maria Goodell, diary entry May 27, 1854, in Kenneth L. Holmes, ed., *Covered Wagon Women,* vol. 7: *Diaries and Letters from the Western Trails, 1854–1860* (Lincoln: University of Nebraska Press, 1998), 98.

26. See Madison Berryman Moorman, *The Journal of Madison Berryman Moorman, 1850–1851,* ed. Irene D. Paden (San Francisco: California Historical Society, 1948), entry June 11 (1850), 20.

27. Washington, "California Pioneers of African Descent," 73, 139–41; Carter, *Story of the Negro Pioneer,* 18–19; Bagley, "Black Youths Helped Blaze Mormon Trail," *Salt Lake Tribune,* August 27, 2000; Cataldo, "Lizzy Flake Rowan." For Bridget "Biddy" Mason, also see Taylor, *In Search of the Racial Frontier;* 72; Dolores Hayden, "Biddy Mason's Los Angeles," *California History* 63, no. 3 (Fall 1989): 89, 148n8. For the constant attention required in managing mules, see Moorman, *The Journal,* entries May 8, 6, May 14, 7–8, 94n7.

28. Loren Schweninger and John H. Rapier, "The Dilemma of a Free Negro in the Ante-bellum South," *Journal of Negro History* 62, no. 3 (July 1977): 283–88, especially see 286; Loren Schweninger, "John H. Rapier Sr.: A Slave and Freedman in the Ante-bellum South," *Civil War History* 20, no. 1 (March 1974): 23–34, especially see 26–27; Loren Schweninger, "Thriving within the Lowest

Caste: The Financial Activities of James P. Thomas in the Nineteenth-Century South," *Journal of Negro History* 63, no. 4 (October 1978): 353–64; Loren Schweninger, "A Slave Family in the Ante Bellum South," *Journal of Negro History* 60, no. 1 (January 1975): 29–44; John H. Rapier Sr. to Richard Rapier, letter dated April 8, 1845, original in the Rapier Papers, Moorland-Spingarn Collection, Howard University, Washington, D.C., reprinted in John Hope Franklin and Loren Schweninger, *In Search of the Promised Land: A Slave Family in the Old South* (New York: Oxford University Press, 2006), 274.

29. Franklin and Schweninger, *In Search of the Promised Land,* 99–100; Moorman, *The Journal,* entry April 27, 1850, 1. See Durham, *Volunteer Forty-Niners,* 253–54n39 for a brief discussion of the slave Ben.

30. Franklin and Schweninger, *In Search of the Promised Land,* 95–101; Moorman, *The Journal,* entries April 27 (1850), 1; May 13 (1850), 7; May 14 (1850), 7–8; Durham, *Volunteer Forty-Niners,* 100.

31. For Walker's and John's participation in the company, see entries for July 6, 37, Aug. 1, Aug. 2 , 57–58, Aug. 27, 75; Moorman, *The Journal,* entry May 20 (1850), 11; italics in original.

32. Moorman, *The Journal,* entry June 25 (1850), 30–31; Franklin and Schweninger, *In Search of the Promised Land,* 102–3.

33. Moorman, *The Journal,* entries July 20–Sept. 8 (1850), 48–81; Mattes, *Platte River Road Narratives,* 282; Durham, *Volunteer Forty-Niners,* 102–3; Franklin and Schweninger, *In Search of the Promised Land,* 103–6.

34. Durham, *Volunteer Forty-Niners,* 156; Franklin and Schweninger, *In Search of the Promised Land,* 106–8; Moorman, *The Journal,* entries Sept. 22 (1850); 84, Oct. 19 (1850), 85–86; Feb. 4 (1851), 88.

35. John H. Rapier Sr. to John Rapier Jr. letter, September 15, 1856, quoted in Franklin and Schweninger, *In Search of the Promised Land,* 107–8, 142–46 (regarding James Thomas Rapier's gambling and religious conversion). See also John H. Rapier Sr. to John H. Rapier Jr., St. Paul, Minnesota Territory letter, Florence, Alabama, Dec. 28, 1858, reprinted in Schweninger and Rapier, "The Dilemma of a Free Negro," 288.

36. Records from the Placer County Court, Warrant for Henry Rapier for Murder, September 22, 1856; Arrest of Henry Rapier, February 13, 1859, originals located in the Placer County Archives, Auburn, California, both quoted in Franklin and Schweninger, *In Search of the Promised Land,* 229–30.

37. Dick Rapier's $350 would be the present-day equivalent of $5,250, "Measuring Worth," CPI 2014; Franklin and Schweninger, *In Search of the Promised Land,* 236–37. See especially 247n20 regarding marriage, real estate, and probate matters.

38. John Rapier Sr. to John Rapier Jr., letter, August 6, 1857, quoted in Franklin and Schweninger, *In Search of the Promised Land,* 133. The $800 crop

loss would be the present-day equivalent of $22,400, and the total loss of $2,000 is the equivalent of $56,000 in present-day money, "Measuring Worth," CPI 2014.

39. Dick Rapier to James P. Thomas letter, Dec. 14, 1877, in the Rapier Papers, box 84-2, folder 92, Moorland-Spingarn Collection, Howard University, Washington D.C.

40. *Placer Argus,* February 10, 1887, quoted in Franklin and Schweninger, *In Search of the Promised Land,* 237. The value of Rapier's remaining $700 estate would be worth $18,000 today, "Measuring Worth," CPI 2014.

41. Bagley quoted in *So Rugged and Mountainous,* 168, 270–71.

42. Minto, "Reminiscences of Experiences on the Oregon Trail," II, 219, 241.

43. Lapp, *Blacks in Gold Rush California,* 29; Hugh Brown Heiskell, *A Forty-niner from Tennessee: The Diary of Hugh Brown Heiskell,* ed. Edward M. Steel (Knoxville: University of Tennessee Press, 1960), entry Friday, August, 17, 1849, 10.

44. Moorman, *The Journal,* entry July 6 (1850), 37.

45. Theodore Edgar Potter, *The Autobiography of Theodore Edgar Potter* (Concord, N.H.: Rumford Press, 1913), 28, digitized version from the HathiTrust Yale University, http:/hdl.handle.net/2027/yale.39002028259050 (accessed April 13, 2014).

46. Sandra L. Myres, *Westering Women and the Frontier Experience, 1800–1915* (Albuquerque: University of New Mexico Press, 1982), see especially chapter 5, "Westward Ho! Women on the Overland Trail," 98–106. See also Porter, *By Ox Team to California,* 1–2.

47. Porter, *By Ox Team to California,* 1.

48. Catherine Haun, "A Woman's Trip across the Plains in 1849," quoted in Myres, *Westering Women and the Frontier Experience,* 103. Haun's original diary is in the Henry E. Huntington Library, San Marino, California.

49. Benjamin Butler Harris, *The Gila Trail: The Texas Argonauts and the California Gold Rush,* ed. Richard H. Dillon (Norman: University of Oklahoma Press, 1960), 78.

50. Bruff, *Gold Rush Journals,* 44, 378, 380, 381 (italics in original).

51. Heiskell, *Forty-niner from Tennessee,* entry dated August 17, 1849, 10.

52. Potter, *Autobiography of Theodore Edgar Potter,* 60.

53. Lapp, *Blacks in Gold Rush California,* 26–27.

54. Bruff, *Gold Rush Journals,* 360.

55. Sylvia Stark interview, part 2.

56. Heiskell, *Forty-niner from Tennessee,* entry dated September 2, 1849, 25.

57. Ibid., entry dated October 6, 1849, 61.

58. Ibid., entry dated October 9, 1849, 64.

59. Harris, *The Gila Trail,* 83–84.

60. Potter, *Autobiography of Theodore Edgar Potter,* 53.

61. John Doble, *John Doble's Journal and Letters from the Mines: Mokelumne Hill, Jackson, Volcano and San Francisco, 1851–1865*, ed. Charles Camp (Denver: Old West, 1962), entries dated Sept. 16, Sept. 17 (1852), 115. Also see Lapp's summary of this incident in *Blacks in the California Gold Rush*, 27.

62. Robert Eccleston, *Overland to California on the Southwestern Trail, 1849: The Diary of Robert Eccleston*, ed. George P. Hammond and Edward H. Howe (Berkeley: University of California Press, 1950), 95–96.

63. Ibid.

64. Hyde, *Empires, Nations and Families*, 160–62, 164–70.

65. National Park Service, "Bent's Old Fort National Historic Site: History & Culture" (National Park Service: U.S. Department of the Interior, February 22, 2007), http://www.nps.gov/beol/historyculture/index.htm (accessed August 28, 2010); William W. Gwaltney, "Beyond the Pale: African-Americans in the Fur Trade West," http://www.coax.net/people/lwf/FURTRADE.HTM (accessed September 11, 2009), originally published in *Lest We Forget* (Trotwood, Ohio: LWF, January 1995); Maurice Kenny, *Backward to Forward: Prose Pieces* (Freedonia, N.Y.: White Pine Press, 1997), 35–41; Gail M. Beaton, *Colorado Women: A History* (Boulder: University Press of Colorado, 2012), 12.

66. Charlotte Green quoted in Gwaltney, "Beyond the Pale: African-Americans in the Fur Trade West." For a brief summary of Charlotte Green's life at the fort, see also Beaton, *Colorado Women*, 12. For the "glib-tongued" quote and a description of Charlotte's dancing, see Lewis H. Garrard, *Wah-to-Yah and the Taos Trail: Or, Prairie Travel and Scalp Dances, with a Look at Los Rancheros from Muleback and the Rocky Mountain Camp-Fire* (Cincinnati: H. W. Derby & Co.; New York: A. S. Barnes & Co., 1850), 79–80. For a description of the table setting at the fort, see Kenny, *Backward to Forward*, 36.

67. Marc Simmons, *New Mexico Mavericks: Stories from a Fabled Past* (Santa Fe: Sunstone Press, 2005), 5–53, especially see 52 for Dick Green as "manservant" for Gov. Charles Bent; Kenneth W. Porter, "Notes Supplementary to 'Relations between Negroes and Indians,'" *Journal of Negro History* 18, no. 3 (July 1933): 316. See Gwaltney, "Beyond the Pale," 2, for the "large black man" quote and discussion of Dick's work at the fort and Andrew's status.

68. Gwaltney, "Beyond the Pale," 2. Historian Mark L. Gardner found that the 1850 census for St. Louis showed that Charlotte Green was living there without her husband, Dick. See Simmons, *New Mexico Mavericks*, 53.

Chapter 6

Epigraph 1. Robert Ball Anderson, 125th Colored Infantry (Buffalo Soldiers), quoted in Darold D. Wax, "The Odyssey of an Ex-Slave: Robert Ball Anderson's

Pursuit of the American Dream," *Phylon* 45, no. 1 (1960 reprint, 1st quarter 1984): 67–68.

Epigraph 2. Sylvia Stark interview, part 2

1. Bagley, *So Rugged and Mountainous*, 354. For accounts of overlanders relying on Natives, see David H. De Jong, "'Good Samaritans of the Desert': The Pima-Maricopa Villages as Described in California Emigrant Journals, 1846–1852," *Journal of the Southwest* 47, no. 3 (Autumn 2005): 457–96, see especially 457–62; John Phillip Reid, "Punishing the Elephant: Malfeasance and Organized Criminality on the Overland Trail," *Montana The Magazine of Western History* 47, no. 1 (Spring 1997): 2–21, see especially 14–17; Unruh, *The Plains Across*, 192–94.

2. For embellishments and lurid accounts of Indian violence, see Glenda Riley, "The Specter of a Savage: Rumors and Alarmism on the Overland Trail," *Western Historical Quarterly* 15, no. 4 (October 1984): 427–44.

3. Unruh, *The Plains Across*, 118–20, especially table 1 (119), "Overland Emigration to Oregon, California, Utah, 1840–48," and table 2 (120), "Overland Emigration to Oregon, California, Utah, 1849–60," and 156–200, especially 175–85, also table 4 (185), "Estimated Overland Emigrants Killed by Indians, and Indians Killed by Overland Emigrants, 1840–1860." For robbers, thieves, bandits, and "white Indians," see 192–98 in the same source.

4. Rieck's revisions rely only on overlanders identified by name and exclude anonymous victims found on the trail. He does not offer figures for Indians killed by emigrants. See a discussion of Rieck's revised figures in Bagley, *With Golden Visions*, 396.

5. The quote from Lasselle is in "The 1849 Diary of Stanislaus Lasselle, entries for April 5, 1849, and April 10, 1849, 8–9. For the Indians' perception of African American skin color and hair texture, also see Kenneth W. Porter, "Contacts in Other Parts: Relations between Negroes and Indians," *Journal of Negro History* 17, no. 3 (July 1932): 365. Andrew Green, the brother-in-law of Charlotte Green of Bent's Old Fort, had a very dark complexion and the Cheyenne gave him the name "Black Whiteman." This name, "out of compliment to Andrew," later became a common Cheyenne name. See Kenneth W. Porter, "Notes Supplementary to 'Relations between Negroes and Indians,'" 16.

6. Sarah Winnemucca Hopkins, *Life among the Piutes: Their Wrongs and Claims* (1883 repr., Reno: University of Nevada Press, 1994), 8.

7. Reader, "Uncle Dave's Story," part 1.

8. John Walton Caughey, ed., *Rushing for Gold* (Berkeley: University of California Press, 1949), 27. Pownall incorrectly spelled the name of the leader of the Chiricahua Apache. The correct spelling is Mangas Coloradas, meaning in Spanish, "Red Sleeves." See Edwin R. Sweeney, *Mangas Coloradas: Chief of the Chiricahua Apaches* (Norman: University of Oklahoma Press, 1998), 17–18, 73.

9. Caughey, *Rushing for Gold*, 28, 31.

10. Guenther, "Could These Bones Be from a Negro?" 49–50, 53.

11. Bruff, *Gold Rush Journals,* 382 (italics in original). Also see Odell A. Thurman, *The Negro in California before 1890* (master's thesis, College of the Pacific, 1945, reprint, San Francisco: R & E Research Associates, 1973), 25; Shirley Ann Wilson Moore, "'Do You Think I'll Lug Trunks?': African Americans in Gold Rush California," in Kenneth N. Owens, ed., *Riches for All: The California Gold Rush and the World* (Lincoln: University of Nebraska Press, 2002), 166.

12. *Daily Alta California,* vol. 3, no. 334, December 1852, has the description of the posse. For Andy's reputation as an Indian hunter, see Bruff, *Gold Rush Journals,* 389. For animosity between blacks and Indians in the West, see John Bratt, *Trails of Yesterday* (Chicago: University Publishing, 1921), especially 126–30; Potter, *Autobiography of Theodore Edgar Potter,* 71; Porter, "Notes Supplementary to 'Relations between Negroes and Indians,'" 314–15. For pursuit-and-vengeance posses, see Lapp, *Blacks in Gold Rush California,* 87.

13. Coffey, "Autobiography of Alvin A. Coffey," 69; Molson interview.

14. For quotes from John Durivage, see Lapp, *Blacks in Gold Rush California,* 29. See also *New Orleans Picayune,* June 17, 1849; C. C. Cox, "From Texas to California in 1849: Diary of C. C. Cox (Concluded)," ed. Mabelle Eppard Martin and C. C. Cox, *Southwestern Historical Quarterly* 29, no. 3 (January 1926): 202; italics in original.

15. Sylvia Stark interview, part 2.

16. Eva L. Yancey, Laws Railroad Museum, Laws, California, "History of the McGee Family" file folder, typewritten copy, subheading "Charlie's Butte." I am indebted to Guy Washington of the National Park Service for making this information available to me. The document, part of the online AfriGeneas Genealogy and History Forum Archives, http://www.afrigeneas.com/forum-aarchive/index_3//cgi?noframes;read=19359, was generated by Clarence Caesar, of the State of California Historic Preservation Department, Sacramento. For more detail about the fate of Charley Tyler and the white families with whom he traveled, also see W. A. Chalfant, *The Story of Inyo* (Chicago: self-published, 1922), 136–38. Library of Congress online digitized edition, https://archives.org/stream/storyofinyo00chal/storyofinyo (accessed January 3, 2016).

17. Guenther, "Could These Bones Be from a Negro?" 44–48, quote found on 43.

18. This is from a summary of a preliminary osteological report and laboratory analyses of the 1987 findings of archeological and anthropological excavating teams from the University of Wyoming who discovered the bones at the Rock Ranch site. The findings are summarized in Guenther, "Could These Bones Be from a Negro?" 43–44.

19. Ibid., 51–52.

20. William J. Pleasants, *Twice across the Plains* (San Francisco: Walter N. Brunt, 1906), 21–23, 155–60.

21. Ibid., 103. Amos Kusic's $3,000 would be equivalent today to $95,800. See "Measuring Worth," CPI 2014.

22. Vincent Geiger and Wakeman Bryarly, *Trail to California: The Overland Journal*, ed., David Morris Potter (New Haven: Yale University Press), 10–12; Robert Hunh Jones, *Guarding the Overland Trails: The Eleventh Ohio Cavalry in the Civil War* (Spokane, Wash.: Arthur H. Clark, 2005), 14–16, 73–97, 308–9; William Hayes, *"Devotion to the Good Cause": Nebraska in the Civil War* (master's thesis, University of Nebraska at Kearney, 2008 reprinted by ProQuest, UMI Dissertation Publishing, Ann Arbor, Michigan, 2011). See also National Park Service, "Fort Union National Monument: Cultural Encounters," n.d., http://www.nps.gov/found/historyculture/cultural-encounters.htm (accessed January 24, 2014).

23. How the name Buffalo Soldier became attached to black western troops is open to debate. One theory holds that Indians gave the name to black soldiers because their skin color and hair texture resembled that of the plains animal. Another suggests that the name derived from the black soldiers' wintertime habit of donning buffalo robes for warmth. Some have theorized that black cavalrymen on horseback looked like bison when viewed from a distance; yet others have suggested that Indians bestowed this name on black troops to honor the courage both man and animal displayed in fighting. For discussion of the origin of the name Buffalo Soldier, see "Buffalo Soldiers in the American West, 1865–1900," in *African Americans on the Western Frontier*, Monroe Lee Billington and Roger D. Hardaway, eds. (Niwot: University Press of Colorado, 1998), 56–57.

24. In July 1866, the Ninth Cavalry, under the command of Col. Edward Hatch, began recruiting in Louisiana and Kentucky. On September 21, 1866, the Tenth Cavalry was organized at Fort Leavenworth, Kansas, and was headed by Col. Benjamin H. Grierson. The 38th Infantry, under the leadership of Col. William H. Hazen, was assembled at Jefferson Barracks, Missouri, in 1866. The Thirty-ninth Infantry, led by Col. Joseph A. Mower, began recruiting at Alexandria, Louisiana. Col. Nelson A. Miles, commanded the Fortieth Infantry, which was organized in Washington, D.C., and recruits for the Forty-first Infantry were drawn from Louisiana, Alabama, and Ohio. In 1869, the Thirty-ninth and Fortieth Infantries were disbanded and reorganized as the Twenty-fifth and Forty-first Infantries. See Ron Field and Alexander Bielakiowski, *Buffalo Soldiers: African American Troops in the U.S. Forces, 1866–1945* (New York: Osprey, 2008), 24–25; Ravage, *Black Pioneers*, 41.

25. Arlen L. Fowler, *The Black Infantry in the West, 1869–1891* (Norman: University of Oklahoma Press, 1996), xi–xii, 3–5; Field and Bielakiowski, *Buffalo Soldiers*, 27; Taylor, *In Search of the Racial Frontier*, 165; Bruce A. Glasrud and

Michael N. Searles, eds., *Buffalo Soldiers in the West: A Black Soldiers Anthology* (College Station: Texas A&M University Press, 2007), 33.

26. Katz, *The Black West*, 201–2; William A. Dobak and Thomas D. Phillips, *The Black Regulars, 1866–1898* (Norman: University of Oklahoma Press, 2001), 15.

27. Katz, *The Black West*, 201; John H. Nankivell, *Buffalo Soldier Regiment: History of the Twenty-fifth United States Infantry, 1869–1926* (Lincoln: University of Nebraska Press, 2001), 13–14, 185–86; Ravage, *Black Pioneers*, 43–44; Jones, *Guarding the Overland Trails*, 308–9; Leckie's quote about "burying their dead" is in Fowler, *The Black Infantry in the West*, xii.

28. For military attitudes and hostility toward African American soldiers, see Fowler, *The Black Infantry in the West*, especially 114–39. For civilian attitudes and hostility toward African American soldiers, see Katz, *The Black West*, 201–6; Ravage, *Black Pioneers*, 41–44; Fowler, *The Black Infantry in the West*, 21–27; James N. Leiker, "Black Soldiers at Fort Hayes [sic], Kansas, 1867–69: A Study in Civilian and Military Violence," in Glasrud and Searles, eds., *Buffalo Soldiers in the West*, 158–60; Billington, *Buffalo Soldiers in the American West*, 66–69; Harriet Bunyard, "Diary of Miss Harriet Bunyard: From Texas to California in 1868," ed. Percival J. Cooney, *Annual Publication of the Historical Society of Southern California* 13, no. 1 (1924): 99.

29. For Waller, Harris, and Creek, see Taylor, *In Search of the Racial Frontier*, 169; Dobak and Phillips, *The Black Regulars*, 20. Bruin's quote is from original WPA interview in George P. Rawick, ed., *The American Slave: A Composite Autobiography* (Westport, Conn.: Greenwood Press, 1972), vol. 4, part 1, 171.

30. Wax, "Odyssey of an Ex-Slave," 67–70.

31. Ibid., 72–73. Anderson's money would be the present-day equivalent of $4,130, "Measuring Worth," CPI, 2014. After a brief sojourn in Kentucky, Anderson relocated to Davenport, Iowa, where he worked at various jobs. But bad land investments wiped him out financially, and he was forced to seek employment in neighboring cities. In 1870, after several years of frugality, he purchased eighty acres of land in Butler County, Nebraska, just south of the Platte River. Despite the tough economic times of the 1870s, he also managed to buy a team of oxen and started a freighting business. Later, he purchased a homestead in western Nebraska, and in time, became a successful and well-respected Nebraska rancher. When he died in 1930, the *Hemingford (Nebraska) Ledger* reported that "having a good business judgment, he gained much of this world's goods." Wax, "Odyssey of an Ex-Slave," 74–79; *Hemingsford (Nebraska) Ledger*, December 4, 1930, quoted in Wax, 79. For a description of the location of Fort Union, see National Park Service, "Fort Union National Monument: Cultural Encounters."

32. Leckie quoted in Fowler, *The Black Infantry in the West*, 10–11.

33. Leiker, "Black Soldiers at Fort Hayes [sic], Kansas," 158–60.

34. Of the 230 reported cholera deaths, some 146 occurred in Kansas forts or "among troops en route across the state," hitting African American soldiers especially hard. At Fort Hays, where 464 men (mostly black) were stationed in August, the "Negro troops suffered the deaths recorded at that post." From July to September 1867, 33 cases and at least 23 deaths were reported among the African American troops at the fort. Seven black soldiers, most from two companies of the Thirty-eighth Infantry (which totaled 215 men), succumbed to the disease; the Tenth Cavalry lost more than 20. White soldiers at the fort seem to have fared better. In September 1867, one white soldier was stricken but recovered, and the remaining 34 white troops were not affected. When six companies of the Thirty-eighth Infantry set out from Fort Leavenworth for New Mexico, cholera ravaged their ranks, killing many as they trudged across the Kansas plains. Soldiers well enough to report for duty had the grim task of burying the dead each morning before resuming their march. See Wax, "Odyssey of an Ex-slave," 67–68. For the scurvy outbreak at Fort Davis, see Robert Wooster, *Frontier Crossroads: Fort Davis and the West* (College Station: Texas A&M University Press, 2005), 79; National Park Service, Fort Davis National Historic Site, "Record of Deceased Officers and Soldiers at Fort Davis, Texas, 1867–1879," online summary, http://www.nps.gov/foda/forteachers/upload/Pre-Visit-E (accessed January 27, 2014). For cholera epidemic of 1867 and its impact on African American troops, see Ramon Powers and Gene Younger, "Cholera on the Plains: The Epidemic of 1867 in Kansas," *Kansas Historical Quarterly* 37 (Winter 1971): 351–93, especially 357 for the total numbers of deaths and the number of deaths in Kansas forts or "among troops en route across the state," as well as 380–82, 392 for cholera's toll on black soldiers at Fort Hays; U.S. Surgeon-General's Office, Joseph K. Barnes, and John Maynard Woodworth, *The Cholera Epidemic of 1873 in the United States* (Washington, D.C.: Government Printing Office, 1865), 675–80; Leiker, "Black Soldiers at Fort Hayes [sic]," 158–59; Monroe Lee Billington, *New Mexico's Buffalo Soldiers, 1866–1900* (Niwot: University Press of Colorado, 1991), xvii, 7.

35. Leiker, "Black Soldiers at Fort Hays," 160; George A. Forsyth, *The Story of the Soldier* (New York: D. Appleton and Company, 1900), 151–152, digitized edition, Hathi Trust http://hdl.handle.net/2027/uc2.ark:/13960/t9j38ms7f (accessed January 13, 2016). Also see Nankivell, *Buffalo Soldier Regiment*, 19–20.

36. Franz Huning, *Trader on the Santa Fe Trail: The Memoirs of Franz Huning* (Albuquerque: University of Albuquerque, in collaboration with Calvin Horn, 1973), 89.

37. All quotes from Huning, *Trader on the Santa Fe Trail*, 89.

38. Ibid., 89, 92, 94.

39. Forbes, *Afro-Americans in the Far West*, 33 (italics in original).

40. Taylor, *In Search of the Racial Frontier*, 164. For more on controversy over the legacy of Buffalo Soldiers, see Leiker, "Black Soldiers at Fort Hays," 158; Vernon Bellecourt, "The Glorification of Buffalo Soldiers Raises Racial Divisions between Blacks, Indians," *Indian Country Today* (Oneida, N.Y.: May 4, 1994): A-5; Frank Shubert, "The Myth of the Buffalo Soldier," The Black Past: Remembered and Reclaimed, Online Reference Guide to African American History, http://www.blackpast.or/perspectives/myth-buffalo-soldiers (accessed January 29, 2004).

41. Fowler, *The Black Infantry in the West*, 10–11; Field and Bielakowski, *Buffalo Soldiers*, 32–33; Taylor, *In Search of the Racial Frontier*, 169–70; Elizabeth B. Custer, *Tenting on the Plains, or General Custer in Kansas and Texas* (New York: Harper & Brothers, 1895): 387–88.

42. McCombs quoted in Taylor, *In Search of the Racial Frontier*, 164.

43. Unruh, *The Plains Across*, 379–80; Richard L. Rieck, "A Geography of Death on the Oregon-California Trail, 1840–1860," *Overland Journal* 9, no. 1 (1991): 13–14; Carter, "Sometimes When I Hear the Winds Sigh," especially 147–56; Peter D. Olch, "Treading the Elephant's Tail: Medical Problems on the Overland Trails," *Bulletin of the History of Medicine* 59, no. 2 (Summer 1985): 196–210.

44. See Unruh, *The Plains Across*, 408, 516n75, for the varying estimates of overland death rates, 408–9, for disease accounting for nine of ten trail deaths. See also Carter, "Sometimes When I Hear the Winds Sigh," 153–54; Mattes, *Great Platte River Road*, 82–88; Rieck, "Geography of Death," 13–14, see especially table 1, "Selected Estimates of Oregon-California Trail Deaths, 1840–1860." Mattes estimated that in the year 1850, about 55,000 people traveled the Oregon-California Trail. Mattes, *Great Platte River Road*, 23, as quoted in Olch, "Treading the Elephant's Tail," 196.

45. For Cecelia Adams and other emigrant reports of trailside graves, see Unruh, *The Plains Across*, 408.

46. For McCollum quote, see National Park Service, *Across Wyoming*, 28. McCollum was describing an area where cholera was most prevalent. Beyond Fort Laramie, the disease virtually disappeared, since from that point on, emigrants relied mostly on running water sources—creeks and rivers—where the cholera *vibrio* (bacterium) did not exist. Thanks to Kenneth N. Owens for this information. See also Charles Rosenberg, *The Cholera Years: The United States in 1832, 1849, and 1866* (Chicago: University of Chicago Press, 1962), especially 1–4.

47. For a succinct discussion of health and mortality factors on the Oregon Trail, see Peter D. Olch and Rogert P. Blair, "Plenty of Doctoring to Do: Health Related Problems on the Oregon Trail," *Overland Journal* 33, no. 3 (Fall 2015): 96–113. Also see Olch, "Treading the Elephant's Tail," 205–7; John Edwin Banks, *The Buckeye Rovers in the Gold Rush: An Edition of Two Diaries*, ed. H. Lee Scamehorn (Athens: Ohio University Press, 1965), entry for July 6, 1849. See also

Unruh, The Plains Across, 413, for deaths occurring from wagon and animal mishaps.

48. Mary Stuart Bailey, "A Journal of Mary Stuart Bailey, Wife of Dr. Fred Bailey: From Ohio to California, April–October, 1852," in *Ho For California!: Women's Overland Diaries from the Huntington Library,* ed. Sandra L. Myres (San Marino, Calif.: Henry E. Huntington Library, 1980), 73.

49. Heiskell, *A Forty-niner from Tennessee,* vii, xxxiii–xxxiv, 38, 57.

50. Rieck, "Geography of Death," 15. Also see Olch and Blair, "Plenty of Doctoring," 105.

51. All quotes from John Hawkins Clark, "Overland to the Gold Fields of California in 1852: The Journal of John Hawkins Clark, Expanded and Revised from Notes Made during the Journey," ed. Louise Barry, *Kansas Historical Quarterly* 11, no. 3 (August 1942): 256–59, http://www.kancoll.org/khq/1942/42_3 _barry.htm (accessed July 19, 2011). The phrase "three cheers and a tiger" refers to a congratulatory cheer dating back to at least the early nineteenth century that started with three "hurrahs." The "tiger" came on the final "hurrah," which was more prolonged and intense than the other two. Alternately, the tiger might be a growl from the crowd that slowly rose in volume and pitch, or culminated with the shouted words "Hi, hi, hi, hullah!" See WordReference.com Language Forums, "Three Cheers and a Tiger," http://forum.wordreference.com/showthread.php?t -1186094 (accessed July 1, 2011).

52. Carter, "Sometimes When I Hear the Winds Sigh," 152–56; Unruh, *The Plains Across,* 408–9; Bagley, *So Rugged and Mountainous,* 363–64, 395–96. See also Clark, "Diary of a Journey," 4, 25. For the state of medical knowledge in the mid-nineteenth century, see Charles E. Rosenberg, "The Therapeutic Revolution: Medicine, Meaning, and Social Change in Nineteenth-Century America," *Perspectives in Biology and Medicine* 20 (Summer 1977): 485–506, especially 485–92; Gregg Mitman and Ronald L. Numbers, "From Miasma to Asthma: The Changing Fortunes of Medical Geography in America," *History and Philosophy of the Life Sciences* 25, no. 3 (2003): 391–412, especially 392–404; Myron Echenberg, *Africa in the Time of Cholera: A History of Pandemics from 1917 to the Present* (New York: Cambridge University Press, 2011), 10–11.

53. Unruh, *The Plains Across,* 408; Olch, "Treading the Elephant's Tail," 199–205; Rieck, "Geography of Death," especially 14, table 2, "Selected Causes of Emigrant Deaths"; Carter, "Sometimes When I Hear the Winds Sigh," 151–52. Also see Olch and Blair, "Plenty of Doctoring," 106–13. As overlanders pushed farther west, especially past Fort Laramie, the threat of cholera diminished. See Carter, "Sometimes When I Hear the Winds Sigh," 146–50; Rieck, "Geography of Death," 14–15, especially table 3, "Cholera Deaths East of South Pass," and table 4, "Cholera Deaths per 100 Miles of Trail"; Olch, "Treading the Elephant's Tail," 200–202. See Unruh for the story reported in the *Liberty* (Missouri) *Weekly*

Tribune, September 13, 1850, of a gold seeker who was the only surviving member of his wagon train after cholera struck the company. The disheartened argonaut abandoned his western trek and headed back east to his home state. *The Plains Across,* 124. Overlander Ezra Meeker recalled that, while on the trail in 1852, the "ravages of cholera carried off thousands. One family of seven a little further down the Platte, lie all in one grave; forty-one persons of one train dead in one day and two nights tells but part of the dreadful story." See Ezra Meeker, *The Busy Life of Eighty-Five Years of Ezra Meeker: Ventures and Adventures* (Seattle: self-published, 1916), 295. John Hawkins Clark recorded his meeting with three overlanders who were "returning to the states" after a disastrous encounter with the disease. Clark's journal entry for June 7, 1852, noted, "the three are all that are left out of a total company of seventeen men who left Ash Hollow [on the south side of the North Platte River in Nebraska] a few days ago, bound for California. Sickness commenced soon after leaving the Hollow, and by the time Fort Laramie was reached fourteen of their number were dead. The remaining three concluded to return. . . . The road has been thickly strewn with graves." See Clark, "Overland to the Gold Fields," 249.

54. Carter, "Sometimes When I Hear the Winds Sigh," 146–48. See also Unruh, *The Plains Across,* 124; National Park Service, "Year of Disaster: The Great St. Louis Fire and Cholera Epidemic of 1849," http://www.nps.gov/archive/jeff/disaster_year.html (accessed August 8, 2010); Olch, "Treading the Elephant's Tail," 200; Powers and Younger, "Cholera on the Plains," 353; Pleasants, *Twice across the Plains,* 33–37.

55. Annette W. Curtis, *Jackson County, Missouri in Black & White,* vol. 2: *Jabez Smith, His Slaves, Plantations, Estate, and Heirs* (Independence, Mo.: Two Trails, 1998), 1.

56. Carter "Sometimes When I Hear the Winds Sigh," 146–48; Unruh, *The Plains Across,* 124.

57. Lapp, *Blacks in Gold Rush California,* 29.

58. Coffey, "Autobiography of Alvin A. Coffey," *The Pioneer,* 11.

59. Finley McDiarmid, letter dated June 5, 1850, quoted in Lapp, *Blacks in the California Gold Rush,* 29. For the original, see Finley McDiarmid letters to his wife, Constantia McDiarmid, Wiota, Lafayette County, Wis., BANC MSS C-B 605, Bancroft Library.

60. Sylvia Alden Roberts, *Mining for Freedom: Black History Meets the California Gold Rush* (New York: IUniverse, 2008), 34. Also see "A Negro in Sonora," interview of Vernon Sugg McDonald by Neil Mill, September 9, 1975, in the Tuolumne County Historical Society. Hereafter cited as the McDonald interview.

61. Vernon Sugg McDonald, "The Pioneer Sugg Family: The Saga of an Early Day Family of Tuolumne County History of One of Sonora's Outstanding

Gold Rush Homes," *Quarterly of the Tuolumne County Historical Society* 4, no. 1 (July–September 1964): 98.

62. Carter, "Sometimes When I Hear the Winds Sigh," 148; Echenberg, *Africa in the Time of Cholera*, 10; McDonald, "The Pioneer Sugg Family," 98; Leonard J. Arrington, "LDS Girls in the Pioneer West," *New Era* (July 1982) 16, digital copy regarding asafoetida, http://lds.org/ldsorg/v/index.jsp?hideNav=1&locale =0&sourceId=d020ad74be99b010Vgn (accessed September 26, 2010).

63. Carter, "Sometimes When I Hear the Winds Sigh," 148; Olch, "Treading the Elephant's Tail," 201.

64. John Lowery Brown, "Journal of John Lowery Brown of the Cherokee Nation en Route to California in 1850," in *Chronicles of Oklahoma* 12, no. 2, ed. Muriel H. Wright (June 1934): 209. For the range of diseases that afflicted overlanders, see Carter, "Sometimes When I Hear the Wind Sigh," 151–52; Bagley, *With Golden Visions*, 268–71; Olch, "Treading the Elephant's Tail," 201–5; Unruh, *The Plains Across*, 408–9.

65. Bruff, *Gold Rush Journals*, 373, 374, 380.

66. George Mifflin Harker, "Morgan Street to the Old Dry Diggins,' 1849," in Stella M. Drum, "Glimpses of the Past," *Missouri Historical Society* 6, no. 52 (April–June 1939): 45.

67. Carter, "Sometimes When I Hear the Winds Sigh," 152–53. See also Lillian Schlissel, ed., *Women's Diaries of the Westward Journey* (New York: Schoken Books, 1982), 35, 106–9.

68. Carter, "Sometimes When I Hear the Winds Sigh," 152–53; Sylvia D. Hoffert, "Childbearing on the Trans-Mississippi Frontier, 1830–1900," *Western History Quarterly* 22, no. 3 (August 1991): 271–74, 276–80, 284–85; Lillian Schlissel, "Women's Diaries on the Western Frontier," *American Studies* 18, no. 1 (Spring 1977): 88–89. See also Nancy Theriot, "Diagnosing Unnatural Motherhood: Nineteenth-Century Physicians and 'Puerperal Insanity,'" *American Studies* 30, no. 2 (Fall 1989): 69–88.

69. Hayden, "Biddy Mason's Los Angeles," 88–89, 91–92; Coleman, "History of Blacks in Utah," 34, 36, 66n20.

70. See Carter, *Story of the Negro Pioneer*, 33, for "excellent horsewoman" quote and "responded to calls day or night."

71. See Beasley, *Negro Trail Blazers*, 109, for "confinement nurse" and Mason's pay rate. Mason's pay of $2.50 would today be worth $72, "Measuring Worth," CPI 2014.

72. Albert E. Williams, *Black Warriors: Unique Units and Individuals* (Haverford, Penn.: Infinity Publishing.com, 2003), 112, for the quote. Irene Schubert and Frank N. Schubert, *On the Trail of the Buffalo Soldier II: New and Revised Biographies* (Lanham, Md.: Scarecrow Press, 2004): 17, provides the description of the parents. See also Guenther, "Could These Bones Be from a

Negro?" 46; Bob Pool, "Bringing a Buffalo Soldier Back to Life," *Los Angeles Times,* September 26, 2008, http://articles.latimes.com/print/2008/sep/26/local/me-honor26 (accessed February 5, 2014); Kwame Anthony Appiah and Henry Lewis Gates Jr., *Africana: The Encyclopedia of the African and African American Experience* (New York: Oxford University Press, 2d ed., 2004), s.v. "Baker, Edward Lee, Jr.," 335.

73. Taylor, *In Search of the Racial Frontier,* 82; National Park Service, "George Washington Bush and the Human Spirit of Westward Expansion"; McLaglan, *A Peculiar Paradise,* 20; John Minto, "Reminiscences of Experiences on the Oregon Trail in 1844," I, *Quarterly of the Oregon Historical Society* 2, no. 2 (June 1901): 142, 163; Minto, "Reminiscences of Experiences on the Oregon Trail," II, 212, 219, 241; Murray C. Morgan, "George W. Bush and the Simmons Party," in *Murray's People: A Collection of Essays,* Tacoma: Tacoma Public Library Northwest Room, 1960, http://ww2.tacomapubliclibrary.org/v2/nwroom/morgan/Bush.htm (accessed September 21, 2010). For evidence of Bush helping new arrivals, see Bagley, *So Rugged and Mountainous,* 336; Darrell Millner, "George Bush of Tumwater: Founder of the First American Colony on Puget Sound," *Columbia Magazine* 8, no. 4 (Winter 1994–95): 14–19, especially 18–19, http://columbia.washigtonhistory.org/anthology/settlers/georgeBush.aspx (accessed September 21, 2010); Lenore Ziontz, "George and Isabella Bush: Washington's First Family" (Tumwater: City of Tumwater, Washington, 2005), http://www.ci.tumwater.wa.us/research%20&%20isabella%bush.tm (accessed July 29, 2010).

74. Clackamas Heritage Partners, Historic Oregon City Presents: End of the Oregon Trail Interpretive Center, "Black Pioneers and Settlers—Rose Jackson," http://www.historicoregoncity.org/HOC/index.php?option=com_content&view=article&i (accessed December 29, 2008); Gayle Karol, "1849: Rose Jackson's Trip to Oregon in a Box," published originally in *The Oregonian,* Saturday, February 23, 2008, OregonLive.com, http://blog.oregonlive.com/blackhistory_impact/print.html?entry=/2008/02/1849_rose_jacks (accessed December 29, 2008). See also Martha Anderson, *Black Pioneers of the Northwest, 1800–1918* (self-published), 1980. In present-day terms, Mrs. Allen's daily earnings would amount to $63.90, and Rose's to $383.00, "Measuring Worth," CPI, 2014.

75. Stuart, "Notes on a Trip," diary entry 14–16, September 1849.

76. All quotes from Parkman, *The California and Oregon Trail,* 132–33. Pommes blanches are edible tuberous roots, akin to Indian breadroots, a perennial of central North America. See Dictionary.com (accessed February 26, 2014).

77. M. Durivage (regarding Isaac) and Lorton (regarding General Blodgett) are quoted in Lapp, *Blacks in Gold Rush California,* 35; De Jong, "Good Samaritans of the Desert," 461. See original for M. Durivage in *New Orleans Picayune,* August 7, 1849; originals for Lorton are in the University of California Bancroft Library, Lorton Diaries, transcript.

78. Bayard Taylor, *El Dorado; or Adventures in the Path of Empire: Comprising a Voyage to California, via Panama; Life in San Francisco and Monterey; Pictures of the Gold Region, and Experiences of Mexican Travel* (New York: G. P. Putnam, 18th ed., 1861), 48. The quote "his old companions hesitated to go to his relief," and Whittier's review of Taylor's book and his remark about the incident are in *National Era,* July 4, 1850, vol. 4, reprinted in *The Black Experience in America: Negro Periodicals in the United States, 1840–1960* (New York: Negro Universities Press, 1969), 106.

79. *Sacramento Transcript,* vol. 1, no. 123, September 23, 1850. Lapp refers to Louis as Ed Lewis, *Blacks in Gold Rush California,* 37–38; Moore, "Do You Think I'll Lug Trunks?" 163.

80. Pleasants, *Twice across the Plains,* 36–39.

81. Sylvia Stark interview, part 2.

Chapter 7

1. The 1860 census reported some 4,479 black people living in the Far West (California, Colorado, Nevada, New Mexico, Oregon, Utah, and Washington), with the largest black western population by far residing in California. In 1850, 962 African Americans lived in California, and in 1870 that number had risen to 4,272 (approximately 1 percent of the state's total population). During the early years of the gold rush alone, nearly 3,000 African Americans, enslaved and free, lived in California. By 1870, with the inclusion of Arizona, Dakota Territory, Idaho, Montana, and Wyoming, an estimated 6,474 African Americans were living in the Far West. In Jessie Carney Smith and Carrell Peterson Horton, eds., *Historical Statistics of Black America: Media to Vital Statistics,* vol. 2 (New York: Gale Research, 1995), see "Slaves and Free Blacks: Distribution, by States, 1790–1860—I, 1844." Smith and Horton's figures were compiled from the U.S. Bureau of the Census, *Negro Population in the United States, 1790–1915,* "Negro Population, Slave and Free, at Each Census by Division and States: 1790–1860," 57. Also see White, *It's Your Misfortune,* 187; Taylor, *In Search of the Racial Frontier,* 76.

2. Charles W. Wesley and Patricia W. Romero, *Negro Americans in the Civil War: From Slavery to Citizenship* (New York: Publishers Company, under the auspices of The Association for the Study of Negro Life and History, 1967), 19, compiled from the 1860 census; Ravage, *Black Pioneers,* xix.

3. See Patricia A. Etter's comments in Lasselle, "The Diary of Stanislaus Lasselle," 27n3.

4. Heiskell, *A Forty-niner from Tennesee,* entry of May 17, 1849, 10.

5. See Bruff, *Gold Rush Journal,* 44, for the "colored man and woman" quote, and 242, for the "three men with packed oxen and a negro" quote. See same

source, 374, 378, and 380 for references to Andy, and 485 for the quote about the "Danish Captain."

6. Brown, *Journal of John Lowery Brown*, 183.

7. For the Fort Smith bulletin and quotes regarding the Georgia and Tennessee wagons trains, see Lapp, *Blacks in Gold Rush California*, 26, 27. For Fort Smith as a departure point for California-bound emigrants, see Grant Foreman, "Early Trails through Oklahoma," *Chronicles of Oklahoma* 3, no. 2 (June 1925): 105–6. Goodell is quoted in Holmes, *Covered Wagon Women*, 98.

8. McLagan, *A Peculiar Paradise*, 32; Hayden, "Biddy Mason's Los Angeles," 88, 90; Carter, *Story of the Negro Pioneer*, 21. For an exact count of the Mormon expedition, see Brown, *Autobiography of Pioneer John Brown*, especially Brown's report of the Mississippi Company, entry of Saturday, May 27, 1848, 96, and see 145 for reference to Betsy Flewellen.

9. The phrase "sweet Freedom's plains" is from the lyrics of an abolitionist song called the "Flying Slave," in William Wells Brown's *The Anti-Slavery Harp*. An excerpt of the "Flying Slave" with slightly different wording is also reprinted in Beasley, *Negro Trail Blazers*, 69.

10. Beasley, *Negro Trail Blazers*, especially 69–70.

11. William Dulany to Susan Dulany, May 1, 1850, in the William Henry Fields Dulany Papers, box 1, folder 3, Missouri History Museum Archives, St. Louis, Missouri. The present-day equivalent of Lee's selling price would be $21,900. Dulany's "pile" of $2,000 would today be $62,500, "Measuring Worth," CPI 2014.

12. Joseph Warren Wood, "Diary, May 6 to December 10, 1849," digital typescript, pages 1–95, transcribed by Richard L. Rieck, September 2004, pages 96–154, transcribed by Kay Threlkeld, National Park Service, May 2007. The original is in the Huntington Library, San Marino, California.

13. Banks, *Buckeye Rovers in the Gold Rush*, entry of May 9, 1849, 5, and entry of September 8, 1850, 136.

14. Washington, "California Pioneers of African Descent," 89; State of California Department of Parks and Recreation, "Monroe House Site," not paginated, n.d.; Osborne West, "The Monroe Family," *Teaching Students to Read Nonfiction* (New York: Scholastic Professional Books, 2002), 86; Anthony Belli, "California Legends: Chattel Hood to Freedom—Black Pioneers Help Settle California," http://www.legendsofamerica.com/ca-blackpioneers.html (accessed July 9, 2008); California State Parks, "Black Pioneer Families of Coloma: Highlighting the Gooch-Monroe Families," pamphlet printed for the Marshall Gold Discovery State Historic Park, Coloma, California, 2001.

15. Washington "California Pioneers of African Descent," 89. See also Beasley, *Negro Trail Blazers*, 71; State of California Department of Parks and Recreation, "Monroe House Site"; West, "The Monroe Family," 86; Belli, "California

Legends"; California State Parks, "Black Pioneer Families of Coloma." Peter Gooch's payment of $1,000 for the property would be the present-day equivalent of $29,700, "Measuring Worth," CPI 2014.

16. Washington, "California Pioneers of African Descent," 89.

17. Sylvia Stark interview, part 1. The $1,000 Howard Estes earned would today be worth $31,300.

18. Sylvia Stark interview, part 1. The $800 awarded to Tom Estes today would be $25,000, "Measuring Worth," CPI 2014.

19. Sylvia Stark interview, part 1.

20. Ibid. The purchase price of $1,000 each for Hannah and Jackson would today be $63,900 (for both), and the $900 price for Sylvia would be $28,800, "Measuring Worth," CPI 2014.

21. Sylvia Stark interview, part 2.

22. Ibid.

23. Ibid. This account of Salt Lake City, Brigham Young, and Mountain Meadows may be a confused recollection on the part of Sylvia Estes Stark, who at the time her daughter Marie Albertina Stark Wallace interviewed her, was in her late eighties or early nineties. It is tempting to assume that an elderly woman at the time of the interviews was alluding to the Mountain Meadows Massacre, in which most of an Arkansas wagon train (except children under six) were murdered by Mormon leaders in the vicinity of Cedar City, Utah. That shocking event, however, took place in 1857, six years after Stark's party had passed through Salt Lake City. Ascribing "future history" to past events is one of the most challenging problems researchers face when using oral history accounts. However, Stark's recollections, confused as they are, of the group's time in Salt Lake City serve two purposes. First, her reminiscences stand as further documentation of black overlanders' reaction to stories about Indian violence against emigrants. Second, her memory of this incident, though mistaken in some very key facts, nonetheless reveals that western emigrants, black and white, still viewed Mormon society with a mixture of curiosity and suspicion.

24. Ibid.

25. Thurman, *Pioneers of Negro Origin*, 21.

26. Roberts, *Mining for Freedom*, 56; Beasley, *Negro Trail Blazers*, 117. Roberts spells Daniel's wife's name as Artemisa. Beasley's work shows her name spelled Artimisa and this is the way it appears in the primary source documents that are reproduced in Beasley's book, *Negro Trail Blazers*, 87. Therefore, I use the spelling shown in Beasley.

27. Beasley, *Negro Trail Blazers*, 117; Thurman, *Pioneers of Negro Origin*, 21. The price of Daniel Rodgers freedom papers varies according to different accounts. Thurman states that Redmond Rodgers demanded a fee of $1,000 for his slave's freedom, 17; Phil Reader, "To Know My Name: A Chronological History of

African Americans in Santa Cruz County, part 2, Chronology, 1542–1860," Santa Cruz Public Library, 1995, http://www.santacruzpl.org/history/articles/127/ (accessed August 3, 2010); Roberts, *Mining for Freedom*. Roberts states that Redmond Rodgers demanded a fee of $1,200 for his slave's freedom, 56. Present-day equivalent of $1,100 is $35,100; $1,200 is $38,300, "Measuring Worth," CPI 2014.

28. Thurman, *Pioneers of Negro Origin*, 17–18; Beasley, *Negro Trail Blazers*, 71, 117; Roberts, *Mining for Freedom*, 56.

29. Roberts, *Mining for Freedom*, 57.

30. Artimisa Penwright Daniels's manumission papers, reprinted in Beasley, *Negro Trail Blazers*, 87.

31. The note is quoted in Roberts, *Mining for Freedom*, 57.

32. The certificate is dated Dardanell, Yell County, Arkansas, April 30, 1859, and it is signed by Robert E. Walters, George Williams, Joseph Miles, W. H. Spirey, L. D. Parish, George L. Kimble, Samuel Dickens, Haunis A. Hawill, A. Ferril, James A. Baird, William A. Ross, C. M. Mundock, A.H. Fulton, Joseph P. Williams, and B. I. Jacoway, reprinted in Beasley, *Negro Trail Blazers*, 87.

33. Thurman, *Pioneers of Negro Origin*, 20; Roberts, *Mining for Freedom*, 58. Reader, "To Know My Name, part 2."

34. Roberts, *Mining for Freedom*, 58–59

35. Ibid.; Beasley, *Negro Trail Blazers*, 117–18.

36. Daniel Rodgers quoted in Leon Rowland, "Uncle Dan Rodgers," Santa Cruz Historical Society Archives, undated paper, reprinted in Roberts, *Mining for Freedom*, 60. Daniel Rodgers quoted in Thurman, *Pioneers of Negro Origin*, 21.

37. Beasley, *Negro Trail Blazers*, 118; Roberts, *Mining for Freedom*, 60.

38. Thurman, *Pioneers of Negro Origin*, 21.

39. Coffey's description is in his deed of emancipation, issued November 5, 1856, and quoted in Jeanette L. Molson and Eual D. Blansett Jr., *The Torturous Road to Freedom: The Life of Alvin Aaron Coffey* (Linden, Calif: self-published, 2004), 74. See Molson interview, for the "in hopes" quote; see Thurman, *Pioneers of Negro Origin*," 15, for the "my pretty Mahala" quote.

40. Beasley, *Negro Trail Blazers*, 70. See also Molson and Blansett, *Torturous Road to Freedom*, 66. Coffey's $700 earnings would today have a value of $22,400, "Measuring Worth," CPI 2014.

41. Molson and Blansett, *Torturous Road to Freedom*, 66. Coffey's shoe soling would have a value today of $575, and his savings would be worth $19,000 to $19,700, "Measuring Worth," CPI 2014.

42. Coffey, "Autobiography," *The Pioneer*, 12. In present-day terms, Coffey earned Bassett $176,000, and the gold Bassett stole from his slave would equal $19,700. Bassett sold him for $31,900 (in present-day terms), and Bassett's "clear profit" totaled $220,000, "Measuring Worth," CPI 2014. Coffey's "clear profit" figures actually total $227,600 in today's money; his estimates of "clear profit" were

just slightly off the mark by $7,600 in today's money, but his point and his outrage are perfectly valid.

43. Both quotes are found in Molson and Blansett, *Torturous Road to Freedom*, 66.

44. Molson interview. The present-day equivalent of Coffey's gold is $18,600 to $19,100, "Measuring Worth," CPI 2012.

45. Coffey, quoted in Molson and Blansett, *Torturous Road to Freedom*, 70–71. Molson and Blansett note that the actual fee Tindall demanded for the slave's liberty is unclear. Different sources place it between $1,000 and $2,000. Molson and Blansett believe that the "price may have been only $1,000," 70–71. His emancipation price of $1,000 would today have a value of $29,100, "Measuring Worth," CPI 2014.

46. Molson and Blansett, *Torturous Road to Freedom*, 74; Thurman, *Pioneers of Negro Origin*, 15. The present-day equivalent of Coffey's $5,000 worth of gold is $140,000, "Measuring Worth," CPI 2014.

47. Molson interview. See also Molson and Blansett, *Torturous Road to Freedom*, 74.

48. Thurman, *Pioneers of Negro Origin*, 15; Beasley, *Negro Trail Blazers*, 70; Molson and Blansett, *Torturous Road to Freedom*, 79–85; see 75–76 for a discussion of Canada. See also Jeannette Molson, "Coffey, Alvin Aaron (1822–1902)," The Black Past: An Online Reference Guide to African American History, BlackPast.org, http://www.blackpast.org/?q=aaw/coffey-alvin-aaron-1822-1902 (accessed July 10, 2011); Society of California Pioneers obituary for Alvin Coffey quoted in Thurman, *Pioneers of Negro Origin in California*, 17.

49. Reader, "Uncle Dave's Story," part 2. The $1,000 Boffman paid for his freedom has a present-day value of $31,900, "Measuring Worth," CPI 2014.

50. The price Boffman and McAdams planned to get for the lumber would today equal $3,190, "Measuring Worth," CPI 2014.

51. Reader, "Uncle Dave's Story," part 2. The $200 the sheriff won in court has a present-day value of $5,540. Otto's payment of $100 would today be $2,940, and the auction price of Boffman's land and livestock would be $22,200, "Measuring Worth," CPI 2014.

52. Reader, "Uncle Dave's Story," part 2.

53. Both quotes from the *Santa Cruz Sentinel* are found in Reader, "Uncle Dave's Story," part 2.

54. Taylor, *In Search of the Racial Frontier*, 75–76; Fred Lockley, "The Case of Robin Holmes vs. Nathaniel Ford," *Quarterly of the Oregon Historical Society* 23, no. 2 (June 1922): 111. For brief narratives of Lewis Southworth and Amanda Johnson, see George P. Rawick, ed., *The American Slave: A Composite Autobiography*, supp. series 1, Arkansas, Colorado, Minnesota, Missouri, Oregon and Washington Narratives, vol. 2 (Westport, Conn.: Greenwood, 1977), 273–78. See also

"Lou Southworth," *Oregon Encyclopedia,* Oregon History and Culture, http://www.oregonencyclopedia.ort/entry/view/southworth_louis_1829_1917 (accessed August 28, 2010).

55. Lewis Southworth, as quoted in Peggy Baldwin, "A Legacy beyond the Generations" (Genealogical Forum of Oregon Annual Writing Contest, 2006), http://www.gfo.org/writecontest/2006-1st.pdf. Also see John B. Horner, "Uncle Lou and His Violin," *Days and Deeds in the Oregon Country* (Portland: J. K. Gill, 1928), 139–46. The $300 Lewis earned would have a present-day value of $8,480, and the cost of his rifle today would be $1,440, "Measuring Worth," CPI 2014.

56. Baldwin, "A Legacy beyond the Generations."

57. Vivian T. Williams, "Louis Alexander Southworth," *Northwest Pioneer Fiddlers, 1830–1917"* (Seattle: Voyager Recordings & Publications, 2010), http://www.voyagerrecords.com/arNWFiddlers.htm (accessed July 14, 2011).

58. Lewis's $400 payment would today have a value of $11,700; the $1,000 total would today be worth $29,400, "Measuring Worth," CPI 2014; Baldwin, "A Legacy beyond the Generations," especially n. 17 for the "Petition of James B. Southworth and Others Praying the Recognition of the Right of Legislative Protection of Slave Property," January 4, 1859, item no. 10974, Oregon Territorial and Provisional Papers, microfilm reel 73, Oregon Territorial and Provisional Records, U.S. Department of State (Salem, Ore.: Oregon State Archives).

59. Lewis Southworth, quoted in Baldwin, "A Legacy beyond the Generations." Also see Horner, "Uncle Lou and His Violin," 130–46; Williams, *Northwest Pioneer Fiddlers.*

60. McLagan, *Peculiar Paradise,* 83–84; "Louis A. Southworth (1830–1917)," Oregon Northwest Black Pioneers: Celebrating the Contributions of Oregon's African-American Pioneers, http://www.oregonnorthwestblackpioneers.org/historybriefs.htm (accessed August 8, 2010).

61. Coleman, "Blacks in Utah History"; Coleman, "A History of Blacks in Utah," 37; Carter, *Story of the Negro Pioneer,* 20–26.

62. All quotes are from Henry C. Bruce, *The New Man: Twenty-Nine Years a Slave. Twenty-Nine Years a Free Man, Recollections of H.C. Bruce* (York, Penn.: P. Anstadt & Sons, 1895), 108–9. See also Katz, *The Black West,* 178–79. Katz erroneously refers to Henry C. Bruce as "Howard C. Bruce." Henry Clay Bruce's more famous brother, Blanche K. Bruce, served in the U.S. Senate from Mississippi (1875–81) and as the register of the treasury from 1881–1898.

63. Bruce, *The New Man,* 108–9.

64. Ibid., 109–10, 112–13, 155–58. See also Bill Lohse, "Bruce, Henry Clay (1836–1902)," The Black Past: An Online Reference Guide to African American History, BlackPast.org, http://www.blackpast.org/?q=aaw/bruce-henry-clay-1836-1902 (accessed January 17, 2012); Katz, *The Black West,* 178–79.

65. For all the quotes regarding Bluford, see Bruce, *The New Man,* 34–36. Also see Katz, *The Black West,* 178–79.

66. Peter Brown to Mrs. Alley Brown, St. Genevieve City, Missouri, December 1, 1851, original in the Oregon-California Collection, 1832–1943, folder 14, Missouri Historical Society, St. Louis. The $80 he paid out then would today be worth $2,370, the $300 he earned would be $9,580, and $4 a day paid at some diggings would have a present-day value of $128 a day, "Measuring Worth," CPI, 2014.

67. Michael Rafferty, "Nelson Ray—A Story of the West: Placerville Miner Bought His Family Out of Slavery in Missouri," Placerville *Mountain Democrat,* October 8, 1998. Ray's earnings of $3,700 are the 2014 equivalent of $117,000, "Measuring Worth," CPI 2014. Also see Samuel H. Williamson and Louis P. Cain, "Measuring Slavery in $2009," http://www.measuringworth.com/slavery/php (accessed July 9, 2011).

68. Rafferty, "Nelson Ray."

69. Harold and Gay Alexander and family, interview with Shirley Ann Wilson Moore, August 1, 2009. Hereafter cited as Alexander Family interview; San Francisco African American Historical & Cultural Society, "Charles and Nancy Alexander," *Monographs: Blacks in the West* (San Francisco: African American Historical & Cultural Society, no. 1 Manuscript Series, 1976), 87–88. This article is an excerpt from James William Pilton, "Negro Settlement in British Columbia, 1858–1871" (master's thesis, University of British Columbia, 1951). The article also contains a reprint of a 1909 newspaper interview (newspaper unidentified) with Charles and Nancy Alexander. This original document is in the personal collection of Barton Alexander, Victoria, British Columbia. Hereafter cited as Charles and Nancy Alexander interview.

70. Alexander Family interview; Pilton, "Negro Settlement in British Columbia," 87; Doug Hudlin video interview, conducted by Dale Hitchcocks, British Columbia Black History Awareness Society, April 23, 2010 (hereafter cited as Hudlin interview), http://www.youtube.com/watch?v=Yp5IM9Qs_0g (accessed February 28, 2011). See also "Charles and Nancy Alexander," in "A Resource Guide on Black Pioneers in British Columbia" (Victoria, B.C.: The British Columbia Black History Awareness Society, n. d.), 64–65.

71. The quote "fighting Indians" is from the Alexander Family interview; the "occasionally a menace" quote is from Pilton, "Negro Settlement in British Columbia," 87–88.

72. For Indians on the Humboldt River route, see Unruh, *The Plains Across,* 165; Bagley, *So Rugged and Mountainous,* 51; Hudlin interview.

73. Pilton, "Negro Settlement in British Columbia," 88 Alexander Family interview.

74. Alexander Family interview; Hudlin interview; Pilton, "Negro Settlement in British Columbia," 88–89. Harold Alexander's carpentry earnings of $6 a day has the present-day value of $173, "Measuring Worth," CPI 2014.

75. Alexander Family interview.

76. Hudlin interview.

77. Sylvia Stark interview, part 2.

78. For the impact of the Civil War on slavery in Missouri, see Taylor, *In Search of the Racial Frontier*, 95–97. For the quotes from the 1964 interview with Belle Fisher and details about the McDonalds and the tin box, see Gail Schontzler, "McDonald House Holds History of Freed Slaves Who Helped Settle Bozeman," *Bozeman Daily Chronicle*, February 13, 2011. See also Simon Shaw with Linda Peavy and Ursula Smith, *Frontier House* (New York: Atria Books, 2002), 43; Phyllis Smith, *Bozeman and the Gallatin Valley: A History* (Essex, Conn.: Globe Pequot Press), 91–92.

79. Schontzler, "McDonald House"; Shaw, Peavy, and Smith, *Frontier House*, 43; Phyllis Smith, *Bozeman and the Gallatin Valley*, 91–92.

80. Mary gave birth to seven children—two boys who died as infants, two boys who died by the age of fifteen, and three girls who lived well into adulthood. Schontzler, "McDonald House."

81. Katz, *The Black West*, 178. For Nancy Lewis's date of birth, her "job as a cook," and her employment in the Tabor household, see "Lewis Family Matriarch–Nancy Lewis Obituary," *Colorado Statesman*, September 9, 1944, courtesy of the Denver Public Library, Blair-Caldwell African American History Collection.

82. David Brown's documents were officially certified and attested to by John B. White, clerk of the Hampshire County Court, and John Brady, "a Justice of the Peace for the said county," on October 27, 1834. See Beasley, *Negro Trail Blazers*, 87.

83. John Mark Lambertson, "I Remain Your Affectionate Wife: David and Rachel Brown and the California Gold Rush," from notes "What We Know of David and Rachel Brown." Notes compiled for the exhibit at the National Frontier Trails Museum, Independence, Missouri. Hereafter cited as Lambertson, "David Brown Exhibit Notes." Thanks to John Mark Lambertson for providing me with this material.

84. "Recommendation for David Brown, about to Migrate to Ohio, Signed by Certain County Residents, Oct. 27, 1834, Hampshire County, Virginia." The document is located in the Robert B. Honeyman Collection, Bancroft Library.

85. Lambertson, "David Brown Exhibit Notes."

86. Ibid.

87. "Brown Letters," Mrs. Rachel A. Brown to Mr. David Brown, letters dated May 22, 1853, and May 26, 1853, Lancaster, Ohio.

88. Ibid., Mrs. Rachel A. Brown to Mr. David Brown, letters dated April 1853[?] and May 22, 1853, Lancaster, Ohio. The question mark accompanying the April 1853 letter appears on the transcribed typescript copy sent to the author from John Mark Lambertson, National Frontier Trails Museum, indicating that the date is illegible on the original document.

89. Lambertson, "David Brown Exhibit Notes." Thomas Sturgeon and Samuel Crim were two prominent white Lancaster, Ohio, businessmen. Another source states that Brown's company started out with one hundred horses and mules and forty-four riders on horseback. See E. H. Colburn, *History of Fairfield County, Ohio, Past and Present* (1883; repr., Knightstown, Ind.: Bookmark, 1977), 334, 374. Brown's outfitting cost of $150 is the present-day equivalent of $4,740, "Measuring Worth," CPI 2014.

90. Document of agreement between Thomas Sturgeon, Samuel Crim and David Brown, February 28, 1852, in Beasley, *Negro Trail Blazers*, 87–88.

91. Lambertson, "David Brown Exhibit Notes."

92. Bill to David Brown, March 4, 1853, David Brown Papers, 1853–1887, from the Edwin Grabhorn Collection, Bancroft Library. Hereafter cited as the "Brown Papers, Grabhorn Collection." Brown's $10 tab would today amount to $316, "Measuring Worth," CPI 2014.

93. Bill of Sale of a watch from Ernest Zoller, April 30, 1853, "Brown Papers, Grabhorn Collection" Bancroft Library. Brown's $20 watch would today cost $632, "Measuring Worth," CPI 2014.

94. Bill of Sale to David Brown signed by John Calvert, Josiah Calvert, Matthew Corothers, July 26, 1853, "Brown Papers, Grabhorn Collection" Bancroft Library. David Brown's two mining claims of $50 would today have a value of $1,580, "Measuring Worth," CPI 2014.

95. Bill of Sale to David Brown and George M. Rollin, signed by Geo. A. Booth and I. Hixson, dated May 1, 1854, Honeyman Collection, Bancroft Library. Hereafter cited as the "Brown Papers, Honeyman Collection." The $440 hydraulic and drifting claims purchase is the present-day equivalent of $12,800, "Measuring Worth," CPI 2014.

96. Bill of Sale to David Brown, signed by Moses I. Harris, dated June 2, 1855, "Brown Papers,Grabhorn Collection" Bancroft Library. Brown's quarter interest in the claim would today have a value of $4,240, "Measuring Worth," CPI 2014.

97. Article of Agreement entered into by David Brown and Stephen Campbell and William A. Jackson, dated July 27, 1857, "Brown Papers, Grabhorn Collection," Bancroft Library.

98. Receipt for "Cayotoville, December 1st 1855"; Charles Thomas Millard agreement with David Brown, February 23, 1857, both documents in the "Brown Papers, Grabhorn Collection, "Bancroft Library. Brown's final payment of

$180 would today be the equivalent of $5,090 and the $225 installments would be $6,300, "Measuring Worth," CPI, 2014.

99. David Brown's bar bill, "Mr. Wm. Wilkerson in a/c with David Brown," December, 1856–January 1857, "Brown Papers, Grabhorn Collection," Bancroft Library. Brown's $2.50 bar tab would today amount to $70.00, "Measuring Worth," CPI 2014.

100. C. Millard to Mr. David Brown, letter dated Downieville, June 28, 1855, "Brown Papers, Grabhorn Collection," Bancroft Library. In present-day terms, the $18.52 debt is the equivalent of $523, and the $12 Millard collected is the equivalent of $339, "Measuring Worth," CPI 2014.

101. See "Notice," Colored American Joint Stock Quartz Mining Company, February 26, 1866, "Brown Papers, Grabhorn Collection," Bancroft Library. Also see Lambertson, "David Brown Exhibit Notes."

102. "Brown Letters," R. A. Brown to Mr. D. Brown, letter dated January 3, 1853, Lancaster Ohio.

103. Ibid.

104. Ibid., letter dated October 14, 1853.

105. Ibid. letter dated May 26, 1853.

106. Ibid., letter dated May 22, 1853.

107. Ibid., letters dated January 3, 1853; May 22, 1853; and May 26, 1853.

108. Ibid., letter dated Oct 14, 1853.

109. Ibid., letters dated May 26, 1853, and May 22, 1853.

110. Ibid., letter dated May 26, 1853.

111. Ibid., letters dated January 3, 1853, and May 26, 1853.

112. Ibid., letter dated May 26, 1853.

113. Ibid., letter dated May 22, 1853.

114. Ibid., letters dated January 3, 1853, and May 26, 1853.

115. Ibid., letter dated April 1853[?].

116. Ibid., letters dated January 3, 1853; May 26, 1853; and October 14, 1853. The "two thousand" dollars would have the present-day value of $63,200, "Measuring Worth," CPI 2014.

117. Ibid., letter dated April 1853[?].

118. Lambertson, "David Brown Exhibition Notes." The $20 noted for funeral expenses would today amount to $537, "Measuring Worth," CPI 2014.

119. Lambertson, "David Brown Exhibition Notes."

Chapter 8

Epigraph 1. Rudolph M. Lapp, *Archy Lee: A California Fugitive Slave Case* (Berkeley, Calif.: Heyday Books, 2008), 9.

Epigraph 2. "Change of Sentiment," article in the *The Pacific Appeal*, vol. 1, no. 20, August 16, 1862.

1. McLagan, *A Peculiar Paradise*, 33. Taylor, *In Search of the Racial Frontier*, 77; Fred Lockley, "The Case of Robin Holmes vs. Nathaniel Ford," *Quarterly of the Oregon Historical Society* 23, no. 2 (June, 1922): 111–37.

2. McLagan, *A Peculiar Paradise*, 34. Robin's $900 would have the present-day value of $28,100, "Measuring Worth," CPI 2014; Lockley, "The Case of Robin Holmes vs. Nathaniel Ford," 117–18.

3. McLagan, *A Peculiar Paradise*, 34; Taylor, *In Search of the Racial Frontier*, 77; Lockley, "The Case of Robin Holmes vs. Nathaniel Ford," 114.

4. McLagan, *A Peculiar Paradise*, 34–35. The $3,000 bond would have the present-day value of $92,000, and the $1,000 bond the value of $31,300, "Measuring Worth," CPI 2014.

5. McLagan, *A Peculiar Paradise*, 33–35; Taylor, *In Search of the Racial Frontier*, 77.

6. Nathaniel Ford to James A. Shirley, letter dated June 22, 1852, in Frederic A. Culmer, ed., "Emigrant Missourians in Mexico and Oregon," *Missouri Historical Review* 25 (1931): 287.

7. McLagan, *A Peculiar Paradise*, 80–81; Tricia Martineau Wagner, "Drake, Mary Jane Holmes Shipley (1841–1925)," The Black Past: An Online Reference Guide to African American History, BlackPast.org, http://www.blackpast.org/?=aaw/drake-mary-jane-holmes-shipley-1841-1925 (accessed July 25, 2008). Robin Holmes's personal property valuation would be equivalent to $19,000 today; Reuben Shipley's freedom price of $1,500 would be $42,000; and $750 extortion demanded by Ford would be $21,000, "Measuring Wealth," CPI 2014.

8. McLagan, *A Peculiar Paradise*, 81.

9. Ibid., 82.

10. Young, quoted in Taylor, *In Search of the Racial Frontier*, 79.

11. Taylor, *In Search of the Racial Frontier*, 79–80; Hayden, "Biddy Mason's Los Angeles," 86–99, especially 88–90. See also Tricia Martineau Wagner, "Mason, Bridget 'Biddy' (1818–1891)," The Black Past: An Online Reference Guide to African American History, BlackPast.org, http://www.blackpast.org/?=aaw/mason-bridget-biddy-1818-1891 (accessed July 10, 2011).

12. Hayden, "Biddy Mason's Los Angeles," 89.

13. Ibid., 90; Taylor, *In Search of the Racial Frontier*, 80; Wagner, "Mason, Bridget 'Biddy.'"

14. All quotes in this paragraph are found in Hayden, "Biddy Mason's Los Angeles," 91.

15. Ibid.

16. Wagner, "Mason, Bridget 'Biddy'"; Hayden, "Biddy Mason's Los Angeles," 91–99.

17. Lapp, *Archy Lee*. This is the best, most detailed account of the Archy Lee case. For this quote, see "Affidavit of C.A. Stovall," filed March 29, 1858, in BACM Research, "African-American Slavery: California Fugitive Slave Case: Stovall v. Archy Lee Legal Papers," http://www.paperlessarchives.com/FreeeTitles/StovallvArchy.pdf (accessed May 5, 2011).

18. The newspaper interview is reprinted in Lapp, *Archy Lee*, 9, 52–53. For the original newspaper interview, see the *Alta California*, "Archy's Story," March 31, 1858. Original of the *Alta California* newspaper is in the California State Library, Sacramento, California Room collection.

19. For Stovall's and Lee's differing versions of events, see "Petition and Affidavit of C. A. Stovall," January 8, 1858, "Affidavit of C. A. Stovall," filed March 29, 1858, and "Brief for Respondent and Statement of Facts," April 1858, all in BACM Research, "Archy Lee Legal Papers." Also see National Archives, "Slavery in California, the Case of *Stovall v. Archy, a Slave*," especially "Petition and Affidavit of C. A. Stovall," January 8, 1858 (ARC Identifier 295969), "Brief for Respondent (and Statement of Facts)," ca. April 1858 (ARC Identifier 295967), all in Our Archives: Our Voices. Our History. Our National Archives, an online project of the U.S. National Archives, http://www.ourarchives.wikispaces.net/Slavery inCaliforniatheCaseofStovallv.Archy (accessed May 3, 2011). Also see Lucile Eaves, *A History of California Labor Legislation: With an Introductory Sketch of the San Francisco Labor Movement* (Berkeley: University of California Press, 1910), especially "The Last California Fugitive-Slave Case," 99–104.

20. Lapp, *Archy Lee*, 9, 52–53; *Alta California*, "Archy's Story," March 31, 1858; BACM Research, "Archy Lee Legal Papers," "Petition and Affidavit of C. A. Stovall," January 8, 1858, "Affidavit of C. A. Stovall" filed March 17, 1858, and "Brief for Respondent and Statement of Facts," April 1858; National Archives, "Slavery in California."

21. Moore, "We Feel the Want of Protection," 109–11; "Affidavit of C. A. Stovall," filed March 29, 1858, and "Affidavit of S. J. Noble," filed March 29, 1858, in BACM Research, "Archy Lee Legal Papers"; Eaves, *History of California Labor Legislation*, 100–104; Pilton, "Negro Settlement in British Columbia," excerpted in San Francisco African American Historical and Cultural Society, Manuscript Series, No. 1, "Monographs: Blacks in the West" (San Francisco: African American Historical and Cultural Society, 1976), 53–56, hereafter cited as Pilton excerpt, "Negro Settlement in British Columbia."

22. Lapp, *Archy Lee*, 3–7, 9 (for Lee's quote). Also see Pilton, "Negro Settlement in British Columbia," 54. In present-day money, Lee would have been worth $44,500, "Measuring Worth," CPI 2014.

23. Lapp, *Archy Lee*, 11–13; Robert F. Heizer and Alan F. Almquist, *The Other Californians: Prejudice and Discrimination under Spain, Mexico, and the*

United States to 1920 (Berkeley: University of California Press, 1971), 127–28; Eaves, *History of California Labor Legislation,* 100–101.

24. Lapp, *Archy Lee,* 21–39, 48–62; Eaves, *History of California Labor Legislation,* 100–104; Pilton excerpt, "Negro Settlement in British Columbia," 57–58. Also see the *Alta California,* "The Case of Archy," for Riker's petition for a writ of habeas corpus, "City Items—The Denouement of the Archy Case—Great Excitement on Steamer Day," both articles, March 6, 1858; *Alta California,* "City Items—The Release of Archy Lee and the End of It," April 15, 1858. For community fund-raising activities on behalf of Archy Lee, see *Alta California,* "Archy: To the Friends of the Constitution and Laws!," March 20, 1858.

25. Moore, "We Feel the Want of Protection," 111; Lapp, *Archy Lee,* 64. For Lee's life in Victoria, B.C., see Broussard, *Expectations of Equality,* 19. For a brief account of Archy Lee's final days, see the *San Francisco Elevator,* vol. 9, no. 32, "A Bit of History, after 15 Years," November 15, 1873.

26. Coleman, "Is There No Blessing for Me?" 144.

27. The father of Jane Elizabeth's baby was reputed to be either a white Presbyterian minister or a white Methodist minister. See Coleman, "Is There No Blessing for Me?" 145.

28. Coleman, "Is There No Blessing for Me?" 145, 147; Coleman, "A History of Blacks in Utah," 56.

29. Coleman, "A History of Blacks in Utah," 7; Church of Jesus Christ of Latter-day Saints. Church History, "Mormon Pioneer Overland Travel, 1847–1868," http://lds.org/churchhistory/library/pioneercompany/1,15797,4017-1-285,000 .html (accessed August 28, 2011). Jane Elizabeth Manning James noted in her memoirs, "At Hog Creek, my son Silas was born." "Life History of Jane Elizabeth Manning James," as transcribed by Elizabeth J. D. Round[y], Blackslds.org, A Web Site Dedicated to Black Members of the Church of Jesus Christ of Latter-day Saints, http://www.blacklds.org/manning (accessed January 19, 2012). In his "History of Blacks in Utah," Coleman wrote, "Jane was pregnant with her son Silas, who was born at Hogg Creek, Iowa," 56–57. Also see Coleman, "'Is There No Blessing for Me?'" in which he wrote, "In June 1846 Jane Elizabeth gave birth to a second son, Silas, at the family's temporary homesite, Keg Creek, Iowa," 147.

30. Coleman, "A History of Blacks in Utah," 7; Coleman, "Is There No Blessing for Me?" 147–48, 152.

31. Coleman, "Is there No Blessing for Me?" 148.

32. Eliza Lyman's journal, quoted in Carter, *Story of the Negro Pioneer,* 9–10.

33. Coleman, "Blacks in Utah, 1825–1910," 57. See also Coleman, "Is There No Blessing for Me?" 148–50.

34. Coleman, "Is There No Blessing for Me?" 151–55; The LDS Endowment, "About the Endowment," http://www.ldsendowment.org/about.html (accessed August 29, 2011).

35. Coleman, "Is There No Blessing for Me?" 147–49, 150–57. See also Carter, *Story of the Negro Pioneer*, 9–13.

36. Coleman, "Is There No Blessing for Me?" 147–49, 150–57.

37. Emma Belle Bush interview by Paul Thomas, 1960, see Paul Thomas, "George Bush" (master's thesis, University of Washington, 1965), quoted in Darrell Millner, "George Bush of Tumwater: Founder of the First American Colony on Puget Sound," *Columbia Magazine* 8, no. 4 (Winter 1994–95): 14–19, http://columbia.washigtonhistory.org/anthology/settlers/georgeBush.aspx (accessed September 21, 2010).

38. Minto, "Reminiscences of Experiences on the Oregon Trail," II, 212; Taylor, *In Search of the Racial Frontier*, 82.

39. Taylor, *In Search of the Racial Frontier*, 82; Millner, "George Bush of Tumwater," 16–19; National Park Service, "George Washington Bush: The Spirit of Westward Expansion."

40. Millner, "George Bush of Tumwater"; George Washington Bush quoted in McLaglan, *A Peculiar Paradise*, 20. See also Bagley, *So Rugged and Mountainous*, 336.

41. Millner, "George Bush of Tumwater," 18–19.

42. Ibid.; "An Act for the Relief of George Bush, of Thurston County, Washington Territory," approved February 10, 1855, *Appendix to the Congressional Globe for the Second Session, Thirty-Third Congress: Containing Speeches, Important State Papers, Laws, Etc.*, ed. Francis Preston Blair, John Cook Rives and Franklin Rives (City of Washington: Office of John C. Rives, 1855), 418. Also see U.S. Congress, *Journal of the House of Representatives of the Thirty-Third Congress, Begun and Held at the City of Washington, December 4, 1854*, H.R. 707, "An Act for the Relief of George Bush, of Thurston County, Washington Territory" (Washington, D.C.: A. O. P. Nicholson, Printer, 1854), 299, 302, 338, 346, 352. Meeker quoted in Bagley, *So Rugged and Mountainous*, 336.

43. Millner, "George Bush of Tumwater," 18–19.

44. Kit Oldham, "George and Mary Jane Washington Found the Town of Centerville (now Centralia) on January 8, 1875," HistoryLink.org Online Encyclopedia of Washington State History, http://www.historylinnk.org/essays/output.cfm?file_id=5276 (accessed July 18, 2011). Hereafter cited as Oldham, "George and Mary Jane Washington." Also see Kit Oldham, "Washington, George (1817–1905)," The Black Past: An Online Reference Guide to African American History, BlackPast.org, http://www.blackpast.org/?q-aaw/washington-george-1817-1905. Hereafter cited as Oldham, "Washington, George (1817–1905)." Also see Clackamas Heritage Partners, Historic Oregon City, "Black Pioneers and Settlers—George Washington," http://www.historicoregoncity.org/HOC/index.php?option=com_content&view=article&i (accessed December 29, 2008). Hereafter cited as Historic Oregon City, "Black Pioneers and Settlers—George Washington."

45. Oldham, "George and Mary Jane Washington"; Clackamas Heritage Partners, Historic Oregon City, "Black Pioneers and Settlers—George Washington."

46. Oldham, "George and Mary Jane Washington."

47. Clackamas Heritage Partners, Historic Oregon City, "Black Pioneers and Settlers—George Washington."

48. Oldham, "George and Mary Jane Washington."

49. Roberts, *Mining for Freedom,* 34. Also see Neil Mill, "A Negro in Sonora," interview of Vernon Sugg McDonald by Neil Mill, September 9, 1975, in the Tuolumne County Historical Society. Hereafter cited as the McDonald interview.

50. Vernon Sugg McDonald, "The Pioneer Sugg Family: The Saga of an Early Day Family of Tuolumne County and the History of One of Sonora's Outstanding Gold Rush Homes," *Quarterly of the Tuolumne County Historical Society* 4, no. 1 (July–September 1964): 97–98.

51. All quotes by Mary Elizabeth are in McDonald, "The Pioneer Sugg Family," 98; see also Roberts, *Mining for Freedom,* 34–35.

52. Beth L. Savage, *African American Historic Places,* National Register of Historic Places, National Park Service (New York: John Wiley & Sons, 1994), 119; Roberts, *Mining for Freedom,* 82; Francis Trale to William Sugg, Deed of Manumission, Tuolumne County, Deed Book 2, page 908, Recorded June 14, 1854. Sugg's $1 free price is the present-day equivalent of $29.10, "Measuring Worth," CPI 2014.

53. McDonald, "The Pioneer Sugg Family," 98.

54. Ibid. 98–99; Savage, *National Register of Historic Places,* 119; Roberts, *Mining for Freedom,* 35, 82. See also the Historical Marker Data Base: Bite-Size Bits of Local, National, and Global History, "Sugg House," http://www.hmdb.org/marker.asp?marker=31861 (accessed September 25, 2010); Jeff Jardine, "Mining Mother Lode's Black History," *Modesto Bee,* January 20, 2008. Description of the contents of the house is derived from a personal tour of the Sugg House (April 5, 2004) and my discussions with Bob and Sherry Brennan, current owners of the Sugg House and the collection, 2004–5. The Sugg and McDonald Family Papers are in the Yale Collection of Western Americana, Beinecke Rare Book and Manuscript Library.

55. Unfortunately, I have been unable to identify William Sugg's specific fraternal order, or discover the meaning of G.O.R.

56. Moore, "We Feel the Want of Protection," 116–17.

57. Roberts, *Mining for Freedom,* 35, 66–72, 83, 122–30 (for description of the "fancy dress ball" fund-raiser); Jardine, "Mining Mother Lode's Black History." For African Americans' fight against segregation in California's public schools, see Taylor, *In Search of the Racial Frontier,* 215–16; Marilyn K. Demas, *Ungraded School No. 2 Colored: The African American Struggle for Education in Victorian*

Sacramento (Sacramento: Sacramento County Historical Society, 1999), especially 21–78; Susan Bragg, "Knowledge is Power: Sacramento Blacks and the Public Schools, 1854–1860," *California History* 75, no. 3 (Fall 1996): 214–21.

58. McDonald, "The Pioneer Sugg Family," 99; Roberts, *Mining for Gold*, 35.

59. See, for example, Julia Henning Larsen, "Ben Palmer (c. 1817–1908)," The Black Past: An Online Reference Guide to African American History, BlackPast.org, http://www.blackpast.org/?q=aaw/palmer-ben-c-1817-1908 (accessed September 23, 2010); Joyce Devore, "Old Alpine County Barn Finds New Purpose as a Home," Gardnerville, Nevada *Record Courier*, January 29, 2010, http://www.recordcourier.com/article/20100129/ALPINE/100129646 (accessed September 24, 2010); Ed Johnson and Elmer R. Rusco, "The First Black Rancher: Ben Palmer and a Group of Black Pioneers Made Their Marks in the 1800s," *Historical Nevada Magazine: Outstanding Historical Features from the Pages of Nevada Magazine* (Carson City: Nevada Magazine, a Division of the Nevada Commission on Tourism, 1998), 82. This article was originally published in *Nevada Magazine* (January–February, 1989): 26–27; Grace Dangberg, *Carson Valley—Historical Sketches of Nevada's First Settlement* (Reno: A. Carlisle and Co., 1972), 60. According to Elmer R. Rusco, Ben Palmer may have brought Charlotte and her children out to his ranch sometime after his arrival in 1853. This and the 1875 state census is quoted in Rusco, *"Good Time Coming?"* 143.

60. Larsen, "Ben Palmer"; Devore, "Old Alpine County Barn."

61. Johnson and Rusco, "The First Black Rancher," 82–84.

62. *Territorial Enterprise* quoted in Johnson and Rusco, "The First Black Rancher," 83. Assessed valuations of $5,000 is the present day equivalent of $140,000, "Measuring Worth," CPI 2014.

63. Johnson and Rusco, "The First Black Rancher," 83–84. For the quote regarding Charlotte's hospitality and her reputation as a "prophetess," see Sally Zanjani, *Devils Will Reign: How Nevada Began* (Reno: University of Nevada Press, 2006), 15.

64. The "white men" quote was made by a Nevada territorial assemblyman. See Rusco, *"Good Time Coming?"* 22.

65. For a detailed discussion of territorial and state antiblack legislation in Nevada, see Rusco, *"Good Time Coming?"* especially 21–38; Larsen, "Palmer, Ben (c. 1817–1908)," The Black Past; Senator Harry Reid of Nevada, "Black History Month," speech to the U.S. Senate focusing on African Americans in Nevada, February 27, 2004, *Cong. Rec.* 108th Cong., 2d sess., 2004, 150, pt. 3: 2915–16, hereafter cited as Reid, "Black History Month," *Congressional Record*.

66. Rusco, *"Good Time Coming?"* 143–44; Ben Palmer's obituary in the *Record-Courier* quoted in Reid, "Black History Month," *Congressional Record*, 2916. Miller's real estate valued at $4,000 would have the present-day equivalence

of $74,900; her $1,000 personal worth would have a value of $18,700 today, "Measuring Worth," CPI 2014.

67. For a brief discussion of the Miller ranch, Sophia's management of it after Winfield's death, and Winfield Miller's horsemanship, see Johnson and Rusco, "The First Black Rancher," 84. For the value of Sophia Miller's real estate and personal holdings and a discussion of other African Americans who settled in the area, see Rusco, *"Good Time Coming?"* 143–44.

68. For a detailed account of Clara Brown's life, see Roger Baker, *Clara: An Ex-Slave in Gold Rush Colorado* (Boulder, Colo: Black Hawk, 2003). An older, cliché-ridden, but still useful biography of Clara Brown is Bruyn's *"Aunt" Clara Brown*, especially 1–4, 13–35.

69. Bruyn, *"Aunt" Clara Brown*, 21–25; Lapp, *Blacks in Gold Rush California*, 27; Shanti Zaid, "Aunt Clara Brown," Colorado Historical Society, http://www.historycolorado.org/sites/default/files/files/Kids_Students/Bios/Aunt_Clara_Brown.pdf (accessed September 24, 2010); Katz, *The Black West*, 77; Schlissel, *Women's Diaries*, 136–38.

70. Baker, *Clara: An Ex-slave in Gold Rush Colorado*, 32–33.

71. For discussion of Bowman and Lee, see ibid., 44–45, 48–51, 69.

72. Zaid, "Aunt Clara Brown"; Tricia Martineau Wagner, "Clara Brown (1803–1885)," The Black Past: An Online Reference Guide to African American History, BlackPast.org, http://www.blackpast.org/?=aaw/brown-clara-1803-1885 (accessed September 24, 2010); Lisa Keipp, "Clara Brown, a Colorado Pioneer, Part 1," Colorado History Examiner, Examiner.com. February 18, 2010, http://www.examiner.com/history-in-denver/clara-brown-a-colorado-pioneer (accessed September 24, 2010).

73. Baker, *Clara: An Ex-slave in Gold Rush Colorado*, 36–37; Zaid, "Aunt Clara Brown." See also Keipp, "Clara Brown, Part 1." The $100 donation is the present-day equivalent of $1,500, and the $50 dollar contribution is the present-day equivalent of $750, "Measuring Worth," CPI 2014.

74. Coleman, "A History of Blacks in Utah, 1825–1910," 53–56. The $4,000 Brown spent on one of her wagon caravans would be the present-day equivalent of $60,000, "Measuring Worth," CPI 2014.

75. Joseph Atkins, *Human Relations in Colorado* (Denver: Colorado State Department of Education, 1961), 15. This 1961 interview was done for a pamphlet on ethnic diversity in Colorado. The quotes from Gilmore are also in Baker, *Clara: An Ex-slave in Gold Rush Colorado*, 57.

76. Katz, *The Black West*, 77–79; Baker, *Clara: An Ex-slave in Gold Rush Colorado*, 57–61, 75–84; Zaid, "Aunt Clara Brown"; Wagner, "Clara Brown"; Lisa Keipp, "Clara Brown, A Colorado Pioneer, Part Two," Colorado History Examiner, http://www.examiner.com/history-in-denver/clara-brown-a-colorado-pioneer-part-two (accessed September 24, 2010).

77. The *Denver Republican,* February 18, 1882, story reprinted in Baker, *Clara: An Ex-slave in Gold Rush Colorado,* 89; Karen A. Johnson, "Undaunted Courage and Faith: The Lives of Three Black Women in the West and Hawaii in the Early 19th Century," *Journal of African American History* 91, no. 1 (Winter 2006), 11–12. The $100 train ticket would today cost $2,390, "Measuring Worth," CPI, 2014.

78. *Council Bluffs NonPareil,* quoted in the *Denver Republican,* March 4, 1882. See Baker, *Clara: An Ex-slave in Gold Rush Colorado,* 87.

79. Clara Brown interview, *Denver Tribune Republican,* June 26, 1885.

80. Newspaper accounts quoted in Baker, *Clara: An Ex-slave in Gold Rush Colorado,* 97–98.

81. Ibid., 43; Forbes Parkhill, *Mister Barney Ford: A Portrait in Bistre* (Denver: Sage Books, 1963), 79–91. The profits from the sale of Ford's business would today represent $64,600, "Measuring Worth," CPI 2014.

82. For a description of Denver and the mountain mining districts, see Baker, *Clara: An Ex-slave in Gold Rush* Colorado, 25–26, 43; Parkhill, *Mr. Barney Ford,* 97; Modupe Labode, Chief Historian, Colorado Historical Society, "Barney Ford's Legacy Still a Presence Today," Colorado Historical Society, February 16, 2006, http://www.denver.yourhub.com/Littleton/Stories/News/Print-Content~53835 (accessed September 23, 2010); Brooke Cleary, "Barney L. Ford: Runaway Slave, Denver Pioneer," Colorado Historical Society, adapted from "Barney Ford—From Plantation Slave to Denver Leader," by David F. Halaas, *Colorado History NOW,* October 2000, http://www.docstoc.com/docs/44329510/BARNEY-FORD (accessed September 23, 2010); Kenneth Jessen, "Former Slave Barney Ford Became a Colorado Millionaire," *Loveland* (Colorado) *Reporter-Herald,* February 26, 2012, http://www.reporterherald.com/ci_20031588 (accessed January 14, 2016).

83. Baker, *Clara: An Ex-slave in Gold Rush Colorado,* 43; Labode, "Barney Ford's Legacy." The quote is from Cleary, "Barney L. Ford."

84. Labode, "Barney Ford's Legacy"; Taylor, *In Search of the Racial Frontier,* 203.

85. Baker, *Clara: An Ex-slave in Gold Rush Colorado,* 43; Cleary, "Barney L. Ford"; People's Restaurant advertisement, quoted in Labode, "Barney Ford's Legacy." The $9,000 loan Ford took out has the present-day value of $175,000, "Measuring Worth," CPI 2014.

86. Baker, *Clara: An Ex-slave in Gold Rush Colorado,* 43–44; Cleary, "Barney L. Ford"; Taylor, *In Search of the Racial Frontier,* 203. The original quote regarding the Inter-Ocean hotel is found in Frank Hall, *History of the State of Colorado,* vol. 4 (Chicago: Blakely Printing, 1895): 441; Moya Hansen, "Ford, Barney L. (1822–1902)" The Black Past: An Online Guide to African American

History. BlackPast.org. *http://www.blackpast.org/?q=aaw/ford-barney-1-1822 -1902* (accessed August 8, 2010); John Hafnor, "Colorado's Black Baron Stood Tall," in *Strange But True, Colorado: Weird Tales of the Wild West* (Fort Collins, Colo.: Lone Pine Productions, 2005), 26. See also National Park Service, "Barney L. Ford Building."

87. Parkhill, *Mister Barney Ford,* 111–14, 124–25; Taylor, *In Search of the Racial Frontier,* 123–25.

88. Taylor, *In Search of the Racial Frontier,* 124–25; Parkhill, *Mr. Barney Ford,* 134–38; Moya Hansen, "Wagoner, Henry O. (1816–1901)," The Black Past: An Online Guide to African American History. http://www.blackpast.org/aaw /wagoner-henry-o-1816-1901 (accessed February 10, 2016).

89. Cleary, "Barney L. Ford"; Labode, "Barney Ford's Legacy"; Hansen, "Barney L. Ford"; Hafnor, "Colorado's Black Baron," 26; Eugene H. Berwanger, "Reconstruction on the Frontier: The Equal Rights Struggle in Colorado, 1865–1867," *Pacific Historical Review* 44, no. 3 (August 1975): 314–18, 320–28; Eugene H. Berwanger, "Hardin and Langston: Western Black Spokesmen of the Reconstruction Era," *Journal of Negro History* 64, no 2 (Spring, 1979): 103–5, 109–13.

90. Zion Baptist Church, "Historical Sketch," Zion Baptist Church & Ministries, 2008, http://www.zionbaptistchurchdenver.org/index.php?option=com _content&view=article&id (accessed September 23, 2010); Labode, "Barney Ford's Legacy"; Parkhill, *Mister Barney Ford,* 7–12. See also Five Points Business District, "The History of Five Points," http://www.fivepointsbiz.org/history -culture.html (accessed September 23, 2010).

91. Barney L. Ford, quoted in the Barney Ford House Museum, Town of Breckenridge, http://www.townofbreckenridge.com/index.aspx?page=211 (accessed September 23, 2010), hereafter cited as Breckenridge, "Barney Ford House Museum." This saying is posted over the door at the museum, which is located in the Ford home in the city of Breckenridge, Colorado.

92. *Pacific Appeal,* August 16, 1862.

93. Thomas Detter, *Pacific Appeal,* November 26, 1870, and letter to the *San Francisco Elevator,* June 26, 1868, quoted in Rusco, *"Good Time Coming?"* 10, 155–56.

94. I am indebted to historian Eric Gardner for this analysis of Jenny Carter's work. See Eric Gardner, ed., *Jennie Carter: A Black Journalist of the Early West* (Jackson: University Press of Mississippi, 2007), ix, xxix.

95. That date marked the sixth anniversary of the Emancipation Proclamation. See "Semper Fidelis," from Nevada County, Mud Hill, August 4, to the *San Francisco Elevator,* August 16, 1867; "Semper Fidelis," letter from Mud Hill, January 8, 1869, to the *Elevator,* and January 15, 1869, in Gardner, *Jennie Carter,* 4, 55–56.

96. Robert J. Chandler, *San Francisco Lithographer: African American Artist Grafton Tyler Brown:* (Norman: University of Oklahoma Press, 2014), 15, 17 (for "day-to-day" quote).

97. Lizzetta LeFalle-Collins, "Grafton Tyler Brown: Selling the Promise of the West," *International Review of African American Art* 12, no. 1 (1995): 27–32.

98. Lizzetta LeFalle-Collins, "Grafton Tyler Brown: Visualizing California and the Pacific Northwest," Exhibition Catalog (digital copy), California Historical Society, San Francisco, Calif. 2003, http://www.californiahistoricalsociety.org/exhibits/gtb.html (accessed July 14, 2011); Douglas Frazer Fine Art, Ltd., "Biography of Grafton Tyler Brown, 1841–1918," http://www.askart.com/AskART/artists/biography.aspx?searchtype=BIO&artist=1201 (accessed July 14, 2011); Chandler, *San Francisco Lithographer,* 27–30, 41–48; Robert J. Chandler, "From Black to White: Lithographer and Painter Grafton Tyler Brown," *California Territorial Quarterly* no. 86 (Summer 2011): 4–29; Dreck Spurlock Wilson, ed., *African American Architects: A Biographical Dictionary, 1856–1945* (New York: Routledge, 2004) s.v. "Grafton Tyler Brown"; LeFalle-Collins, "Selling the Promise of the West," 26–44.

99. Chandler, "From Black to White," 14–19; Rusco, "Good Time Coming?," 142; LeFalle-Collins, "Selling the Promise of the West," 32.

100. Chandler, *San Francisco Lithographer,* 153–78; LeFalle-Collins, "Selling the Promise of the West," 26–44.

101. Joe Louis Moore, "In Our Own Image: Black Artists in California, 1880–1970, Sample Portfolio of the Works of Grafton Tyler Brown, Sargent Claude Johnson, Emmanuel Joseph, Samella Lewis, Ruth Waddy, Emory Douglas," in *California History* 75, no. 3 (Fall 1996): 265–71; LeFalle-Collins, "Selling the Promise of the West," 26–44. For quality reproductions of Brown's work, see Chandler, *San Francisco Lithographer,* especially 6–8, 48, 173–77.

102. Quintard Taylor, *The Forging of a Black Community: Seattle's Central District from 1870 through the Civil Right Era* (Seattle: University of Washington Press, 1994), 21, 22, 45.

Epilogue

Epigraph 1. Dr. W. H. C. Stephenson quoted in Rusco, *"Good Time Coming?"* 75

1. Daniels, *Pioneer Urbanites,* 59, 62–74.

2. Ibid., 68.

3. George W. Bush, quoted in Minto, "Reminiscences of Experiences of the Oregon Trail," II, 212.

4. Broussard, *Expectations of Equality,* 19.

5. Dr. W. H. C. Stephenson, as quoted in Rusco, *"Good Time Coming?"* 75.

6. I am indebted to Blake Allmendinger's discussion of a representative black western experience and the notion of the West and the American Dream. See Blake Allmendinger, *Imagining the African American West* (Lincoln: University of Nebraska Press, 2005), xvi, 15.

Bibliography

Archival Collections

Benton County Historical Society Museum Collection. Lewis Southworth and his violin photograph. Philomath, Oregon.

Brown, Peter, to Mrs. Alley Brown, December 1, 1851. Oregon-California Collection, 1832–1943, F 14, Missouri Historical Society, St. Louis.

California State Library, Sacramento, California History Room. Picture Catalogue Collection, African American Miners.

California State Parks, Marshall Gold Discovery State Historic Park Archives. Gooch-Monroe Family photographs. Coloma, California.

California State University, Sacramento. Library Special Collections. T. H. Jefferson Map and *Accompaniment* and John Doble's *Journal and Letters from the Mines*.

Clarissa Hundley Wildy Collection. Nelson Ray materials, Sacramento History Center.

Curtis, William J. and Annette Curtis. "Searching for the Real Hiram Young." Curtis Family private collection, Independence, Missouri.

David Brown Papers, 1853–1887. Edwin Grabhorn Collection, Bancroft Library, University of California, Berkeley.

———. Robert B. Honeyman Jr. Collection, Bancroft Library, University of California, Berkeley.

Denver Public Library. Western History Collection. Clara Brown and Barney Ford photographs. Denver, Colorado.

Horner Collection. Lewis Southworth at his fireplace photograph. Benton County Historical Society Museum. Philomath, Oregon.

Hubert Howe Bancroft Collection. Nineveh Ford, "The Pioneer Road Makers." Salem Oregon, 1878. Bancroft Library, University of California, Berkeley.

Los Angeles Public Library. Security Pacific National Bank Collection. Bridget "Biddy" Mason photograph. Los Angeles, California.

Salt Spring Island Archives. Estes-Stark family photographs. Salt Spring Island, British Columbia, Canada.

University of Nevada, Reno, Libraries. Special Collections. Ben Palmer photograph. Reno, Nevada.

Yancey, Eva L. "History of the McGee Family." File folder, typewritten copy, subheading "Charlie's Butte." Laws Railroad Museum, Laws, California.

Public Records

The following list includes both printed and digital U.S. census reports, National Archives documents, state and local government documents, and Supreme Court and congressional records. It also includes publications and documents of the federal executive branch. Interpretive information from National Park Service is found under "Online Sources" below.

Bureau of Land Management. "Old Spanish Trail/Mormon Road Historic District." *National Register of Historic Places Registration Form,* prepared by Terri McBride, Nevada State Historic Preservation Office, in collaboration with Stanton D. Rolf, Las Vegas Field Office. National Park Service: Washington, D.C., 2001. http://pdfhost.focus.nps.gov/docs/NRHP/Text/01000863.pdf (accessed 9/1/2011).

Kimball, Stanley B. *Historic Resource Study: Mormon Pioneer National Trail,* Denver: Denver Service Center, National Park Service, 1991.

National Archives. Affidavit of Hiram Young; *Estate of Hiram Young, Deceased v. the United States* [No. 7320 Cong.].

———. "Slavery in California, The Case of *Stovall v. Archy, a Slave.*" Our Archives Wiki. National Records and Archives Administration. http://www.ourarchives.wikispaces.net/SlaverinCaliforniatheCaseofStovallv.Archy (accessed May 3, 2011).

National Park Service. "California Pioneers of African Descent," compiled by Guy Washington, regional manager, National Park Service, Underground Railroad Network to Freedom Program. Oakland, Calif., December 17, 2010. http://home.nps.gov/subjects/ugrr/discover_history/upload/California-Pioneers-of-African-Descent.pdf (accessed July 15, 2011).

———. Comprehensive Management and Use Plan/Final Environmental Impact Statement, California National Historic Trail, Pony Express National Historic Trail; and Management and Use Plan Update/Final Environmental Impact Statement, Oregon National Historic Trail, Mormon Pioneer National Historic Trail. Salt Lake City: Long Distance Trails Office, National Park Service, 1999.

———. Fort Davis National Historic Site, "Record of Deceased Officers and Soldiers at Fort Davis, Texas 1867–1879." http://www.nps.gov/foda/forteachers/upload/Pre-Visit-E (accessed January 27, 2014).

———. "Freedom Suits." Jefferson National Expansion Memorial/Missouri. http://www.nps.gov/jeff/learn/historyculture/freedom-suits.htm (accessed September 12, 2015).

———. "George Washington Bush and the Human Spirit of Westward Expansion." Jefferson National Expansion Memorial. *Museum Gazette* (February), 1999.

———. *National Historic Trails Auto Tour Route Interpretive Guide: Nebraska and Northeastern Colorado,* by Lee Kreutzer. Salt Lake City: National Trails System-Intermountain Region, August 2006.

———. *National Historic Trails Auto Tour Route Interpretive Guide: Western Missouri through Northeastern Kansas,* by Lee Kreutzer. Salt Lake City: National Trails System-Intermountain Region, September 2005.

———. *National Historic Trails Auto Tour Route Interpretive Guide across Wyoming,* by Lee Kreutzer. Salt Lake City: National Trails System-Intermountain Region, July 2007.

———. National Register of Historic Places. "Historic Resources of the Santa Fe Trail, 1821–1880." Washington, D.C.: U.S. Department of the Interior, May 11, 1995.

———. "Stories: The Santa Fe Story." http://www.nps.gov/safe/historyculture/stories.htm (accessed March 31, 2013).

———. "Suits for Freedom, St Louis, 1804–1865." http://www.nps.gov/jeff/historyculture/loader.cfm?csModule=security/getfile&PageID=166963 (accessed September 12, 2015).

State of Missouri, General Assembly. *Laws of the State of Missouri: Revised and Digested.* Vol. II, 1825. St Louis: E. Charles, for the state, 1825.

———. *The Revised Statutes of the State of Missouri,* 1845. St. Louis: J. W. Dougherty, for the state, 1845.

U.S. Bureau of the Census. *Fourth Census of the United States, 1820.* Washington, D.C.: Government Printing Office, 1822. http://www.census.gov/prod/www/abs/decennial/1820.html.

———. *Eighth Census of the United States, 1860.* Washington, D.C.: Government Printing Office, 1864. http://www.census.gov/prod/www/abs/decennial/1860.html.

———. *Negro Population of the United States, 1790–1915.* Washington, D.C.: Government Printing Office, 1918. http://www2.census.gov/prod2/decennial/documents/00480330_TOC.pdf.

———. *Ninth Census of the United States, 1870.* Washington, D.C.: Government Printing Office, 1872. http://www.census.gov/prod/www/abs/decennial/1870.html.

———. *Seventh Census of the United States, 1850.* Washington, D.C.: Government Printing Office, 1851. http://www.census.gov/prod/www/abs/decennial/1850.html.

———. *The Social and Economic Status of the Black Population in the United States: An Historical View, 1790–1978.* Washington, D.C.: Government Printing Office, 1979.

———. "Utah—Race and Hispanic Origin: 1850 to 1990." Online project of the Population Division, Working Paper Series, No. 56, September 2002.

http://www.census.gov/population/wwwdocumentation/twps0056/twps0056.html.
U. S. Congress. *The Congressional Globe* (Appendix). vol. 31, part 2. Washington, D.C. 1854–1855. Washington, D.C.: John C. Rives, 1855.
———. *The Congressional Globe.* 33d Cong., 2d session, January 9, 1855. Washington, D.C.: John C. Rives, 1855.
———. *The Congressional Globe.* 33d Cong., 2d session, January 31, 1855. Washington, D.C.: John C. Rives, 1855.
———. *The Congressional Globe.* 34th Cong., 1st session. January 8, 1856. Washington, D.C.: John C. Rives, 1856.
———. *The Congressional Globe.* 34th Cong., 1st session. February 12, 1856. Washington, D.C.: John C. Rives, 1856.
———. *The Congressional Globe.* 34th Cong., 1st session. February 21, 1856. Washington, D.C.: John C. Rives, 1856.
———. *The Congressional Globe.* 34th Cong., 1st session. April 17, 1856. Washington, D.C.: John C. Rives, 1856.
———. *The Congressional Globe.* 34th Cong., 1st session. April 21, 1856. Washington, D.C.: John C. Rives, 1856.
———. *The Congressional Record: Proceedings and Debates, Senate.* 108th Cong., 2d session. February 27, 2004. Speech of Sen. Harry Reid on African Americans in Nevada, given in honor of Black History Month.
———. *Journal of the House of Representatives.* 1854. 33d Cong., 2d session. Washington, D.C.: A.O.P. Nicholson, 1854.
U.S. Supreme Court. *Dred Scott v. Sandford,* 60 U.S. 393 (1856). http://laws.findlaw.com/us/60/393./html (accessed May 20, 2011).
———. *Scott v. Sandford,* 60 U.S. 393, Cornell University Law School, Legal Information Institute. http://www.law.cornell.edu/supct/html/historics/USSC_CR_0060_0393_ZO.html.

Primary Sources: Published, Unpublished, and Online

Alexander, Eveline M. *Cavalry Wife: The Diary of Eveline M. Alexander, 1866–1867, Being the Record of Her Journey from New York to Fort Smith to Join Her Cavalry-Officer Husband Andrew J. Alexander and Her Experiences with Him on Active Duty among the Indian Nations and in Texas, New Mexico and Colorado.* Edited by Sandra L. Myres. Reprint, College Station: Texas A&M University Press, 1977.
Bailey, Mary Stuart. "A Journal of Mary Stuart Bailey, Wife of Dr. Fred Bailey: From Ohio to California, April-October, 1852." In *Ho for California!: Women's Overland Diaries from the Huntington Library.* Edited by Sandra L. Myres. San Marino, Calif.: Henry E. Huntington Library, 1980.

Banks, John Edwin. *The Buckeye Rovers in the Gold Rush: An Edition of Two Diaries.* Edited by H. Lee Scamehorn. Athens: Ohio University Press, 1965.

Bartlett, Henry. "Henry Bartlett's Diary to Ohio and Kentucky." *Virginia Magazine of History and Biography* 19, no. 1 (January 1911): 68–86.

Beckwourth, James P. *The Life and Adventures of James P. Beckwourth, As Told to Thomas D. Bonner.* 1856. Reprint, Lincoln: University of Nebraska Press, 1972.

Blassingame, John, ed. *Slave Testimony: Two Centuries of Letters, Speeches, Interviews and Autobiographies.* Baton Rouge: Louisiana State University Press, 1977.

Boyd, Julian P., ed. *The Papers of Thomas Jefferson,* vol. 13. Princeton: Princeton University Press, 1953–1958.

Bratt, John. *Trails of Yesterday.* Chicago: University Publishing Company, 1921.

Brown, Adam Mercer. "Over Barren Plains and Rock-Bound Mountains: Being the Journal of a Tour by the Overland Route and South Pass of the Rocky Mountains, across the Great Basin and through California, with Incidents and Scenes of the Homeward Voyage, in the Years 1850 and 1851 by Adam Mercer Brown of Pittsburgh." Edited by David M. Kiefer. *Montana: The Magazine of Western History* 22, No. 4 (Autumn 1972): 16–29.

Brown, John. *Autobiography of Pioneer John Brown, 1820–1896.* Edited by John Zimmerman Brown. Salt Lake City: Stevens and Walls, 1941.

Brown, John Lowery. "The Journal of John Lowery Brown, of the Cherokee Nation En Route to California in 1850." Edited by Muriel H. Wright. *Chronicles of Oklahoma* 12, no. 2 (June 1934): 177–213.

Brown, Rachel. "'I Remain Your Affectionate Wife, Until Death . . .': Seven Letters Written to David Brown, 'a Colored Man' from his Wife and Mother-in-law, Rachel Ann Brown and Sarah Smith (in Lancaster, Fairfield County, Ohio), 1853." Merrill J. Mattes Research Library, National Frontier Trails Museum, Independence, Missouri.

Brown, William Wells. *The Anti-Slavery Harp: A Collection of Songs for Anti-Slavery Meetings. Compiled by William W. Brown, A Fugitive Slave.* Boston: Bela Marsh, No. 25 Cornhill, 1848. Digital reprint, http://www.fullbooks.com/The-Anti-Slavery-Harp.html (accessed September 29, 2010).

———. *My Southern Home: or The South and Its People.* 1880. Digital reprint, Chapel Hill: University of North Carolina Press, 2000. http://docsouth.unc.edu/neh/brown80/brown80.html (accessed August 4, 2010).

———. *Narrative of William W. Brown, A Fugitive Slave. Written by Himself.* 1847. Digital reprint, Chapel Hill: University of North Carolina Press, 2001. http://docsuouth.unc.edu/neh/brown47/brown47.html (accessed August 4, 2010).

———. *The Travels of William Wells Brown: Narrative of William W. Brown, a Fugitive Slave and the American Fugitive in Europe. Sketches of Places and People Abroad.* 1847, 1853. Reprint. Edited by Paul Jefferson. New York:

Marcus Weiner, 1991. http://bboks.google.com/books?id=021VODKyz7KC&pg=PA238&lpg=PA238&dq=William+Wells+Brown+Narrative+of+a+Fugitive+Slave (accessed July 26, 2011).

Bruce, Henry C. *The New Man: Twenty-Nine Years a Slave. Twenty-Nine Years a Free Man. Recollections of H.C. Bruce.* York, Penn: P. Anstadt & Sons, 1895.

Bruff, J. Goldsborough. *Gold Rush: The Journals, Drawings, and Other Papers of J. Goldsborough Bruff, Captain, Washington City and California Mining Association.* Edited by Georgia Willis Read and Ruth Gaines. New York: Columbia University Press, 1949.

Bryant, Edwin. *What I Saw in California: Being the Journal of a Tour in the Years 1846, 1847 by the Emigrant Route and South Pass of the Rocky Mountains, across the Continent of North America, the Great Basin and through California, 1846, 1847.* 1849. Reprint. Minneapolis: Ross & Haines, 1967.

Bunyard, Harriet. "Diary of Miss Harriet Bunyard: From Texas to California in 1868." Edited by Percival J. Cooney. *Annual Publication of the Historical Society of Southern California.* 13, no. 1 (1924): 92–124.

Burnett, Peter H. *Recollections and Opinions of an Old Pioneer.* New York: D. Appleton, 1880.

Campbell, J. L. *Idaho: Six Months in the New Gold Diggings, The Emigrant's Guide Overland.* Chicago: John R. Walsh, 1864.

Castañeda, Pedro de. "The Narrative of the Expedition of Coronado." In *Spanish Explorers in the Southern United States, 1528–1543.* New York: C. Scribner's Sons 1907. Digital reprint. from the Early Americas Digital Archive, 2002. http://mith.umd.edu/eada/html/display.php?docs=castaneda_account.xml&action=show (accessed March 23, 2013).

Caughey, John Walton, ed. *Rushing for Gold.* Berkeley: University of California Press, 1949.

Cherokee Nation. *Declaration of the People of the Cherokee Nation of the Causes Which Have Impelled Them to Unite Their Fortunes with Those of the Confederate States of America, Talequah, C.N., October 28, 1861.* Digital reprint excerpted from Emmet Starr, *History of the Cherokee Indians and Their Legends and Folk Lore.* Oklahoma City: The Warden Company, 1921. United Native America, n.d. http://www.unitednativeamerica.com/cherokee.html (accessed April 13, 2011).

Child, Lydia Maria Francis. "Lewis Clark[e], Leaves from a Slave's Journal of Life." From the *Anti-Slavery Standard,* October 20 and 27, 1842, 78–79, 83. Digital reprint, University of North Carolina, Chapel Hill, 2004. http://docsouth.unc.edu/neh/clarke/support1.html (accessed March 25, 2013).

Clark, Bennett C. "Diary of a Journey from Missouri to California in 1849." Edited by Ralph P. Bieber. *Missouri Historical Review* 23 (1928): 3–43.

Clark, Eva Turner, ed. *California Letters of William Gill.* New York: Downs, 1922.

Clark, John Hawkins. "Overland to the Gold Fields of California in 1852: The Journal of John Hawkins Clark, Expanded and Revised from Notes Made during the Journey." Edited by Louise Barry. *Kansas Historical Quarterly* 11, no. 3 (August 1942): 227–96. http://www.kaancoll.org/khq/1942/42_3_barry.htm (accessed July 19, 2011).

Clayton, William. *The Latter-Day Saints' Emigrants' Guide*. 1848. Reprint. Edited by Stanley Kimball. Gerald, Mo.: Patrice Press, 1983.

Clyman, James. "James Clyman: His Diaries and Reminiscences." Edited by Charles Camp. *California Historical Society Quarterly* 4, no. 3 (September 1925): 272–83.

Coffey, Alvin Aaron. "The Autobiography of Alvin A. Coffey." *Overland Journal* 20, no. 2 (Summer, 2002): 64–73.

———. *The Autobiography of Alvin Coffey*. 1901. Reprint. *Pioneer* 23, no. 1 (December 2000): 11–13.

Colburn, E. H. *History of Fairfield County, Ohio, Past and Present*. 1883. Reprint. Knightstown, Indiana: Bookmark, 1977.

Collier, Fred C., ed. *The Teachings of President Brigham Young*, vol. 3, 1852–1854. Salt Lake City: Collier's, 1987.

Cox, C. C. [Cornelius C.]. "From Texas to California in 1849: Diary of C. C. Cox." Edited by Mabelle Eppard Martin and C. C. Cox. *The Southwestern Historical Quarterly* 29, no. 1 (July 1925): 36–50.

———. "From Texas to California in 1849: Diary of C. C. Cox (Concluded). Edited by Mabelle Eppard Martin and C. C. Cox. *The Southwestern Historical Quarterly* 29, no. 3 (January 1926): 201–223.

Custer, Elizabeth B. *Tenting on the Plains, or General Custer in Kansas and Texas*. New York: Harper & Brothers Publishers, 1895.

Davies, John Johnson. "Historical Sketch of My Life." *Utah Historical Quarterly* 9, nos. 3–4 (July-October 1941): 155–67.

Demarest, David Durie. "Diary and Related Material of Trip in Bark, Norumbego to Galveston, Texas, then Overland to California, Experiences in the Mines, etc. March 8, 1849—May 1850." Typed transcript, partial microfilm reel (12 exposures): negative (Rich.94:12) and positive. (C-F, Reel 14.) Bancroft Library, University of California, Berkeley.

Doble, John. *John Doble's Journal and Letters from the Mines: Mokelumne Hill, Jackson and San Francisco, 1851–1865*. Edited by Charles L. Camp. Denver: Old West Publishing., 1962.

Dulany, William, to Susan Dulany, May 1, 1850. William Henry Fields Dulany Papers, Missouri History Museum Archives, St. Louis.

Eccleston, Robert. *Overland to California on the Southwestern Trail 1849: The Diary of Robert Eccleston*. Edited by George P. Hammond and Edward H. Howe. Berkeley: University of California Press, 1950.

Evans, George W. H. *Mexican Gold Trail: The Journal of a Forty-Niner.* San Marino, Calif.: Huntington Library, 1945.

Ford, Nathaniel. Letter to James A. Shirley, June 22, 1852. In "Emigrant Missourians in Mexico and Oregon." Edited by Frederic A. Culmer. *Missouri Historical Review* (1931): 281–288.

Forsyth, George A. *The Story of the Soldier.* New York: D. Appleton and Company. 1900. Digital reprint. Hathi Trust http://hdl.handle.net/2027/uc2.ark:/13960/t9j38ms7f (accessed January 13, 2016).

Frémont, John Charles. *Geographical Memoir upon Upper California in Illustration of His Map of Oregon and California.* 1848. Reprint. Fairfield, Wash.: Ye Galleon Press, 1995.

Gardner, Mark L., and Mark Simmons, eds. *The Mexican War Correspondence of Richard Smith Elliott.* Norman: University of Oklahoma Press, 1997.

Garrard, Lewis H. *Wah-To-Yah and the Taos Trail: Or, Prairie Travel and Scalp Dances, with a Look at Los Rancheros from Muleback and Rocky Mountain Camp-Fire.* Cincinnati: H. W. Derby and New York: A. S. Barnes, 1850.

Geiger, Vincent, and Wakeman Bryarly. *Trail to California: The Overland Journal.* Edited by David Morris Potter. New Haven: Yale University Press, 1945.

Gibbs, Mifflin Wistar. *Shadow & Light: An Autobiography.* 1902. Reprint. Lincoln: University of Nebraska Press, 1995.

Greeley, Horace. "Two Hours with Brigham Young: Brigham Young Interview, Salt Lake City, Utah, July 13, 1859." Reprinted in the *Salt Lake Tribune,* August 15, 1993. http://www.utlm.org/onlineresources/sermons_talks_interviews/brighamgreeleyinterview_july131859.htm [accessed May 12, 2011].

Grimsley, Thornton, to Honorable John Bell, Secty. of War, 16th April, 1841, in "Colonel Grimsley's Proposed Expedition to Oregon, in 1841." Edited and with introduction by T. C. Elliott, *Quarterly of the Oregon Historical Society* 24, no. 4 (December 1923): 434–35.

Harris, Benjamin Butler. *The Gila Trail: The Texas Argonauts and the California Gold Rush.* Edited by Richard H. Dillon. Norman: University of Oklahoma Press, 1960.

Harker, George Mifflin. Edited by Stella M. Drum, *Glimpses of the Past.* "Morgan Street to the Old Dry Diggings." *Missouri Historical Society,* 6, no. 52 (June-April, 1939): 35–76.

Hastings, Lansford W. *The Emigrants' Guide to Oregon and California: The 1845 Pioneers' Guide for the Westward Traveler.* 1845. Reprint. Bedford, Mass.: Applewood Books, 1994.

Hayes, Benjamin. *Pioneer Notes from the Diaries of Judge Benjamin Hayes, 1849–1875.* Edited by Marjorie Tisdale Wolcott. Los Angeles: Private printing, 1929. Reprinted online by the Library of Congress, American Memory

Project. http://lcweb2.loc.gov/cgii-bin/query/r?ammem/calbk:@field(DOCID +@lit9lit(calbk026div0)) (accessed June 21, 2013).

Heiskell, Hugh Brown. *A Forty-Niner from Tennessee: The Diary of Hugh Brown Heiskell.* Edited by Edward M. Steel. Knoxville: University of Tennessee Press, 1998.

Hopkins, Sarah Winnemucca. *Life among the Piutes: Their Wrongs and Claims.* 1883. Reprint. Reno: University of Nevada Press, 1994.

Hudson, John. *A Forty-niner in Utah with the Stansbury Expedition of Great Salt Lake: Letters and Journals of John Hudson, 1848–50.* Papers edited by Brigham D. Madsen. Salt Lake City: University of Utah Tanner Trust Fund, 1981. Transcription by Kay Threlkeld, National Park Service, 2008.

Huning, Franz. *Trader on the Santa Fe Trail: Memoirs of Franz Huning.* 1894. Reprint. Albuquerque: University of Albuquerque in collaboration with Calvin Horn, 1973.

Jacobs, Harriet. *Incidents in the Life of a Slave Girl.* Edited by Nellie Y. McKay and Frances Smith Foster. New York: W. W. Norton, 2001.

James, Jane Elizabeth Manning. "Life History of Jane Elizabeth Manning James." Transcribed by Elizabeth J. D. Roundy. Blacklds.org, A Web Site Dedicated to Black Members of the Church of Jesus Christ of Latter-day Saints. http://www.blacklds.org/manning (accessed January 19, 2012).

Jefferson, T. H. *Map of the Emigrant Road from Independence, Mo., to St. Francisco, California and Accompaniment.* 1846. Reprint. Special Publication No. 20. Oakland: Oakland Press for the California Historical Society, 1945.

Korns, J. Roderic. "West from Fort Bridger: The Pioneering of the Immigrant Trails across Utah, 1846–1850." *Utah Historical Quarterly* 19 (1951).

———, and Dale L. Morgan, eds. *West from Fort Bridger: The Pioneering of the Immigrant Trails across Utah, 1846–1850, Original Diaries and Journals.* 1951. Reprint. Revised by Will Bagley and Harold Schindler. Logan: Utah State University Press, 1994.

Laselle, Stanislaus. "The 1849 Diary of Stanislaus Lasselle." Edited by Patricia A. Etter. *Overland Journal* 9, no. 2 (1991): 2–33.

Leonard, Zenas. *The Adventures of Zenas Leonard, Fur Trader.* Edited by John C. Ewers. Norman: University of Oklahoma Press, 1959.

Lewis, Enoch, ed. *The African Observer* 1, no. 13 (Seventh Month, 1827): 103.

Lippincott, Benjamin S. "Letter to John L. Stephens, Esq., Feby. 6, 1847." Familytales.org, http://www.familytales.org/dbDisplay.php?id=ltr_bs1838&person=bsl [accessed July 4, 2011].

Magoffin, Susan Shelby. *Down the Santa Fe Trail and into Mexico: The Diary of Susan Shelby Magoffin, 1846–1847.* Reprint. Edited by Stella Drumm. Lincoln: University of Nebraska Press, 1982.

Majors, Alexander. *Seventy Years on the Frontier: Alexander Majors' Memoirs of a Lifetime on the Border.* Chicago: Rand, McNally, 1893.

Malvin, John. *Autobiography of John Malvin: A Narrative Containing an Authentic Account of His Fifty Years' Struggle in the State of Ohio in Behalf of the American Slave, and the Equal Rights of All Men before the Law without Reference to Race or Color; Forty-Seven Years of Said Time Being Expended in the City of Cleveland.* Cleveland: Leader Printing Company, 1879.

Manly, William Lewis. *Death Valley in '49: The Autobiography of a Pioneer, Detailing His Life from a Humble Home in the Green Mountains to the Gold Mines of California; and Particularly Reciting the Sufferings of the Band of Men, Women and Children Who Gave "Death Valley" Its Name.* 1894. Digital reprint, Project Gutenberg, 2004. http://www.gutenberg.org/files/12236/12236-h/12236-h.htm (accessed December 12, 2008).

Marcy, Randolph B. *The Prairie Traveler: The Classic Handbook for America's Pioneers.* 1859. Reprint. New York: Perigee Books, 1994.

Marsh, Andrew J. *Letters from Nevada Territory, 1861–1862.* Edited by William C. Miller, Russell W. McDonald, and Ann Rollins. Carson City: Legislative Counsel Bureau, State of Nevada, 1972.

Meeker, Ezra. *The Busy Life of Eighty-Five Years of Ezra Meeker: Ventures and Adventures.* Seattle: Self Published, 1916.

Minto, John. "Reminiscences of Experiences on the Oregon Trail in 1844, I." *Quarterly of the Oregon Historical Society* 2, no. 2 (June 1901): 118–65.

———. "Reminiscences of Experiences on the Oregon Trail in 1844, II." *Quarterly of the Oregon Historical Society* 2, no. 3 (September 1901): 209–54.

Moorman, Madison Berryman. *The Journal of Madison Berryman Moorman, 1850–1851.* Edited by Irene Paden. San Francisco: Westgate Press, 1948.

National Era, July 4, 1850. The Black Experience in America: Negro Periodicals in the United States, 1840–1960. New York: Negro Universities Press, 1969.

Northup, Solomon. *Twelve Years a Slave.* 1853. Reprint. Edited by Sue Eakin and Joseph Logsdon. Baton Rouge: Louisiana State University Press, 1968.

Parkman, Francis, Jr. *The California and Oregon Trail: Being Sketches of Prairie and Rocky Mountain Life.* New York: A. L. Burt, Publisher, 1847.

Parkman, Francis. *The Oregon Trail: Sketches of Prairie and Rocky Mountain Life.* 6th ed. Boston: Little, Brown, 1877.

Patterson, Edward H. N. "Overland Journal, Impressions by E. H. N. Patterson." *Oquawka Spectator* (Summer–Fall) 1850. University of Illinois at Urbana-Champaign, Illinois Newspaper Project, *Oquawka Spectator* (Henderson County). Digital transcript, Ancestry.com. http://freepages.genealogy.rootsweb.ancestry.com/~bbunce77/1849GoldRush.html (accessed August 3, 2010).

Perry, William Henry, J. H. Battle, and Weston Arthur Goodspeed. *The History of Medina County and Ohio.* 1881. Reprint. Evansville, Ind.: Unigraphic, 1972.

Pleasants, William J. *Twice across the Plains.* San Francisco: Walter N. Brunt, 1906.

Porter, Lavinia Honeyman. *By Ox Team to California: A Narrative of Crossing the Plains in 1860.* Oakland, Calif.: *Oakland Enquirer*, 1910.

Potter, Theodore Edgar. *The Autobiography of Theodore Edgar Potter.* Concord, N.H.: Rumford Press, 1913. http://hdl.handle.net/2827/yale.390020 28259050 (accessed April 13, 2014).

Reid, Bernard J. *Overland to California with the Pioneer Line: The Gold Rush Diary of Bernard J. Reid.* Edited by Mary McDougall Gordon. Stanford: Stanford University Press, 1983.

Ruxton, George Frederick. *Life in the Far West.* 1859. Reprint. Edited by LeRoy Hafen. Norman: University of Oklahoma Press, 1951.

Sabin, Henry, and Edwin L. Sabin. *The Making of Iowa.* Chicago: Flanagan Co. 1900.

Sherman, Jacob. Summary of the *Narrative of the Sufferings of Lewis Clarke, during a Captivity of More than Twenty-Five Years, among the Algerines of Kentucky, One of the So Called Christian States of North America.* Boston: David H. Ela, 1845. Digital reprint, University of North Carolina Press, Chapel Hill, 2004. http://docsouth.unc.edu/neh/clarke/summary.html (accessed March 25, 2013).

Smith, Joseph. *General Smith's Views on the Government and Policy of the U.S.* Nauvoo: John Taylor, 1844. The Joseph Smith Home Page, Church of Jesus Christ of Latter-day Saints, from the L. Tom Perry Special Collections, Brigham Young University. http://contentdm.lib.byu.edu/cdm4/document.php?CISOROOT=/NCMP1820–1846&CISOPTR=2836 (accessed May 10, 2011).

Stover, Jacob. "The Jacob Y. Stover Narrative: History of the Sacramento Mining Company of 1849, Written by One of Its Number." Edited by John Walton Caughey. *Pacific Historical Review* 6, no. 2 (June 1937): 165–81.

Thomas, James. *From Tennessee Slave to St. Louis Entrepreneur: The Autobiography of James Thomas.* Edited by Loren Schweninger. Columbia: University of Missouri Press, 1984.

Union Historical Company. *The History of Jackson County, Missouri: Containing a History of the County, Its Cities, Towns, Etc.* Kansas City, Mo.: Birdsall, Williams, 1881.

United States War Department. *The War of the Rebellion: A Compilation of the Official Records of the Union and Confederate Armies.* Series 3, vol. 1. Compiled by John Sheldon Moody, Calvin Duvall Cowell, Frederick Clayton

Ainsworth, Robert N. Scott, Henry Martyn Lazelle, George Breckenridge Davis, Leslie J. Perry, Joseph William Kirkley. Washington, D. C.: Government Printing Office, 1880–1901. Cornell University Library Digital Collections. http://ebooks.library.cornell.edu/cgi/t/text/pageviewer-idx?c=moawar;cc=moawar;ql=Jacob (accessed July 2, 2013).

Wallace, Mary Albertina Stark. Marie Albertina (Stark) Wallace, "Recollections of Sylvia Stark, Parts 1 and 2." Great Unsolved Mysteries in Canadian History. Online collection of the Salt Spring Island Historical Society Archives, Add. Mss. 91, Salt Spring Island, British Columbia. http://www.canadianmysteries.ca/sites/robinson/archives/diaryjournalreminiscece/3109en (accessed July 14, 2009).

Wittenmyer, Lewis Cass. "The Autobiography and Reminiscence of Lewis Cass Wittenmyer." Society of California Pioneers, Typescript, Martinez, California, 1901. Digital reprint by Calisphere, University of California Libraries, California Digital Library. http://content.edlib.org/ark:13030/kt0q2nc5jv/?order=3&brand=calisphere (accessed July 13, 2013).

Wood, Joseph Warren. "Diary, May 6 to December 10, 1849." Digital Typescript, 1–95 transcribed by Richard L. Rieck, September 2004; 96–154 transcribed by Kay Threlkeld, National Park Service, Salt Lake City, May 2007.

Works Projects Administration. Interview with Charlie Richardson, "Slave Narratives: A Folk History of Slavery in the United States from Interviews with Former Slaves, 1936–1938: Volume X, Missouri Narratives." Federal Writers Project Washington, D.C.: Library of Congress, 1941. Released by Project Gutenberg, February 23, 2011.

Yetman, Norman R., ed. *Voices from Slavery: The Life of American Slaves.* New York: Holt, Rinehart and Winston, 1970.

Books

Allmendinger, Blake. *Imagining the African American West.* Lincoln: University of Nebraska Press, 2005.

Anderson, Martha E. *Black Pioneers of the Northwest, 1800–1918.* Publisher and place of publication not indicated, 1980.

Appiah, Kwame Anthony, and Henry Lewis Gates Jr., *Africana: The Encyclopedia of the African and African American Experience*, 2d ed., s.v. "Baker, Edward Lee, Jr." New York: Oxford University Press, 2004.

Atkins, Joseph. *Human Relations in Colorado.* Denver: Colorado State Department of Education, 1961.

Bagley, Will. *So Rugged and Mountainous: Blazing the Trails to Oregon and California, 1812–1848.* Norman: University of Oklahoma Press, 2010.

———. *With Golden Visions Bright before Them: Trails to the Mining West, 1849–1852.* Norman: University of Oklahoma Press, 2012.

Baker, Roger. *Clara: An Ex-Slave in Gold Rush Colorado.* Central City, Colo:. Black Hawk, 2003.
Bancroft, Caroline. *Historic Central City: Gold! And Now Glamour.* Boulder, Colo.: Johnson, 1974.
Bandelier, A. D. F., ed., *The Journey of Álvar Nuñez Cabeza de Vaca.* New York: A. S. Barnes, 1905.
Barbour, Barton H. *Jedediah Smith: No Ordinary Mountain Man.* Norman: University of Oklahoma Press, 2009.
Barnes, Joseph K., and John Maynard Woodworth. *The Cholera Epidemic of 1873 in the United States.* Washington, D.C.: Government Printing Office, 1875.
Barr, Alwyn. *Black Texas: A History of African Americans in Texas, 1528–1995*, 2d ed. Norman: University of Oklahoma Press, 1996.
Beasley, Delilah L. *The Negro Trail Blazers of California.* Los Angeles: University of California Press, 1919.
Beaton, Gail M. *Colorado Women: A History.* Boulder: University Press of Colorado, 2012.
Berg, William. *Sacramento's K Street: Where Our City Was Born.* Charleston, S.C.: History Press, 2012.
Berlin, Ira. *Many Thousand Gone: The First Two Centuries of Slavery in North America.* Cambridge, Mass.: Belknap, 1998.
Bigler, David L., and Will Bagley. *The Mormon Rebellion: America's First Civil War, 1857–1858.* Norman: University of Oklahoma Press, 2011.
Billington, Monroe Lee. *New Mexico's Buffalo Soldiers, 1866–1900.* Niwot: University Press of Colorado, 1991.
———, and Roger D. Hardaway, eds. *African Americans on the Western Frontier.* Niwot: University Press of Colorado, 1998.
Bowes, John P. *Exiles and Pioneers: Eastern Indians in the Trans-Mississippi West.* New York: Cambridge University Press, 2007.
Bringhurst, Newell G. *Saints, Slaves and Blacks: The Changing Place of Black People Within Mormonism.* Westport, Conn.: Greenwood, 1981.
———, and Darron T. Smith, eds. *Black and Mormon.* Chicago: University of Illinois Press, 2006.
The British Columbia Black History Awareness Society. "A Resource Guide on Black Pioneers in British Columbia." Victoria: British Columbia Black History Awareness Society, n.d.
Brock, Richard K., ed. *Emigrant Trails West: A Guide to the Applegate Trail, the South Road to Oregon, from Lassen Meadows to Southern Oregon.* Reno, Nev.: Trails West, 2004.
Brodie, Fawn M. *Thomas Jefferson: An Intimate History.* New York: Bantam, 1974.

Broussard, Albert S. *African-American Odyssey: The Stewarts, 1853–1963.* Lawrence: University Press of Kansas, 1998.

———. *Expectations of Equality: A History of Black Westerners.* Wheeling, Ill.: Harlan Davidson, 2012.

Brown, Hallie Q. *Homespun Heroines and Other Women of Distinction.* Xenia, Ohio: Aldine, 1926.

Bruyn, Kathleen. *"Aunt" Clara Brown: Story of a Black Pioneer.* Boulder, Colo.: Pruett, 1970.

Bunch, Lonnie, III. *Black Angelenos: The Afro-American in Los Angeles, 1850–1950.* Los Angeles: California Afro-American Museum, 1988.

Burns, John F., and Richard J. Orsi, eds. *Taming the Elephant: Politics, Government, and Law in Pioneer California.* Berkeley: University of California Press with the California Historical Society, 2003.

Bush, Lester E., Jr., and Armand L. Mauss, eds. *Neither White nor Black: Mormon Scholars Confront the Race Issue in a Universal Church.* Midvale, Utah: Signature Books, 1984.

Calarco, Tom, Cynthia Vogel, Kathryn Grover, Rae Hallstrom, Sharron L. Pope, and Melissa Waddy-Thibodeaux. *Places of the Underground Railroad: A Geographical Guide.* Santa Barbara: Greenwood, 2011.

Campbell, Stanley W. *The Slave Catchers: Enforcement of the Fugitive Slave Law, 1850–1860.* New York: W. W. Norton, 1970.

Carter, Kate B. *The Story of the Negro Pioneer.* Salt Lake City: Daughters of Utah Pioneers, 1965.

Chan, Sucheng, and Douglas Henry Daniels, Mario T. García, Terry P. Wilson, eds. *Peoples of Color in the American West.* Lexington, Mass.: D. C. Heath, 1994.

Chandler, Robert J. *San Francisco Lithographer: African American Artist, Grafton Tyler Brown.* Norman: University of Oklahoma Press, 2014.

Chinn, Jennie. *The Kansas Journey.* Layton, Utah: Gibbs Smith, 2005.

Christensen, Lawrence O., William E. Foley, Gary R. Kremer, and Kenneth H. Winn. *Dictionary of Missouri Biography.* Columbia: University of Missouri Press, 1999.

Cunningham, Roger D. *The Black Citizen-Soldiers of Kansas, 1864–1901.* Columbia: University of Missouri Press, 2008.

Curry, Leonard P. *The Free Black in Urban America, 1800–1850: The Shadow of the Dream.* Chicago: University of Chicago Press, 1986.

Curtis, Annette W. *Jackson County, Missouri in Black and White: Jabez Smith, His Slaves, Plantations, Estate and Heirs.* 2 vols. Independence, Mo.: Two Trails, 1998.

Curtis, William J. *A Rich Heritage: A Black History of Independence, Missouri,* vol. 1. Kansas City, Mo.: Better Impressions, 1985.

Dangberg, Grace. *Carson Valley—Historical Sketches of Nevada's First Settlement*. Reno, Nev.: A. Carlisle, 1972.

Daniels, Douglas. *Pioneer Urbanites: A Social and Cultural History of Black San Francisco*. Philadelphia: Temple University Press, 1980.

Dary, David. *The Oregon Trail: An American Saga*. New York: Oxford University Press, 2004.

———. *The Santa Fe Trail: Its History, Legends and Lore*. New York: Penguin Books, 2002.

De Graaf, Lawrence B., Kevin Mulroy, and Quintard Taylor. *Seeking El Dorado: African Americans in California*. Los Angeles: Autry Museum of Western Heritage in association with Seattle: University of Washington Press, 2001.

Demas, Marilyn K. *Ungraded School No. 2 Colored: The African American Struggle for Education in Victorian Sacramento*. Sacramento: Sacramento County Historical Society, 1999.

Denton, Ivan. *Old Brands and Lost Trails: Arkansas and the Great Cattle Drives*. Fayetteville: University of Arkansas Press, 1992.

Dobak, William A., and Thomas D. Phillips. *The Black Regulars, 1866–1898*. Norman: University of Oklahoma Press, 2001.

Durham, Walter T. *Volunteer Forty-Niners: Tennesseans and the California Gold Rush*. Nashville: Vanderbilt University Press, 1997.

Eaves, Lucile. *A History of California Labor Legislation: With an Introductory Sketch of the San Francisco Labor Movement*. Berkeley: University Press, 1910.

Echenberg, Myron. *Africa in the Time of Cholera: A History of Pandemics from 1917 to the Present*. New York: Cambridge University Press, 2011.

Etulain, Richard W. *Western Lives: A Biographical History of the American West*. Albuquerque: Center for the Southwest, University of New Mexico, 2005.

Federal Writers' Project of the Works Progress Administration. *The Oregon Trail: The Missouri River to the Pacific Ocean*. Washington, D.C.: Oregon Trails Memorial Association, 1939.

Fehrenbacher, Don E. *The Dred Scott Case: Its Significance in American Law and Politics*. New York: Oxford University Press, 1979.

Field, Ron, and Alexander Bielakiowski. *Buffalo Soldiers: African American Troops in the U.S. Forces, 1866–1945*. New York: Osprey Publishing, 2008.

Flamming, Douglas. *African Americans in the West*. Santa Barbara, Calif.: ABC-CLIO, 2009.

Forbes, Jack. *African Americans in the Far West: A Handbook for Educators*. Berkeley, Calif.: Far West Laboratory for Educational Research and Development, 1970.

Fowler, Arlen L. *The Black Infantry in the West, 1869–1891*. Norman: University of Oklahoma Press, 1996,

Francaviglia, Richard V. *Mapping and Imagination in the Great Basin: A Cartographic History.* Reno: University of Nevada Press, 2005.
Franklin, John Hope, and Alfred A. Moss Jr. *From Slavery to Freedom: A History of African Americans,* 7th ed. New York: McGraw-Hill, 1994.
Franklin, John Hope, and Loren Schweninger. *In Search of the Promised Land: A Slave Family in the Old South.* New York: Oxford University Press, 2006.
Gardner, Eric, ed. *Jennie Carter: A Black Journalist of the Early West.* Jackson: University Press of Mississippi, 2007.
Gardner, Mark L. *Wagons for the Santa Fe Trade: Wheeled Vehicles and Their Makers, 1822–1880.* Albuquerque: University of New Mexico Press, 2000.
Genovese, Eugene D. *Roll, Jordan, Roll: The World the Slaves Made.* New York: Vintage Books, 1974.
Gillis, Delia C. *Kansas City.* Charleston, S.C.: Arcadia Publishing, 2007.
Glasrud, Bruce A., and Michael N. Searles, eds., *Buffalo Soldiers in the West: A Black Soldiers Anthology.* College Station: Texas A&M University Press, 2007.
Gordon-Reed, Annette. *The Hemingses of Monticello: An American Family.* New York: W. W. Norton, 2008.
Greene, Lorenzo J., Gary R. Kremer, and Antonio F. Holland. *Missouri's Black Heritage.* Columbia: University of Missouri Press, 1993.
Gutiérrez, Ramón A. *When Jesus Came, the Corn Mothers Went Away: Marriage, Sexuality, and Power in New Mexico, 1500–1846.* Stanford, Calif.: Stanford University Press 1991.
Gutman, Herbert G. *The Black Family in Slavery and Freedom, 1750–1925.* New York: Vintage Books, 1976.
Hafen, LeRoy R., ed. *The Mountain Men and the Fur Trade of the Far West,* vol. 4. Glendale, Calif.: Arthur H. Clark, 1966.
———. *Trappers of the Far West: Sixteen Biographical Sketches.* Lincoln: University of Nebraska Press, 1983.
Hafen, LeRoy R., and Francis Marion Young. *Fort Laramie and the Pageant of the West, 1834–1890.* Reprint. Lincoln: University of Nebraska Press, 1984.
Hafnor, John. *Strange But True, Colorado: Weird Tales of the Wild West.* Fort Collins, Colo.: Lone Pine Productions, 2005.
Hagedorn, Ann. *Beyond the River: The Untold Story of the Heroes of the Underground Railroad.* New York: Simon & Schuster Paperbacks, 2002.
Hall, Frank. *History of the State of Colorado,* vol. 4. Chicago: Blakely Printing, 1895.
Hammond, Andrew, and Joanne Hammond. *Following the Beckwourth Trail: A Guide to the 1851 Emigrant Trail and to the Route Markers Placed by Trails West, Inc.* 1994. Chico, Calif: self-published, 1994.

Harrold, Stanley. *Border War: Fighting over Slavery before the Civil War.* Chapel Hill: University of North Carolina Press, 2010.
Heikell, Iris White. *The Wind-Breaker: George Washington Bush, Black Pioneer of the Northwest.* New York: Vantage Press, 1980.
Heizer, Robert F., and Alan F. Almquist, *The Other Californians: Prejudice and Discrimination under Spain, Mexico, and the United States to 1920.* Berkeley: University of California Press, 1971,
Hine, Darlene Clark, William C. Hine, and Stanley Harrold. *The African American Odyssey.* Combined vol. 4th ed, 5th ed. Upper Saddle River, N. J.: Pearson, 2008, 2011.
Holmes, Kenneth L., ed. *Covered Wagon Women,* vol. 7: *Diaries and Letters from the Western Trails, 1854–1860.* Lincoln: University of Nebraska Press, 1998.
Hoover, Herbert T., and Larry J. Zimmerman, eds. *South Dakota Leaders: From Pierre Choteau, Jr. to Oscar Howe.* Vermillion: University of South Dakota Press, 1989.
Horner, John B. *Days and Deeds in the Oregon Country.* Portland: J. K. Gill, 1928.
Howard, Thomas Frederick. *Sierra Crossing: First Roads to California.* Berkeley: University of California Press, 1998.
Howe, Octavius T. *Argonauts of '49.* Cambridge, Mass.: Harvard University Press, 1923.
Hudson, Lynn M. *The Making of "Mammy Pleasant": A Black Entrepreneur in Nineteenth-Century San Francisco.* Urbana: University of Illinois Press, 2003.
Hurtado, Albert L. *John Sutter: A Life on the North American Frontier.* Norman: University of Oklahoma Press, 2006.
Hyde, Anne F. *Empires, Nations and Families: A History of the North American West, 1800–1860.* Lincoln: University of Nebraska Press, 2011.
Isserman, Maurice. *Exploring North America, 1800–1900.* New York: Chelsea House, 2010.
Jackson, David W. *Kansas City Chronicles: An Up-To-Date History.* Charleston, S.C.: History Press, 2010.
Jameson, Elizabeth, and Susan Armitage. *Writing the Range: Race, Class, and Culture in the Women's West.* Norman: University of Oklahoma Press, 1997.
Johnson, Walter. *Soul by Soul: Life inside the Antebellum Slave Market.* Cambridge, Mass.: Harvard University Press, 1999.
Jones, Robert Huhn. *Guarding the Overland Trails: The Eleventh Ohio Cavalry in the Civil War.* Spokane, Wash.: Arthur H. Clark Company, 2005.
Jordan, Winthrop D. *White over Black: American Attitudes toward the Negro, 1550–1812.* Chapel Hill: University of North Carolina Press, 1968.
Katz, William Loren. *The Black West: A Pictorial History,* 3d ed. Seattle: Open Hand, 1987.

Kenny, Maurice. *Backward to Forward: Prose Pieces.* Freedonia, N.Y,: White Pine Press, 1997.
Kleber, John E., ed. *The Kentucky Encyclopedia.* Lexington: University Press of Kentucky, 1992.
Konig, Thomas, Paul Finkelman, and Christopher Alan Bracey, eds. *The Dred Scott Case: Historical and Contemporary Perspectives on Race and Law.* Athens: Ohio University Press, 2010.
Lapp, Rudolph M. *Archy Lee: A California Fugitive Slave Case.* Berkeley: Heyday Books, 2008.
———. *Blacks in Gold Rush California.* New Haven: Yale University Press, 1977.
LaSalle, Michael E. *Emigrants on the Overland Trail: The Wagon Trains of 1848.* Kirksville, Mo.: Truman State University Press, 2011.
Lebsock, Suzanne. *The Free Women of Petersburg: Status and Culture in a Southern Town, 1784–1860.* New York: W. W. Norton, 1984.
Leckie, William H., and Shirley A. Leckie. *The Buffalo Soldiers: A Narrative of the Black Cavalry in the West.* Norman: University of Oklahoma Press, 2003.
Limerick, Patricia Nelson. *The Legacy of Conquest: The Unbroken Past of the American West.* New York: W.W. Norton, 1987.
Litwack, Leon F. *North of Slavery: The Negro in the Free States, 1790–1860.* Chicago: University of Chicago Press, 1961.
Low, Augustus, and Virgil A. Clift, eds. *Encyclopedia of Black America.* New York: Da Capo Press, 1981.
Lucas, Marion Brunson. *A History of Blacks in Kentucky: From Slavery to Segregation, 1760–1891.* Lexington: University Press of Kentucky, 2003.
Lyman, Edward Leo. *The Overland Journey from Utah to California: Wagon Travel from the City of Saints to the City of Angels.* Reno: University of Nevada Press, 2004.
Mattes, Merrill J. *The Great Platte River Road: The Covered Wagon Mainline via Fort Kearny to Fort Laramie,* 2d ed., 1979. Reprint. Lincoln: University of Nebraska Press, 1987.
———*Platte River Road Narratives: A Descriptive Bibliography of Travel over the Great Central Overland Route to Oregon, California, Utah, Colorado, Montana, and Other Western States and Territories, 1812–1866.* Urbana: University of Illinois Press, 1988.
McLagan, Elizabeth. *A Peculiar Paradise: A History of Blacks in Oregon, 1788–1940.* Portland, Ore.: Georgian Press, 1980.
McLynn, Frank. *Wagons West: The Epic Story of America's Overland Trails.* New York: Grove Press, 2002.
McPherson, James M. *The Negro's Civil War: How American Blacks Felt and Acted during the War for the Union.* New York: Ballantine Books, 1991.

Melish, Joanne Pope. *Disowning Slavery: Gradual Emancipation and "Race" in New England, 1780–1860.* Ithaca: Cornell University Press, 1998.

Menard, Russell R. *Migrants, Servants and Slaves: Unfree Labor in Colonial British America.* Aldershot, United Kingdom: Ashgate, 2001.

Michno, Gregory, and Susan Michno. *A Fate Worse than Death: Indian Captives in the West, 1830–1885.* Caldwell, Idaho: Caxton Press, 2007.

Molson, Jeannette L., and Eual D. Blansett Jr. *The Torturous Road to Freedom: The Life of Alvin Aaron Coffey.* Linden, Calif.: self-published, July 2009.

Montoya, Maria. *Translating Property: The Maxwell Land Grant and the Conflict over Land in the American West, 1840–1900.* Berkeley: University of California Press, 2002.

Morgan, Dale. *Jedediah Smith and the Opening of the West.* Reprint. Lincoln: University of Nebraska Press, 1964.

———, ed. *Overland in 1846: Diaries and Letters of the California-Oregon Trail.* 2 vols. Lincoln: University of Nebraska Press, 1963.

Morgan, Edmund S. *American Slavery, American Freedom: The Ordeal of Colonial Virginia.* New York: W. W. Norton, 1975.

Myres, Sandra L. *Westering Women and the Frontier Experience, 1800–1915.* Albuquerque: University of New Mexico Press, 1982.

Nankivell, John H. *Buffalo Soldier Regiment: History of the Twenty-fifth United States Infantry, 1869–1926.* Lincoln: University of Nebraska Press, 2001.

Nash, Gary B. *Race and Revolution.* Madison, Wisc.: Madison House, 1990.

Nevada Magazine. *The Historical Nevada Magazine: Outstanding Historical Features from the Pages of Nevada Magazine.* Carson City: Nevada Commission on Tourism, 1998.

Nugent, Walter. *Into the West: The Story of Its People.* New York: Vintage Books, 1999.

Oakes, James. *The Ruling Race: A History of American Slaveholders.* New York: W. W. Norton, 1998.

Owens, Kenneth N., *Gold Rush Saints: California Mormons and the Great Rush for Riches.* Norman: University of Oklahoma Press, 2004.

———, ed. *Riches for All: The California Gold Rush and the World.* Lincoln: University of Nebraska Press, 2002.

Parkhill, Forbes. *Mister Barney Ford: A Portrait in Bistre.* Denver: Sage Books, 1963.

Peters, Arthur King. *Seven Trails West.* New York: Abbeville Press, 1996.

Porter, Kenneth Wiggins, ed. *The Negro on the American Frontier.* New York: Arno Press and the *New York Times,* 1971.

Price, Daniel O. *Changing Characteristics of the Negro Population.* U.S. Bureau of the Census. Washington, D.C.: Government Printing Office, 1969.

Quarles, Benjamin. *The Negro in the American Revolution*. Chapel Hill: University of North Carolina Press, 1961.

Quinn, D. Michael. *The Mormon Hierarchy: Extensions of Power*. Salt Lake City: Signature Books, 1997.

———. *The Mormon Hierarchy: Origins of Power*. Salt Lake City: Signature Books, 1994.

Ravage, John W. *Black Pioneers: Images of the Black Experience on the North American Frontier*. Salt Lake City: University of Utah Press, 1997.

Rawick, George P., ed. *The American Slave: A Composite Autobiography,* vol. 1; *Arkansas, Colorado, Minnesota, Missouri, Oregon and Washington Narratives*, vol. 2. Westport, Conn.: Greenwood, 1977.

Roberts, Sylvia Alden. *Mining for Freedom: Black History Meets the California Gold Rush*. New York: iUniverse, 2008.

Rohrbough, Malcolm J. *The Days of Gold: The California Gold Rush and the American Nation*. Berkeley: University of California Press, 1997.

Rosenberg, Charles. *The Cholera Years: The United States in 1832, 1849, and 1866*. Chicago: University of Chicago Press, 1962, reprinted 1987.

Ross, Marvin C., ed. *The West of Alfred Jacob Miller (1937), From the Notes and Water Colors of the Walters Art Gallery*. Norman: University of Oklahoma Press, 1951.

Rusco, Elmer R. *"Good Time Coming?": Black Nevadans in the Nineteenth Century*. Westport, Conn.: Greenwood Press, 1975.

Savage, Beth. *African American Historic Places*. National Register of Historic Places, National Park Service. New York: John Wiley & Sons, 1994.

Schubert, Irene, and Frank Schubert. *On the Trail of the Buffalo Soldier II: New and Revised Biographies*. Lanham, Md.: Scarecrow Press, 2004.

Schlissel, Lillian. *Women's Diaries of the Westward Journey*. New York: Schoken Books, 1982.

Scott, Victoria, and Ernest Jones. *Sylvia Stark: A Pioneer*. Seattle: Open Hand, 1991.

Shaw, Simon, with Linda Peavy and Ursula Smith. *Frontier House*. New York: Atria Books, 2002.

Sides, Hampton. *Blood and Thunder: An Epic of the American West*. New York: Doubleday, 2006.

Simmons, Marc. *New Mexico Mavericks: Stories from a Fabled Past*. Santa Fe: Sunstone Press, 2005.

Smith, Jessie Carnie, ed. *Notable Black American Women*. Book II. Detroit: Gale Research, 1996.

———, and Carrell Peterson Horton, eds. *Historical Statistics of Black America: Media to Vital Statistics*. New York: Gale Research, 1995.

———, Millicent Lownes Jackson, and Linda T. Wynn, eds. *Encyclopedia of African American Business*. Westport, Conn.: Greenwood Press, 2006.

Smith, Phyllis. *Bozeman and the Gallatin Valley: A History*. Essex, Conn.: Globe Pequot Press, 1996.

Stampp, Kenneth M. *The Peculiar Institution: Slavery in the Ante-Bellum South*. New York: Vintage Books, 1956.

Starr, Emmet. *History of the Cherokee Indians and Their Legends and Folk Lore*. Oklahoma City: Warden Company, 1921.

Stewart, George R. "Introduction and Notes" to *Maps of the Emigrant Road, from Independence, Mo., to St. Francisco, California, and Accompaniment*, by T. H. Jefferson, i-xi. Reprint. San Francisco: California Historical Society, 1945.

Stillson, Richard T. *Spreading the Word: A History of Information in the California Gold Rush*. Lincoln: University of Nebraska Press, 2006.

Sweeney, Edwin R. *Mangas Coloradas: Chief of the Chiricahua Apaches*. Norman: University of Oklahoma Press, 1998.

Taylor, Quintard. *The Forging of a Black Community: Seattle's Central District from 1870 through the Civil Rights Era*. Seattle: University of Washington Press, 1994.

———. *In Search of the Racial Frontier: African Americans in the American West, 1528–1990*. New York: W. W. Norton, 1998.

———, and Shirley Ann Wilson Moore, eds. African American Women Confront the West, 1600–2000. Norman: University of Oklahoma Press, 2003.

Thurman, Sue Bailey. *Pioneers of Negro Origin in California*. 1949. Reprint. San Francisco: R and E Research Associates, 1971.

Turner, Robert F., ed. *The Jefferson-Hemings Controversy: Report of the Scholars Commission*. Durham, N.C.: Carolina Academic Press, 2011. http://www.tjheritage.org/newscomfiles/front_matter_and_report.pdf (accessed July 5, 2013).

Unruh, John D., Jr. *The Plains Across: The Overland Emigrants and the Trans-Mississippi West, 1840–60*. Urbana: University of Illinois Press, 1979.

Utley, Robert M. *A Life Wild and Perilous: Mountain Men and the Paths to the Pacific*. New York: Henry Holt, 1997.

Vanepps-Taylor, Betti. *Forgotten Lives: African Americans in South Dakota*. Pierre: South Dakota State Historical Society Press, 2008.

Wagner, Tricia Martineau. *African American Women of the Old West*. Helena, Mont.: Two Dot, 2007.

———. *It Happened on the Oregon Trail*. Guilford, Conn.: Morris, 2005.

Wesley, Charles W., and Patricia W. Romero. *Negro Americans in the Civil War: From Slavery to Citizenship*. New York: Publishers Company, 1975.

Wheeler, Keith. *The Scouts.* New York: Time-Life, 1980.
White, Deborah Gray. *Ar'n't I a Woman?: Female Slaves in the Plantation South.* New York: W. W. Norton, 1985.
White, Richard. *It's Your Misfortune and None of My Own: A New History of the American West.* Norman: University of Oklahoma Press, 1991.
Williams, Albert E. *Black Warriors: Unique Units and Individuals.* Haverford, Penn.: Infinity, 2003.
Williams, Jean Kinney. *Bridget "Biddy" Mason: From Slave to Businesswoman.* Minneapolis: Compass Point, 2006.
Williams, Vivian T. *Northwest Pioneer Fiddlers.* Seattle: Voyager Recordings & Publications, 2010. http://www.voyagerrecords.com/arNWFiddlers.htm (accessed July 14, 2011).
Willoughby, Robert J. *The Great Western Migration to the Gold Fields of California, 1849–1850.* Jefferson, N.C.: McFarland, 2003.
Wilson, Carol. *Freedom at Risk: The Kidnapping of Free Blacks in America, 1780–1865.* Lexington: University Press of Kentucky, 1994.
Wilson, Dreck Spurlock, ed. *African American Architects: A Biographical Dictionary, 1856–1945.* New York: Routledge, 2004.
Wilson, Elinor. *Jim Beckwourth: Black Mountain Man, War Chief of the Crows, Trader, Trapper, Explorer, Frontiersman, Guide, Scout, Interpreter, Adventurer, and Gaudy Liar.* 1972. Reprint. Norman: University of Oklahoma Press, 1988.
Wishart, David J., ed. *Encyclopedia of the Great Plains.* Lincoln: University of Nebraska Press, 2004.
Wood, Peter H. *Black Majority: Negroes in Colonial South Carolina from 1670 through the Stono Rebellion.* New York: Knopf, 1974.
Woodson, Byron W. *A President in the Family: Thomas Jefferson, Sally Hemings, and Thomas Woodson.* Westport, Conn.: Praeger, 2001.
Wooster, Robert. *Frontier Crossroads: Fort Davis and the West.* College Station: Texas A&M University Press, 2006.
Yellin, Jean Fagan. *Harriet Jacobs: A Life.* New York: Basic Civitas, 2004.
Zanjani, Sally. *Devils Will Reign: How Nevada Grew.* Reno: University of Nevada Press, 2006.

Articles and Book Chapters

Anthony, Arthé. "'Lost Boundaries': Racial Passing and Poverty in Segregated New Orleans." *Louisiana History: Journal of the Louisiana Historical Association* 36, no. 3 (Summer 1995): 291–312.
Arrington, Leonard J. "Black Pioneer Was Union Fort Settler." *Pioneer* 28 (September-October 1981): 8–9.

Athearn, Robert G. "West of Appomattox: Civil War beyond the Great River, a Stage-Setting Interpretation." *Montana The Magazine of Western History* 12, no. 2 (Spring 1962): 2–11.

Behan, Barbara Carol. "Forgotten Heritage: African Americans in the Montana Territory, 1864–1889." *Journal of African American History* 91, no. 1 (Winter 2006): 23–40.

Bellamy, Donnie D. "The Education of Blacks in Missouri Prior to 1861." *Journal of Negro History* 59, no.2 (April 1974): 143–57.

———. "Free Blacks in Antebellum Missouri, 1820–1860." *Missouri Historical Review* 67 (January 1973): 198–226.

Bellard, Jequetta. "For Many Enslaved San Bernardino Was the First Stop." *The Black Voice News: The California Connection to the Underground Railroad* (March 23, 2006): 11–12.

Bellecourt, Vernon. "The Glorification of Buffalo Soldiers Raises Racial Divisions between Blacks, Indians." *Indian Country Today* (May 4, 1994): A-5.

Beller, Jack. "Negro Slaves in Utah." *Utah Historical Quarterly* 2 (October 1929): 122–26.

Bergman, G. M. "The Negro Who Rode with Fremont in 1847." *Negro History Bulletin* 28, no. 2 (November 1964): 31–32.

Berlin, Ira, and Herbert G. Gutman. "Natives and Immigrants, Free Men and Slaves: Urban Workingmen in the Antebellum American South." *American Historical Review* 88, no. 5 (December 1983): 1175–1200.

Berry, Daina Ramey. "'In Pressing Need of Cash': Gender Skill, and Family Persistence in the Domestic Slave Trade." *Journal of African American History* 92, no. 1 (Winter 2007): 22–36.

Berwanger, Eugene H. "The Black Law Question in Ante-Bellum California." *Journal of the West* 6 (April 1967): 205–20.

———. "Hardin and Langston: Western Black Spokesmen of the Reconstruction Era." *Journal of Negro History* 64, no. 2 (Spring 1979): 101–15.

———. "Reconstruction on the Frontier: The Equal Rights Struggle in Colorado, 1856–1867." *Pacific Historical Review* (August 1975): 313–29.

Billings, Warren M. "The Cases of Fernando and Elizabeth Key: A Note on the Status of Blacks in Seventeenth-Century Virginia." *William and Mary Quarterly* 30, no. 3 (July 1973): 467–74.

Boman, Dennis K. "The Dred Scott Case Reconsidered: The Legal and Political Context in Missouri." *American Journal of Legal History* 44, no. 4 (October 2000): 405–28.

Bragg, Susan. "Knowledge Is Power: Sacramento Blacks and the Public Schools, 1854–1860." *California History* 75, no. 3 (Fall 1996): 215–21.

Brigandi, Phil. "The Southern Emigrant Trail." *Overland Journal* 28, no. 1 (Fall 2010): 99–116.

Bright, Verne. "Black Harris, Mountain Man, Teller of Tales." *Oregon Historical Quarterly* 52, no. 1 (March 1951): 3–20.

Bringhurst, Newell G. "'The Missouri Thesis' Revisited: Early Mormonism, Slavery, and the Status of Black People." In *Black and Mormon,* edited by Newell G. Bringhurst and Darron T. Smith, 13–33. Urbana: University of Illinois Press, 2006.

———. "The Mormons and Slavery: A Closer Look." *Pacific Historical Review* 50, no. 3 (August, 1981): 329–38.

Brodie, Fawn M. "Thomas Jefferson's Unknown Grandchildren: A Study in Historical Silences." *American Heritage Magazine* 27, no. 6 (October 1976): 23–33, 94–99. http://www.americanheritage.com/print/53472 (accessed July 3, 2013).

Buchanan, Thomas C. "Rascals on the Antebellum Mississippi: African American Steamboat Workers and the St. Louis Hanging of 1841." *Journal of Social History* 34, no. 4 (Summer 2001): 797–816.

Bush, Lester E., Jr. "Mormonism's Negro Doctrine: An Historical Overview." *Dialogue* 8 (1973): 11–68.

Bynum Victoria E. "'White Negroes' in Segregated Mississippi: Miscegenation, Racial Identity, and the Law." *Journal of Southern History* 64, no. 2 (May 1998): 247–76.

Carey, Charles W., Jr. "'These Black Rascals': The Origins of Lord Dunmore's Ethiopian Regiment." *Virginia Social Science Journal 31* (1996): 65–77.

Carlton, Robert L. "Blacks in San Diego County: A Social Profile, 1850–1880." *Journal of San Diego History* 21, no. 4 (Fall 1975): 7–20.

Carter, Harvey Lewis, and Marcia Carpenter Spencer. "Stereotypes of the Mountain Man." *Western History Quarterly* 6, no. 1 (January 1975): 17–32.

Carter, Robert W. "'Sometimes When I Hear the Winds Sigh': Mortality on the Overland Trail." *California History* 74, no. 2 (Summer 1995): 146–61.

Cashin, Joan E. "Black Families in the Old Northwest." *Journal of the Early Republic* 15, no. 3 (Autumn 1995): 449–75.

Catterall, Helen Tunnicliff. "Some Antecedents of the Dred Scott Case." *American Historical Review* 30, no. 1 (October 1924): 56–71.

Chan, Sucheng. "A People of Exceptional Character: Ethnic Diversity, Nativism, and Racism in the California Gold Rush." *California History* 79, no. 2 (Summer 2000): 44–85.

Chandler, Robert J. "From Black to White: Lithographer and Painter Grafton Tyler Brown." *California Territorial Quarterly,* no. 86 (Summer 2011): 4–29.

Chaplin, Joyce E. "Expansion and Exceptionalism in Early American History." *Journal of American History* (March 2003): 1431–55.

Christensen, James B. "Negro Slavery in the Utah Territory." *Phylon Quarterly* 18, no. 3 (Third Quarter 1957): 289–305.

Coleman, Deirdre. "Janet Schaw and the Complexions of Empire." *Eighteenth-Century Studies* 36, no. 2 (Winter 2003): 169–93.

Coleman, Ronald G. "'Is There No Blessing for Me?': Jane Elizabeth Manning James, a Mormon African American Woman." In *African American Women Confront the West,* edited by Quintard Taylor and Shirley Ann Wilson Moore, 144–62. Norman: University of Oklahoma Press, 2003.

Conyers, James E., and T. H. Kennedy. "Negro Passing: To Pass or Not to Pass." *Phylon* 24, no. 3 (Third Quarter, 1963): 215–23.

Crofts, Daniel W. "Late Antebellum Virginia Reconsidered." *Virginia Magazine of History and Biography* 107, no. 3 (Summer 1999): 253–86.

Crothers, A. Glenn., and Tracy E. K'Meyer. "'I Was Black When It Suited Me: I Was White When It Suited Me': Racial Identity in the Biracial Life of Marguerite Davis Stewart." *Journal of American Ethnic History* 26, no. 4 (Summer 2007): 24–49.

Curtis, William J. "Emily Fisher: First Independence Black Business Woman." *Kansas City Genealogist* (Fall 1995): 76–77.

Day, Judy, and M. James Kendro. "Free Blacks in St. Louis." *Missouri Historical Society Bulletin* 30 (January 1974): 117–35.

De Graaf, Lawrence B. "Recognition, Racism and Reflections on the Writing of Western Black History." *Pacific Historical Review* 44, no. 1 (February 1975): 22–52.

De Jong, David H. "'Good Samaritans of the Desert': The Pima-Maricopa Villages as Described in California Emigrant Journals, 1846–1852." *Journal of the Southwest* 47, no. 3 (Autumn 2005): 457–96.

Doran, Michael F. "Population Statistics of Nineteenth Century Indian Territory." *Chronicles of Oklahoma* 53, no. 4 (Winter 1975): 501.

Ellington, J. Stephen. "Understanding the Dialectic of Discourse and Collective Action: Public Debate and Rioting in Antebellum Cincinnati." *American Journal of Sociology* 101, no. 1 (July 1995): 100–144.

Ellis, Joseph J. "Jefferson: Post-DNA." *William and Mary Quarterly,* Third Series 57, no. 1 (January 200): 125–38.

Farrison, W. Edward. "Phylon Profile, XVI: William Wells Brown." *Phylon* 9, no. 1 (First Quarter 1948): 13–23.

Ford, Lacy. "Reconfiguring the Old South: 'Solving' the Problem of Slavery, 1787–1838." *Journal of American History* 95, no. 1 (June 2008): 95–122.

Foreman, Grant. "Early Trails through Oklahoma." *Chronicles of Oklahoma* 3, no. 2 (June 1925): 99–119.

Franklin, V. P. "The African American Experience in the Western States." *Journal of African American History* 91, no. 1 (Winter 2006): 1–3.

Gardner, Eric. "'You Have No Business to Whip Me': The Freedom Suits of Polly Wash and Lucy Ann Delaney." *African American Review* 41, no. 1 (Spring 2007): 33–50.

Genovese, Eugene D. "The Medical and Insurance Costs of Slaveholding in the Cotton Belt." *Journal of Negro History* 45, no. 3 (July 1960): 141–55.

Golub, Mark. "'Passing': Judicial Responses to Ambiguously Raced Bodies in *Plessy v. Ferguson*." *Law and Society Review* 39, no. 3 (September 2005): 563–600.

Gordon, Mary McDougall. "Overland to California in 1849: A Neglected Commercial Enterprise." *Pacific Historical Review* 52, no. 1 (February 1983): 17–36.

Gudmestad, Robert H. "The Troubled Legacy of Isaac Franklin: The Enterprise of Slave Trading." *Tennessee Historical Quarterly* 62, no. 3 (Fall 2003): 193–217.

Guenther, Todd. "'Could These Bones Be from a Negro?': Some African American Experiences on the Oregon-California Trail." *Overland Journal* 19, no. 2 (Summer 2001): 42–55.

———. "Lucretia Marchbanks: A Black Woman in the Black Hills." *South Dakota History* 31 (Spring 2001): 1–25.

Hall, Lewis D. W. "A Summation of Events." *Montana The Magazine of Western History* 12, no. 2 (Spring 1962): 12–15.

Hall, Martin Hardwick. "*The Mesilla Times:* A Journal of Confederate Arizona." *Arizona and the West* 5, no. 4 (Winter 1963): 337–51.

Hammond, Andrew, and Joanne Hammond. "Mapping the Beckwourth Trail." *Overland Journal* 12, no. 3 (1994): 10–18.

Handlin, Oscar and Mary F. "Origins of the Southern Labor System." *William and Mary Quarterly* 7, no. 2 (April 1950): 199–222.

Hansen, Klaus J. "The Millennium, the West, and Race in the Antebellum Mind." *Western Historical Quarterly* 3, no. 4 (October 1972): 373–90.

Hartley, William G. "LDS Emigration in 1853: The Keokuk Encampment and Outfitting Ten Wagon Trains for Utah." *Mormon Historical Studies* (Fall 2003): 43–76.

Hayden, Dolores. "Biddy Mason's Los Angeles, 1856–1891." *California History* 63, no.3 (Fall 1989): 86–99.

Hazelett, Stafford. "'Let Us Honor Those to Whom Honor Is Due.'" *Oregon Historical Quarterly* (Summer 2010): 220–48. http://www.historycooperative.org/journals/ohq/111.2/hazelett.html (accessed August 12, 2010).

Herr, Pamela, and Mary Lee Spence. "'I Really Had Something Like the Blues': Letters from Jessie Benton Frémont to Elizabeth Blair Lee." *Montana The Magazine of Western History* 41, no. 2 (Spring 1991): 16–31.

Hickman, Christine B. "The Devil and the One Drop Rule: Racial Categories, African Americans, and the U.S. Census." *Michigan Law Review* 95, no. 5 (March 1997): 1161–1265.

Hill, D. G. "The Negro as a Political and Social Issue in the Oregon Country." *Journal of Negro History* 33, no. 2 (April 1948): 130–45.

Hill, James L. "Migration of Blacks to Iowa, 1820–1960." *Journal of Negro History* 66, no. 4 (Winter 1981–1982): 289–303.
Hoffert, Sylvia D. "Childbearing on the Trans-Mississippi Frontier, 1830–1900." *Western Historical Quarterly* 22, no. 3 (August 1991): 272–88.
Hollinger, David A. "Amalgamation and Hypodescent: The Question of Ethnoracial Mixture in the History of the United States." *American Historical Review* 108, no. 5 (December 2003); 1363–90.
Holton, Woody. "'Rebel against Rebel': Enslaved Virginians and the Coming of the American Revolution." *Virginia Magazine of History and Biography* 105, no. 2 (Spring 1997): 157–92.
Hoover, Herbert T. "The Arrival of Capitalism on the Northern Great Plains: Pierre Choteau, Jr., and Company." In *South Dakota Leaders: From Pierre Choteau, Jr., to Oscar Howe*, edited by Herbert T. Hoover and Larry J. Zimmerman, 6–10. Vermillion: University of South Dakota Press, 1989.
Horner, John B. "Uncle Lou and His Violin." In *Days and Deeds in the Oregon Country*, 139–46. Portland: J. K. Gill, 1928.
Horton, Lois E. "From Class to Race in Early America: Northern Post-Emancipation Racial Reconstruction." *Journal of the Early Republic* 19, no. 4 (Winter 1999): 629–49.
Hudson, J. Blaine. s.v. "Education, Afro-Americans." *The Kentucky Encyclopedia*, edited by John, E. Kleber, 284–287. Lexington: University Press of Kentucky, 1992.
Hudson, Nicholas. "Nation to 'Race': The Origin of Racial Classification in Eighteenth-Century Thought." *Eighteenth-Century Studies* 29, no. 3 (Spring 1996): 247–64.
Hurtado, Albert L. "When Strangers Met: Sex and Gender on Three Frontiers." In *Writing the Range: Race, Class and Culture in the Women's West*, edited by Elizabeth Jameson and Susan Armitage, 122–42. Norman: University of Oklahoma Press, 1997.
Hyde Anne F. "Cultural Filters: The Significance of Perception in the History of the American West." *Western History Quarterly* 24, no. 3 (August 1993): 351–74.
Jackson, David W. "African American Neighborhood of Steptoe Vanishing," in *Kansas City Chronicles: An Up-to-Date History*. Charleston, S.C.: The History Press, 2010.
Johnson, Ed, and Elmer R. Rusco. "The First Black Rancher: Ben Palmer and a Group of Black Pioneers Made their Marks in the 1800s." *Historical Nevada Magazine: Outstanding Historical Features from the Pages of Nevada Magazine* (no volume) (1998): 82–85.
Johnson, Karen A. "Undaunted Courage and Faith: The Lives of Three Black Women in the West and Hawaii in the Early 19th Century." *Journal of African American History* 91, no. 1 (Winter 2006): 4–22.

Johnson, Walter. "The Slave Trader, the White Slave, and the Politics of Racial Determination in the 1850s." *Journal of American History* 87, no. 1 (June 2000): 13–38.
Jordan, Winthrop. "Modern Tensions and the Origins of American Slavery." *Journal of Southern History* 28, no. 1 (February 1962): 18–30.
Kelley, Sean. "'Mexico in His Head': Slavery and the Texas-Mexico Border, 1810–1860." *Journal of Social History* 37, no. 3 (Spring 2004): 709–23.
Kiple, Kenneth F. and Virginia H. "Black Tongue and Black Men: Pellagra and Slavery in the Antebellum South." *Journal of Southern History* 43, no. 3 (August 1977): 411–28.
Konig, David Thomas. "The Long Road to *Dred Scott:* Personhood and the Rule of Law in the Trial Court Records of St. Louis Slave Freedom Suits." *University of Missouri, Kansas City, Law Review* 75, no. 1 (Fall 2006): 54–79. Reprinted online, http://www.s1.sos.mo.gov/CMSImages/MDH/TheLongRoadtoDredScott.pdf (accessed September 13, 2015).
LeFalle-Collins, Lizzetta. "Grafton Tyler Brown: Selling the Promise of the West." *International Review of African American Art* 12, no. 4 (1995): 26–44.
——. "Grafton Tyler Brown: Visualizing California and the Pacific Northwest." Art Exhibit Brochure, California African American Museum in Los Angeles, 2003.
Lewis, David Rich. "Argonauts and the Overland Trail Experience: Method and Theory." *Western Historical Quarterly* 16, no. 3 (July 1985): 285–305.
Lewis, Jan. "Introduction: Thomas Jefferson and Sally Hemings Redux." *William and Mary Quarterly,* 3d series, 57, no. 1 (January 2000): 121–24.
Lockley, Fred. "The Case of Robin Holmes vs. Nathaniel Ford." *Quarterly of the Oregon Historical Society* 23, no. 2 (June 1922): 111–37.
Lythgoe, Dennis L. "Negro Slavery in Utah." *Utah Historical Quarterly* 39 (Winter 1977): 40–54.
Malone, Dumas, and Steven H. Hochman. "A Note on Evidence: The Personal History of Madison Hemings." *Journal of Southern History* 41, no. 4 (November 1975): 523–28.
Mathias, Frank F. "John Randolph's Freedmen: The Thwarting of a Will." *Journal of Southern History* 39, no. 2 (May 1973): 263–72.
May, Robert E. "Invisible Men: Blacks and the U.S. Army in the Mexican War." *The Historian* 49 (1987): 463–77.
McCarthy, Michael P. "The Philadelphia Consolidation of 1854: A Reappraisal." *Pennsylvania Magazine of History and Biography* 110, no. 4 (October 1986): 531–48.
McCoy, Raymond. "Arizona Early Confederate Territory." *Montana The Magazine of Western History* 12, no. 2 (Spring 1962): 16–20.

McDonald, Dedra S. "To Be Black and Female in the Spanish Southwest." In *African American Women Confront the West,* edited by Quintard Taylor and Shirley Ann Wilson Moore, 32–52. New York: W. W. Norton, 1998.

McDonald, Vernon Sugg. "The Pioneer Sugg Family: The Saga of an Early Day Family of Tuolumne County and the History of One of Sonora's Outstanding Gold Rush Homes." *Quarterly of the Tuolumne County Historical Society* 4, no. 1 (July-September 1964): 97–100.

Melish, Joanne Pope. "The 'Condition' Debate and Racial Discourse in the Antebellum North." *Journal of the Early Republic* 19, no. 4 (Winter 1999): 651–72.

Middleton, Stephen. "The Fugitive Slave Crisis in Cincinnati, 1850–1860: Resistance, Enforcement, and Black Refugees." *Journal of Negro History* 72, nos. 1–2 (Winter-Spring 1987): 20–32.

Miller, Randall M. "The Fabric of Control: Slavery in Antebellum Southern Textile Mills." *Business History Review* 55, no. 4 (Winter 1981): 471–90.

Millner, Darrell. "George Bush of Tumwater: Founder of the First American Colony on Puget Sound." *Columbia Magazine* 8, no. 4 (Winter 1994–1995): 14–19. http://columbia.washingtonhistory.org/anthology/settlers/georgeBush.aspx (accessed September 21, 2010).

———. "York of the Corps of Discovery: Interpretations of York's Character and His Role in the Lewis and Clark Expedition." *Oregon Historical Quarterly* (Fall 2003): 302–33. http://www.historycooperative.org/journals/ohq/104.3/millner.html (accessed September 18, 2010).

Mills, Marilyn. "True Community: Latter-day Saints in San Bernardino, 1851–1857." *Ensign* (February 2003): 36–45.

Mitman, Gregg, and Ronald L. Numbers. "From Miasma to Asthma: The Changing Fortunes of Medical Geography in America." *History and Philosophy of the Life Sciences* 25, no. 3 (2003): 391–412.

Montesano, Phil. "A Black Pioneer's Trip to California." *Pacific Historian* 13 (1969): 58–62.

Moore, Joe Louis. "In Our Own Image: Black Artists in California, 1880–1970, A Sample Portfolio of the Works of Grafton Tyler Brown, Sargent Claude Johnson, Emmanuel Joseph, Samella Lewis, Ruth Waddy and Emory Douglas." *California History* 75, no. 3 (Fall 1996): 265–71.

Moore, Robert, Jr. "A Ray of Hope, Extinguished: St. Louis Slave Suits for Freedom." *Gateway Heritage Magazine* 14, no. 3 (Winter 1993–94. Reprinted online, https://www.google.com/collections.mohistory.org/media/CDMgateway/86.pdf (accessed September 13, 2015).

Moore, Shirley Ann. "African American Women." In *Encyclopedia of Social History,* edited by Peter N. Stearns, 9–10. New York: Garland Publishing, 1994.

Moore, Shirley Ann Wilson. "We Feel the Want of Protection: The Politics of Law and Race in California, 1848–1878." In *Taming the Elephant: Politics, Government, and Law in Pioneer California,* edited by John F. Burns and Richard J. Orsi, 108–109. Berkeley: University of California Press, 2003.

Morehouse, George P. "Padilla and the Old Monument near Council Grove." *Kansas Historical Collection* 10 (1908): 472–79.

Moss, Rick. "Not Quite Paradise: The Development of the African American Community in Los Angeles through 1950." *California History* 75, no. 3 (Fall 1996): 222–35.

Nadelhaft, Jerome. "The Somersett Case and Slavery: Myth, Reality, and Repercussions." *Journal of Negro History* 51, no. 3 (July 1966): 193–208.

Nash, Gary B. "African Americans in the Early Republic." *Magazine of History* 14, no. 2 (Winter 2000): 12–16.

Nugent, Walter. "Western History, New and Not So New." *OAH Magazine of History* 9, no.1 (Fall 1994): 5–9.

Nunis, Doyce B. "Milestones in California History: The 150th Anniversary of the Bidwell-Bartleson Party." *California History* 70 (Summer 1991): Inside front cover.

O'Brien, William Patrick. "Hiram Young: Black Entrepreneur on the Santa Fe Trail." *Wagon Tracks* 4, no. 1 (November 1989): 1–4. http://www.santafetrail.org/the-trail/history/best-of-wagon tracks/Hiram_Young.pdf (accessed May 30, 2011).

———. "Hiram Young: Pioneering Black Wagon Maker for the Santa Fe Trade." *Gateway Heritage* 14 (Summer 1993): 56–67.

———. "'Olam Katan' (Small World): Jewish Traders on the Santa Fe Trail." *Journal of the Southwest* 48, no. 2 (Summer 2006): 211–31.

Olch, Peter D. "Treading the Elephant's Tail: Medical Problems on the Overland Trails." *Bulletin of the History of Medicine* 59, no. 2 (Summer 1985): 196–212.

———, and Roger P. Blair. "Plenty of Doctoring to Do: Health Related Problems on the Oregon Trail." *Overland Journal* 33, no. 3 (Fall 2015): 96–113.

Oliver, Mamie O. "Idaho Ebony: The African American Presence in Idaho State History." *Journal of African American History* 91, no. 1 (Winter 2006): 41–54.

Oman, Kerry R. "Winter in the Rockies: Winter Quarters of the Mountain Men." *Montana The Magazine of Western History,* 52, no 1 (Spring 2002): 34–47.

Onuf, Peter S. "Every Generation Is an 'Independant Nation': Colonization, Miscegenation, and the Fate of Jefferson's Children." *William and Mary Quarterly,* 3d series, 57, no. 1 (January 2000): 153–70.

Oswald, Delmont R. "James P. Beckwourth." In *Trappers of the Far West,* edited by LeRoy R. Hafen, 162–85.Lincoln: University of Nebraska Press, 1983.

O'Toole, James M. "Passing: Race, Religion, and the Healy Family, 1820–1920." *Proceedings of the Massachusetts Historical Society* 108 (1996): 1–34.

Owens, Kenneth N. "The Mormon-Carson Emigrant Trail in Western History." *Montana The Magazine of Western History* 42, no. 1 (Winter, 1992): 14–27.

Parrish, William E. "The Mississippi Saints." *Historian* 50, no. 4 (August 1988): 489–506.

Peltier, Jerome. "Moses 'Black' Harris." In *The Mountain Men and the Fur Trade of the Far West,* Vol. 4, edited by LeRoy R. Hafen, 103–17. Glendale, Calif.: Arthur H. Clark, 1966.

A Pioneer. "A Negro Pioneer in the West." *Journal of Negro History* 8, no. 3 (1920): 333–35.

Porter, Kenneth W. "Contacts in Other Parts: Relations between Negroes and Indians." *Journal of Negro History* 17, no. 3 (July 1932): 359–67.

———. "Notes Supplementary to 'Relations between Negroes and Indians.'" *Journal of Negro History* 18, no. 3 (July 1933): 282–321.

Powers, Ramon, and Gene Younger. "Cholera on the Plains: The Epidemic of 1867 in Kansas." *Kansas Historical Quarterly* 37 (Winter 1971): 351–93.

Prince, Carl E. "The Great 'Riot Year': Jacksonian Democracy and Patterns of Violence in 1834." *Journal of the Early Republic* 5, no. 1 (Spring 1985): 1–19.

Pritchett, Jonathan B. "Quantitative Estimates of the United States Interregional Slave Trade, 1820–1860." *Journal of Economic History* 61, no. 2 (June 2001): 467–75.

Rafferty, Michael. "Nelson Ray—A Story of the West: Placerville Miner Bought His Family Out of Slavery in Missouri." *Mountain Democrat* (Placerville, California), October 8, 1998.

Reid, John Phillip. "Binding the Elephant: Contracts and Legal Obligations on the Overland Trail." *American Journal of Legal History* 21, no. 4 (October 1977): 285–315.

———. "Punishing the Elephant: Malfeasance and Organized Criminality on the Overlnd Trail." *Montana The Magazine of Western History* 47, no. 1 (Spring 1997): 2–21.

Reid, Margaret Ann. "Charlotta Gordon Pyles." In *Notable Black American Women,* Book II, edited by Jessie Carney Smith, 534–35. Detroit: Gale Research, 1996.

Richards, Kent D. "Rudimentary Government in Nevada." *Arizona and the West* 11, no. 3 (Autumn 1969): 213–32.

Rieck, Richard L. "A Geography of Death on the Oregon-California Trail, 1840–1860." *Overland Journal* 9, no. 1 (1991): 13–21.

Riforgiato, Leonard R. "Bishop Timon, Buffalo, and the Civil War." *Catholic Historical Review* 73, no. 1 (January 1987): 62–80.

Riley, Carroll L. "Blacks in the Early Southwest." *Ethnohistory* 19, no. 3 (Summer 1972): 247–60.

Riley, Glenda. "American Daughters: Black Women in the West." *Montana: The Magazine of Western History* 38, no. 2 (Spring 1988): 14–27.

———. "The Specter of a Savage: Rumors and Alarmism on the Overland Trail." *Western Historical Quarterly*, 15, no. 4 (October 1984): 427–44.

Robbins, Karen. "Power among the Powerless: Domestic Resistance by Free and Slave Women in the McHenry Family of the New Republic." *Journal of the Early Republic* 23, no. 1 (Spring 2003): 47–68.

Rosenberg, Charles E. "The Therapeutic Revolution: Medicine, Meaning, and Social Change in Nineteenth-Century America." *Perspectives in Biology and Medicine* 20 (Summer 1977): 485–506.

Sacks, B. "The Creation of the Territory of Arizona," Part 1. *Arizona and the West* 5, no. 1 (Spring 1963): 29–62.

———. "The Creation of the Territory of Arizona," Part 2. *Arizona and the West* 5, no. 2 (Summer 1963): 109–48.

San Francisco African American Historical and Cultural Society. *Blacks in the West*. Manuscript Series, No. 1. San Francisco: African American Historical and Cultural Society, 1976.

Savage, W. Sherman. "The Negro in the History of the Pacific Northwest." *Journal of Negro History* 13, no. 3 (July 1928): 255–64.

———. "The Negro in the Westward Movement." *Journal of Negro History* 25, no. 4 (October 1940): 531–39.

Schlissel, Lillian. "Women's Diaries on the Western Frontier." *American Studies* 18, no. 1 (Spring 1977): 87–100.

Schmidt, Louis Bernard. "Manifest Opportunity and the Gadsden Purchase." *Arizona and the West* 3, no. 3 (Autumn 1961): 245–64.

Schwaller, Robert C. "'Mulata, Hija de Negro y India': 'Afro Indigenous Mulatos' in Early Colonial Mexico." *Journal of Social History* 44, no. 3 (Spring 2011): 889–914.

Schweninger, Loren. "Black-Owned Businesses in the South, 1790–1880." *Business History Review* 63, no. 1 (Spring 1989): 22–60.

———. "John H. Rapier, Sr.: A Slave and Freedman in the Ante-Bellum South." *Civil War History* 20, no. 1 (March 1974): 23–34.

———. "A Slave Family in the Ante Bellum South." *Journal of Negro History* 60, no. 1 (January 1975): 29–44.

———. "Thriving within the Lowest Caste: The Financial Activities of James P. Thomas in the Nineteenth-Century South." *Journal of Negro History* 63, no. 4 (October 1978): 353–64.

———. "The Vass Slaves: County Courts, State Laws, and Slavery in Virginia, 1831–1861." *Virginia Magazine of History and Biography* 114, no. 4 (2006): 464–97.

———, and John H. Rapier. "The Dilemma of a Free Negro in the Ante-Bellum South." *Journal of Negro History* 62, no. 3 (July 1977): 283–88.

Sheeler, J. Reuben. "The Struggle of the Negro in Ohio for Freedom." *Journal of Negro History* 31, no. 2 (April 1946): 208–26.

Shore, Laurence. "The Enduring Power of Racism: A Reconsideration of Winthrop Jordan's *White over Black*." *History and Theory* 44, no. 2 (May 2005): 195–226.

Smith, Ross A. "The Southern Route Revisited." *Oregon Historical Quarterly* (Summer 2004) 105, no. 2: 292–307. http://www.historycooperative.org/journals/ohq/105.2/smith.html (accessed August 12, 2010).

Spedden, Rush. "The Fearful Long Drive: The 1846 Hastings Cutoff." *Overland Journal* 12, no. 2 (1994): 3–16.

———. "Who Was T. H. Jefferson?" *Overland Journal* 8, no. 3 (Fall 1990): 2–8.

Stewart, James Brewer. "The Emergence of Racial Modernity and the Rise of the White North, 1790–1840." *Journal of the Early Republic* 18, no. 2 (Summer 1998): 181–217.

Swagerty, William R. "Marriage and Settlement Patterns of Rocky Mountain Trappers and Traders." *Western Historical Quarterly* 11, no. 2 (April 1980): 159–80.

Taylor, Nikki. "Reconsidering the 'Forced' Exodus of 1829: Free Black Emigration from Cincinnati, Ohio, to Wilberforce, Canada." *Journal of African American History* 87 (Summer 2002): 283–302.

Taylor, Quintard. "Freedmen and Slaves in Oregon Territory, 1840–1860." In *Peoples of Color in the American West*, edited by Sucheng Chan, Douglas Henry Daniels, Mario T. Garcia, and Terry P. Wilson, 77–79. Lexington, Mass.: D. C. Heath, 1994.

———. "From Esteban to Rodney King: Five Centuries of African American History in the West." *Montana The Magazine of Western History* 46, no. 4 (Winter 1996): 2–23.

Theriot, Nancy. "Diagnosing Unnatural Motherhood: Nineteenth-Century Physicians and 'Puerperal' Insanity.'" *American Studies* 30, no. 2 (Fall 1989): 69–88.

Thompson, Gerald. "Another Look at Frontier versus Western Historiography." *Montana The Magazine of Western History* 40, no. 3 (Summer 1990): 68–71.

Vance, James E., Jr. "The Oregon Trail and Union Pacific Railroad: A Contrast in Purpose." *Annals of the Association of American Geographers* 51, no. 4 (December 1961): 357–79.

Van Cleve, George. "'Somerset's Case' and Its Antecedents in Imperial Perspective." *Law and History Review* 24, no. 3 (Fall 2006): 601–45.

VanderVelde, Lea. "The Dred Scott Case as an American Family Saga." *OAH Magazine of History* 25, no. 2 (April 2011): 24–28. Reprinted online, http://www.doi:10.1093/oahmag/oar010 (accessed September 13, 20015).

Wade, Richard C. "The Negro in Cincinnati, 1800–1830." *Journal of Negro History* 39, no. 1 (January 1954): 43–57.

Wallach, Jennifer Jensen. "The Vindication of Fawn Brodie." *Massachusetts Review* 43, no. 2 (Summer 2002): 277–95.

Wax, Darold D. "The Odyssey of an Ex-Slave: Robert Ball Anderson's Pursuit of the American Dream." *Phylon* 45, no. 1 (First Quarter 1984): 67–79.

West, Osborne. "The Monroe Family." In *Teaching Students to Read Nonfiction*. 86. New York: Scholastic Professional Books, 2002.

Whaley, Gray H. "Oregon, Illahee, and the Empire Republic: A Case Study of American Colonialism, 1843–1858." *Western Historical Quarterly*, 36, no. 2 (Summer 2005): 157–78.

Wheat, Carl I. "The Forty-Niners in Death Valley: A Tentative Census." *Historical Society of Southern California Quarterly* 21 (December 1939): 102–17. http://www.scvhistory.com/scvhistory/wheat-49ers.htm (accessed January 10, 2012).

Whitaker, Matthew C. "The Rise of Black Phoenix: African-American Migration, Settlement and Community Development in Maricopa County, Arizona 1868–1930." *Journal of Negro History* 85, no. 3 (Summer 2000): 197–209.

Williams, John A. "The Long Hot Summers of Yesteryear." *History Teacher* 1, no. 3 (March 1968): 9–23.

Wood, Peter. "Jefferson-Hemings Revisited." *Chronicle of Higher Education* (blog). September 1, 2011. http://chronicle.com/blogs/innovations/jefferson-hemings-revisited/30273 (accessed July 5, 2013).

Wood, Timothy L. "The Prophet and the Presidency: Mormonism and Politics in Joseph Smith's 1844 Presidential Campaign." *Journal of the Illinois State Historical Society* 93, no. 2 (Summer 2000): 167–93.

Worster, Donald. "New West, True West: Interpreting the Region's History." *Western Historical Quarterly* 18, no. 2 (April 1987): 141–56.

Wright, Donald R. "Recent Literature on Slavery in Colonial North America." *Magazine of History* 17, no. 3 (April 2003): 5–9.

Wright, Gavin. "Slavery and American Agricultural History." *Agricultural History* 77, no. 4 (Autumn 2003): 527–52.

Wright, George C. s.v. "Afro-Americans." *The Kentucky Encyclopedia,* edited by John, E. Kleber, 3–5. Lexington: University Press of Kentucky, 1992.

———. "Oral History and the Search for the Black Past in Kentucky." *Oral History Review* 10 (1982): 73–91.

Wyman, Walker. "Bullwhacking: A Prosaic Profession Peculiar to the Great Plains." *New Mexico Historical Review* 7, no. 4 (October 1932): 297–310.

———. "Freighting: A Big Business on the Santa Fe Trail." *Kansas Historical Quarterly* 1, no. 1 (November 1931): 17–27.

———. "The Outfitting Posts." *Pacific Historical Review* 18, no. 1 (February 1949): 14–23.
Zackodnik, Teresa. "Fixing the Color Line: The Mulatto, Southern Courts, and Racial Identity." *American Quarterly* 53, no. 3 (September 2001): 420–51.

Dissertations and Theses

Coleman, Ronald G. "A History of Blacks in Utah, 1825–1910." Ph.D. diss., University of Utah, 1980.
Bresee, Floyd Edgar. "Overland Freighting in the Platte Valley, 1850–1870." Master's thesis, University of Nebraska, Lincoln, 1937.
Fisher, James. "A History of the Political and Social Development of the Black Community in California, 1850–1950." Ph.D. diss., State University of New York, Stony Brook, 1971.
Hayes, William. "Devotion to the Good Cause: Nebraska in the Civil War." Master's thesis, University of Nebraska at Kearney, 2008. Reprinted by UMI Dissertation Publishing, Ann Arbor, 2011.
Paul, Thomas. "George Bush." Master's thesis, University of Washington, 1965.
Pilton, James William. "Negro Settlement in British Columbia, 1858–1871." Master's thesis, University of British Columbia, 1951.
Ricks, Nathaniel R. "A Peculiar Place for the Peculiar Institution: Slavery and Sovereignty in Early Territorial Utah." Master's thesis, Brigham Young University, 2007.
Thurman, Odell A. "The Negro in California before 1890." Master's thesis, College of the Pacific, 1945. Reprinted by R & E Associates, San Francisco, 1973.

Interviews

Alexander, Harold, Gay and Family. Interview by author, August 1, 2009. Transcript on file at National Park Service, National Trails Intermountain Region, Salt Lake City.
Brown, Clara. Interview. *Denver Tribune Republican,* June 26, 1885.
Curtis, William J. Telephone interviews by author, August 12 and August 29, 2009.
Hudlin, Doug. Video interview by Dale Hitchocks, British Columbia Black History Awareness Society, April 23, 2010, http://www.youtube.com/watch?v=Yp5IM9Qs_0g (accessed February 28, 2011).
Molson, Jeannette. Interview by author, June 24, 2009. Transcript on file at National Park Service, National Trails Intermountain Region, Salt Lake City.
Richardson, Constance Moore. Telephone interview by author, September 11, 2009.

Online Sources

BACM Research. "African-American Slavery: California Fugitive Slave Case: *Stovall v. Archy Lee* Legal Papers." Paperless Archives. http://www.paperlessarchives.com/FreeTitles/StovalvArchy.pdf (accessed May 5, 2011).

Bagley, Will. "Black Youths Helped Blaze Mormon Trail." History Matters (column), *Salt Lake Tribune,* August 27, 2000. Utah History to Go, State of Utah website. http://historytogo.utah.gov/salt_salt_lake_tribune/history_matters/082700.html. (accessed August 22, 2010).

———. "Pioneer Map leads Jefferson Scandal to West." History Matters (column), *Salt Lake Tribune,* May 6, 2001. Utah History to Go, State of Utah website. http://histortogo.utah.gov/salt_lake_tribune/history_mattters/050601.html (accessed August 10, 2010).

Baldwin, Peggy. "A Legacy beyond the Generations." Genealogical Forum of Oregon. Annual Writing Contest, 2006. http://www.gfo.org/writecontest/20006--1st.pdf (accessed December 27, 2010).

Belli, Anthony. "California Legends: Chattel Hood to Freedom—Black Pioneers Help Settle California." Legends of America. http://www.legendsofamerica.com/ca-blackpioneers.html (accessed July 9, 2008).

Betts, William J. "Early Pioneer's Faith Finally Rewarded." *The Olympian* [Olympia, Washington], April 19, 1964. http://www.ci.tumwater.wa.us/research%20early%20pioneers.htm (accessed December 12, 2008).

Cataldo, Nicholas R. "Lizzy Flake Rowan: Former Slave Played Major Role in San Bernardino's Early History." City of San Bernardino, 1998. http://www.sbcity.org/about/history/lizzy_flake_rowan___slave.asp (accessed August 22, 2010).

Chalfant, W. A. *The Story of Inyo*. Chicago: self-published, 1922. Library of Congress, online digitized edition https://archivesorg/stream/storyofinyo00chal/storyofinyo (accessed January 3, 2016).

Chipman, Donald E. "Estevanico." Handbook of Texas Online. Texas State Historical Association. http://www.tshaonline.org/handbook/online/articles/fes08 (accessed January 3, 2012).

Choate, Jane McBride, "Heroes and Heroines: Green Flake—Black Pioneer." *Liahona* (June 1989). http://www.lds.org/ldsorg/v/index.jsp?vgnextoid=f318118dd536c010VgnVCM1000004d8 (accessed August 23, 2008).

Clackamas Heritage Partners. Historic Oregon City Presents: End of the Oregon Trail Interpretive Center, "Black Pioneers and Settlers—George Washington." http://www.historicoregoncity.org/HOC/index.php?option=com_content&view=article&i (accessed December 29, 2008).

Cleary, Brooke. "Barney L. Ford: Runaway Slave, Denver Pioneer." Colorado Historical Society, 2001. http://www.docstoc.com/docs/44329510/BARNEY-FORD (accessed September 23, 2010).

Church of Jesus Christ of Latter-day Saints. "Mormon Pioneer Overland Travel, 1847–1868." Church History. http://lds.org/churchhistory/library/pioneercompany/1,15797,4017-1-285,00.html (accessed August 28, 2011).
Coleman, Ronald G. "Blacks in Utah History: An Unknown Legacy." Utah History to Go, State of Utah website. http://historytogo.utah.gov/people/ethnic_cultures/the_peoples_of_utah/blacksinutahhistory.html (accessed December 27, 2009).
Devore, Joyce. "Old Alpine County Barn Finds New Purpose as a Home." (Gardnerville, Nevada) *Record Courier,* January 29, 2010. http://www.recordcourier.com/article/20100129/ALPINE/100129646 (accessed September 24, 2010).
Dickey, Michael. "George Caleb Bingham's Missouri." Friends of Arrow Rock. *Summer Newsletter,* 2007. http://www.friendsar.org/binghamsmo2.lhtml (accessed July 26, 2010).
First Baptist Church of St. Louis. "Our History: The First Baptist Church Story." http://firstbaptistchurchstlouis.org/history (accessed March 31, 2013).
Five Points Business District. "The History of Five Points." http://www.fivepointsbiz.org/history-culture.html (accessed September 23, 2010).
Flint, Richard, and Shirley Cushing Flint. "Dorantes, Esteban de." New Mexico Office of the State Historian. http://www.newmexicohistory.org/filedetails.php?fileID=464 (accessed March 2, 2013).
Freeman, Ron. "James Madison Flake, 1815–1850." https://famiysearch.org/patron/v2/TH-300-41879-6-92/dist.pdf?ctx=ArtCtxPublic (accessed January 16, 2016).
Goodnow, Cecelia. "State Owes Much to George W. Bush—A Black Pioneer." *Seattle Post Intelligencer,* February 5, 2002. http://seattlepi.nwsource.com/lifestyle/56993_blackhistory05_2.shtml (accessed December 19, 2008).
Gray, Beverly J. "The Hemings Family of Monticello," from Ross County Historical Society *Magazine Recorder,* February 1994, updated in 1998. Thomas Woodson Family Web Site. http://woodson.org/Hemingshistory.shtml (accessed July 5, 2013).
Grinde, Donald, Jr. "Rose, Edward (ca. 1780– ca. 1833)." The Black Past: An Online Guide to African American History. BlackPast.org. http://www.blackpast.org/?q=aaw/rose-edward-c-1780-c-1833 (accessed March 8, 2013).
Gwaltney, William W. "Beyond the Pale: African-Americans in the Fur Trade West." In *Lest We Forget* (January). Trotwood, Ohio: LWF Publications, 1995. http://people.coax.net/lwf/FURTRADE.HTM (accessed September 11, 2009).
Hague, Harlan. "The Search for a Southern Overland Route to California." Life Is a Soft Adventure, Harlan Hague. http://www.softadventure.net/roadcal.htm (accessed September 4, 2010).

Hansen, Moya. "Ford, Barney L. (1822–1902)." The Black Past: An Online Guide to African American History. BlackPast.org. http://www.blackpast.org/?q=aaw/ford-barney-1-1822-1902 (accessed August 8, 2010).

Historical Marker Data Base. "Sugg House." Bite-Size Bits of Local, National, and Global History. http://www.hmdb.org/marker.asp?marker=318619 (accessed September 25, 2010).

Holdredge, Sterling M. *State Territorial and Ocean Guide Book of the Pacific: Containing the Time and Distance Tables on or Connecting with the Pacific Coast and the Interior to Which Are Added Nine Large and Reliable Maps Showing Principal Towns, Routes of Communication, etc.* Illustrated title page by Grafton Tyler Brown. San Francisco: Sterling M. Holdredge, 1866. In the David Rumsey Historical Map Collection, http://www.davidrumsey.com/luna/servlet/detail/RUMSEY~8~1~860~50032?printerFriendly (accessed January 22, 2012).

Jensen, Kenneth. "Former Slave Barney Ford Became a Colorado Millionaire," *Loveland (Colorado) Reporter-Herald*, February 26, 2012. http://www.reporterherald.com/ci_20031588 (accessed January 14, 2016).

Jackson, David W. "Portals to the Past: Westport Steptoe Neighborhood Stepping into History." Jackson County, Missouri Historical Society. http://www.jchs.org/education/Kansas%20City%20Star%20Articles/Westport%20Steptoe.htm (accessed March 31, 2013).

Kansas State Historical Society and the Kansas Collection of the University of Kansas. "Immigration and Early Settlement." Territorial Kansas Online 1854–1861: A Virtual Repository for Territorial Kansas History. http://www.territorialkansasonline.org/~imlskto/cgibin/index.php?SCREEN=immigration (accessed April 14, 2011).

Karol, Gayle. "1849: Rose Jackson's Trip to Oregon in a Box." OregonLive.com. http://blog.oregonlive.com/blackhistory_impact/print.html?entry=/2008/02/1849_rose_jackson (accessed December 29, 2008).

Kaubisch, Barret. "New Mexico Territory Slave Code (1859–1867)." The Black Past: An Online Guide to African American History. BlackPast.org. http://www.blackpast.org/?q-aaw/new-mexico-territory-slave-code-1859-1867 (accessed April 14, 2011).

Keipp, Lisa. "Clara Brown, a Colorado Pioneer, Parts 1–2." Colorado History Examiner, February 18, 2010. http://www.examiner.com/history-in-denver/clara-brown-a-colorado-pioneer (accessed September 24, 2010).

Labode, Modupe. "Barney Ford's Legacy Still a Presence Today." http://denver.yourhub.com/Littleton/Stories/News/Story~53935.aspx (accessed September 23, 2010).

LaFayette County, "LaFayette County History." http://www.lcmogov.com/P-100/History.aspx (accessed January 8, 2012).

Lamb, Blaine P. "Travelers on the California Leg of the Southern Route 1849–1852." California State Parks. http://www.parks.ca.gov/?page_id=24680 (accessed September 4, 2010).
Larsen, Julia Henning. "Ben Palmer (ca. 1817–1908)." The Black Past: An Online Guide to African American History. BlackPast.org, http://www.blackpast.org/?q=aaw/palmer-ben-c-1817–1908 (accessed September 23, 2010).
LeFalle-Collins, Lizzetta. "Grafton Tyler Brown: Visualizing California and the Pacific Northwest." Exhibition Catalog. California Historical Society, San Francisco. 2003. http://www.californiahistoricalsociety.org/exhibits/gtb.html (accessed July 14, 2011).
Lohse, Bill. "Bruce, Henry Clay (1836–1902)." The Black Past: An Online Guide to African American History. BlackPast.org. http://www.blackpast.org/?q=aaw/bruce-clay-1836–1902 (accessed January 17, 2016).
Mars, Shaun Michael. "Dodson, Jacob (1825-?)." The Black Past: An Online Guide to African American History. BlackPast.org. http://www.blackpast.org/?q=aaw/dodson-jacob-1825? (accessed September 18, 2010).
Mattox, Joe Louis. "Taking Steps to Record Steptoe, Westport's Vanishing African American Neighborhood." *Journal of the Jackson County Historical Society* (Autumn 2004). http://jchs.org/Journal/Autumn%202004/steptoe.htm (accessed March 31, 2013).
McWilliams, Dorothy. "Oregon Territory Attracted Black Pioneer," *The Tumwater Olympian,* n.d. Reprint, City of Tumwater, Washington, March 4, 2008. http://www.ci.tumwater.wa.us/research%20oregon%20territory.htm (accessed September 21, 2010).
Measuring Worth. "Seven Ways to Compute the Relative Value of a U.S. Dollar Amount, 1774 to Present." http://www.measuringworth.com/uscompare (accessed May 30, 2011).
Mid-Missouri Civil War Round Table. "'Uncle' Fil Hancock." Hancock Slave Narrative. Missouri Slave Narratives. http://mmcwrt.missouri.org/SlaveNarrativeHancock.htm (accessed July 21, 2010).
Millner, Darrell. "York." The Black Past: An Online Guide to African American History. BlackPast.org. http://www.historycooperative.org/journals/ohq/104.3/millner.html (accessed September 18, 2010).
Missouri State Archives. "Before Dred Scott: Freedom Suits in Antebellum Missouri: *Rachel v. William Walker* (1836)." Missouri Digital Heritage. http://s1.sos.mo.gov/archives/education/aahi/beforedredscott/rachel-petition (accessed September 11, 2015).
———. "Missouri's Early Slave Laws: A History in Documents. Laws Concerning Slavery in Missouri Territory to 1850s." Missouri Digital Heritage. http://www.sos.mo.gov/archives/education/aahi/earlyslavelaws/slavelaws.asp (accessed August 1, 2010).

———. "Missouri's Dred Scott Case, 1846–1857." Missouri Digital Heritage. http://www.sos.mo.gov/archives/resources/africanamerican/scott/scott.asp (accessed May 19, 2011).

Molson, Jeannette. "Coffey, Alvin Aaron (1822–1902)." The Black Past: An Online Guide to African American History. BlackPast.org. http://www.blackpast.org/?aaw/coffey-alvin-aaron-1822–1902 (accessed July 10, 2011).

Murphy, Miriam B. "Those Pioneering African Americans." *Beehive History 22.* Utah History to Go, State of Utah Website. http://www.historytogo.utah.gov/utah_chapters/pioneers_and_cowboys/thosepioneeringafricanamercans (accessed August 23, 2008 and March 24, 2011).

National Park Service. "Barney L. Ford Building." A National Register Travel Itinerary. Aboard the Underground Railroad. http://www.cr.nps.gov/nr/travel/underground/co1.htm (accessed June 25, 2011).

———. "Bent's Old Fort National Historic Site: History and Culture." Bent's Old Fort National Historic Site, February 22, 2007. http://www.nps.gov/beol/historyculture/index.htm (accessed August 8, 2010).

———. "Black Forty-niners." Death Valley National Park. History and Culture: People. http://www.nps.gov/deva/historyculture/people.htm (accessed August 29, 2011).

———. "James P. Beckwourth, Black Mountain Man." Stories of Exploration, Stories to Be Told: African American History in Your National Parks. http://www.nps.gov/untold/banners_and_backgrounds/adventurbanner/adventurestories/beckwourth.htm (accessed December 19, 2008).

———. CWSAC Battle Summaries. "Glorieta Pass." Heritage Preservation Services, the American Battlefield Protection Program. http://www.nps.gov/hps/abpp/battles/nm002.htm (accessed April 26, 2011).

———. "Year of Disaster: The Great St. Louis Fire and Cholera Epidemic of 1849." http://www.nps.gov/archive/jeff/disaster_year.html (accessed August 8, 2010).

National Underground Railroad Network to Freedom. "The Wigglesworth Kidnapping." Clermont County, Ohio, Freedom Trail. Underground Railroad and Abolitionist Sites: Legacies of Liberty . . . the People and the Places. Clermont County Convention & Visitors Bureau, Batavia, Ohio. http://www.firstohio.com/maps/tours_pdf/Underground_Railroad_Tour.pdf (accessed July 27, 2011).

Oldham, Kit. "George and Mary Jane Washington found the town of Centerville (now Centralia) on January 8, 1875." HistoryLink.org The Free Online Encyclopedia of Washington State History, February 23, 2003. History Ink, Seattle. http://www.historylink.org/essays/output.cfm?file_id=5276 (accessed July 18, 2011).

———. "Washington, George (1817–1905)." The Black Past: An Online Guide to African American History. BlackPast.org. http://www.blackpast.org/?q=aaw/washington-george-1817-1905 (accessed July 18, 2011).

Olsen, Winnifred. "Bush, George (1789?-1863)." The Black Past: An Online Guide to African American History. BlackPast.org. http://www.blackpast.org/?q=aaw/bush-george-1789-1863 (accessed September 21, 2010).

Oregon-California Trails Association. Paper Trail: A Guide to Overland Pioneer Names and Documents. Independence, Mo. http://www.paper-trail.org/ (accessed January 2008-July 2011).

———. "Virtual Tour. Independence Rock." Virtual Trail: Online Adventures on the Oregon Trail. http://www.octatrails.org/learn/virtual_trail/virtual_tour/independence_rock/index.php (accessed August 19, 2010).

Oregon Northwest Black Pioneers. "Louis A. Southworth (1830–1917)." History Briefs. http://www.oregonnorthwestblackpioneers.org/historybriefs.htm (accessed August 8, 2010).

Portland State University, the Oregon Council of Teachers of English, and the Oregon Historical Society. "Louis Southworth (1829–1970)." Oregon Encyclopedia Project. Oregon History and Culture. http://www.oregonencyclopedia.ort/entry/view/southworth_louis_1829_1917 (accessed August 28, 2010).

Pool, Bob. "Bringing a Buffalo Soldier Back to Life." *Los Angeles Times.* September 26, 2008. http://articles.latimes.com/print/2998/sep/26/local/me-honor26 ([accessed February 5, 2004).

Reader, Phil. "To Know My Name: A Chronological History of African Americans in Santa Cruz County." Santa Cruz Public Libraries. Santa Cruz County History—Public Diversity. http://www.santacruzpl.org/history/articles/127/ (accessed August 3, 2010).

Reader, Phil. "Uncle Dave's Story: The Life of Ex-Slave Dave Boffman," Parts 1 and 2. Santa Cruz Public Library. http://www.santacruzpl.org/history/articles/207 (accessed July 21, 2010).

Reid, John. "Peter Ranne of the Jedediah Strong Smith Party." *One: The Online Nevada Encyclopedia.* http://www.onlinenevada.org/peter_ranne_of_the_jedediah_strong_smith_party (accessed March 9, 2013).

Roberts, Sylvia Alden. "Sugg Family of Sonora Left Their Mark." City of Sonora. http://www.sonoraca.com/visitsonora/History/people-thesuggfamily.htm (accessed September 25, 2010).

Ruffin, Herbert G., II. "*Sistema de Castas* (1500s–ca.1829)." The Black Past: An Online Guide to African American History. BlackPast.org. http://www.blackpast.org/?q-aaw/sistema-de-castas-1500s-ca-1829 (accessed July 4, 2011).

San Bernardino Historical and Pioneer Society. "The Area's First Black College Graduate: Alice Rowan Johnson." The City of San Bernardino, California,

1983. http://www.sbcity.org/about/history/pioneer_women/alice_rowan_johnson.asp (accessed August 2, 2013).

Sharp, Jay W. "Desert Trails: Kit Carson and the Santa Fe Trail." Desert USA. http://www.desertusa.com/mag03/trails/trails08.html (accessed August 9, 2010).

Shubert, Frank. "The Myth of the Buffalo Soldier." The Black Past: An Online Guide to African American History. BlackPast.org.http://www.blackpast.or/perspectives/myth-buffalo-soldiers (accessed January 29, 2014).

St. Louis Circuit Court Historical Records Project. "Freedom Suits Case Files, 1814–1860." http://www.stlcourtrecords.wustl.edu/about-freedom-suits-series.php (accessed September 12, 2015).

———. "History of Freedom Suits in Missouri." http://stlcourtrecords.wustl.edu/about-freedom-suits-history.php (accessed September 12, 2015).

Stillwell, Ted. "Sam Shepard and the Broadaxe." Independence, Missouri *Examiner,* January 3, 2002. http://nl.newesbank.com/nlarch/we/Archives?p_action=doc&p_docid=1228BC45B1A41 (accessed July 23, 2010).

Taylor, Quintard. "African-American Dreams Helped Shape This Region." *Seattle Times.*

February 29, 2004. http://community.seattletimes.nwsource.com/archive/?date=20040229&slug=sunquintard29 (accessed September 21, 2010).

Trails West, Inc. "Markers of the California Trail: Historical Development of the California Trail. http://www.emigranttrailswest.org/caltrail.htm (accessed August 8, 2010).

Trexler, Harrison Anthony. *Slavery in Missouri, 1804–1865.* 1914. Digital reprint, Internet Archive. http://www.dinsdoc.com/trexler-1-0b.htm (accessed April 12, 2011).

Truneh, Sophia. "The Ilfelds: A Family Story of Jewish Pioneers in New Mexico." *Southwest Jewish History* 3, no. 2 (Winter 1995). http://parentseyes.arizona.edu/bloom/sjhilfeld.htm (accessed May 3, 2011).

Utah State Division of Parks and Recreation. "The Mormon Pioneer Trail." http://www.americanwest.com/trails/pages/mormtrl.htm (accessed August 8, 2010).

Wagner, Patricia Martineau. "Clara Brown (1803–1885)." The Black Past: An Online Guide to African American History. BlackPast.org. http://www.blackpast.org/?q=aaw/brown-clara-1803-1885 (accessed September 24, 2010).

———. "Drake, Mary Jane Holmes Shipley (1841–1925)." The Black Past: An Online Guide to African American History. BlackPast.org. http://www.blackpast.org/?=aaw/drake-mary-jane-holmes-shipley-1841-1925 (accessed July 25, 2008).

Yee, Shirley. "National Negro Convention Movement (1831–1864)." The Black Past: An Online Guide to African American History. BlackPast.org. http://www

.blackpast.org/aah/national-negro-convention-movement-1831-1864 (accessed September 19, 2015).
Young, Margaret Blair. "Abel, Elijah (1810–1884)." The Black Past: An Online Guide to African American History. BlackPast.org. http://www.blackpast.org/?q=aaw/abel-elijah-1810-1884 (accessed July 7, 2011).
———. "Flake, Green (1828–1903), The Black Past: An Online Guide to African American History. BlackPast.org. http://www.blackpast.org/?q=aaw/flake-green-1828-1903 (accessed July 24, 2008).
———. "Green Flake: Who Can Tell His Story?" Patheos Mormon: Hosting the Conversation on Faith. http://www.patheos.com/Mormon/Green-Flake-Margaret-Blair-Young (accessed January 14, 2016).
Zaid, Shanti. "Aunt Clara Brown." Colorado Historical Society, http://www.historycolorado.org/sites/default/files/files/Kids_Students/Bios/Aunt_Clara_Brown.pdf (accessed September 24, 2010).
Zion Baptist Church. "Zion Baptist Church—Historical Sketch." Zion Baptist Church & Ministries, Denver, 2008. http://www.zionbaptistchurchdenver.org/index.php?option=com_content%view=article&id (accessed September 23, 2010).
Ziontz, Lenore. "George and Isabella Bush: Washington's First Family." City of Tumwater, Washington, March 4, 2008. http://www.ci.tumwater.wa.us/reserch%20george%20&%20isabella%20bush.htm (accessed July 29, 2010).

Newspapers

Border Star (Westport, Missouri). "To Correspondents," January 1, 1859. Digital reprint, the State Historical Society of Missouri, Missouri Digital Heritage: Hosted Collections. http://cdm.sos.mo.gov/cdm4/browse.php?CISOROOT (accessed March 28, 2013).
Bozeman (Montana) Daily Chronicle. Gail Schontzler. "McDonald House Holds History of Freed Slaves Who Helped Settle Bozeman," February 13, 2011.
Daily Alta California. December 4, 1852.
Far West (Liberty, Missouri). "The Mormons-Unparalleled Impudence." August 18, 1836. Digital reprint, The State Historical Society of Missouri, Missouri Digital Heritage: Hosted Collections. http://cdm.sos.mo.gov/cdm4/document.php?CISOROOT (accessed March 28, 2013).
Independence Examiner. Adrianne DeWeese, "Top 10: The People and Places Who Made Up a Rich Black History in Independence," February 19, 2010.
Modesto (California) Bee, "Mining Mother Lode's Black History," January 20, 2008.
Pacific Appeal. August 16, 1862.
Sacramento Transcript. September 23, 1850.

Salt Lake Tribune. Hal Schindler. "Bullwhacking Was No Snap: Occupied Lowest Rung on the Social Ladder." October 29, 1995.

Maps

Franzwa, Gregory. "Covered Wagon Roads to the American West." Tucson: The Patrice Press, 1998.

Tennessee Genealogy & History. "Trails West: A Map of Early Western Migration Trails." TNGenNet, 2000. http://www.tngenweb.org/tnletters/usa-west.htm (accessed June 26, 2011).

Index

References to illustrations appear in italic type.

Abel, Elijah, 251n50
Absarokas. *See* Crows
accidents, 143–45, 156
Adams, Cecelia, 143
African Observer, 32, 52
Alex (slave), 121, 144
Alexander, Charles and Nancy, *101*, 180–82, 230
Alexander, Gay, *102*, 181–82
Alexander, Harold, *102*, 180, 181, 182
Allen, William, 150–51
Alta California, 200
Alvarez, Manuel, 59
American Society of Free Persons of Color, 50
American West. *See* West, American
Amesti, Don José, 165
Anderson, Robert Ball, 130, 138–39, 140, 284n31
Andy (black man in J. Goldsborough Bruff's party), 16, 123, 133, 148, 158
Anthony, Elihu, 172
antiblack laws: in Arizona, 42–43; in California, 198, 201–2, 212; in Colorado, 221, 222; in Connecticut, 40; in Indiana, 41; in Massachusetts, 40; in Missouri, 35, 61, 208, 245n12; in Montana, 42; in Nevada, 43, 215; in New Jersey, 40; in New Mexico, 42; in New York, 40–41; in Ohio, 41; in Oregon, 43–44, 173–74, 207, 249n43; in Pennsylvania, 41; in Utah, 47, 253n60; in Wisconsin, 41

Applegate Trail, 30, 79–80, 114
Arikaras, 25
Arizona, 42–43, 138, 248n36, 291n1
Arnett, John, 136
Ashley, William, 26, 29
Atchison, Kans., 177
Austin, Stephen, 39

Bagley, Will, 15, 85, 121, 130
Bailey, Mary Stuart, 144
Baker, Edward Lee, Jr., 149–50
Baker, Roger, 68–69, 264n56
bandits: overlanders killed by, 136; "white Indians" as, 16, 131, 155
Bankhead, Alexander, 176
Bankhead, John H., 55, 57
Bankhead, Marinda Redd, 175–76
Banks, John Edwin, 143–44, 160
Barber, David and Charlotte, 213, 214
Bartleson, John, 86
Bassett, William, 77, 114, 146, 169, 294n42
Batchelder, Amos, 111–12
Baughman, Henry, 71
Baughman, Newton, 71–72
Beale's Wagon Road, 81, 82
Beasley, Delilah, 11, 161, 168
Beck, Sorepaw, 220
Beckwourth, James Pierson, 18, 26–29, *96*, 239n37
Beckwourth Trail, 27–28, 238n30
Bellevue, Nebr., 76
Bent, Charles, 127, 128

357

Bent, William, 127, 128
Benton, Thomas Hart, 87–88
Bent's Old Fort, 127–28
Berryman, George, 15, 115
Bidwell, John, 86
Bidwell-Bartleson Party, 86
Big Meadows, 80, 81
black elected officials, 223–24
black entrepreneurs, 59–60, 62–66, 74, 207, 213–15, 216–18, 221–24, 230
Blackfeet, 27
black rights, struggle for, 50, 60–61, 212, 225; for Archy Lee's freedom, 202; for education, 167–68; for voting rights, 222–23, 231
Blair, Gus, 109
Blodgett, General, 152
Bluford (slave), 178, 230
Boffman, Dave, 71–72, 131–32, 171–73, 230
Bonga, George, 240n38
Bonner, Thomas, 28
Booker, Louis, 161
border states, 35–39
Bowman, Jonathan P., 179
Bowman, Lorenzo, 217
Boyle, Charles, 110
Bozeman, Mont., 183–84
Brewer, Eliza Jane, 216, 219–20
British Columbia, 181, 182–83, 202
Broad Ax, 176
Broussard, Albert S., 22, 231
Brown, Adam Mercer, 66
Brown, Clara, 70, *104*; and Barney Ford, 220, 221, 224; search for daughter by, 216, 219–20; story of, 68–69, 216–20
Brown, David, 69, 70, 184–91
Brown, Elizabeth Crosby, 159
Brown, Grafton Tyler, 226–28
Brown, Henry, 55–57, 256n3
Brown, John (Mormon convert), 55, 56–57
Brown, John Lowery, 147, 158

Brown, Peter, 178–79
Brown, Rachel, 68, 184–86, 188–91
Brown, William Wells, 70–71
Bruce, Henry Clay, 176–78, 230
Bruff, J. Goldsborough, 16, 89, 123, 133, 148, 158
Bruin, Madison, 138
Brunner, Jacob, 216
Bryant, Edwin, 86–87, 92, 116
Buffalo Soldiers, 15, 137–43, 283n23; and disease, 140, 285n34; organization of, 283n24; racial prejudice faced by, 142; reasons for joining, 138–39
Buller, Vardaman, 112
Bunyard, Harriet, 138
Burnett, Peter H., 43
Bush, George W., 70, 262n51; congressional act on, 207–8; generosity of, 67–68, 150; in Oregon Country, 206–8; as skilled overlander, 30, 121, 230
Bush, Isabella, 206, 207, 208
Bushman, Ben, 84, 94
Byrnes, Edward, 140–41

Cabeza de Vaca, Álvar Nuñez, 20
California: African American population in, 291n1; antiblack laws in, 198, 201–2, 212; Fugitive Slave Act in, 45–46, 201, 202; and slavery, 44–45, 182, 199, 211, 250n47; southern trails to, 81–84
California gold rush, 27, 71, 82, 117, 180, 186–88
California Trail, 71, 78, 79, 80–81, 94, 180. *See also* Oregon-California Trail
Call, Asa Cyrus, 87
Campbell, Alex, 144
Campbell, Donald, 121
Campbell, J. L., 66
Canada: British Columbia, 181, 182–83, 202; emigration societies and, 48–49

INDEX

Carrington, Henry, 28–29
Carson, Kit, 84, 138
Carson River, 80, 81, 181
Carson Valley, 200, 213–15
Carter, Jennie, 226
Carter, Robert W., 109
Casner, George, 26
Casper, Wyo., 77, 145
Castañeda, Pedro de, 18
Central City, Colo., 184, 216–17, 218
Centralia, Wash., 209, 262n51
Chaffee, Calvin, 52
Cherokees, 40, 82
Cherokee Trail, 82
Cheyenne, Wyo., 222
Cheyennes, 131–32, 141–42, 281n5
childbirth, 148–50
cholera: black troops and, 140, 285n34; in Independence, Mo., 30, 146; overlanders and, 145–47, 286n46, 287–88n53
Churchill, C. C., 121, 146
Cimarron Cutoff, 84, 94
Cincinnati, Ohio, 48–49, 50
Civil War, 40, 48, 65, 66, 138, 224; and slave emancipation, 176, 183; transformation of trail security by, 137, 155–56
Clark, Bennett C., 110
Clark, John Hawkins, 288n53
Clark, William, 23
Clarke, Lewis Garrard, 32, 33
Claycome, Reverend, 72
Clayton, William, 86
Clyman, James, 29, 240n39
Cochrane, James and Anna, 208, 209
Coffey, Alvin Aaron, 77, 97, 133, 137, 146, 230, 294n42, 295n45; as driver, 109, 114–15; story of, 168–71
Coffey, Mahala Tindall, 98, 169, 170
Colbourne, John, 48
Coleman, Ronald G., 203, 205, 257n9

Colorado, 28, 223, 224; antiblack law in, 221, 222. *See also* Denver, Colo.
Colored American Joint Stock Quartz Mining Company, 188
Columbia River, 30, 79, 207, 209
Connecticut, 40
Continental Divide, 77–78, 82
Convention of Colored Citizens of the State of California, 212, 225
cooks, 122–23, 127–28
Coolbrith, Ina, 27
Cooness (Cornie), Mary Jane, 209
Coronado, Francisco Vásquez de, 21
Corvallis, Ore., 175, 197
Corvallis Daily Gazette, 174
cotton, 37, 71, 244n10
Council Bluffs (Kanesville), Iowa, 57, 58, 61, 76, 219
Council Bluffs Nonpareil, 219
Cox, Cornelius C., 134
Creek, Charles, 138
Crim, Samuel, 186
Crimson, Charles, 55
Crissup, Thomas, 48, 254n65
Crocker, Edwin B., 201
Crosby, Oscar, 55, 112, 256n3
Crows, 25, 27, 29
Curtis, William, 64–65
Custer, Elizabeth, 142

Dalton, John, 115
Daniels, Douglas, 70, 229
Davies, John Johnson, 115
Death Valley, 82
de Graaf, Lawrence B., 14
Demarest, David, 110–11
Denver, Colo., 28, 85, 184, 216–18, 219–20; Clara Brown and Barney Ford in, 216–17, 218, 219–24
Denver Republican, 219
Denver Tribune Republican, 220
de Olvera, Isabel, 22
Derrick, John, 166, 167
Detter, Thomas, 225–26

Devil's Gate, 77–78
Dick (slave), 125
disease: Buffalo Soldiers and, 140, 145–48, 156, 285n34; caring for victims of, 148; cholera, 140, 145–47, 285n34, 286n46, 287–88n53; pneumonia and influenza, 56
Doble, John, 126
Dodson, Jacob, 87, 95
Donation Land Claim Act, 150, 207, 209
Donner Party, 78, 112
Doolittle, James R., 42
Dorantes de Carranza, Andrés, 19
Drake, R. G., 197
Dred Scott decision, 51–52, 53, 255n76
Drisdom, Annie, 172, 173
drivers, 111–20
drownings, 144–45
Dulany, William, 160
Dunleavy, James, 92
Durivage, John E., 134, 152
Duval, P. S., 227

Eccleston, Robert, 126–27
Echo Canyon, 112
Eddy, Josiah, 161
education, 61, 167–68, 224
Elko, Nev., 225
Emanuel (slave), 136, 154
Emerson, John, 51
Emigrants' Guide to California, The (Ware), 87
Emigrants' Guide to Oregon and California, The (Hastings), 86
Emigration Canyon, 112
Emory, William, 87
Empires, Nations, and Families: A New History of the North American West, 1800–1860 (Hyde), 15
Esteban, 18, 19–20, 236n3
Estes, Agnes, 162, 163

Estes, Hannah, 76, *100*, 154, 162, 163, 164; work ethic of, 123, 182–83
Estes, Howard, *100*, 162–65, 182–83, 230
Estes, Jackson, 76, 134, 137, 162, 164
Estes, Sylvia. *See* Stark, Sylvia Estes
Estes, Tom, 162–63
Etter, Patricia, 157
Evans, Lewis, 82
Ewers, John C., 237n13

Fairchild, Lucius, 58
family separation, 184–91
Farmer, Allen, 176
Fifteenth Amendment, 42, 215, 223
Finley, Henry, 69, 70
Fisher, Adam, 62
Fisher, Belle, 183, 184
Fisher, Emily, 62–63, *96*, 230
Fisher, James, 14
Flake, Elizabeth "Lizzy," 112, 113–14
Flake, Green, 112–13, 256n3
Flake, James and Agnes, 112
Flanagan, Daniel, 65
Flewellen, Betsy and Kate, 159
Flitch, Joseph, 203
food prices, 66–68
Forbes, Jack, 14, 142
Ford, Barney Launcelot, 84–85, *104*, 220–24
Ford, Julia, 220, 224
Ford, Julia Lyoni, 85
Ford, Nathaniel, 30, 159, 194–95, 196
Forsyth, George A., 140
Fort Bridger, Wyo., 67, 78, 179, 180
Fort Laramie, Wyo., 28, 72, 77, 141, 143
Fort Leavenworth, Kans., 65, 68, 139, 177, 178, 184
forts, 127, 140, 285n34
Fort Smith, Ark., 81, 158
Fort Smith–Santa Fe Trail, 157
Fort Wallace, Kans., 142
Forty Mile Desert, 80, 81, 181
Fourteenth Amendment, 42

Francaviglia, Richard V., 15, 93
freedom suits, 36–37, 245n15, 246n16
Frémont, John C., 87–88
Frink, Margaret, 81
Fugitive Slave Act (national), 44, 200–201, 250n46
Fugitive Slave Law (California), 45–46, 201, 202
fur trade, 24–25, 26–27, 59

Garrard, Lewis H., 128
Genovese, Eugene, 56
Gila Trail, 75, 122, 126, 134, 152; about, 82–83
Gill, William, 112
Gilliam-Simmons-Bush-Ford wagon company, 29–30
Gilmore, Eliza Smith, 218–19
Gilpin, William, 87
Gooch, Andrew, 99, 162
Gooch, Nancy and Peter, 99, 160–61, 162
Gooch, William D., 161
Goodell, Anna Maria, 116, 159
Gordon, Frances, 72, 73
Gray, W. H., 29
Great Platte River Road, 54, 76–78
Green, Andrew, 128, 281n5
Green, Charlotte, 127–28
Green, Dick, 128
Green, Edmund, 110
Green, Lorenzo, 60
Grierson, Benjamin H., 283n24
Guadalupe Pass, 157
guard duty, 133–34
Guenther, Todd, 132
Guerra de Resa, Juan, 22
guides, 110–11
Gutiérrez, Ramón A., 20

Hackett, Charles, 200
Haight, Isaac C., 67
Hannah (slave), 149, 198–99
Hardin, William Jefferson, 223–24

Hardy, James H., 201
Harker, George Mifflin, 148
Harmony, Manuel X., 59
Harris, Benjamin Butler, 122–23, 125
Harris, Moses "Black," 29–30, 239–40nn37–40; and Applegate Trail, 79–80; as guide, 30, 241n43
Harris, Samuel, 138
Hastings, Lansford W., 66, 78, 86
Hastings Cutoff, 78
Hatch, Edward, 283n24
Haun, Catherine, 122
Hayes, Benjamin Ignatius, 82, 198–99
Hazen, William H., 283n24
Heiskell, Hugh Brown, 121, 123, 124, 144, 158
Hell Gate (Devil's Gap), 139
Hemings, Sally, 89–90
hemp, 37, 246n19
Hensley, William, 154
herders, 116–18
Hickman, W. Z., 111
Hickok, Wild Bill, 138
hiring-out arrangements, 38
Holmes, Harriet, 194, 195
Holmes, James, 194, 195
Holmes, Mary Jane, 30, 159, 195, 196–97
Holmes, Polly, 30, 159, 194, 196
Holmes, Robin, 30, 159, 193–97
Holmes, Roxanna, 194, 195
Holmes v. Ford, 195–96
Hudlin, Doug, 180, 181, 182
Humboldt River, 79, 80, 164, 181
Humboldt Sink, 80, 81, 111–12
Huning, Franz, 140–41
hunters, 121–22
Hurtado, Albert L., 4
Hyde, Anne F., 4, 15, 19, 59, 127

Ice Slough, 77–78
Ilfeld, Charles, 59

Independence, Mo., 73, 84, 91, 117; black community in, 61–66; cholera in, 30, 146; as outfitting town, 57, 59, 64, 111, 260n28
Independence Daily Union, 30
Independence Rock, 77, 240n40
Indiana, 41
Indians: black views toward, 132–33; Buffalo Soldiers engagement against, 139, 142; charity and assistance rendered by, 151–52, 155; legal rights of, 43, 222; raids on overlanders conducted by, 25, 26, 84, 130–31, 134–36, 141, 181; relocation of, 40; view of blacks by, 3, 131–32, 155, 261n5, 281n5; violence against, 13, 16, 133
In Search of the Racial Frontier: African Americans in the American West, 1528–1900 (Taylor), 14–15
intermarriage, 19
invisibility, 8, 12, 156, 158–59
Isaac (slave), 134, 152
Ivory, Matthew, 55

Jackson (ranch manager), 83, 94, 270n26
Jackson, John, 151
Jackson, Rose, 150–51
James, Isaac, 203, 204–5
James, Jane Elizabeth Manning, 203–6
James, Richard, 187
Jefferson, T. H., 75, 78, 89–94, 95, 229
Jefferson, Thomas, 89–90
Jenkins, George, 180
Johnson, Amanda and Benjamin, 173
Johnson, Jack, 124
Johnson, Jacob and Sarah, 161–62
Johnson, Robert, 166, 167
Johnston, George Pen, 202
Jordan, Winthrop, 242–43n2
Journal of Negro History, 14
jumping-off places, 54–74; black communities in, 60–66; definition of, 54–55; diversity in, 58–60; exploitation of emigrants in, 57–58; getting to, 55–57; racial hostility and discrimination in, 62, 70–73, 74; and trade, 57, 59, 259n22
Junction City, Kans., 140–41

Kanesville (Council Bluffs), Iowa, 57, 58, 61, 76, 219
Kansas, 138, 176–78, 218–19; Bleeding Kansas struggle, 50; overland trails through, 75–76, 84, 87
Kansas City, 55, 63, 75, 260n32
Kansas-Nebraska Act, 50, 52
Katz, William Loren, 14, 41, 137–38, 184, 250n47
Keemle, Charles, 25
Kelawatsets, 26
Kelsey, John, 174
Kentucky, 36–38, 246nn18–19
Kinkaid, James, 90
Kinney Cutoff, 78
Kiowa, 141
Knowlton, Miss, 168
Korns, Roderic, 92
Kountze, Luther, 221
Kuchel, C. C., 227
Kusick, Amos, 136, 137
Kusick, Sam, 136

Labrosse, Polette, 26
LaFayette County, Mo., 73, 265–66n74
Lambertson, John Mark, 185
Lander Road, 78
Lapp, Rudolph, 14, 123, 146, 263n55
Lasselle, Stanislaus, 131
Lassen (Nobles) Trail, 79
Lay, Hark, 55, 112, 256n3
Leavenworth, Kans., 75, 216, 218, 219. *See also* Fort Leavenworth
Leckie, William H., 15
Lee (slave), 160
Lee, Archy, 193, 199–202, 230

Lee, Jeremiah, 217
LeFalle-Collins, Lizzetta, 227
Leonard, Zenas, 23, 25, 237–38n18
Leopold, Charles, 123, 163–64
Lewis, Israel, 48, 254n65
Lewis, Meriwether, 23, 90
Lewis, Nancy, 184
Liberty, Mo., 63
Lippincott, Benjamin S., 91–92
Lisa, Manuel, 24, 237n13
Little Blue River, 64, 75
Little Mountain, 112
"Little West," 82, 269n23
Lorton, William, 82–83, 152
Los Angeles, Calif., 21–22, 198–99
Louis, Edward, 153
Love, John, 69
Lovelock, Nebr., 80
Lower Emigrant Road, 81–82
Lyman, Eliza, 205

MacKenzie, Kenneth, 265n68
Malvin, John, 32, 48
Mangas Coloradas, 132, 281n8
Manly, William Lewis, 73
Mapping and Imagination in the Great Basin (Francaviglia), 15
maps, 85–88, 89–94
Marcos de Niza, 20
Mason, Bridget "Biddy," *102*, 116, 149, 159, 197–99
Massachusetts: antiblack laws in, 40
Mattes, Merrill J., 3, 15, 54, 76, 286n44
McAdams, Samuel, 171
McCollum, T., 143, 286n46
McCombs, Henry, 142–43
McCoy, William, 63
McDiarmid, Finley, 146
McDonald, Dedra S., 21
McDonald, Richard and Mary, 58, *107*, *108*, 183–84
McDonald, Vernon Sugg, 210, 211, 213

McGee, Alney, 134
McKune, John H., 201
McNair, Clem, 158
Meachum, John Berry, 60–61
Meeker, Ezra, 208, 288n53
Meeks, Stephen, 30
Mendoza, Don Antonio de, 20
Mexican War, 88
Mexico, 39, 157
Miles, Nelson A., 283n24
Millard, Charles Thomas, 187–88
Miller, Alfred Jacob, 29, 239n38
Miller, Sophia and Winfield, 215
Millner, Darrell, 208
Minersville, Nebr., 76
Minto, John, 67, 121, 206, 262n51
Mission San Gabriel, 21
"Mississippi Boys" party, 82, 269n23
"Mississippi Saints," 55–56, 256–57n3
Missouri, 59, 246n19; black population in, 60–66; and *Dred Scott* case, 51–52, 255n76; freedom suits filed in, 36–37, 245n15, 246n16; slave code and antiblack laws in, 35, 61, 208, 245n12; slavery in, 35–36, 183, 244n10, 245n12; Supreme Court on slaves in, 70, 265n68
Missouri Republican, 91
Missouri River, 146, 177, 178, 186; as jumping-off place, 54–55, 61, 70, 73–74, 75, 76
mob violence, 47–50, 53
Molson, Jeannette, 114, 133
Monroe (Gooch) family, 99
Montana, 42, 183–84
Moorman, Madison Berryman, 117, 118, 119, 121–22
Morgan, Dale L., 15, 89
Mormon Road, 83
Mormons, 203–4, 205, 293n23; attacks on emigrants by, 164, 210–11, 293n23; maps produced by, 86; Salt Lake Valley as destination of,

364　　　　　　　　　　　　　INDEX

Mormons (cont.)
  47, 76, 78, 112, 130–31, 204, 241n43;
  settlements by, 76; and slavery,
  45–46, 197, 251n50, 253n56; slaves
  during migration of, 55–56, 256n3;
  westward migration of, 55–56, 67,
  130–31, 204, 241n43, 256–57n3
Mormon Trail, 76, 77, 78, 94
mortality rates, 143, 156, 286n44
Moss, Rick, 242n47
motives and expectations, 3–4, 5, 8–9,
  159, 165, 173, 191–92, 225–28; of
  free blacks, 4, 178–84; of slaves, 4,
  160–78
Mountain Meadows Massacre, 164,
  293n23
mountain men, 24–26
Mower, Joseph A., 283n24
Murieta, Joaquin, 136

Narváez, Pánfilo de, 19
Nauvoo, Ill., 45–46, 112, 204,
  253n60
Nebraska City, Nebr., 76
"Negro Joe," 82, 269n23
Negro on the American Frontier, The
  (Porter), 14
Negro Trail Blazers of California
  (Beasley), 11
Nevada, 43, 213–15
New Jersey, 40
New Market, Wash., 207
New Mexico, 59, 81, 84, 128;
  African Americans in, 42, 157,
  248n36
New Spain: Esteban in, 18, 19–20,
  236n3; expeditions to, 21–22,
  236–37n8; as geographic region,
  18; racial classification in, 33,
  241–42n47; women of African
  descent in, 21–22
New York City draft riot (1863), 50
New York State, 40–41
Nicaragua, 84, 85, 220

Nobles Trail, 79, 114
Nowlin, Bryant, 55

Ohio, 41, 48–49, 185
Oklahoma, 40
Old Spanish Trail, 27, 81, 83, 157–58
Old Wyoming, Nebr., 76
Olney, Cyrus, 195
one-drop rule, 33, 35, 52–53
Onorato (Franciscan friar), 20
Oregon: antiblack laws in, 43–44,
  173–74, 207, 249n43; and slavery,
  43, 195–96
Oregon-California Trail, 77, 78–79,
  135, 143, 150, 230
Oregon City, Ore., 208–9
Oregon Spectator, 79–80
Oregon Trail, 77–79, 87
Otto, George, 172
overland journeys, 109–29, 191–92;
  abusive treatment of blacks
  during, 125–27; accidents during,
  143–45; childbirth during, 148–50;
  cooks on, 122–23, 127–28; cost of,
  66–70; disease during, 56, 145–48,
  156, 287–88n53; drivers on, 111–21;
  guides on, 110–11; hunters on,
  121–22; mortality rates during, 143,
  156, 286n44; servants on, 124–27;
  statistics on, 3, 157–58, 233n1, 291n1;
  wagon companies and, 68–69,
  263n55, 264n56; wagons and
  carriages for, 57
overland parties: Gilliam-Simmons-
  Bush-Ford, 29–30; "Mississippi
  Boys," 82, 269n23; "Mississippi
  Saints," 55–56, 256–57n3;
  Southwest Expedition (1826–27),
  25–26; Whitman-Spalding, 29
overland routes, 6–7, 75–95, 157–58;
  Applegate Trail, 30, 79–80, 114;
  Beckwourth Trail, 27–28, 238n30;
  California Trail, 71, 78, 79, 80–81,
  94, 180; Cherokee Trail, 82; Gila

Trail, 75, 82–83, 122, 126, 134, 152; Humboldt River Trail, 79, 80, 181; Lassen Trail, 79; maps of, 85–88, 89–94; Mormon Trail, 76, 77, 78, 94; Nobles Trail, 79, 114; Old Spanish Trail, 27, 81, 83, 157–58; Oregon-California Trail, 77, 78–79, 135, 143, 150, 230; Oregon Trail, 77–79, 87; Santa Fe Trail, 59, 63–64, 81, 83–84, 127, 157; Sonora route, 153; Southern Trail, 81–82, 157
Owens, Charles, 198, 199
Owens, John, 135
Owens, Kenneth N., 257n3
Owens, Robert and Minnie, 197–98, 199
oxen, 64, 77, 79, 82, 113–14, 115–16, 166, 183, 200, 218; about, 111; prices of, 67, 262n50

Pacific Appeal, 193, 202, 225
Padilla, Juan de, 21
Paiutes, 181
Palmer, Ben, *106*, 213–15
Parker, Charles W., 200, 201
Parkhill, Forbes, 220
Parkman, Francis, 57, 58, 151–52
Pate, Henry Clay, 61
Patterson, Edward H. N., 54, 58
Patterson, E. M., 117
Patterson, Hugh E., 117
Pennsylvania, 41, 50
Pepper, Manuel, 198
Philadelphia, Pa., 50
Pico, Don Jesus, 88
Pierce, Franklin, 88
Pilton, James William, 180
Placer Argus, 120
Placerville, Calif., 119, 165, 180
Platte River, 75, 76–78, 144–45, 157
Plattsmouth, Nebr., 76
Pleasants, William J., 136, 154
pneumonia, 56

Point of Rocks (N.Mex.), 84
Porter, John T., 172
Porter, Kenneth Wiggins, 14
Porter, Lavinia Honeyman, 115–16, 122
Portsmouth, Ohio, 49, 91
posses, 133
Potter, Theodore Edgar, 109, 122, 123, 125
Powell, Capt. A., 125
Powell, David, 55
Pownall, Joseph, 132
Pratt, Orson, 112
Price, Jemima, 90–91, 93
prices, 66–68, 241n44
Prudomme, Victor, 83
Punch, John, 242–43n2
Pyle, Benjamin, 73, 265n74
Pyle, Charlotta Gordon and Harry MacHenry, 72–73

racial identity, 31; in New Spain, 33, 241–42n47; and one-drop rule, 33, 52–53
Raft River, 79
Randolph, John, 49
Ranne, Peter, 25–26
Rapier, Henry, 119–20
Rapier, James Thomas, 117, 119
Rapier, John H., Sr., 116, 119
Rapier, Richard G. (Dick), 116–20, 121
Ravage, John W., 14, 157
Ray, Nelson and Lucinda, 179–80
Record-Courier (Gardnerville, Nev.), 215
Red, White and Blue Smelting Company, 217
Redmond (colored) v. Murray et al., 245n12
Reid, Bernard, 30
Richardson, Charlie, 70
Richardson, Constance Moore, 89
Rieck, Richard L., 131
Riker, James, 202

Rio Grande, 20, 82, 157
Rivera, Fernando X., 21
Robinson, Harriet, 51–52
Robinson, Robert, 201
Rock Ranch, 135–36, 282n18
Rocky Mountains, 5, 26, 29, 30, 88; emigrant trails through, 75, 77, 78, 92
Rodgers, Artimisa Penwright, 165, 293n26
Rodgers, Daniel, 165–68, 230, 293–94n27
Rodgers, Redmond, 165, 166
Rollin, George M., 187
Roman Nose (Cheyenne), 142
Rose, Edward, 24–25, 237n13, 237–38n18
Rowan, Charles H., 113–14, 197
Rusco, Elmer R., 43
Russell, William, 91–92
Ruxton, George Frederick, 29, 239–40n38

Sacramento Transcript, 153
Salt Lake City and Valley, 112, 118–19; African Americans in, 45, 250n48; black overlanders traveling to, 149, 164–65, 203, 204, 293n23; as Mormon destination, 47, 76, 78, 112, 130–31, 204, 241n43
Sanderlin, Edward, 223
Sanford, Eliza Irene, 51
San Francisco Elevator, 225, 226
Santa Cruz Sentinel, 173
Santa Fe, N.Mex., 22, 81
Santa Fe Trail, 59, 63–64, 81, 83–84, 127, 157
Savage, W. Sherman, 14, 63
security needs, 133–37; Buffalo Soldiers and, 139–41, 156
sexual assault and abuse, 16, 126, 129, 133
Shipley, Reuben, 196–97

Shirley, James A., 196
Shoshone River, 25
Shoshones, 181
Siegmann, Herman, 171
Simmons, Michael, 67
Sioux, 151–52
slave codes, 34; in Kentucky, 37; in Missouri, 35, 245n12; in New Mexico, 42; in Utah, 47; in Virginia, 38–39. *See also* antiblack laws
slave hunters, 70–73
slavery, 34, 242–43n2; Arizona and, 43; California and, 44–45, 182, 199, 211, 250n47; and *Dred Scott* case, 51–52, 53, 255n76; and fugitive slave laws, 44, 45–46, 200–201, 202, 250n46; Kansas struggle over, 50; Kentucky and, 36–38, 246nn18–19; and manumission prices, 162, 163, 166, 170, 174, 175, 211; Missouri and, 35–36, 183, 244n10, 245n12; Missouri court cases concerning, 36–37, 245n15, 246n16; Mormons and, 45–47, 197, 251n50, 253n56; Nevada and, 43; Oregon and, 43, 195–96; and slave auctions, 38, 71, 73, 166; Texas and, 39–40; Utah and, 45–47; Virginia and, 38–39, 242–43n2, 247n21
Sloan, Old Uncle Dick, 136
Smith, Gladys Owens, 199
Smith, Jabez, 64, 146
Smith, Jackson, 219
Smith, Jedediah, 25–26
Smith, Joseph, 204; and slavery, 45–46, 251n50
Smith, Robert, 149, 159, 197, 198
Smith, Thomas, 27
Smith, Tornelia Williams, 98
Snake River, 78–79
Snelling, Mary Elizabeth, 146–47, 210–11
Sonora, Calif., *105*, 166, 210, 211–12
Southern Trail, 81–82, 157

South Pass, 77–78, 82, 92, 180
Southwest Expedition of 1826–27, 25–26
Southworth, Lewis Alexander, *103*, 173–75
Spedden, Rush, 90
Split Rock, 77–78
Stark, Louis, 182
Stark, Sylvia Estes, *101*, 123, 163; in British Columbia, 182–83; overland recollections of, 76–77, 94, 130, 134, 154–55; in Salt Lake City, 164–65, 293n23
Stephenson, W. H. C., 229, 231
Stewart, George R., 93
St. Joseph, Mo., 73, 146; as jumping-off place, 57, 58, 59, 186; as outfitting town, 61, 66, 260n28
St. Joseph Gazette, 30
St. Louis, Mo., 24, 51, 52, 72, 146, 180, 216; black community in, 60–61; as jumping-off place, 54–55, 59, 91, 117; slave auctions in, 73
Stone, Nathan, 72
Story, Middleton, 154
Stovall, Charles, 200, 201–2
Stover, Jacob, 83, 94, 270n26
Stratton, Joseph, 55
Stuart, Joseph Alonzo, 80, 94, 151
Sturgeon, Thomas, 186
St. Vrain, Ceran, 127
Sublette, William, 240n40
Sublette Cutoff, 78
Sugg House, *105*, 211–13
Suggs, Mary Elizabeth and William, *105*, 210–13
Summers, Mr. and Mrs., 134
Sutton, John L., 26
Sweetwater River, 77

Tabor, Horace Austin Warner, 184
Taney, Roger B., 52
Taylor, Bayard, 152–53
Taylor, Henry, 28
Taylor, James, 160
Taylor, Quintard, 14–15, 19, 142, 228
Territorial Suffrage Act, 42, 223
Texas, 81–82, 157
The Dalles, Ore., 30, 79, 207
Thomas, Daniel M., 55
Thomas, Henry K., 116–17
Thomas, James, 59–60, 64, 65, 259nn22–23
Thomas, Mr., 124
Thompson, Mr., 124
Thornton, J. Quinn, 54, 59
Thurman, Sue Bailey, 14, 167, 168
Tindall, Ben, 170
Tindall, Mary, 169–70, 295n45
Trail of Tears, 40
Trale, Francis, 211
travelcraft, 229
Trexler, Harrison Anthony, 35
Truckee River, 80, 81, 93
Turner, David, 142
Turner, John, 177
Twohy, Emma Belle Bush, 206
Twyman, Leo, 146
Tyler, Charley, 134–35, 137

Udell, Bertha, 113
Unruh, John D., Jr., 15, 87, 130
Upper Emigrant Road, 82
Utah, 45–47, 250–51n48; slave codes and antiblack laws in, 47, 253n60. *See also* Salt Lake City and Valley
Utley, Robert M., 24

Vasquez, Louis, 27
violence: antiblack mob, 47–50, 53; by bandits and criminals, 16, 58, 131, 136, 155; Indian raids on overlanders, 25, 26, 84, 130–31, 134–36, 141, 181; against Indians, 13, 16, 133
Virginia, 38–39, 242–43n2, 247n21
Virginia City, Nev., 43, 174, 183–84, 231

Virginia City Territorial Enterprise, 214
voting rights: in Missouri, 183; in North, 40–41; struggle for, 222–23, 231; Territorial Suffrage Act and, 42, 223; in West, 42, 44, 208, 214–15

Waddell, W. B., 179, 180
Wagner, Tricia Martineau, 62
wagon companies, 68–69, 263n55, 264n56
Wagoner, Henry O., 85, 223
wagon manufacturing, 64
wagon trains, 3, 56, 140–41, 233n2
Waldo, William, 153
Walker (slave), 117, 121
Waller, Reuben, 138
Ware, Joseph E., 87
Wash (slave), 124–25
Washington, George (black overlander), 208–10, 262n51
Washington County Gold Mining Company, 82
Washington Territory, 207–8, 209
Weller, John B., 88
West, American: African Americans' status in antebellum, 41–47; black overlanders in, 206–24; early black presence in, 18–31; location of, 234n6; and promise of freedom, 4, 71, 115, 160–61, 168–69, 170, 182, 190, 192, 193, 196, 209, 211, 225, 228; statistics on migration to, 3, 157–58, 233n1, 291n1; traditional narrative of migration to, 3, 231–32. *See also* overland journeys
Western Emigration Society, 85–86
Westport, Mo., 59–60, 61, 117, 259n23

What I Saw in California (Bryant), 86–87
Wheat, Carl I., 269n23
White, Ann and Virginia, 84
White, James M., 84
"white Indians," 16, 131, 155
Whitman-Spalding missionary party, 29
Whittier, John Greenleaf, 153
Wigglesworth, Fanny and Vincent, 73
Wilcox, Lufina Williams, 98
Wilhite, Nancy, 173
Willamette Valley, 30, 79, 80, 194, 207
Wilberforce settlement, 45–49
Williams, George A., 195–96
Williams, Louis James, 98
Williams, William, 98
Winans, Joseph W., 201
Winnemucca, Sarah, 131
Winny v. Whitesides, 246n16
Winter Quarters (Omaha), Nebr., 76, 112
Wisconsin, 41
Withe, Harry, 69, 70
women: childbirth by, 148–50; in New Spain, 21–22, 236–37n8; sexual assault and abuse of, 16, 126, 129, 133
Wood, Joseph Warren, 160
Woodson, Drury, 90
Woodson, John, 90
Wyoming, 25, 29, 78, 135–36, 150, 222, 224

York (slave), 23
Young, Brigham, 55, 112, 204, 205; on blacks and slavery, 46, 197, 253n56
Young, Hiram, 62, 63–66, 97, 230

Zoller, Ernest, 186
Zunis, 20

www.ingramcontent.com/pod-product-compliance
Lightning Source LLC
Chambersburg PA
CBHW020827160426
43192CB00007B/559